SEXUAL
CITIZENS

SEXUAL CITIZENS

A LANDMARK STUDY OF SEX, POWER, AND ASSAULT ON CAMPUS

JENNIFER S. HIRSCH
&
SHAMUS KHAN

W. W. NORTON & COMPANY
Independent Publishers Since 1923

FOR THE STUDENTS WHO SHARED THEIR STORIES

AND THEIR LIVES WITH US

CONTENTS

INTRODUCTION

A NEW APPROACH

Why do campus sexual assaults happen? And what should be done to prevent them? *Sexual Citizens* offers parents, students, school administrators, policy makers, and the public a new way to understand sexual assault and an approach to prevention that extends far beyond the campus gates. Our perspective is based upon a landmark research project: the Sexual Health Initiative to Foster Transformation, or SHIFT. Along with nearly thirty other researchers, we've spent the last five years undertaking one of the most comprehensive studies of campus sex and sexual assault. *Sexual Citizens* draws upon that research, providing detailed portraits of a wide range of sexual experiences—from consensual sex to sexual assault—of undergraduates at Columbia University. We'll hear about men like Austin, whose attentiveness to his girlfriend's pleasure contrasts starkly with the night he assaulted a woman he barely knew, when both were drunk in her room. We'll discuss why Adam never talked to his boyfriend about how pushy and forceful he was about sex, even after his boyfriend came home one evening after a long night of drinking and "basically raped" him. We'll write about Michaela, a queer Black woman, who refused to accept as normal being touched, brushed up against, and grabbed on a dance floor—experiences that heterosexual women (and some heterosexual men) see as an inevitable part of being in those spaces. And we'll meet women like Luci, who was raped by Scott, a senior, when she was a freshman, and a virgin. As Scott took off Luci's pants, she exclaimed, "No! Don't!" His response was, "It's okay."

We spoke with many students whose pre-college sex education consisted primarily of instruction about the perils of sex. Once on campus, they had all learned about "affirmative consent"; they dutifully told us that in order for sex to be consensual, both parties have to say "yes," and be sober enough to know what they're saying yes to. But over the course of our research we found that the moment of consent frequently looks more like this, often drunken, text exchange:

U up?

Yep

Can I come over?

Sure

We have to do better. *Sexual Citizens* shows how.

Since the fall of 2014, we have been part of SHIFT's research on campus sexual assault. Jennifer codirected SHIFT with her friend and colleague clinical psychologist Claude Ann Mellins, an expert in adolescent and young adult development, mental health, substance use, and trauma.[1] *Sexual Citizens* primarily draws on the ethnographic component of the SHIFT research, which Jennifer and Shamus led together. Our ethnographic research, conducted between the late summer of 2015 and January of 2017, consisted of over 150 interviews, about two hours each, eliciting young people's broad accounts of their lives and how sex fit into them. We combined these interviews with talking to students in groups, and having SHIFT research team members spend time with students in dorms, the bus to the athletic fields, fraternity basements, and spaces of worship. SHIFT also included a large survey of over 1,600 undergraduates' histories, relationships, and experiences with sex and assault, and another that surveyed nearly 500 students daily for 60 days, asking them about stress, sleep, socializing, sex, sexual assault, and substance use in the prior twenty-four hours. (Throughout the book, the term "substance use" includes alcohol, illegal drugs, or legal drugs used outside the supervision of a physician; the primary substance on which we focus is alcohol.) *Sexual Citizens* builds on the work of others who have conducted research on campus sexual assault using interviews and observations. But the design—deep ethnographic engagement, nested within the work of a large research team—has allowed us to contextualize and enrich our findings, yielding fresh insights.[2]

It isn't just the amount or type of data that makes us different. It's how we think about the problem. Our focus is on the social roots of sexual assault. This is a starkly different starting point than the two major themes of public discussion. The first directs attention to predators, or toxic masculinity, as the problem. The second is the focus on what to do after assaults occur—how to adjudicate those "he said/she said" moments. Instead of thinking in terms of predators or post-assault procedures, SHIFT examined the social drivers of assault, in order to develop new approaches to making assault a less common feature of college life. We deployed what public health scholars call an "ecological model." This approach situates individuals, along with their problem behaviors, in the broader context of their relationships, their pre-college histories, the organizations they are a part of, and the culture that influences them.[3]

Thinking about sexual assault as a public health problem expands the focus from individuals and how they interact, to systems. If we know that people are drinking water that is polluted, one solution is to try and educate every person about how to use that water in safe ways. Another is to go upstream and remove the toxins from the water, reducing the need to change individual behavior one person at a time. Effectively, this book asks, "What would the 'clean water' approach to sexual assault look like?" The creation of a context that nudges people toward making decisions that are good for themselves and others, or "choice architecture," a theory for which Richard Thaler won the Nobel Prize in economics, calls attention to how much impact can come from working at the system and community level.[4] In her prior work on HIV, Jennifer has argued for prevention approaches that go beyond working "one penis at a time."[5] In the case of sexual assault, in addition to instructing students, "Don't rape anyone; don't get raped; don't let your friends get raped," what if prevention work did more to address the social context that makes rape and other forms of sexual assault such a predictable element of campus life?

This perspective yields a new language for sexual assault, based on analyzing the ecosystems in which it occurs: the forces that influence young adults' sexual lives; the relationships people share; the power dynamics between them; how sex fits into students' lives, and how physical spaces, alcohol, and peers create not just the opportunities for sex, but also the ways in which sex is subsequently interpreted and defined by those having it. Our approach mines everything from sexual literacy (or more precisely, illiteracy), to underage drinking, social cliques, stress, shame, and the spaces where they sleep. It incorporates feminist writing on sexual assault, emphasizing gender inequality, sexuality, and power. But it expands upon that approach by exploring how race, socioeconomic status, and age, to name just a few intersecting forms of social inequality, are also essential to understanding assault. These factors deeply affect people's sexual lives. This points to another way in which our approach is unique. While many insist that rape and sex are fundamentally different things, we maintain that understanding what young people are trying to accomplish with sex, why, and the contexts within which sex happens are all essential for a comprehensive analysis of sexual assault.

Better prevention is urgently needed. An analysis of SHIFT survey data led by Claude Mellins found that over one in four women, one in eight men, and more than one out of three gender-nonconforming students said that they'd been assaulted.[6] Columbia is like other schools; similar rates of assault have been confirmed time and again by surveys in many different higher education contexts.[7] The risk of assault is highest freshman year, but it accumulates over time; among seniors who completed the SHIFT survey, one in three women and almost one in six men had experienced an assault.[8] And for many, it's not just one assault; students who had been assaulted were assaulted, on average, three times. It's not that college is particularly dangerous, compared to other settings. While the evidence is mixed, some studies suggest that young women in higher education settings are less likely to be assaulted than those of the same age who are not in school; and no study that we know of finds that women in college are more likely to be assaulted.[9]

The stories that students—and not just women—shared with us made clear the harms of sexually assault, and how parts of that suffering ripple through the whole campus community. If preventing sexual assault's emotional and social harms is insufficient to justify more attention to prevention, we can also point to sexual assault's vast economic impact. In 2017 researchers from the Centers for Disease Control estimated that across the population of the United States, the economic cost of rape was over $3 trillion.[10]

We seek to move readers beyond simply being shocked by these statistics, or saddened by the stories that follow. Our goal is to impel action, but from a position of empathy and understanding, rather than fear.

SEXUAL PROJECTS, SEXUAL CITIZENSHIP, SEXUAL GEOGRAPHIES

We explain students' experiences—with pleasurable sex, sex that is consensual but not so pleasurable, and sexual assault—through three concepts: sexual projects, sexual citizenship, and sexual geographies. Together, these help us understand why sexual assault is a predictable consequence of how our society is organized, rather than solely a problem of individual bad actors. This sad reality has a hopeful implication: in working to better articulate sexual projects for young people, to cultivate their sexual citizenship, and to rearrange campus sexual geographies, we can make sexual assault far less likely. The conceptual framework that animates our analysis charts the path forward.

A *sexual project* encompasses the reasons why anyone might seek particular sexual interactions or experiences.[11] Pleasure is an obvious project; but a sexual project can also be to develop and maintain a relationship; or it can be a project to *not* have sex; or to have sex for comfort; or to try to have children; or because sex can advance our position or status within a group, or increase the status of groups to which we belong. A sexual project can also be to have a particular kind of experience, like sex in the library stacks; sex can be the goal rather than a strategy toward another goal. People don't just have one sexual project. They can have many. Wanting intimacy doesn't mean not wanting other things, like to hook up from time to time.

Plenty of young people, driven by sexual anxieties, described college as a time to acquire sexual experience. In the words of one young man, he wanted to learn to "give good dick." Other students' projects were about their own gender or sexual identity. For those who might be exploring their trans, or queer, or gay identities, sex wasn't just about who to have sex with. It was a project of coming to understand the person they were, or wanted to be. Still other projects were about status and building relationships with peers, sometimes with an edge of competition. Men and women would ask each other "What's your number?" meaning, "How many people have you had sex with?" In that question, to be sure, "sex" is a purposefully vague umbrella term, encompassing a range of practices.[12] For some students it meant penetrative intercourse, whereas others, particularly LGBTQ students, counted oral or manual stimulation as sex. But regardless of what they count, students strive for numbers high enough to convey expertise, but low enough to dodge being labeled a "fuckboy" or "whore." Some students are far more interested in finding a relationship within which sex can happen. Others want intimacy but imagine that a partner can take up too much time, and so they satisfy their desire for a sexually intimate connection—or rather, as we show, partially satisfy it—outside of relationships, finding warmth and pleasure that feels otherwise missing in their achievement-oriented lives.

The young people in whose world we were immersed were frequently figuring out their sexual projects through trial and error, to no small degree because no one had spent much time talking to them about what a sexual project might be. Some, ashamed of their desires or their bodies, drink heavily to escape their rational, deliberate, considered state in order to be in a place where they can have sex. For others, alcohol silences confusion rather than shame; they're totally unclear on their projects, unable to answer, for themselves, the question "What is sex for?" Getting drunk is a good way to avoid thinking about it.

As we map the range of students' sexual projects, we shy away from judgment about the morality of different projects, about what sex should be for. Our goal is to encourage families and institutions to initiate conversations about what kinds of sexual projects fit with their values. We heard about so many missed opportunities to shape and clarify young people's values about sex. Many students told us that all their parents did was to hand them a book; at best, children were told, with some degree of discomfort, that they could ask questions later if they had them. Children themselves got the lesson—sex was something uncomfortable, something not to be spoken about. Learning that it was best not to talk about sex played out, sometimes with disastrous consequences, in their future sexual experiences. Almost no one related an experience where an adult sat them down and conveyed that sex would be an important and potentially joyful part of their life, and so they should think about what they wanted from sex, and how to realize those desires with other people in a respectful way.

Time and again, we thought of how disappointed we were, not in young people, but in the communities that had raised them. And failed them. Students we spoke with had been bombarded with messages about college and career, but had generally received little guidance for how to think about sexually intimate relationships. Hungry for guidance, young people gleaned lessons from elsewhere: from their peers who are similarly in the dark, or from pornography.[13]

Crucially, sexual projects are embedded within other projects—like college projects—which together make up people's life projects.[14] A college project can be to learn, to fall in love, to get a job, to get drunk and do drugs, to discover what's meaningful in life, or to figure out how to live on one's own, away from one's family, and in ways one desires. We adopt a "lifecourse perspective," which acknowledges people's multiple, emergent aims over the course of their lives, and examines how future aims and past experiences impact their present and future.[15]

Though forged in communities, sexual projects are intensely personal. And yet how partners fit within one's sexual project is a critical moral question. Sadly, sexual partners often fit in as objects, rather than fully imagined, self-determining humans. We found that students whose sexual goal is connecting with another person are much more attentive to whether or not their partner wants to have sex than those whose goal is pleasure or status accrual. Treating people like objects doesn't necessarily mean a student will inadvertently assault someone, but not treating people like objects is a good way to make sure not to.

Our second grounding concept, *sexual citizenship,* denotes the recognition of one's own right to sexual self-determination and, importantly, acknowledges the equivalent right in others. Sexual citizenship isn't something some are born with and others are born without. Rather, sexual citizenship is fostered, and institutionally and culturally supported. We do not use the term *sexual citizenship* as it is sometimes used, wherein the government designates people as citizens or noncitizens, allocating rights and benefits dependent on sexual identity. Rather, we mean a socially produced sense of enfranchisement and right to sexual agency.[16]

Sexual citizenship focuses attention on how some people feel entitled to others' bodies, and others do not feel entitled to their own bodies. As a social goal, promoting sexual citizenship entails creating conditions that promote the capacity for sexual self-determination in all peo-

ple, enabling them to feel secure, capable, and entitled to enact their
sexual projects; and simultaneously insisting that all recognize others'
right to self-determination. Sexual citizenship is a community project;
it requires developing individual capacities, social relationships founded
in respect for others' dignity, organizational environments that seek to
educate and affirm the citizenship of all people, and a culture of respect.
In contrast to sexual projects, where out of respect for diversity and
the freedom of self-expression the role of public institutions should be
limited, promoting sexual citizenship is a project in which the state has
a fundamental role.

All but the most progressive American sex education consistently
denies young people's sexual citizenship—communicating, in the words
of one of our mentors, the notion that "sex is a dirty rotten nasty thing
that you should only do to someone you love after you are married."
Plenty of young people told us that they had had sex ed, but that it was
taught by a teacher who was mortified to be teaching it, or whose message was one of fear: of pregnancy, of sexually transmitted infections, of
all the terrible things that sex could bring into their lives. Whether from
school-based sex education, from their families, or from their religious
upbringing, many students we spoke with had absorbed the lesson that
sex was something potentially terrible and most certainly dangerous.
But in the United States today there's likely more than a full decade
between a young person's first sexual experience and marriage. And
that's if they ever marry, which is decreasingly likely.[17] It's not that people are having sex younger; the average age at first sex, around 17 in the
United States, hasn't changed much for over four decades.[18] If anything,
young people today are having less sex, overall.[19] What has changed
significantly, however, is the age at which young people are getting married.[20] In 1960 the average age at first marriage was twenty-three for
men and twenty for women. Today, men first marry, on average, when
they're thirty, and women when they're twenty-eight.[21]

Social policies that communicate that young people are not legitimate sexual citizens date back at least to President Reagan's "Just Say

No" approach, which was not just about drugs; the Adolescent Family Life Act of 1981, otherwise known as the "chastity" program, discouraged premarital sex.[22] Abstinence-only programs enacted as part of President Clinton's 1996 Personal Responsibility and Work Opportunity Reconciliation Act (known as "welfare reform") teach "abstinence from sexual activity outside marriage as the expected standard for all school age children." Federal support for abstinence-only-until-marriage (now rebranded as "sexual risk avoidance") has ebbed and flowed to some extent with partisan shifts in power. The widespread belief among elected officials seems to be that it would be better if adolescents did not have sex at all; even a Democratically controlled Congress under President Obama maintained some funding for abstinence-only programs.[23] Proponents of comprehensive, medically accurate, age-appropriate sex education have sometimes hesitated to directly challenge the framing of young people's sexual activity as intrinsically bad, preferring a more health-focused middle ground that emphasizes the benefits of comprehensive sex education to prevent pregnancy or sexually transmitted infections.[24]

Analysis of nationally representative data shows a worsening landscape for sex education, with significant declines in the proportion of adolescent women in America saying that they had received formal instruction about birth control, about saying no to sex, about sexually transmitted diseases, and about HIV/AIDS, and significant declines in young men's instruction in birth control.[25] Fewer and fewer students are receiving sex education that covers topics such as the right to make one's own reproductive decision, how to resist peer pressure, or how to use condoms.

In addition to the overall declines in delivery of key topics that would help cultivate sexual citizenship, some of the most disadvantaged are getting the least information. Only 6% of LGBTQ youth—those most at risk of assault—report that their sex education included information on LGBTQ topics.[26] Young people growing up in poor families and in rural areas in the United States are less likely to receive comprehensive, medically accurate sex education.[27] This is part of the normalization of educational inequality in the United States: some students experience K–12 education where they're lucky to have adequate heat and air conditioning, while others are educated in places bursting with computers, AP classes, and arts options. Some of the students we spoke with revealed stunning ignorance about basic elements of sex and reproduction. One young woman recounted that no one had ever spoken to her about sex, other than to instill fear; as a result, she said, "I didn't even know where my holes were." If the goal is ignorance, the policy is a resounding success—but that sexual illiteracy reflects a denial of young people's sexual citizenship, with a consequent climate of shame and silence that are part of the social context of campus sexual assault.

The final piece of our conceptual framework is *sexual geographies*. This concept integrates the built environment into our perspective. Yes, we literally mean things like space and furniture, but also a lot more. Sexual geographies encompass the spatial contexts through which people move, and the peer networks that can regulate access to those spaces. Far more than many of us realize—and particularly in college settings— sexual outcomes are intimately tied to the physical spaces where they unfold. Put simply, space is inextricably intertwined with sexuality. It's not just a backdrop, where certain behaviors are more likely to occur in certain places. Instead, space has a social power that elicits and produces behavior. Within the social sciences there's an enormous amount of work that points to how space influences actions and interactions.[28] Someone in a mosque will probably act differently than they will at their best friend's house. We tap these insights to think about what might explain sexual assault, and how we could potentially address it.[29]

Think for a moment about two young people flirting at a party, who both want some privacy. They're not sure what more they want. Let's say they both have roommates. It's a pretty big request for one of them to text their roommate asking them to leave the room for an hour at, say, 2 a.m. It's suddenly more awkward to head to that now-vacated space, chat for a bit, and then just leave. It shouldn't be that way, but it is.

Or, let's say one of them has a single. In that room is a desk, a chair, a bureau, and a bed. To sit apart would be awkward. But sitting together means sharing a bed.

The physical landscape is a critical player in young people's futures, and is intertwined with all kinds of inequalities. Think about being "stuck" somewhere more than an hour from home, with public transportation running sporadically and without the money to pay for a cab home, and feeling compelled to spend the night at someone else's place, despite not wanting to. A wealthy student stranded the same distance from campus can open up a phone, click on an app, and be whisked safely back to the dorm, all because their parents have the capacity to pay that bill for them. Access to and control over space, like so many other things, isn't equally shared. We refer to "geographies" in the plural, to indicate both the range of spaces that shape sexual interactions and the ways in which a student's resources and social position affects their experience of the same space.

Space is a central dimension of institutional power, on campus and beyond, and power is central to understanding assault. The presence of roommates, the taken-for-granted idea that more advanced students should get better housing, including single rooms, and national Greek-life policies that ban sororities—women-controlled spaces—from throwing parties that serve alcohol, all are part of the campus sexual geography. These spatial dynamics—control, access, feeling at ease— are major players in sexual assault. To tackle this problem, we need to think about people, the communities they're a part of, and how these can support sexual projects and citizenship. We also need to think about the landscape and the built environment that augment or moderate power inequalities, that support or deny projects and citizenship, and that remove or pose barriers to satisfying sexual lives.[30] Students may arrive on campus clear about their own sexual projects, having grown to young adulthood in families and communities that help them understand themselves as sexual citizens—and yet once at school they navigate sexual geographies that produce vulnerability and they encounter others who do not recognize their right to sexual self-determination, or for whom they are nothing more than a prop in the quest to realize a sexual project centered on accumulating experience, or prestige, or pleasure.

A BRIEF HISTORY OF SEXUAL ASSAULT ACTIVISM, RESEARCH, AND POLICYMAKING

Understanding what to do requires that we recognize where we are, and how we got here—specifically, the interplay of advocacy, research, and policymaking around sexual assault. A complete history is beyond the scope of this book. Nevertheless, some context is essential to situate our work in relation to those shoulders we stand upon and to indicate ways in which our perspective is distinct from other, more common understandings. We also seek to recognize key insights that have slipped from center stage in recent decades.

Although the label that circulates in the policy world—"gender-based violence"—suggests that socially unequal relations between men and women are the primary form of inequality relevant to understanding sexual assault, a core message of *Sexual Citizens* is that it is only possible to make sense of campus sexual assault by looking at the intersection of gender with other forms of inequality.[31] America's history of organized public action on sexual assault reveals that racial inequality has always been central to understanding both the circumstances in which men sexually assault women and the meaning of confronting that violence. In the 1860s, brave African American women testified before Congress about a gang rape by a white mob.[32] Decades before she refused to give up her bus seat to a white man, Rosa Parks was organizing against sexual violence as a tool for racial domination. In 1931 she helped defend the Scottsboro Boys, nine young African American men accused of raping two white women on an Alabama train. In 1944, as the NAACP's chief rape investigator, Parks stood by the side of Recy Taylor, who refused to be silent after being raped by six white boys in

Alabama.[33] Black women's organized opposition to racialized sexual violence, grounded in an analysis of sexual violence not as a problem of individual pathology but as part of the social organization of society, laid a foundation for the civil rights movement, and for the kind of approach we take in this book.[34]

That work also paved the way for more public attention to sexual assault in the 1970s.[35] In 1975 the term "date rape" first appeared in print, in Susan Brownmiller's *Against Our Will: Men, Women and Rape*, and the 1970s also saw the emergence of annual "Take Back the Night" marches, calling attention to violence against women in cities and on campuses around the world.[36]

The history of sexual assault on campus has been written primarily with a focus on women students being assaulted; until recently little attention has been paid to men's assaults of other men, to say nothing of women's assaults of men, or the experiences of LGBTQ students. This focus on women's victimization by men is in part because men commit the vast majority of assaults, and women are overwhelmingly the people being assaulted. Coeducation and campus sexual assault are, for rather obvious reasons, intimately intertwined. By implication, the problem of campus sexual assault is likely far older than many realize. In 1833, Oberlin College was founded as the first coeducational institution of higher education in the United States, and by the end of the nineteenth century, around seventy percent of colleges were coed. We likely have readers in their sixties, seventies, and eighties for whom this book is not just sad, or thought-provoking, but also distinctly discomfiting, as they recall their own college days and reassess long-dormant memories of assault, or realize that they may have assaulted someone. But the ways in which those older readers understood sexual assault at the time they were in college was likely quite different. Part of the history of campus sexual assault is tracing changing understandings of the very nature of the problem. Research led by Desiree Abu-Odeh, as part of SHIFT, found that when Columbia and Barnard's campus newspaper, the *Columbia Spectator*, first began covering the topic in the 1950s, the focus was on a stranger coming from outside the gates. [37] In Columbia's case, student reporters wrote about the Black men in nearby Harlem, as a risk to the innocent white Barnard women. Gradually, other images would be layered onto this racialized view of a stranger lurking in the bushes: the athlete who drags a drunken woman behind a dumpster, the campus as a "hunting ground"; or even, as in the title of Peggy Sanday's 1990 classic, *Fraternity Gang Rape*.[38]

Research recognizing the problem of campus sexual assault began as early as the 1950s. In 1957, the *American Sociological Review* published "an investigation of sexual aggressiveness in dating-courtship relationships on a university campus."[39] The modern era of campus sexual assault research began in 1985, with *Ms.* magazine's publication of pioneering work conducted under the direction of Mary Koss.[40] A survey of over 7,000 women students at thirty-five schools showed that one in four women had experienced rape or attempted rape, mostly by friends or intimate partners. What began as just a trickle of papers annually examining sexual assault among college students, mostly written by psychologists, behavioral scientists, and criminologists, became first a steady flow—dozens per year—and then a veritable flood since 2014, the recent period in which campus sexual assault has been a major focus of public discussion.[41] The scholars producing this work reflected the core approach of their academic disciplines, concentrating on the individual attitudes, attributes, behaviors, and histories of those who either committed assault, or were themselves assaulted, and issues related to adjudication. We are interested in these individual factors, but our work responds to calls dating back two decades for analysis that examines the broader ecology of sexual assault.[42]

At least as influential as the scholarship and activism around sexual assault is the legal terrain, mostly shaped by the federal government. Three pieces of federal legislation from the 1970s through the 1990s have fundamentally shaped how we think about sexual assault, what institutions are required to address it, and how the federal government can be called upon to act: Title IX (passed in 1972, mandating gender equality in educational institutions); the Clery Act (passed in 1990, mandating reporting about campus crime), and the Violence Against Women Act (passed in 1994, as part of a broader crime bill).[43] The federal government paid little attention to lowering the rate of sexual violence; instead, its focus was on the aftermath: adjudication, criminal justice responses, and services for survivors.[44] In 2011 the US Department of Education fundamentally transformed the landscape for colleges and universities with a "Dear Colleague" letter. This letter, written to institutions of higher education, suggested that in failing to fully respond to sexual assault, colleges and universities could be violating Title IX. Because women were disproportionately experiencing assault, and assault was known to have significant life impacts, women were not enjoying equal access to educational opportunities.[45] While most of the emphasis in that 2011 guidance continued to focus on the aftermath (standards for grievance, investigations, and adjudication, including evidence and representation), that more recent federal guidance included requirements for education and prevention. The impact of the "Dear Colleague" letter upon colleges and universities was profound. In the spring of 2014, the Obama administration released a list of 55 schools under investigation by the Department of Education's Office for Civil Rights for violations of Title IX related to sexual violence, later expanding that list to 304 investigations at 223 institutions of higher education. In September of 2014 the White House launched the "It's on Us" campaign against campus sexual assault.[46]

Activists have seized upon this policy landscape. Students are using federal laws to advance claims that the administrative responses to sexual assault are generating a climate of gender inequality affecting women's access to and experience of education. Many are demanding swifter justice for the victims of sexual assault, and harsher punishments for the respondents. The stakes are high: schools under federal investigation for potential Title IX violations, Columbia included, risk losing hundreds of millions of dollars in federal support: everything from subsidized loans for students to federal grant money for faculty researchers.

The focus isn't just on what schools should do. Increasingly, both states and schools are creating policies to more precisely define how people must act for sex to be consensual. The most common of these policies is "affirmative consent," which requires ongoing and explicit consent as a sexual interaction proceeds. Developed by student activists at Antioch College in the early 1990s, the idea was initially mocked, even in a 1993 *Saturday Night Live* skit, but its broader influence has been profound; hundreds of schools across the country now have affirmative consent policies, and it is enshrined in law for all people, on and off campus, in four states (New York, California, Illinois, and Connecticut).[47] Frequently through online pre-orientation courses, college students today are taught that the absence of "no" does not mean that sex is consensual; in fact, the only way it can be is if both parties explicitly say "yes." But as we'll show, promoting affirmative consent is insufficient to prevent sexual assault.

While feminists have dominated activism around sexual assault, and psychologists have had the most influence upon scholarship, legal voices have weighed most heavily on the policy-making terrain. By implication, the questions asked center around law, legal procedure, and legal remedies. How should we investigate these cases? And how should we punish people? This focus reflects the power of feminist lawyers such as Catharine MacKinnon in mapping out sexual harassment, and by extension, campus sexual assault, as forms of discrimination, creating an institutional responsibility for redress that provides an alternative to engagement with the criminal justice system.[48] And yet there is something of the 1980s and 1990s approach to criminal justice, with its emphasis on adjudication and punishment rather than prevention, and in the focus on an adversarial legal approach rather than a community-oriented one. The characterization of those who commit assault as sociopathic perpetrators and the portrayal of the greatest risk as coming from serial predators echo the 1990s "superpredator" conversation.[49] Both are built on a sometimes racialized imagination about a predatory other. Our work stands in striking contrast to this, by suggesting that questions about race and campus sexual assault should focus on racial inequality and differences in power and status in specific campus contexts.

Unquestionably, there are "bad guys" out there who intentionally and violently seek to harm others through sex, both within the student body and outside of it.[50] But thinking of men as predators and women as prey misses so much. It flattens women into passive victims in need of protection, renders invisible the experiences of lesbian, gay, bisexual, transgender, and queer (LGBTQ) students, who experience far higher rates of assault than their heterosexual peers, and provides little in the way of conceptual tools to understand, or even recognize, instances in which men are assaulted by women.[51]

FROM FEAR TO EMPATHY AND HOPE

Our analysis of the social dimensions of campus sexual assault suggests that in addition to focusing on predators, we need also to focus on ourselves. Until we look at how our society raises children, organizes our schools, and structures the transition to adulthood, we're not going to make much headway. But if we are part of the problem, we can also be part of the solution.

The focus on fear—the old dangers of pregnancy and sexually transmitted infections, combined with the newly recognized dangers of campus sexual assault—reflects an underlying refusal to acknowledge young people's sexual citizenship. It's magical thinking to believe that young people can learn to put their bodies close to other bodies, safely and without anyone getting hurt, when for most kids the only message that they get from their parents is "not under my roof."[52] Most parents whose children want to learn to drive spend a great deal of time teaching them—talking about the rules of the road, how to drive defensively, how to protect pedestrians and cyclists. They don't sit kids down, awkwardly explain the role of spark plugs in the internal combustion engine, and consider the job done. And with much younger children, parents and caregivers expend enormous energy helping them to move safely in the street. Don't cross against the red, and walk facing traffic. On a bike, always wear a helmet, and ride single file, moving with traffic. It takes a lot of work to teach kids to move their own bodies safely through the world. We know this about everything except, it seems, sex.[53]

This may be why there has been so little progress in actually reducing campus assault. No research that we have seen documents a substantial campus or population-level decline in rates of sexual assault, although several prevention interventions have demonstrated some level of efficacy.[54] The lack of progress reflects, in part, a failure of imagination. What if, instead of scaring young people, we cultivated them so that they might grow into people who have a satisfying intimate life? With some states banning gender-neutral restrooms and others mandating LGBTQ-inclusive sex ed, there is substantial disagreement across the United States about the sexual citizenship of queer youth. The antipathy toward birth control, abortion services, and even the vaccine that prevents sexual transmission of the cancer-causing human papillomavirus, makes it clear that some people believe that it is morally necessary for unmarried heterosexual sex to have dire consequences. But who wishes a future of sexual misery on their children, or any child? It may seem foolish to argue that rather than taking on sexual assault prevention, a challenge which society has largely failed to address, we should take on the much bigger task of promoting young people's sexual citizenship. But that is exactly what we must do. And that means expanding the focus beyond adjudication, which has kept all eyes on that tiny proportion of assaults formally reported to institutions of higher education.[55]

OUR UNIQUE PERSPECTIVE

We are experts in overlapping and complementary fields. Jennifer is an anthropologist and professor at the Mailman School of Public Health at Columbia University. She's spent her academic career studying gender, sex, intimacy, and health.[56] She also has two sons whose time in high school and college coincided with her work on SHIFT, and so she thinks and writes with a very personal concern regarding the world that young men and women are growing up in. Shamus is a sociologist at Columbia University who has spent his career studying American elite communities, gender, inequality, and adolescence.[57] Before we began this project we were not experts in sexual assault research; our prior research had been about the social production of gender and sexuality, rather than social pathology. We have brought a different perspective to an old problem, grounded in the research we have done on related topics, in our shared interest in gender and sexuality, and our expertise in ethnographic research. This book draws on all these aspects of our background, training, interests, and perspectives.

Our methodology (which is described in greater detail in the methodological appendix) involves talking to people, spending time with them in places that are meaningful to them, and observing them as they go about their day-to-day lives. For SHIFT's ethnographic component, we led a team that conducted multiple-hour interviews with 151 undergraduates, describing their experiences before coming to college, their relationships with family and friends, their experiences with drugs and alcohol, and, most of all, their experiences with sex and sexual assault. As is typical with on-campus research, students were compensated for participation in ethnographic interviews and focus groups, as they were for the survey components of the SHIFT research.

We asked students why they pursued sex, what they wanted from it, how it fit into their lives, and what their sexual experiences were actually like. And rather than study every possible dimension of sexual misconduct, we focused intensively on sexual assault. By assault, we mean unwanted nonconsensual sexual contact; this includes rape and attempted rape, but also unwanted nonconsensual sexual touching. In this book we use the word "rape" to refer specifically to penetrative oral or genital assault. Rape is a legal term that we did not use in our data collection, for a variety of methodological reasons. But we use it in this book because it's more direct than "nonconsensual penetrative sexual contact." One of the lessons of our project is that assault is not one thing, it's many different kinds of experiences, and "rape" clearly delineates one such kind of experience.

Across the interviews we heard many stories of sexual violence, stories that, for twenty-five of the students, took up to three two-hour interview sessions to tell. We look back on the students who talked to us and marvel at their extraordinary courage in sharing funny stories about the first time; tender ones about exploring their sexuality; terrifying accounts of rape; and heartbreaking stories of racial and queer victimization and abuse.

In addition to talking with individual students, we wanted to know how students talked about sex and sexual violence with one another. To do so, we ran seventeen focus groups of between eight and fourteen students. Some groups were all women, others were all athletes. We ran an LGBTQ group, a group of students of color, and a group of freshmen. These focus group conversations explored students' shared ways of talking about sex, sexual assault, and consent. We observed that students were already educated about the importance of consent, but the rote answers they could so expertly reproduce about the importance of "yes" bore little resemblance to the ambiguous realities of sex as they actually described it unfolding in their lives.

What people say is never the full story; what truly sets our work apart methodologically is the hundreds of hours of in-depth participant observation, conducted while students were socializing with one another—in their rooms, at parties, at the clubs and organizations that were so important to them.[58] It's not just our ages and bedtimes that precluded us from doing that part of the research: as faculty members at Columbia, socializing with our students would be awkward, intrusive, and unlikely to produce good data. As we learned from one attempt at bar-based participant observation that ended up misrepresented on page six of the *New York Post*, the best way to avoid misunderstandings is to draw a bright line.[59] We attended public events like homecoming and basketball games, and spent time in public spaces, for example eating in the dining hall with students. But we didn't go to places that were, or that students considered, "private."

To gather data in such spaces, we hired five younger researchers with graduate training in anthropology, public health, and social work. Always identifying themselves as researchers and seeking students' permission, they spent hundreds of hours at fraternity parties, on athletics team buses, with religious student organizations, socializing at the cafeteria and at bars, in dorm rooms, and around the city with students as they lived their day-to-day lives.

We have taken many steps to protect the identities of students who participated in the research. This includes changing students' names, hometowns, and identifying details, as well as some of their physical descriptions. If information is analytically important, we don't change it. For example, when we talk about the unique experience of Black men navigating consent, all our examples are from Black men. Sexuality and gender identification are never changed. But we change other details to prevent classmates of those we interviewed, and students' families and friends, from recognizing them. Importantly, all the stories of assault remain true to the experiences of students. Demographic and personal information might be purposefully inaccurate, but the description of the physical interaction adheres to what we were told.

The stories we recount are one-sided. With a few exceptions, we only know what one person told us about an encounter. If we were trying to figure out who was responsible, that would matter. But we're not. We're instead interested in how people experience their lives.

Part of that experience is the development of an identity. Our research included students with a wide range of sexual and gender identities. These gender identities included "male," "female," "queer," "genderqueer," "cisgender," and "transgender," and the sexual identities encompassed "gay," "straight," "bisexual," "queer," "polyamorous," "asexual," etcetera. Some readers may be confused by what all of these identities mean. What is the difference between queer and genderqueer? It is difficult to precisely provide a definition. "Queer," for example, is both a gender identity and a sexual identity. People can use the same identity label in different ways. There were many students we spoke with who do not use the traditional gender pronouns of "he"/"him"/"his" or "she"/"her"/"hers," instead preferring "they"/"them"/"theirs." Throughout *Sexual Citizens*, we employ the pronouns, gender, and sexual identity terms that research subjects used for themselves.

In addition to using people's own words to describe their identities, the ethnographic method favors rich detail over representativeness. To balance this, we triangulated our findings with two other sources of information. First and foremost is the SHIFT survey, led by Claude Ann Mellins, and developed by a faculty research team that included both of us, as well as Louisa Gilbert, John Santelli, Melanie Wall, Kate Walsh, and Patrick Wilson. The SHIFT survey, which was drawn from a random sample of the student body and which had one of the highest response rates of any campus sexual assault survey—over 66%—enabled us to situate ethnographic findings in relation to the more representative student experience.[60] We also referred to the broader literature on sexual assault, which helped us see how our case of Columbia University compared with other campus contexts.

Although we refer to our field site as "Columbia," the students in our research came from four distinct undergraduate institutions: Columbia College, Columbia School of Engineering and Applied Sciences, School of General Studies, and Barnard College. Columbia College is a coeducational liberal arts college. The School of Engineering and Applied Sciences teaches engineering and other applied scientific fields. General Studies matriculates joint-degree, nontraditional, and sometimes older students, from ballet dancers to veterans (in 2016 Columbia had 375 veterans enrolled as undergraduate students, far more than any other Ivy League school; Harvard, by comparison, had four).[61] Barnard, just across the street on the west side of Broadway, is an entirely independent women's college, with its own faculty, administration, policies, buildings, students, dorms, endowment, and campus culture. Each of these four institutions have distinct institutional cultures and other differences, which we do not discuss or use within our analysis. Students from all four schools all take classes together, and for traditional-aged college students the social life of the four schools is more or less integrated. The three coeducational colleges have nearly equal gender ratios, but because Barnard is all women, the gender ratio of the student body of the four schools taken together is closer to 60% women, 40% men.[62] As women today make up more than 56% of all college and university undergraduates, this aspect of the campus landscape is not that unusual.[63]

The context of a private, highly selective, research-intensive, urban university is unquestionably very particular. Most US college students do not attend residential institutions, and most American institutions of higher education lack multi-billion-dollar endowments, accept far more than half their applicants, and have student populations that are, on average, far less wealthy. Still, the questions we ask and the ideas that shape our analysis can guide thinking much more generally. The overall dynamics we are interested in—the search to achieve one's goals and connect with others—are a central challenge in everyone's transition to adulthood. In a community college, boarding school, summer camp, or military institution, the same questions apply: how do the spaces to which people have access shape their interactions? How do people's underlying objectives, and their capacity for empathy, shape the way that they interact?

We wrote *Sexual Citizens* to shed new light on how those interactions, and the underlying objectives and context, lead to campus sexual assault—and so, not surprisingly, this book is mostly about assault. We don't say much about students' academic experiences, internships, or research with faculty. Nor do we spend much time talking about students who don't have sex, or students who are only having satisfying and consensual sexual interactions. Analysis of the SHIFT diary survey research, led by Patrick Wilson, suggests that there is a great deal of campus sex that students experience as enjoyable and consensual.[64] Even if more than one in three women and nearly one in six men are assaulted by the time they leave college, that still means the majority of students do not experience assault. And the students who are assaulted can also have pleasurable and consensual sex. We tell some of these stories, yet our focus is primarily on the types of interactions we seek to prevent.

Victim's rights activists, seeking to emphasize that assault is not normal, and that we should not tolerate it, often exclaim, "Rape is not sex!" And we agree—rape is not sex. Yet for three reasons it is vital to study assault in concert with sex. The first is that comparison aids understanding. Sometimes revealing the fundamental properties of something is easiest when we also look at what that thing is not. Comparing assault to sex helps us better understand both phenomena.

The second reason is more important. Notwithstanding the rare instances of a stranger jumping out from behind a bush to drag a victim away, or the "roofieing scenario" of being drugged at a bar, most campus sexual assaults begin as sexual interactions. Many involve sexual situations that are consensual, until they are not. Sometimes the whole interaction takes place with one person still thinking that it is sex, not assault. That's what, "he said/she said" is often all about. In most cases we saw these to be sincerely held positions, even if we also found that there were plenty of signs that one person wasn't okay with what was happening. Unquestionably, assaults happen that involve violence and physical force (analysis of SHIFT survey data found that among those who were assaulted, 35% of women students' experiences and 13% of men's involved physical force).[65] But most assaults don't involve force. And in order to create a context in which young people have sex without harming each other, it's crucial to understand those pivotal moments when encounters change from being sex, to being assault.

The third reason is that by looking at sex and not just assault, we also see the times assaults didn't happen. In students' stories, there were plenty of situations in which one person conveyed that they wanted to stop—either changing their mind, or clearly expressing a limit that had previously not been spoken—and the sex stopped. We need to study these cases in order to understand what's different about those evenings where heavy making out leads to a friendly goodbye—or even to an awkward goodbye—and those where it culminates in an assault. Why is it that sometimes people look at a sexual partner, see that they don't seem okay, and stop and talk about it, rather than just pushing ahead?

Our framework of sexual projects, sexual citizenship, and sexual geographies provides insight into what is happening and serves as a guide for what to do about it. We've written *Sexual Citizens* primarily for parents—both those with young children and those with high school–aged ones headed off to college—and for young people themselves, who are about to go to college or are already there. We've also written it for policymakers, who we hope will look at assault in a new way, and work with their communities to create policies and programs based in empathy and hope, rather than judgment and fear. We hope that our conceptual framework will become part of a new vernacular for understanding both sexuality and sexual assault, one that can be used to improve the lives of young people for generations to come.

SEXUAL
CITIZENS

I

SEXUAL ASSAULT

"THANK GOD IT'S ME."

Esme began college with a clearly defined sexual project: "I wanted to make out with a ton of boys, I wanted to lose my virginity, and I wanted a boyfriend, in that order." That plan didn't include getting raped in the spring of her sophomore year. The night started like many others. With a dozen other friends, she did some shots in a senior's room. Around midnight most of them set out downtown to an off-campus party sponsored by a student group. Some women stayed behind; they were already too "tapped out, too drunk." No one in the group was sober enough to notice that Esme was too.

Esme jumped into the first cab; when they arrived, as some of her group poured into the club, she stayed outside to wait for the others. A man approached her. He seemed "nice," and "kind of cute." He suggested they go back to his place. Esme told him no, she was waiting for her friends. He didn't listen. Grabbing her arm, he pulled her down the street toward his apartment. Esme didn't put up much resistance. She described herself as "kind of laughing . . . with him, 'cause he's like, kind of being charming and I don't really know what's going on."

But this wasn't just a crazy college escapade. Once in his apartment, the man got her to unlock her phone. Pretending to be Esme, he sent a message to her friends saying she was with Monica. But Monica was passed out in her own bed, back at their dorm. "He pushed me on the bed, took my clothes off, and started having sex with me. And I was like, 'hey, stop,' and he was like 'no,' and that continued for a while. . . . I passed out, and woke up again in the middle of the night and threw up a bunch, he gave me a wastebasket,' and then . . . passed out again. And then when I woke up, he was having sex with me, and I was sober and I was like 'stop, this is really bad.'"

After she was raped, Esme had trouble concentrating, and her grades started to slide. She was angry at her friends. They had failed to notice how drunk she was, had left her alone outside the club, and had not even questioned that message about being with Monica, who had passed out earlier in the evening. By the time we interviewed her she'd found a new "crew." Her rape coalesced what she'd been feeling for a while: she needed a more supportive group of friends.

Yet when Esme told us her story, she emphasized her relative privilege. "I'm sure lucky that . . . I mean, this is a fucked up thing to say, but I'm really lucky that I have parents that I can go home to and, like, that day I had the resources to get $60.00 out of the bank and pay for Plan B, and I could go to Health Services and all of that stuff. I feel like my situation is so much less bad than so many other people . . . like if it had to happen to one of the girls that I'm friends with, that I'm close with now—thank God it's me, because it would fuck them up really really bad, but I can take it."

She also expressed gratitude about when it happened: right before spring break. Days later she was back home, being cared for by her family. She could talk with her mom about sex and drinking; they'd had these kinds of conversations before. It wasn't easy, but Esme knew her mother would be supportive. "I haven't cried about it, except for when I told my mom, and I went to a counselor for a while and even then, I was like, 'This is so ridiculous, I'm probably wasting your time, there are people outside that have actual problems.'"

Stories like Esme's are what students conjure up when you ask them to describe a "typical" sexual assault. In focus group discussions, interviews, and casual conversations around campus, a common archetype emerged: a creepy guy lurking in or near a bar, and then a young woman awakening after the rape, groggy and shaken, in an unfamiliar space. But even in narratives that fit that archetype, important pieces are left out. Esme's emphasis is on her friends. In her mind, her loyalty to them set the whole event in motion: the man who raped her approached her while she was waiting alone outside for others. She wondered why no one who shared that first cab with her decided to keep her company as she waited. In her recounting of the aftermath, her resilience, her relative privilege, and her decision to seek out new friends, we see how her social group anchors her story. Sometimes it's the opposite: social isolation, too, can produce vulnerability.

In this chapter, we use the concepts of sexual projects, sexual citizenship, and sexual geographies to walk through a wide range of sexual assaults. The point is not to make an argument, but instead to outline the range of different experiences that make up the category "sexual assault," to demonstrate just how varied those experiences are (which is why sexual assault is so hard to address), and to show the utility of our framework. In subsequent chapters, we move more systematically through both an argument and an explanation.

Lupe, who uses the pronoun "they," was a first-generation college student. Their transition to college had not been an easy one. What they experienced as a "White institution" was so different from their Latino community at home, and they found that so much of social life revolved around drinking in contexts where Lupe did not feel welcome. During their interview, Lupe told us a story about going alone to a club one Thursday night at the end of freshman year, desperate to get away from the drama of the campus's relatively small queer community and the predictable "shitty white music" at student events. Lupe left a campus that never felt quite like home to reconnect with what was important to them, and to recharge.

Lupe does not have sex with cis-gender men (men whose gender identity corresponds to the sex they were assigned at birth), and describes themself as not conventionally attractive. So they were a little taken aback when a man sidled up and offered to buy them a drink. Lupe demurred. The man bought the drink anyway, and Lupe "was like, whatever, a free drink." A single drink in New York might account for ten percent of Lupe's monthly spending money. Maybe they wouldn't have accepted the drink if bar drinks weren't so pricey, if money weren't so scarce, or if there were more people on campus who liked *bachata*. But no one seemed to know the Dominican style of music that Lupe loved—that helped them connect with their past and identity, complicated though that could be. And so Lupe ended up at this club, hoping to sit, listen, and escape. Soon after having that drink, they began to feel sleepy and dizzy—so much that upon leaving the club, they were not sure that they could make it home on the subway. The stranger offered to get a cab. After this, Lupe remembers only fragments. Being almost carried out of the cab into a building. The use of force. Waking the next morning, "freaking out, you know, 'cause I like I have no idea where I am, of how I even got there . . . and also like this guy . . . I'm just not into that at all." They scrambled to find their cellphone and clothes, afraid that "if I don't get out of here like he might hurt me more . . . 'cause in my mind, men don't just like assault you, they probably kill you as well, you know?"

Lupe and Esme's stories share a context—an off-campus bar—and what sexual assault researchers call a "method of perpetration"—intoxication combined with being physically overpowered.[1] In other "stranger in a bar" stories, the turning point is not being hauled staggering into a taxi, but changing one's mind and being ignored.

Jiyoung was in many circumstances a confident sexual agent. She proudly recounted the time she had asked a guy, as they sat eating pizza, if he'd like to go back to his room and have sex. And two summers ago in Paris, naked and making out with a man in bed, she had sat up, told him she was tired, threw on her clothes, and left to go home. "He was a slobbery kisser." She decided she'd rather catch up on her sleep. But Jiyoung's decisiveness and clarity about her sexual project of accumulating fun sexual experiences did not protect her in an encounter that fell on what she described as the other side of the "really thin line between rape and sex." One night when she was very drunk, she approached a man in a bar. After not very much chatting she suggested that they go back to his place. The intercourse didn't feel good, and she wanted him to stop. She tried to convey that, but "he wasn't responsive." When she reflected back on this night, Jiyoung did what many who are assaulted do: blamed herself. "It was a mistake to go up to a person just because you wanted sex." Once they started down the path to having sex, she reasoned, it was nearly impossible to stop, so she just "ended it quickly and left quickly."

Esme's and Lupe's assaults involved physical force, resistance, and being so drunk they passed in and out of consciousness. Jiyoung, by her own account, "tried" to convey that she wanted to stop and that the sex didn't feel good. Her partner didn't use force, but he "wasn't responsive." The differences in these stories matter. Prevention that respects women and queer people as active sexual agents rather than helpless creatures in need of protection requires building a world in which everyone understands that even if someone goes home from a bar with you—even after you put your penis inside them—they can still change their mind. And Lupe's story gestures toward the much broader vision of prevention we will lay out in the pages to come. Of course, Lupe should have been safe sitting at a bar, listening to the bachata, but if there were a space where Lupe felt at home on campus, where they felt they could be and enjoy themself, then they'd never have wandered away, in despair at their isolation. Addressing sexual assault requires talking about more than how people are having sex. Lupe's story, and Tim's which follows later in this chapter, draw attention to how loneliness, sadness, and other aspects of mental health produce risk for all kinds of things, including sexual assault.[2]

SHE SAID, "NO, DON'T." HE RESPONDED, "IT'S OKAY."

Imagine a fraternity: floor sticky with beer, lights low, music too loud to talk. Two people have consumed an astonishing amount of alcohol, and the assault happens in that same building, after the guy has pulled, carried, or cajoled the girl upstairs, in plain sight of many who might have intervened as bystanders. Luci's story fits a prototype—the toxic brew of alcohol, Greek life, women students new to campus, and older, socially powerful men.[3] After years at an elite but very sheltered boarding school in Thailand, she started Columbia eager to lose her virginity, party, and be popular. That first Saturday after classes began, she went out to one of the local bars with another first-year student, Nancy. Their fake ID weren't particularly good, but the bouncer didn't care. The local bars knew that men were their biggest spending customers, and the best way to get men in the door and get them buying drinks was to make sure that there were plenty of women there too.

At the bar they met two seniors. Nancy danced with one, and the other, Scott, bought Luci a drink. After a while, Scott invited Luci back to his fraternity house. She was excited to go with him. This was what college was all about. They stumbled up the busy avenue in the warm early-fall night, turning left on a street toward fraternity row. They stopped for a bit outside of the fraternity's townhouse on the south side of the street. Scott couldn't find his keys. They made out on the sidewalk, waiting for one of Scott's brothers to let them in. Luci's phone rang and rang. She finally answered it. Nancy was coming to find her. Luci convinced Scott to wait, and once Nancy got there the three climbed the steps and walked through the carved entryway, covered with decades of peeling paint. Scott steered Luci up a flight of stairs. Nancy followed. Luci paused on the stairs to chat with someone she knew, excited to see a familiar face after just a few days on campus. It felt as if her college plan was really coming together. Scott seemed annoyed by all of these diversions, but Luci didn't really care. As they sat in a shared space on the second floor, Scott made drinks for both girls. Nancy passed out on the couch, before even touching the drink. Scott asked Luci if she wanted to see his room. She did. She knew what that meant—to her. They went up one more floor. He closed the door, and they started making out again. He pushed her down on the bed and started to unbutton her pants. "No, don't," she said. He responded, "It's okay." As they continued making out, he took off her pants and underwear and penetrated her. Luci remembers saying no again. He continued. She'd never been in this kind of situation before. She was drunk. She'd tried to stop it. But Scott wouldn't stop. And so Luci just gave up and let him finish.

They dozed off. It was later but not yet morning—there were still plenty of people in the fraternity house—when they awoke to loud knocking on the door. Nancy had woken up, remembered Luci, and had gone to find her. Still drunk, Luci hurriedly threw on her clothes. When she stood up, Scott noticed the blood on the sheets. Looking concerned, he asked Luci if it had been her first time. It was, but Luci denied it. As Luci walked out into the hall with Nancy, She saw Scott pull aside a popular member of a prestigious sorority. Luci couldn't hear what he whispered to her, but the girl, whose name she didn't recall, offered to walk her back to her dorm. When we interviewed Luci as a senior, she had never told anyone this story. Or at least, never the full story; right after it happened, she described it to her friends as just a wild night, as consensual. Now, several years later, she said that she would feel weird about changing her story publicly. She blamed herself, at least partially—she shouldn't have gotten that drunk, she said, or she should have told him up front that she was a virgin. Maybe then he wouldn't have been so cavalier about how it was "ok"? And yet she insisted what happened to her wasn't right. To us, she described what Scott did as preying on her. She'd since heard that he'd done the same with others.

III

"Stranger rape" like the kind we described with Esme, Lupe, or Jiyoung looms large in the national imagination; so too does the kind of frat-house rape that Luci experienced, where she'd just met Scott that night, and never really saw him again. But sexual assault is also something that "normal" people do. The SHIFT survey replicated what decades of campus sexual assault research has shown: a substantial proportion of sexual assaults are committed by an acquaintance, friend, or intimate partner.[4] It isn't just that the two people knew each other; often they'd previously had some sexual contact. This is part of what makes it even more complicated.

As the #MeToo movement has gained attention, some have worried that it advances a view of women as in need of the protection both by and from men. That stands in stark contrast to the feminist movements of the 1960s and 1970s, which understood women as fully capable of protecting themselves, provided they lived in a context that enabled them to do so.[5] Our vision is a society in which everyone—not just women, but also men and genderqueer people—is more protected; that includes protecting people who might commit assaults from actually doing so. We believe it's important to understand assaulters as people; as we'll show in Chapter 6, many of those who commit assault think that what they are doing is having sex and who would be horrified to learn that what they did was experienced as assault by the other person.

Jiyoung's and Luci's stories suggest that in some cases the problem is that young women's partners confuse sexual agency with consent. The women wanted some kind of sexual contact, just not the kind they ended up having. And their sexual partners were either blind, ambivalent, or hostile to this. We heard stories of women initiating sexual encounters that went beyond what they wanted. Of women struggling, often with a great deal of self-blame, to reconcile their own role in setting an encounter in motion with their experience of unwanted and nonconsensual sex. And of students of all genders refusing to label an encounter an assault because they felt that doing so might invalidate their self-perception and identity as an assertive, together, sexually modern person.

SOMETIMES, IT'S YOUR FRIEND

Karen's ex-boyfriend was crushed by news of his sister's cancer recurrence. He texted to see if she had time to talk. They met up in Riverside Park, walking over to the boulders just south of 116th Street and climbing up to watch the boats go by on the Hudson River. Karen was weirded out when he pulled her close and started to kiss her. She'd come to meet him thinking she was supporting a friend in crisis. Sex was the last thing on her mind. She still found him very attractive, but she wasn't interested in anything sexual. He didn't notice, or care. He pushed her up against the rock and raped her. He used physical force. She said "no." She was very clear. She laughed nervously as she told us this story, matter-of-factly adding that later that day, when showering, she found dirt in her vagina. It got there when he dragged her to the ground. And yet she was reluctant to label it "rape," much less "assault." She still cared for him. She even noted, confused, that parts of the rape were physically pleasurable. Karen made excuses for him: he knew her to be sexually adventurous, and so perhaps he misunderstood her words and physical resistance. Maybe he thought her "no" was an objection to the discomfort of being pushed against the rock, not to the sex itself. That must have been why, she reasoned, he dragged her onto the ground.

Early in our research our five-person ethnographic team assembled around a conference table at the Columbia School of Social Work to receive the training that the university offers with the goal of developing young people's skills to stop assaults before they happen; these 'bystander' interventions are one of the small number of programs that have shown any effectiveness in reducing campus sexual assault.[6] We wanted to understand what students were learning about assault, and what they were told they could do about it. The educator talked about how perpetrators groom their victims, and together we practiced bystander strategies—how to distract a perpetrator, or disrupt an assault in process. But the role playing, focused on what we might do to interrupt an incident on the subway, presented a much simpler scene—a predatory stranger bothering a person just sitting there minding their own business—than that which young people most often confront. The reality that people know one another, have often been intimate before, that the contact could be read as flirting as much as it could be assault, makes it so much harder. It's confusing, as a bystander, to know if you are keeping someone safe or blocking them from getting lucky. Worse still, sometimes it's the bystander who is the problem.[7]

On a balmy Saturday night in April, Jessica and Kathleen went from an end-of-year dance performance to a neighborhood bar. They were acquaintances but not close friends: in the same performing arts group, and living in the same dorm. Dalton, a senior, had been texting Jessica, saying that he hoped to see her there. Jessica and Kathleen flashed their fake IDs to get in and edged their way to a table Dalton had managed to snag at the back of the bar. Dalton paid for round after round for both of them. Kathleen was falling-over drunk. Dalton offered to help Jessica get Kathleen back to the dorm, and so they staggered up Broadway, practically carrying Kathleen. It was a combination of frustrating and funny, a bonding moment that might well have been something they would chat about in the days to come, perhaps even ribbing Kathleen a bit for getting so drunk. While Jessica signed Dalton in, Kathleen laughed and ran off. Up the stairs and down the hall, they chased after her, taking seriously their responsibility to get her safely to bed. She hid in a stairwell. Eventually, they found her and got her settled. Then Dalton asked Jessica if she wanted to chill in her room. The details after that are hazy; looking back, she was surprised that she didn't throw up, given how drunk she must have been. She wonders, as students often do when they recall feeling drunker than they'd expected, if maybe he put something in her drink. She remembered lying on the bed together, chatting. Suddenly, they were having sex.

At the time, Jessica didn't label what had happened assault. He was cute, and the sex actually felt pretty good. But she wasn't happy about it. She didn't normally have random hookups. She didn't want a boyfriend, but her sexual project typically involved an ongoing connection with someone she liked and knew. In the weeks that followed, Dalton kept texting Jessica. He was eager to see her again. But she ignored his texts, "ghosting him" (not responding to any of his messages) because she just felt so "weird" about what had happened. By the time she shared her story with us, Dalton had graduated. We heard her story as assault: Jessica was very drunk, didn't say she wanted sex, and was clear—to herself at least—that she didn't want it. It's not clear that she said no; but neither did she say yes. We only have Jessica's accounting; it seems likely to us that Dalton had no idea that she experienced their encounter the way she did. His later attempts to connect with Jessica, as she told it, conveyed not that he was worried she was going to report him for assault, but that he was hoping to hang out with her again. He may even have thought that they shared something special—the "taking care of a drunk friend" scenario is sometimes enough to spark romance. When we talked to men and women in our focus groups, there was a notable difference in how they understood assaults. The men imagined that rapes were contexts where women were screaming "no" and fighting for their lives. Perhaps Dalton couldn't imagine their encounter as assault because it didn't look like what men often imagined it looked like.

Jessica is not to blame for lacking the sexual vocabulary to effectively stop what was happening, or after, to think through what had happened to her. In a broader sense, both of them were failed by the communities that raised them. Both had mastered so many lessons on their way to the Ivy League, but some fundamental ones escaped them. Dalton had been drinking in ways that likely clouded his judgment and consideration. It was only much later, after hearing several campus conversations about sexual assault, intoxication, and consent, that Jessica realized that she had been too drunk to consent, and came to think about what had happened as assault. We don't know how Dalton would have described his actions that night. But if he'd acknowledged how drunk she was as well as his own drunkenness, and considered more than the goal of sex that he likely wanted to achieve, and asked Jessica what she wanted, she might have responded to those future texts, and she wouldn't have been thinking back on her experience with him in the way that she did.

"I THOUGHT THE WHOLE POINT WAS, YOU WERE COLD."

When we interviewed Kara in the winter of her senior year, she gave a first impression of wealth and composure: dark jeans, high-heeled brown riding boots, and a cashmere turtleneck complementing her perfectly straight long dark hair, and carefully done light makeup. But she twisted nervously at her class ring from the private school where she'd been a scholarship student, and over the course of the interview, hives crept up her neck and her cheeks reddened; when we probed for details, she repeatedly answered, "I just don't remember." She struggled awkwardly for words to describe her sexual life. Yet she'd reached out to us, one of those who contacted the team to be interviewed because they "had a story to tell." The story she came to share was about a friend's experience. Her own assault—a word she never used—was something she just skimmed over.

She and her freshman-year roommate had shared a double: 150 square feet with two beds, two dressers, and two desks. That February, she crawled into bed, exhausted and "crossed"—having smoked weed and having drunk a little. Her roommate's boyfriend, visiting from Germany, had invited a friend of his from Boston down to New York. Kara wasn't happy about this—she and her roommate had been fighting so much that Kara had asked the resident advisor for help, and she had begun seeing a counselor because the conflict was making her anxious. No one asked Kara if this friend of her roommate's boyfriend could stay in the room; the four of them just crammed in together. She cracked a joke before going to sleep, hoping to break the ongoing tension. "Hey guys, don't do anything, I'm over here." Her roommate snapped back, "What's your problem? We would never do that."

The friend from Boston—Kara never knew his name—woke her up in the night. He told her he was cold and wanted to get in bed with her. Still a little high, drunk, and tired, and thinking that maybe he really was just cold, she let him climb under the covers. Soon he started to kiss her. She described herself as too "spacey" to do anything but go along with it "and, like, maybe kissing, fine, but I didn't—then I ended up giving him a blow job, and I didn't want to." He didn't use much physical force. She stopped kissing him and rested her head on his chest, hoping to fall back asleep. He pushed her head down "a little bit." She doesn't remember the details, just that "it was not—it wasn't like, pleasant. . . . And the worst part was, then he just went back to his bed on the floor, and I was like, 'I thought the whole point was, you were cold!' I definitely felt taken advantage of at that point." Kara's room didn't feel like her own; she was so scared of her roommate that she barely felt justified in claiming ownership over her bed, much less her body.

"PLAN A DIDN'T WORK . . . PLAN B WOULD BE SAYING NO, BUT I JUST DIDN'T KNOW HOW TO."

College students tend to refer to a lot of their sexual encounters as "hookups."[8] The term is ambiguous, denoting quite a range of interactions and relationships. The two people may know each other well—or not. They may have met at a bar, a campus event, or through an app. They may have kissed before, or been sleeping together for months—or maybe not. Hookups involve all kinds of sexual contact, from making out to intercourse, that happen outside a committed relationship. Given that so much sex occurs in the context of hookups, it's not particularly surprising that many unwanted and nonconsensual sexual experiences do, too.[9] A SHIFT paper led by Louisa Gilbert found that assaults that victims identified as happening because they were "incapacitated" were disproportionately likely to be committed by acquaintances (in this case, also known as "hookups"), where the two people had met before-hand at a party.[10] Non-incapacitated assaults—where force or verbal coercion was used—were more likely to happen in the contexts of committed relationships. But to focus on the relationship context alone is to miss how other elements of the context—like sexual geography—shape vulnerability.[11]

Charisma, a Black Latina senior from Albuquerque who was a varsity athlete, was quick to answer the question about what she'd choose for her one college "do-over" if given the chance. She'd love to have back one Saturday night toward the end of her freshman year. She'd met Raymond, who lived out in Brooklyn, through her roommate. After texting back and forth for weeks, he invited her out to his place. There were so many signs that it was not going to be a good night: the subway she was planning to take was closed for the weekend, making her trip almost twice as long; on the walk from the train the skies opened up, a torrential downpour soaking her to the bone, and her cell phone died so she couldn't call him for directions when she got lost. Miraculously, she had his number written on an actual piece of paper, and some change in her pocket; she was lucky enough to find a bodega with a working pay phone, and called him to get her. Sodden and demoralized, she was happy to peel off her shoes and socks and dry out. They watched tv, did a couple of shots, smoked a joint, and then started to make out. She was fine with all that, but clearly had not been expecting more to happen. She was firm in providing us with "evidence": she was wearing "granny panties" and had not brought her oral contraceptives or even a toothbrush. But more did happen. She "didn't really want it to" and she tried to convey that with her body language. When he reached in between in her legs:

> I wasn't expecting that to happen. So I was like "Okay, let me move his hand." And then his hand didn't move so I was like oh, okay, this is happening. So then it's like he started taking his clothes off, I started taking mine off, just like let it happen. 'Cause

it's like I didn't know how to say no. 'Cause it's like my way of
saying no was through body language, trying to move his hand,
'cause that's what had worked in the past to slow things down if
I didn't want to be touched in a certain area. But in this moment
that didn't work. So it was like my plan, I never had a plan B . . .
It's like plan A was always just body language, just move their
hand. Like, they get it. But this time plan A didn't work, and I
didn't, like, plan B would be saying no. But I just, I didn't know
how to, I didn't know what to do. . . . Verbal wasn't really my form
of communication. . . .

Charisma conveyed in nonverbal ways that she wasn't enjoying their
sex. She told him that it hurt, and at one point when it was hurting she
did, in fact, say "no." He may have heard but he didn't listen; instead
of stopping, she told us, he just tried a different position. Refusing sex
can be awkward, but it's a teachable skill—unfortunately, not one that
Charisma had been given an opportunity to learn.[12] Nor, to be sure, had
Raymond understood, or maybe even been exposed to, the practice of
affirmative consent.

There's a distinction between how much someone wants sex (their
internal desire) and their verbalization of that desire.[13] Raymond may
have had no idea how much she did not want to be having sex. However,
his ignoring the way she moved his hands away as he tried to touch her
sexually shows a lack of respect for Charisma's citizenship. Being attentive to the other person's right to sexual self-determination—thinking
about sex as something to share rather than something to get or to
have—may have gone a long way to prevent this kind of encounter.
Geography matters too. Charisma was stuck in Brooklyn late at night
in a downpour. The train would take almost two hours. Some students
wouldn't think twice about a $60 cab ride home, but she wasn't one of
those students. Charisma told us they had "sex," as she called it, twice
that night and then once in the morning. Perhaps anticipating our curiosity about the second and third times, she told us, unprompted,

I didn't stop it the other times 'cause I was like, well, we already did it once. What's another time? I just, like, literally had no energy to open my mouth or say anything, I just laid there. . . . It was just sad. I was probably thinking about my other friends who have casual sex . . . and like it was never a big deal for them when they do it, and maybe it's like really not a big deal. Or I was feeling ho-ish, or easy, or whatever. . . . I was like, my friends do this and it's fine for them, so it's not actually a big deal.

Charisma's only other sexual experience had been with her high school boyfriend; they'd gone out for the last two years of high school, and could read each other's body language. But she barely knew Raymond, and never saw him again. She took the experience as her own introduction to what she described as "hit it and quit it": "Before I could never understand, okay, a guy hooks up with a girl, has sex with her, then he's like done with her. Why can't you just continue to have sex with her? Why do you want to quit it? But then after that experience I was like 'Oh, 'cause you don't feel like it. You're not interested anymore.'"[14] She described the night as "something I would take back for sure," but then added that she "had to try to find a positive out of that. Which was like confirming for me that I want sex to be something meaningful for me, I want to care about the person, like I know I'm not the type to just have casual sex." While it may seem to some that Charisma was avoiding the "truth" of her assault, she made that night in Brooklyn into a lesson about her sexual project. But like a lot of learning, it took some struggle and repetition to master it.

Later, in her sophomore year, she dated a guy she'd met on Tinder for a couple of months. She wasn't crazy about him; even while they were still texting, she thought to herself that she should google "how to break up with someone." He was "a little rude"—telling her, for example, that her arms were fat—and was "disrespectful" to her friends. She recounted, "I hated being with him in public. He would be, just, extra . . . thinking that people are trying to annoy him on purpose or walk in his way and I'm 'This is New York City, It's crowded.'" She said, looking back, that "I should have taken note of those little signs, to end it or whatever. But I wanted to practice being with someone." Charisma thought of this as a time when she "failed"—by tolerating his bad behavior, by failing to express herself fully, and by giving in when he was ready for sex, and she was not. "Even with him I had sex earlier than I wanted to." He kept pushing her to "move to the next level." She was still getting over her experience with Raymond, and also didn't really like him that much. But she didn't know how to keep saying "let's just wait" without it becoming "a thing" in their relationship. "I didn't want to be in another uncomfortable situation. So I just told him to get the condom and let it happen. I was trying to hold off for like a couple of weeks. But I don't know, I just didn't want to be in another awkward situation."

"Tinder guy," as she described him, was verbally abusive over the course of their relationship. For Charisma, having unwanted sex felt easier than having a difficult conversation. She didn't have the vocabulary to talk about her sexual project, or a strong sense of her own right to sexual self-determination. His focus was on moving things to the next level, not on creating a context where she felt comfortable expressing herself. After they first had sex, she decided something was wrong with how she was navigating her sexual project. She wanted someone who recognized her sexual citizenship. The realization was definitive: "Just because I'm dating someone doesn't mean I have to have sex with them. I want sex to be more intimate. I don't want to regret it." By the time we sat down with Charisma, it had been two years since she had dated "Tinder guy," during which time she'd talked with a couple of guys but not had intercourse with anyone. She was happy about this. "I want it to be something serious for me, 'cause then I'm more into it, I have more fun with him. We are comfortable, I'm more willing to try new things." The emerging clarity around her sexual project is evident in her description of a more recent liaison: "I was talking to someone this semester for a couple of months. And I could have had sex with him easily. But I didn't want to. I held on. It was like—it was not a problem for me to say

'No.' Pretty sure he thought I would give in at some point. But I have grown a lot. And I was like, nuh-uh. . . . I'm really glad that I didn't have sex with him, I was able to stick to what I want sex to be for me." Charisma hadn't necessarily found a different kind of guy, she had found a different sense of herself: one with clarity and purpose about her right to have only the kind of sex she wanted.

Charisma's story of being worn down into finally consenting to sex she did not want came up several times with other people we spoke with. It wasn't that they were drunk and didn't have the words—it was that a partner heard their words but didn't listen.

Mattie came to label what happened to her "rape"—but the relationship started out in an exciting way. She had struggled to find people who wanted the same kinds of experiences that she did, but eventually after some searching online she met her girlfriend at a New York kink sex party. Mattie was assigned the gender identity of "male" at birth, but during college began to transition to being a woman. Over the course of her two-month relationship with her girlfriend, Mattie had begun taking hormones and her transition became more and more visible. She was happy, finally feeling like herself. But as Mattie transitioned, her girlfriend kept wanting to have sex that involved Mattie's penis. For Mattie, using her penis during sex made her feel less like a woman. Her girlfriend's determined pursuit of penile penetration felt like a violation—not only of her boundaries, but of her whole self.

> She was very resentful of my transition. She didn't like the fact that I couldn't use my penis anymore and she really wanted that. Every time we would have sex, she would like ask me. . . . When I would remind her, she would like frown. At some point I kind of gave up and I like stopped saying "no." I just stood there and took it and that was really horrible and I would totally classify that as the fact that I was raped because I was emotionally pressured into it. I was coerced to consenting and I didn't want to consent and had she

not been all upset every time I said no, I would have said, "No,"
and—you know—I would've kept saying, "No." But at some point,
it just took too much emotional toll on me, so I started saying "yes."
It was a war of attrition and her wants overtook my—my consent
boundaries, my needs. So she ended up raping me.

In this "war of attrition," Mattie's partner extracted verbal consent, as
had Charisma's. But for Mattie, as she made clear, it was still rape.[15]

Sometimes assaulters ignore a clearly articulated "no." Sometimes it is
the body language, telling them to stop, that they disregard. And sometimes they turn a persistent "no" into an unwanted "yes." A lot of times
the failure is one of empathy and imagination—failure to understand
that someone might go along with something because it feels awkward
to stop, failure to see that one's social power, or the group's, might render another unable to say no, failure to think about how the desire to
avoid an awkward moment could literally overpower the desire not to
have sex—or failure to consider that, given how much the other person
has had to drink, it's absurd to imagine that they can consent. Assaults
are contexts where one person is inattentive to the other person's right
to sexual self-determination: their sexual citizenship. And often those
who are assaulted have not truly developed a sense of themselves as full
sexual citizens.

In hearing these stories, we rarely saw what looked like predation,
but it also never looked like benign neglect. Instead, the neglect of the
other person seemed far more active—sometimes intentional, sometimes just astonishingly self-absorbed. Almost as if the other person
wasn't a person, but instead an object used to satisfy personal desires.
This is the wisdom of emphasizing affirmative consent—teaching people that they should check in with each other, and be clear about what
the other person is up for. But to focus on only the lack of affirmative
consent is to overlook the many other layers of the problem. What kind
of society produces people whose feeling about their own right to sexual

self-determination is so impoverished that they'd spare someone else an awkward interaction, even if it means having a strange and unwelcome penis inside of them?[16] What kind of society produces people whose sexual projects ignore the basic sexual citizenship of others?[17] And what kind of society produces spaces that don't discourage this kind of behavior, but that instead, seem to facilitate it?[18]

"THIS IS GOING TO BE LIKE A WHOLE NEW CAN OF WORMS."

Social organization doesn't just make assault possible. It also makes some assaults more visible than others, in ways that are highly gendered. Men we interviewed who'd been assaulted, like many students, struggled to make sense of their experience. When we first met him, Boutros seemed like a member of the global elite. An aspiring Olympic-level squash player, he speaks English, French, German, and Arabic, and worked for the year before college at a bank in Switzerland. But as his story unfolded we realized the error in our assumptions: his family had fled Lebanon for France, and he had been a scholarship student at a Swiss boarding school. His good looks, language skills, and boarding school contacts helped him find a job as a bank receptionist in Geneva during his pre-college gap year. In response to the question about whether he'd ever had sex where he or the other person did not fully grant consent, he said, "Not sex, no, but this was weird." He warned us that "this is going to be like a whole new can of worms." Boutros described a pub crawl during a long weekend in Edinburgh with his best friend and two women who were several years older. Late at night, the cab dropped his friend off at the hostel. Boutros planned to walk across town to his cousin's house. But one of the women insisted, " 'No, no, no, like you're too drunk. Just come back with me.' And, um, I went back to her house, and it was weird. Like she was trying to get with me and stuff, and I just wanted to go to sleep. And, um, I think that's like the closest to like . . . I guess that's kind of like sexual assault."

We asked Boutros about this woman "trying to get with" him. She undressed, grabbed him, and wouldn't let go. He repeatedly asked her to leave him alone. In our conversation, Boutros kept doubling back on his story, his otherwise coherent discussion becoming more and more muddled.

> I don't think it's sexual assault. Come on, a girl can't really sexually assault a guy. I don't know, maybe . . . I was thinking, "What the hell are you doing? You've got a boyfriend, I like your best friend, just leave me alone." I guess it is, but it just sounds like—sexual assault makes it sound pretty bad. I guess it is, pretty. Okay, fine. It was sexual assault. I just think it was weird. And she's a weirdo. . . . As I said, I really overthink things. I don't think I just got sexually assaulted. "I'm going to sue her and I'm going to like . . ." No. Unless I get grievous bodily harm or come to serious financial detriment.

Boutros eventually pried himself free. She had taken advantage of the fact that he was in her apartment, in a city he didn't know, and that he was drunk. When we tell people that nearly one in six men in the SHIFT survey experienced some form of sexual assault by the time they graduated, they almost invariably follow up by asking: "Who is assaulting them?" In two-thirds of the cases, it's women.[19] This answer is hard for many to make sense of. It's similarly hard for many heterosexual men to see themselves as victims of sexual assault—how could it be assault if they were not afraid or were never physically overpowered?[20]

"I WAS DRINKING 'CAUSE I WAS UPSET."

Tim is tall, athletic, and handsome, and was part of a prestigious group of men on campus; his very active sex life mostly involved getting drunk and hooking up with women ("girls," as he called them). He didn't feel harmed by his assault, but he was indignant about the invisibility of his experience. The evening he wanted to talk with us about happened during his sophomore year. He described himself as having been "really sad." He went out to one of the bars near campus and drank heavily, alone: "My last memory is feeling myself losing control, looking and seeing if any of my friends are there. There was only one guy, eating face with some girl—he's not gonna help me right now. My last memory is face planting on the table. I wake up again maybe like 5:45-ish." He was in an unknown bed. His face was sticky. He checked to see if maybe he'd thrown up—but it wasn't vomit. He realized it was vaginal secretions. He had no memory of what happened.

We asked him how he felt about waking up naked and confused in a stranger's bed. "Well, I don't really care. Like, shit just happens, right? Whatever. I walk back to my room. I sleep it off, wash my face. This bitch probably rubbed my face while I was asleep." The next day, he asked a friend, "What the fuck happened last night?" His friends had seen her drag him, barely able to walk, back to her room. This was not Tim's first interaction with her. Early in the fall of his freshman year, he was, somewhat typically, blackout drunk at a party. "There was an hour I didn't remember . . . I was just like dancing, barely standing up." She approached him, took his phone out of his pocket, and snapped some pictures of them together. He didn't remember any of this. Weeks later she walked up to him in the dining hall and asked him to send the pictures to her. "I was like, 'What do you mean?' She's like, 'You were really fucked up so I took your phone out of your pocket and took pictures.'" Tim shook his head and told her, "'You don't know me, you're not my friend.'" He figured she wanted him to text her the photos so she could get his number. Thinking back on this, and his later story, he told us, "She's a psycho, she's a fucking psycho."

Tim was angry—not at the woman or at his friends who just let him get dragged away, but at the feeling that the kind of experience he had goes unrecognized, and if he brought it up, it could go catastrophically wrong.

Like, shit, I really didn't care to be honest . . . but what was upsetting is obviously if that happened to a girl there'd be a huge fucking deal. . . I don't really care what happens to me—passing out in public, that's dangerous for me, if anything, it's better that she took me home, but here's what got me really angry about it. I didn't give a shit. I've hooked up with a lot of girls when I'm drunk. What was upsetting to me is that say I go to Columbia, right? I'll say "Hey, I blacked out and passed out. Woke up in this girl's bed," right? Say "I blacked out," say "I know I was incapacitated and passed out, and I woke up, in this girl's bed," right? They talk to her. All she has to say is, "He was drunk, he doesn't remember, he raped me," right? And who are they gonna believe? Best case scenario, it's a stalemate. More than likely, she could say, "He was drunk, I remember he was"—and what the fuck do I do? So I feel if any girl says that, they're fine. But a dude doesn't have recourse, it's fucked up. Again, like personally I don't think it's that bad, but I definitely understand how that's like textbook definition of rape, right?

Tim is right: he was assaulted. It may never have occurred to the woman who first stalked and then assaulted Tim that there is sex that men do not want to have, in part because of sexual scripts that suggest that men always want sex.[21] Like many more men than women, Tim did not feel particularly harmed by what happened to him. He was, however, angry about the ways in which, in our terms, prevailing gendered assumptions invalidated his experiences and made them unintelligible—not to him, since he very explicitly noted that "that's like textbook definition of rape"—but, he felt, to the institution and the world around him.

"I WAS LOST ALREADY."

Boutros and Tim found it hard to make sense of their experiences because of gendered ideas about sex and assault, including the notion that men always want sex, and that assault necessarily requires being physically overpowered. Fran's experience also reflected gendered sexual ideals—in her case, the moralistic division of women into saints and sinners. The silencing of Fran's sexual citizenship began at a birthday party when she was five. Her parents, new to Mountain Brook and unfamiliar with the conservative Southern Baptist community's standards of modesty for young girls, had dropped her off at a birthday pool party. She felt like a million bucks in her new bikini from Target, with a matching cover-up. The shaming was immediate, and intense. She didn't even know what a slut or a sinner was, only that the other girls told her she was one. And not just that day; they picked on her all through elementary and middle school, with a social hierarchy that placed her at the bottom because of her perceived moral defects.

A middle school party was a turning point. She was rarely invited anywhere, and she and another ostracized kid—also in a panic about one of their first boy-girl parties—decided it might be easier if they swiped some tequila and did a couple of shots before the party. It was a revelation to have even a brief interlude where she could tune out the worries about what others might think or say. She felt powerful, getting away with and even embracing the transgressions that she had for so long been accused of. The adult chaperones did not seem to notice her intoxication, or perhaps it just confirmed what they already felt about her. And her friend's parents who picked them up may have just thought that she was being silly on the way home.

This was the start of what Fran subsequently described as her descent into being "a bad girl"—sneaking out of the house, frequently stoned and drunk, after her parents went to bed ("which they did at, like, 8 p.m."). Her parents didn't notice; all they cared about, seemingly, was her field hockey and her grades. Fran was raped at 14, in the back of a car, by her boyfriend. They'd only been going out for two weeks, and hadn't done anything other than touch each other's bodies with their clothes on. She doesn't entirely remember what happened, other than that one moment they were clothed and making out, then suddenly, they were naked and his penis was inside of her. This was her first of many rapes. He was a senior, and had turned eighteen months before the incident. She was too young to legally consent. She didn't think about this; all she knew is that she didn't want to be having sex, and had not consented. But then, as she recounted, she decided it was fine. It started to feel good. And anyway, "I was lost already." She had been since she was five.

HOW COULD I NOT KNOW THAT AN INVITATION TO SOMEONE'S ROOM MEANT HOOKING UP?

If sexual shame produces vulnerability, so does silence. And it's not young people's silence we're talking about here, it's our own: failure to talk to them about sex, to articulate a vision for what their projects might be, to lay the groundwork for them to own their sexual citizenship. The refusal to acknowledge young people as legitimate sexual beings causes harm: not feeling as if they have the right to say "yes" causes confusion about when it's legitimate to say "no."[22] We were astonished by the extent to which these otherwise highly educated young people lacked meaningful knowledge about sex, with consequences that were direct and disturbing. This was most acutely at play during those early weeks of school when perhaps the prime directive is: Don't look stupid.

Kimberly's mother, who'd been a waitress in a bar, was murdered by her father when Kimberly was in middle school. Kimberly and her younger sisters, taken in by an aunt in rural Maine, basically raised themselves. Kimberly felt bad leaving her siblings behind in that small, drafty house, but Columbia was her big break, and no one was going to stop her from becoming an engineer. Her second night on campus, a guy from across the hall knocked on the door of her room, inviting her to a party. "Sure!"

she told him. She was not going to drink, she said to herself, but she'd go. But everyone else was drinking, and it felt weird to keep refusing. She doesn't remember very much of what happened—mostly that her roommate, who came to find her later in the guy's room, brought her back to the party. She recalls feeling embarrassed when he announced to everyone that she gave great blow jobs, that he was going to ask her for another one sometime soon.

Only the next day, at the orientation session on consent, did she gain the language to label what had happened: that they hardly even said a word to one another, that he never checked in with her about what was okay, and that she was too drunk to even make sense of what was happening. She said she bore no animosity toward him because he was also a freshman and didn't know any better. What does it mean to be so unsure of one's sexual boundaries, so without a language for physical and sexual autonomy, that you need a workshop on consent to understand that you've been violated?

"BUT YOU'RE HAVING FUN"

Gaslighting—psychological manipulation that sows doubt, making someone question their own memory or sanity—takes advantage of inexperience; and those starting out in college are particularly vulnerable, because they are inexperienced not just with sex but with college life itself. Jamie was the rare kid who'd gotten through boarding school without drinking at all. Short, with straight shoulder-length hair and dark eyes, she was the daughter of poultry workers from Maryland's Eastern Shore. In high school Jamie worried that as a scholarship kid, she might not be given a second chance if she got in trouble. Better to keep her head down and excel. She was not just going to be the first in her family to make it to college—she was going for the Ivy League. Her plan had always been not to do anything illegal—no drugs and no drinking until she was 21. Her life project felt too precarious to take any big risks, and she was particularly cautious about sex.

But it seemed like everyone in her dorm was drunk those first couple of nights. Jamie worried she was missing out on some essential part of the experience. On the third night she gave in and did a couple of shots. Late that night, one of her new friends texted her. Did she want to come see his saxophone? She walked into his room, and looked around. Where should she sit? Sure, it's awkward to sit down on a bed, but where else could she sit? Jamie didn't want to seem uptight or uncool by choosing the desk chair or the floor. They chatted on his bed and then he reached over, dimmed the lights, and started to touch her. He caressed her chest, shoulders, and neck. She told him she didn't want to do anything, and reminded him about her boyfriend from high school, then a freshman at Harvard. Saxophone guy responded, "No, but you're having fun," and kept touching her. She didn't want him to feel like he'd done something wrong, so she just told him she was too tired to fool around, grabbed her shoes, and walked back down the hall to her room.

Jamie felt like an idiot—how could she not know that in college, an invitation to someone's room meant hooking up? She felt awful, that she'd unintentionally cheated on her boyfriend. She was worried about burning bridges—she hadn't made many friends yet, and didn't want to lose one already. She was even more worried about her reputation. People might learn about what happened, and think of her as an inexperienced virgin who didn't have a clue about how to have fun, how to navigate the "real college experience." She didn't call what happened an assault—she called it a "learning experience." She'd never told anyone until she shared it in the interview—she thought people would blame her, say she should've known better. This was the first of three times that Jamie was assaulted. The interview was so difficult that we reached out to her afterwards, to check in and see how she was doing. Jamie insisted that she was fine—that she'd been eager to participate in the research, and was glad she did. Jamie was proud of the months of sobriety she'd logged, and hoped that her story could somehow help make campuses safer. Still, for all her "learning experience," it was sad to hear how much of that learning was done alone, without much help from the communities and institutions whose job it was to raise her.

"I CAME ALL THE WAY UPTOWN AND I'M NOT EVEN GONNA HAVE AN ORGASM?"

Gwen prepared for the interview, bringing a list of all the guys she'd hooked up with—she'd even checked it with her friends—and referred to it from time to time as we chatted. As a tall, beautiful white woman, she'd slid easily into the New York club scene, and spent several nights a week out, downtown. She described herself as "boy crazy," but—other than one threesome she bragged about—she had not actually had intercourse with that many people. The words spilled out, as she shared stories that she thought were "good for the study." She hadn't wanted to have intercourse with the B-list actors, not-that-famous professional athletes, and other guys she met in clubs who invited her back to their hotel rooms—and so she didn't. But her strategy to "not have sex" was to give them a blow job. For her this seemed like a reasonable compromise, a way to get out of a room she no longer wanted to be in, when a guy was pushing for something more. She repeatedly said that she wanted to "restore the intimacy of the make-out." The line seemed fairly well practiced. But it reflected a sentiment that seemed to us sincere: yearning to enact a sexual project in which physical intimacy expresses emotional connection, rather than her feminine obligation to satisfy someone else's physical desire.[23]

Gwen was reluctant to label what happened freshman year an assault. But when asked if she had any regrets, she immediately answered: "Yeah, scary sex regrets." The guy was a senior she'd met at a party; he wanted to go home that night, but she wasn't that interested and decided to just give him her number. The next morning, over Sunday brunch at their favorite local diner, her roommates encouraged her to give him a chance. And she admitted to herself that if she was going to be with someone on campus, it might as well include a freshman's bragging rights of dating a senior. They went on two dates. She had a plan in mind:

> All right, we're going to kiss and it's gonna be great and then that's it and then he's gonna finger me the next time and this is gonna be the slow production . . . But what was I kidding myself? Like, he's a senior in college, that was not what was gonna happen. The moment we start kissing I honestly, at that situation, was just trying to force something that wasn't there.

Her "what was I kidding myself?" refers to two things. First, despite her mental map of moving through the bases with him, she hadn't accounted for how she might feel—and what she was feeling was zero. She recounted her internal dialogue: "This is awful. I hate this. I am not even pity doing anything with this guy." To translate, "pity doing something" might be giving him a blow job, just to end the evening. The second part of "what was I kidding myself" was her realization that "the slow production" might be her ideal, but not his. Her internal dialogue continued: "I'm not even touching his penis, this is not happening." They were in her dorm room, in her bed, and he started taking off her clothes. He unbuckled her jeans, and reached for a condom. She thought to herself, "We were just supposed to make out." She tried to pacify him by suggesting that they cuddle: it would be kind of cozy to fall asleep in each other's arms. She woke up in the middle of the night. "This guy is humping me in my sleep—just, like, gyrating. I'm like, 'What is this?' He was, like, humping, like, my butt and my leg. I was like, 'This is weird.'"

The next day, she talked to a friend. Gwen described it as "weird." Her friend quickly corrected her. "Oh my god that's sexual assault, 'cause as far as he knows you were sleeping!" Then she told her mom. When her mom agreed with her friend, Gwen pushed back against all that the label would mean. She justified his actions, "The lines are kind of blurred. I did let him sleep over, you know." She decided, "I'm not gonna think twice about it." This, combined with the next assault, was the crucible in which her sexual citizenship was forged.

The second assault—also an incident of unwanted touching— illustrates just how scary it can be to fight off a guy who feels entitled to sex. She described it as "my scariest situation where I kind of learned that, like, I have no obligation to men and their sexual needs." Think for a moment, before the story continues, that this woman—from a wealthy background, and close enough to her mom that she reached out unhesitatingly after her first assault—had, until this time, thought she had an obligation to men and their sexual needs. And ask yourself if you think many men in the stories we've told so far feel the same way about women's needs (including the need to be left alone).[24]

The man in this story was not a fellow student; he was a model from Los Angeles, and "gorgeous gorgeous gorgeous" but also "scummy." They had been sending flirtatious texts, but she was busy with exams. The last night before she left for the summer, with her roommate already gone, she'd spent the day packing up her belongings. He said he was going to come uptown to smoke with her.

> I told him, "I'm not having sex with you, by the way." He's like, "Ha, ha, do you give good head?" I was like, "I guess, but don't expect anything."

"LA model club promoter guy," as she referred to him, took the subway uptown. In the sultry press of mid-May, they went to smoke a joint in Morningside Park.

And he's like, "I need to go back to your room." And I was like, "No, let's not." And then he's like, "Yeah, I left my food in there." I was like, "Fine." So, I was very high from not a lot of weed and so we go back to the room. . . .

She was clear—with him, with herself—that she did not want to fool around:

I was only gonna hook up with a guy if it was worth it. Not just for the sake of it. So he kind of starts making out with me and he was a good kisser. I was like, "All right, fine." He takes off my shirt, and I'm like, "All right, fine." Then he's like, "Take off your pants." And I was like—I used my intuition. I just knew—your gut's right one hundred percent of the time. This wasn't right. I was like, "Nothing's happening."

He turned off the lights. She asked him to turn them back on.

And then he said, "Well, we're gonna have sex." I'm like, "No we're not." I was like, "Well, see, look, look at my bed, there's no sheets on bed, it's all in boxes . . ."
He's like, "Whatever. We'll do it here on the floor, we'll do it standing, I don't care.
And, like, blah, blah, blah. I was like, "No, no, no." Then he's like, "Well, suck me off." and I was like, "No." "Oh yeah?" "No." "Are you fucking kidding me? I came all the way uptown to smoke you out and not even gonna have an orgasm."

She couldn't believe it.

And then he starts verbally assaulting me. Telling me, "Oh, you're a bitch. You're" [she paused] the c word. "Fuck you, you think this school actually means something?" You know what I mean? Just, like, trying to put me down. And, like, everything just seems, like, exaggerated, because, like, I'm high.

It continued. He threatened to tell the security guard she'd been smoking marijuana, and she responded that she'd tell the security guard that he tried to rape her.

"You need to get out or I'm gonna call the cops." And he's like, "And then the cops'll know you're high." And I was like, "I have a really better argument than you do." And so he finally leaves and then he says, "I'll catch you later." And I was like, "Fuck you." And I was traumatized, 'cause I was, like, just verbally harassed.

And then I just start crying and I called my mom and I told her about the story and as I'm kind of saying it back it's a lot better than I thought it was in the moment. In the moment it felt like the worst thing in the world, but at the end of the day it was an idiot who was just saying mean things to me; nothing escalated, my pants never came off. I know you're not supposed to blame your-self. But I went against my better judgment. I knew what this guy was all about and I chose to ignore it. Um, yeah, so I—I definitely learned from the situation.

That was a turning point:

"I was like, wow, I wasn't even gonna give him head, you know, was not gonna feel bad about it. Because I had no reason to, you know. He doesn't—what makes him deserve it, right? Definitely a learning experience. I actually ran into him at a club and I was like, to my friend, I was like, "That's my rapist. Or, like, rapist guy."

Later in the interview we asked her about consent. How it works, and how it's worked for her. The juxtaposition, and her description based on her experiences, was astonishing. "You know, guys will pressure you until you do consent. I've never been raped or anything."

No, she'd never been raped. But she'd had her body touched, and had been subject to verbal abuse, by a man who assumed that consent to enter her room equaled consent to enter her vagina.

III

Reading these stories may feel like jumping into a river of pain; there are so many instances of young people failing to see the humanity in each other, to treat each other with kindness and consideration. And there are some moments that seem like real, intentional evil, like telling a vulnerable freshman that "it's okay" when she clearly says "no." But as we wade through into these waters, despite the variety in these stories, there is a constant set of factors operating in the background that produce vulnerability both to being assaulted, and to committing assault. These factors are not just identifiable—they are modifiable. We can build safer campuses, although in part it will require work off-campus, and before students ever arrive on campus. To see how to move forward, we have to learn more about campus geography today.

2

UNDER ONE ROOF

THE RAT RACE

On Saturday mornings at 10 a.m., hours after swimmers, wrestlers, basketball players, and other varsity athletes have crowded through the doors, Dodge Fitness Center opens for Columbia's general members. We start queueing up at about 9:45. Students in the glass entryway are mostly checking their phones, keeping to themselves. When the student working at the check-in booth gives the nod, people start swiping through, and the race is on. There's one thirty-minute cardio machine slot per person. At ten o'clock on the dot all the ellipticals and treadmills are full. Headphones on, ponytails bouncing, sweat dripping onto the machines—the goal is to make every minute count.

When the digital clock's bright red numbers flash 10:29 a.m., people signed up for the next half hour start trying to make eye contact with those on the machines. They are polite, even apologetic: "Um, I think I'm signed up for that machine next?" There's an awkward moment with the switch: does the person leaving machine at 10:30 actually have to stop early to wipe down the machine, so that the next person can start exactly at 10:30? Interactions where two people want different things can be very awkward.

Life on campus, as in the rest of New York, can be intense. We have seen students scarfing down breakfast in the gym locker room—a brief moment of quiet, with a bagel and a thermos of coffee, after a shower and before class or an internship. A sign in the women's locker room reminds students that shaving and urinating inside the sauna are prohibited. Some students circle the jogging track together, but for many, Dodge presents a solitary project—go in, get it done, move on. Those intercollegiate team members, for whom athletics offers not just fitness but a sense of belonging, have separate spaces—rowers saunter out of the crew room, wrestlers with singlets around their waists burst through the doors from the gym's lower level, and swimmers, clustered together in their long swim coats, hair wet, laughing at a shared joke, exit Dodge as the rest of us wait for it to open. Faculty keep to themselves—occasionally greeting a colleague, but mostly hoping to avoid being seen naked in the locker room by a student or, perhaps worse, a dean.

On a Saturday morning walk home back through campus, we catch a snippet of conversation between a man and two young children: "Of course, you'd need to be good enough to be a Columbia student." For many students, the sculpted bodies they cultivate in the gym are just one more expression of the appetite for hard work that got them to campus. When the weather is fair and students join all the other runners down the hill in Riverside Park, the treadmills in the gym are emptier. But there are tourists on the Low Library steps year-round, taking pictures of the famous statue, *Alma Mater*, maybe dreaming that they, or their children, will someday call this campus their own.

And yet the goal of college, and of this moment of transitioning to adulthood, is not just to achieve—it is also to move away from one's childhood family and connect with a new, "chosen" family. Early adulthood is the time of separation—to make a unique life, one's own friends, and set out toward a career. For some students, continuities ease the transition. Students who play "rich people sports"—lacrosse, sailing, tennis, or crew—may know their new teammates from national tournaments, private school leagues, or pricey sports camps. Students from elite public and private high schools will see faces from their own graduating class on campus, as well as those from prior years. Religious structures are another bridge connecting students into campus life; sure, the campus prayer space may not be exactly what they had before, but the underlying institution offers a welcome continuity.

In October 2015, we slowed down at the corner of Broadway and 115th to let two young women in long skirts pass us. We caught a bit of their excited chatter. One referred to "this project of Jewish husbandry." The other laughed, saying, "Isn't husbandry something about taking care of trees?" "No, silly, it's finding a husband," said the first. The guard welcomed them by name as they turned into the warmly lit Jerusalem stone campus center for Jewish student life. Columbia and Barnard have their share of religious students, although nationally, fewer and fewer college students today are religiously affiliated, and of course there are some students, like LGBTQ ones, who find more harm than support in religious spaces.[1] While some fortunate students begin college with a place where they immediately belong, like a team or a religious community, college is a place where young people often find themselves lonely within the crowd.[2]

Student organizations recruit by offering up the hope of connection. A black-and-white flyer for the women's rugby team calls out, in block letters, for students to "Join the Family." The nearly 25% of students on campus involved in Greek life are drawn, in part, by the notion that during that first year on campus, they will be someone's "little," and have someone to go to and somewhere they belong.[3] Even activities like Model UN come with a complete kin structure, including "MUNtors" (older students assigned to mentor new Model UN students), and in some cases "grandMUNtors" (the muntors of one's muntor); they even evoke familial incest taboos with their prohibitions on "muncest."

Students focus so intensely on getting to college that many have not thought about just how wrenching the transition will feel. So much of college life can be seen through the fundamental tension at this developmental stage: a desperate drive for independence coupled with feeling alone and abandoned. Extracurricular organizations and new friendship groups are the glue of college life—where students meet new friends, discover themselves, and find sexual partners. This shapes the landscape of sexual assault—both how people experience and think about it, and also why it can be so hard to address. Whether it's the marching band, a theater group, the Black Students Organization, or a religious group, extracurriculars are both a terrain of accomplishment—offering an opportunity to ascend to leadership, to network, to meet somebody who knows somebody who can help you get through the hell of finding a summer job—and of connection. This context is essential for understanding vulnerability to sexual assault.

UNDERIROOF

Students don't know what kind of world they'll encounter in three years, much less decades in the future. The emotional consequences of such uncertainty are an essential component of today's campus landscape. A 2015 survey of students at 40 schools across the country found that 85% of college students reported being overwhelmed at some point.[4] Research with directors of college counseling programs found that over 40% said that anxiety was the greatest concern for college students today, and one in four of their student clients were taking some kind of psychotropic medication.[5] According to an annual multi-campus survey conducted by the American College Health Association, between 2008 and 2018 the percentage of students diagnosed with or treated for anxiety more than doubled (from 10% to 22%), and the percentage diagnosed with or treated for depression nearly doubled (from 10% to 18%).[6] This is a fundamental feature of the campus ecology. Even students who don't experience anxiety or depression live in a context where many do. Roommates, teammates, sexual partners, lab partners: at least one of them is struggling. The collective emotional burden is considerable, and in some communities, especially those that are already precarious, the weight is particularly heavy.

Even high up in Morningside Heights, the ground on which students walk feels as if it's constantly shifting. We're not suggesting that it's so much worse for college students than it is for others—say, the poor who are excluded from opportunities and whose jobs are tenuous at best. But whereas college was once a privileged space that, in large part, protected young people from such uncertainty, for today's students those protections feel fragile. It's hard to be settled, to feel secure, with so little sense of what the future holds.[7]

Yet the purpose of college, is, in part, to unsettle. As educators, we would be failing if we simply reaffirmed what students already thought and felt, or produced a community of comfort and familiarity. New ideas should be troubling and challenging. This is part of what gives them their power. Mind-expanding experiences are not comforting and soothing like childhood blankets. The possibilities are scary, but often thrilling. It's part of what some students are looking for when they leave home, desperate for something new.

Sundeep's family was so proud of him for getting into Columbia, and so grateful for the scholarship that covered all of his tuition. But his departure meant that the only adult with papers had left the house. There was one less regular salary coming in, and no one to help the younger children with their homework, make sense of what was happening at school, talk to the landlord, or manage the day-to-day things that were so hard to accomplish without speaking English while also being undocumented. For his part, Sundeep could not wait to get away from a home that felt like a space of fear and repression. The constant worry that his parents could be deported made them even more conservative. They didn't want him to draw attention. They also didn't want him to be gay. Sundeep felt relieved, and guilty, when he left.

Sundeep loved his parents; his campus job allowed him to send money home when he could; he recognized and respected all the sacrifices they'd made for him. But he didn't go home anymore. He couldn't face being berated about his sexuality. When he walked into our office, we were concerned that he didn't have a warm enough winter coat. But as his story unfolded, we realized this was just the beginning. Sundeep's interview was harrowing for us—not because of the assaults he experienced, but because of how his homelessness put him at so much risk. Poverty bred precariousness. Sundeep had spent winter break of his sophomore year—from December 20th to January 20th—wandering the streets of New York. After the dorms closed he had nowhere to go. He didn't want to talk to his friends about it. To go home with one of his classmates would lead to questions he didn't really want to answer. He had a plan. He'd scouted out office buildings around Manhattan that had quiet, mostly abandoned spaces in which he could nap during the day: a chair outside an office that wasn't really used, for example. He had a backstory and even some props: if roused by an office worker concerned about his presence, he'd show his Columbia notebook and ID; he was an intern on another floor, and an Ivy League student; he'd fallen asleep; he'd be on his way. Once discovered, he never went back; he had a whole list of buildings he could use. So during the days, Sundeep slept in Manhattan's accessible office spaces and in spaces on campus that were open to the office staff and professors still working on campus.

At night he rode the subways. He didn't feel safe sleeping there, but he would read, zone out, or listen to music. The subway was warm. He didn't always get enough to eat. He didn't sleep nearly enough. But he never felt in much danger. It was certainly better than going home. More than most, he was thrilled with the opening of campus after the break—to have a bed, a meal plan, and a place to be. College unsettled his old life. But that's exactly what he'd signed up for.

Men like Sundeep—queer, poor, nonwhite, with undocumented families—aren't common at Columbia, but neither are they rare. In the last twenty years, they've become a feature of the campus landscape.[8] Elite colleges point to these students with pride, "Yes, we might be exceptionally wealthy institutions, but look at what we make possible for men like Sundeep." In a way that they didn't used to be, elite colleges are now spaces of encounter, where a man whose family owns multiple homes might share a room with a man who'd spent part of his life homeless. Making this possible, so that an intrinsic part of college is navigating difference, has become a critical mission of American higher education.[9] When their students were mostly white people from a narrow socioeconomic background, colleges didn't have to think so much about strategies to create an equitable learning environment for different kinds of students. But today, they have to ask how Sundeep can feel at home alongside men whose families have studied at Columbia since before the American Revolution, when it was called "King's College." How the descendants of slaveholders can study and live alongside the descendants of slaves. How women can thrive on a campus where they have only been able to matriculate as Columbia students since 1983. Today, colleges have to ask what work is necessary so that students who are lesbian, gay, bisexual, or nonbinary will be accorded the same respect as any other student. These transformations don't just happen as a result of meritocratic admissions processes or more generous financial aid policies. They are the product of policies and programs that deliberately embrace, or even seek to engineer through admissions policies, certain kinds of difference.[10] For incoming students, the transition to college presents at least three distinct social challenges: leaving home, remaking their social world, and encountering forms of difference with which they are unfamiliar. For the institution, the challenge is to bridge those differences in experiences, resources, and self-understanding to create a community of learners.

Juan came to Columbia from a middle-class community in the Southwest. Few families there were poor, though the wealthier children tended to go to a different high school, nestled out of sight behind smooth adobe walls. He described coming to Columbia as "definitely a big culture shock." At orientation, he learned that the way he spoke about sex, "making jokes about women," as part of his everyday conversations, was not acceptable. "It was definitely a big jump." In high school it would have been totally normal to talk about sex in ways that "insinuated that a woman was an object," but he quickly learned that "I would get killed if I did something like that." Like most of its peer institutions, Columbia includes in its orientation programming explicit instructions on how students should encounter diversity—with a particular focus on how to have respectful conversations. Called the "Under1Roof" program, it

> explores how we individually and collectively create an inclusive community at Columbia University. It provides the framework on how inter-group understanding and community building are achieved through continual engagement and education about the different social identities that all students bring to campus. It is the exciting beginning of a sustained dialogue that will last throughout a student's education here and beyond.[11]

While at first glance Juan's high school tendency to talk about women as objects indicates a lack of respect across lines of difference, it was those very differences that made him want to be part of the community. He considered other highly selective private colleges, but chose Columbia for its diversity:

> I thought the idea of diversity was really cool even though I didn't know what that meant. I just knew diversity sounds like a good thing to have. Turns out it was one of the best things that could have happened in terms of me liking to be around a lot of people who were very different. I didn't realize I liked it as much as I did until I got to see it. I definitely didn't know what diversity meant, but now I'm, like, a big fan of it. It's, like, addicting.

Juan is not alone in finding this difference so meaningful—or in noting its salience in the community that he joined. Colleges today are often far more diverse than almost any other community students have lived in before, and certainly more diverse than many workplaces that they will join after. Columbia College and Columbia Engineering's class of 2022, for example, is 57% white, 28% Asian, 17% Latino, 16% African

American, 4% Native American, and 16% international.[12] Seventeen percent are the first in their family to go to college. The SHIFT survey found that 78% of the students identified as heterosexual.[13] America's strong pattern of residential segregation means that almost no high school looks like this. It's one of the unsettling and exciting features of college. It's an intentional community of difference that embodies the notion that excellence can come from just about anywhere in society. After college, students will settle back into their more segregated lives. And within college they'll also live in separate worlds—clustering with other members of the queer community, or with friends who are also mostly white and rich, or with their fellow religiously observant students. But they cannot help but experience the encounter with difference. Students find this both valuable and disruptive.

Freshman year, Juan struggled to find "his people." His roommates didn't drink and were dismissive of sports, which were a huge part of his life. Eventually he found a group of men who shared his interests. And for all the diversity on campus, "his people" tended to be people more or less like him. "I'd say I got lucky with the people who I found here. If I didn't get lucky with the people who I found here I would've been miserable. I wanted to transfer in the beginning because I didn't really like the people I had."

There's a lot riding on orientation, when schools prepare incoming students to bridge differences and make connections. It's a flood of guidance, mostly focused on what students shouldn't do. Don't burn candles in your room, because they will set off the fire alarm. Don't assume someone's gender pronouns. A natural impulse—to just ask— might not be the right impulse, because asking can make the other person feel uncomfortable, or out their identity as someone who has a fluid or transgender identity before they're ready. Don't assume that every Black person is poor, or on financial aid. Don't inquire where someone's "weird" name came from. Don't ask Asian people where they are "really" from. Saying "that's so gay" to criticize something or someone is offensive and potentially hurtful to LGBTQ people. There are intercultural differences in things like personal space. Don't tell your roommate, eating a cherished meal from their home country, that their kimchi or curry smells funny. There are students from all fifty states.[14] Those from Maine, one of the whitest states in the union, may never have spent much time with, or even met, a Black person before.[15] They may have sincere curiosity about their roommate's hair, but it's helpful for them to know: don't ask to touch it.

As we sat through these training sessions, the information was overwhelming. Some students were hanging on every word, elated to finally be in an institution where they could show their whole selves. Some were sleepy and inattentive, or profoundly hung over. Others were just scared. And many were trying to play it cool—like they knew it all already. Students learn, in many ways, not to assume and not to offend. For some, much of this is painfully obvious. But for many others, it's not. So many of the lessons are about what not to do. Like most of their sex education, positive lessons about how they should be acting are comparatively rare.[16]

Juan felt no animus toward gay people; he just hadn't known anyone who was out in his suburban high school. Juan only once made the mistake of referring to something he thought was stupid as "gay." "I just, I felt really bad. Yeah, and that kind of happened. I thought it was a really interesting thing that I learned. I remember telling people from high school about that. Like 'dude I can't really even say the word gay anymore. It's crazy.'" He was in shock. The phrase was so much a part of his lexicon that he wasn't sure how he'd even be able to speak. "It was like, 'What am I going to do? How am I going to describe my life now?'" Adjusting to college is hard enough as it is without getting a reputation as your hall's resident homophobe. But his friends didn't ostracize him, and he learned to be careful about how he talked about things. Instead of experiencing this as silencing, Juan embraced these lessons. "I changed the way I perceived a lot of social things." And he thought of himself as better off because of it. He was even helping others avoid some of the mistakes he feels he made. He told us about a student he was mentoring, in whom he saw a younger version of himself. "He's also from the same kind of place I am. And he just says whatever's on his mind like, 'Oh dude I really wanna hook up with this girl!' or, 'Dude, I'm really into Asian girls right now. I really love Asian girls.' I'm like, 'Dude, you probably shouldn't say stuff like that.' He was like, 'What do you mean? It's just the truth.' I was like, 'I wouldn't say it if I were you,' and now he doesn't say it anymore."

While some may bemoan this as the loss of free speech on campus, we see it differently.[17] The students we met chose this campus out of a desire to experience its diversity. They generally sought to connect with one another in ways that are respectful—even if they disagree. If these kinds of disagreements are more common today than before, it is in no small part because campuses of the past were places where a relatively homogeneous population did not encounter much difference, and was unlikely to have its power challenged. Men like Juan and Sundeep weren't there. When prior generations of students said "that's gay," there was no organized LGBTQ student community to challenge them. Students who asserted that Black people had an easier time getting into college were rarely in conversation with Black people. Today, those kinds of statements have to be made in front of a far less disempowered audience. Encounters between different groups are built into the environmental design, and demand some accountability. It's uncomfortable, challenging, and potentially transformative. And as we heard from Juan, those kinds of transformations are not simply forced, they're what students want out of their college experience—valuable lessons they transfer to others.

FINDING ONE'S PLACE

In 2018 just over six percent of applicants were admitted to Columbia College.[18] Those who got in were overwhelmingly ambitious, disciplined, and driven. And, on top of that, lucky. We sometimes hear from our colleagues, both at Columbia and at other highly selective institutions, about how little experience today's college students have with failure. There's an "excellent sheep" narrative about how competitive college admissions, and higher education itself, is producing a generation of conformists.[19] Certainly, it used to be much easier to be admitted to college. Jennifer's children sometimes tell her that she'd never get into Princeton now. When Shamus applied to colleges in 1995, the acceptance rate at the University of Chicago was around 70%.[20] Columbia's admissions rate in the 1990s was about four times as high as it is today—and even that was a sharp decrease from the 40% admission rate prior to coeducation.[21] The grandparents of children today may be proud of their Harvard diplomas, but they might forget that back in their day, about half of the applicants were accepted.[22]

Still, essayists have called this "generation snowflake," suggesting students who melt quickly under the tiniest bit of heat.[23] That critique misses the hardships and challenges that many of them—yes, even the very wealthy ones—face. One young man, as he entered our office for an interview, sporting a thousand-dollar Canada Goose jacket, and mentioning that he'd spent break at his family's "winter home" in the Rockies, seemed the embodiment of privilege. But as his story unfolded, we heard how hard his junior year in high school had been. His girlfriend had been raped just before they started going out. Emotionally supporting her was, at times, overwhelming, as was managing the sexual intimacy she wanted, but had such a hard time having. College was a time for him to start anew.

The opening days on campus are filled with activity and instruction on policies and procedures. How to sign up for classes. How to access Counseling and Psychological Services. The rules around drinking. The "Under1Roof" program about microaggressions, pronouns, and basic respect. Where you can use the "flex-cash" that is associated with your ID. Deadlines for dropping classes. Panel after panel after panel. Many of the policies and procedures in college expose vast differences in socioeconomic status; even laundry is a terrain of social stratification. Some students may have been doing their younger siblings' laundry since they could read. Others, who may never even have washed their own clothes, skip the laundry orientation; they'd already signed up for the private laundry service that picks up and delivers.

Colleges and universities such as Columbia are almost semi-sovereign nations, with their own police force, medical teams, housing, work opportunities, and food supply. Getting up to speed is no small matter. Many students find themselves going to fewer and fewer events, whether because they are too hungover, or because it's overwhelming. As one woman in a focus group told us, her peers nodding their heads, the hardest part of orientation was that there was "nowhere to cry." Her roommate was always around. This sad moment stood out, in a research project that was full of them. What they were so desperately excited about—coming to college—left them not only wanting to cry, but struggling to find someplace to do so without anyone seeing them.

There are structural dimensions to these challenges. First-year students go from being the most senior people in high school—knowing the most and being the most powerful, even if they aren't the cool kids—to being the least again, relatively clueless and at the bottom of the social hierarchy. Students look around, and to some it feels like others, mysteriously, have already made friends. The athletes have already been on campus for a couple of weeks; they may not all love their team members, but they have a ready-made pack to travel with. The students whose families could afford it may have gone on one of the pre-orientation trips: a week in the woods, or doing social service, with a small group of incoming students, offers an opportunity to build deep connections before they've even made their dorm room bed. A few students look around and see their ancestors' portraits on campus, or their family name on a building. An increasing number of others step onto campus as the first one in their family to attend college.

Outside the gates of Columbia is a vast city, waiting for you. But its vastness can also be terrifying, giving a deep sense that you're on your own. The woman who said she had nowhere to cry during the opening days on campus was pointing to the challenge of not having a place to call her own. This "place" is partially metaphoric: she didn't have a community to rely upon, a new, chosen family of support. But it is also literal: in the geography of campus, she didn't have a physical room of her own. Roommates can be the first ones to notice that something is wrong and perhaps intervene in positive ways; they can also serve as ready-made friends.[24] But having a roommate presents challenges, because if one roommate wants to have sex with a partner, that inevitably involves a third party, who might not want to give up their space for that to happen. Built into the landscape of college is this spatial challenge to students' sexual citizenship.

I SORT OF FOUND MY PLACE

Maddox, who'd grown up in the suburbs of the Northeast, had a hard time adjusting to college. His first friends were on his floor, but he didn't click with them after a while. "I moved away from a lot of them because I, I felt a lot of them were pretty shallow." Maddox couldn't quite describe what he didn't like about his roommate, other than the fact that he was "annoying" and always around. That others on the hall seemed to like his roommate so much annoyed him even further. The marching band became a refuge for him, and he particularly enjoyed the trips away from campus. One of his band friends had an off-campus apartment, which gave him a space to escape to away from his hall. But it wasn't his own space, and it was a little far away. Maddox's biggest challenges weren't actually his own. His best friend experienced serious mental health issues, eventually resulting in a medical leave of absence; given everything his friend was going through, he didn't feel he could ask for much emotional support in return. Maddox started to spend more and more time alone off campus, particularly at bars. His family gave him enough money at the start of college that he could afford the high cost of nights out in New York City, as well as to get a fake ID that didn't raise too many eyebrows. His whiteness helped, too, at the local bars. He became a regular at one of the more popular student hangouts. But he felt little comfort there.

When his friend came back from his mental health leave, Maddox hit his stride. "I sort of found my place." He and his friends found a bar that was near campus, but seemingly a world away. He refused to name the place. As it turns out, he'd been sworn to secrecy.

> Uh, I'm a little embarrassed. Uh, it's one of the best-kept secrets. It's populated almost exclusively by, like, fairly old locals, so it's pretty easy for, like, our group of four to eight Columbia students to come in and take a table and just sort of disappear into the background and have our own little area. By now, we're all good friends with the bartenders and, uh, the bouncer, and so we get free drinks pretty frequently. There's a jukebox. There's pool. It's, like, just a really, really solid place.

When we asked why he was so hesitant to tell us the name, he said, "There's a very high bar for any of us to introduce this place to anyone new." We joked that it might become infested. But Maddox was dead serious in his reply. "Yeah, so we don't want that to happen. Then we would have to find somewhere new."

Most students can't use money to help them find a place to feel at home. They stay on campus, with access to physical space opening up over time. As students become more senior, they get access to better living spaces on campus, particularly in their final two years. But for most students, a successful integration into college means having both a private place, a room of one's own, and a social institution through which students "own the place"—or at least some small corner. In college this can be a fraternity or sorority; it can also be a special interest house like Casa Latina, Jazz House, or Muslim student house; or it can be a room, like the LGBTQ lounge, or the band practice room. It's a space that lets students proclaim to themselves, "I belong here." That grounding provides a critical resource as students navigate the terrain of college.

In the fall of 2016 we went to a party celebrating Mexican independence, thrown by the Latino students on campus. We arrived early, around 9:30 p.m., to a darkly lit room and the smell of a home-cooked meal. On the table were bags of tortilla chips and three homemade salsas. Estella told us to try one in particular. "It's amazing." It was. Several young women huddled around a large pot in the kitchen, making horchata. A group of boys—a few of them looked as if they were sixteen—sat beneath a large Mexican flag in the living room. We joked with Estella about the women in the kitchen and the boys hanging out; she brushed us off. They were freshmen, she said, too nervous to talk to anyone else. Four gay men and two women hung out in the middle of the room, eating and chatting. Everyone in the space was Latino but from a wide range of origins, some born in the United States, some abroad, some undocumented; almost everyone seemed at home. Estella explained that they called their event a dinner, not a party, so they didn't have to check for IDs. No one was going to drink that much anyway. They were there to socialize, and mostly, to dance. After about an hour, as the lights were turned off and only Christmas lights remained as illumination, the music was turned up and people started to move their bodies more; it was still a little awkward. But people started to loosen up. It was almost too loud to talk, but Estella brought a parade of people to chat with us. One woman complained about finding roaches in her bed. It was hard to listen to her story; all we could focus on was the line of perfectly spaced scars that ran down her left arm. We figured this was how she dealt with the stresses of her life. We didn't ask about the cutting. But she was open enough about it, wearing a tank top that clearly showed the healed wounds she'd inflicted upon herself.

The room heated up as bodies danced to the music. Mercifully, someone opened a window, but both the smell and the energy kept building.

Estella deftly managed the room, dragging one woman away from us to "go dance with the boys." Estella wanted to break them out of their awkward huddle. When the woman objected, saying that she didn't like boys, Estella didn't flinch. "That's not the point." The woman did as she was told, and soon the freshman boys were dancing. "See, it works!" Estella said with a firm nod of her head. She ran off again.

Slowly the kitchen filled with bottles of vodka and the dance floor filled with people. No one at the party actually lived in this space; it was one of the "Latino frats," the space lent to Estella and her friends to throw this event. When the fraternity brothers arrived, they seemed like guests in their own dorm suite, heading for the vodka rather than the dance floor. Chants of "¡México!" rose from the crowd—and then suddenly the lights were flipped on. The room collectively groaned as a white woman walked in. She called out for the host, eventually finding Estella.

"Okay, I'm not telling you guys to shut it down. There was a noise complaint so I'm just telling you to tone it down. Maybe close the windows to the courtyard, that was probably the problem." Two men closed the windows, and the woman, evidently a resident advisor, left the room, turning off the lights on her way out. As the party started up again we saw something unusual at Columbia: larger women, dressed to the nines and dancing with boys in the center of the room. College is accepting of all kinds of identities and differences, except when it comes to bodies. They had to be athletic, even sculpted. These Latina women were some of the few heavier people we ever saw out, partying with other students. The partying in this space was also different from what happened at most student events, particularly those run by white students. There were a few bottles of Negra Modelo, some white wine; the horchata the women had made earlier had been spiked with some vodka. But it was not enough to get anyone drunk. The altered states of consciousness came more from a collective effervescence of community than from alcohol.

Just before midnight the sound of a high-pitched clarinet blared out of the speakers and the students went wild, singing along to Calle 13's reggaeton hit.

Atrévete-te-te, salte del closet
Destápate, quítate el esmalte . . .

The student voices drowned out the speakers, and as they belted out the lyrics they circled up around a young, heavy-set man. We could barely see him, but the shouts of "Ay! Ay! Ay! Ay!" conveyed that he knew how to move. After "Atrévete" Estella turned the music down, telling the crowd, "Okay. Now it's time for what you came here for!" It was midnight, time for "el Grito." The chanting began, "Viva! Viva! Viva!" Younger students, and those who were not Mexican, looked confused but quickly joined in. A man jumped onto the dining room table, crouching down to keep his head from hitting the ceiling. Glancing at his phone, he began to read the story of Mexico's independence, "Two hundred and six years ago. . . ." At first, it was a dull affair. But it all changed when he reached the formal celebration of Mexico's independence:

¡Mexicanos!
¡Vivan los héroes que nos dieron patria!
¡Víva Hidalgo!
¡Viva Morelos!
¡Viva Josefa Ortiz de Domínguez!
¡Viva Allende!
¡Vivan Aldama y Matamoros!
¡Viva la independencia nacional!
¡Viva México! ¡Viva México! ¡Viva México!

The chants grew progressively louder, more people joining in with each "¡Viva!" At the last "¡Viva México!" the room erupted, transitioning quickly into dancing *el zapateado*. Estella turned to us, her face glowing: "My heart is just full of joy right now with all of this. All my lil' babies together. *This* is a Mexican ass party." With that, we wished her a good night. She was thrilled to show us her community. On our way out the door we were surprised to run into Anna, who was of Dominican descent. She was someone we'd spent some time with; we'd never seen her out, and she'd told us she never goes to parties. She seemed to recognize the surprise on our face, smiled, and explained that she always comes to these parties. Otherwise they'd stop inviting her. And it's these events that remind of her of family, of home, of where she comes from. She told us, referring to one of the most popular songs we heard during our field work, "Trap Queen" by Fetty Wap,

> I don't go to white parties. I don't understand what's happening. I don't understand what they are doing. Here, like, this is a Mexican party but the music I know and understand. So, I just don't feel comfortable at white parties. I don't want to go to a party and just listen to "Fetty Wap." I guess I'm segregating myself but I don't care. White people will say to me "Oh you only hang out with Latinos" but I'm like, "Whatever, all your friends are named 'Brad.'"

There were lots of differences at this party—gay and straight, younger and older, fat and athletic, all together. Most of the students were Latino, though certainly not all Mexican. But a sense of collectivity, of pan-ethnicity, brought them together.[25] These were moments, on what students of color often referred to as a "white campus," where they felt at home. The room's energy was electrifying. Estella had good reason to be proud of the community they made, and the space they shared—only possible because they had secured a physical space with a living room big enough for more than fifty people to cram into. It also helped that the women took over; their focus was far more on making people dance and talk than it was to drink. And, of course, the music helped. We only heard this mixture of bachata, cumbia, salsa, and reggaeton at parties hosted by Latino students. At what Anna experienced as the "white" parties on campus, Fetty Wap's rap "Trap Queen" did indeed seem to be on endless repeat. The women had asked the men to use this space; if they were in a sorority, they'd be unable to serve alcohol, and if they did, their national organization could revoke their charter. While the point of this party wasn't to get drunk, a little bit of booze did loosen the crowd up. Men control far more space on campuses than women. Booze can be expensive. Even if selling it, or collecting a door fee, the hosts never make back what they put in. And so wealthy students, not surprisingly, have more control over social space and the distribution of alcohol than others on campus. As much as the themes of diversity and inclusion dominate campus life, inequality and segregation are stubbornly persistent features of the landscape.

This isn't just because of public spaces; there are also a vast array of private spaces in and around colleges. Coffee shops and fast casual dining—two famous burger chains, the burrito joint, the noodle bar, the fancy salads—offer a range of options for spaces in which to work or chat with a friend, and there are endless options for dates—if you can afford them. A lot of students can't—or at least not on a regular basis. We saw some students enter restaurants as regulars, welcomed back by the staff, for fifteen-dollar grass-fed burgers followed by the famous butterscotch pudding. Others glanced in from the street, some with longing, some with disgust. On campus itself, public spaces have been converted into cafés selling five-dollar coffees—which can exclude those who don't have the money or don't feel entitled to occupy a table without paying. This is, in miniature, the story of New York. It's a playground, for sure, but a lot more so if you have the ability to pay to enter anywhere you want, and to be shuttled there and back with the ease of a private car.

Wealth isn't the only resource for students. There's race too. Some are never asked, "What are you doing here?" either in so many words, or with a look of suspicion. This is, in part, what students of color mean when they describe Columbia as a "white institution." White students' presence on campus is rarely questioned, nor are their capacities as students. Not infrequently students of color hear offhand remarks from peers that imply they're only at Columbia because of affirmative action. They are also far more likely to be stopped by security, asked to show their ID in a way that says to them, "Why are you here? You don't belong."

After one break, Asian students returned to find the name cards that had adorned their dorm rooms torn down and destroyed; the white students' name cards had been left untouched.[26] Another time, the sign an RA had made celebrating LGBTQ diversity was vandalized.[27] Sometimes these experiences, which happen at campuses across the country, involve actual rather than symbolic violence. Recently, a Black student was followed by campus security as he walked into Barnard's campus. Security had asked him for his ID; he refused to show it to them, sick of what he saw as his being policed while white students walked around without interruption. The encounter ended shamefully: campus police persisted in asking him for his ID, eventually grabbing him and pushing his body down onto a café counter when he refused to comply with their requests.[28] These experiences serve as a powerful justification for "special interest" spaces on campus: when a student's belonging upon campus is questioned, having a space where it is not becomes essential.[29] White students certainly have challenges finding a place on campus, but rarely are they subject to racial violence.

Students develop a sense of who they are and connect with others in communities that resonate with their identities or that give them a place where they belong. This is part of what makes fraternities or sororities so appealing. It's the draw of the special interest house, like Casa Latina, for Latino students; Greenborough, for those interested in living sustainably; Manhattan House, for indigenous students; Q House, for LGBTQ students; or Writers House or Pot Luck House, which are both fairly self-explanatory. Sometimes the seniors from a club live together using the common area of their suite—a semi-private room around which a group of single rooms are organized—as a place where club members can head to any time. The problem with space—particularly in Manhattan but almost anywhere—is that it's expensive to create and maintain. It's a fiercely guarded resource.

While some people find their own place on campus, it comes with a troubling condition—making sure it doesn't get too crowded, so overwhelmed that you can't really go there to feel you belong anymore, or filled with people who aren't your community. The Latino student parties like the ones we just described experienced this firsthand. Students at these parties had so much fun they started to text their friends— hoping they'd come share in one of the better parties on campus. As new people started to pile in, as word got around that the Latino student parties were the place to be, the dynamic changed. When too many students arrived who didn't know the words to Calle 13's "Atrévete," or who were more interested in drinking than dancing, the people who had built the vibe of the party suddenly felt like it wasn't their space anymore. They stopped showing up, or started leaving early. Before long it was over. We've all experienced this with our favorite café, bar, or gym. There was a reason Maddox was sworn to secrecy about his favorite bar. While space is an essential element of finding one's place on campus, it's also built upon the premise that not everyone can be there. Home has to be, to some degree, exclusive.

As students find their place on campus, events tend to get a little more "chill." Hanging out in suites, sitting on the floor having cooked some rice and stew, passing around magnums of cheap wine poured into Solo cups, is a fun night for a lot of students. The challenge is that these moments come, for most students, at the end of college, and not at the beginning. They require a common area comfortable enough to host a gathering of ten or so friends, a kitchen with a stove and a fridge, and being able to buy wine, bring it into your dorm, and drink it openly without worrying about getting in trouble with the RA. None of these things are easy for freshmen, or even sophomores, because of the campus geography and institutions rules: RAs are more likely to write them up for drinking, and the kind of housing they are given doesn't have common spaces they can use as their own for these kind of events.[30]

A WORK-HARD, PARTY-HARD LIFE

Groups of men in jackets and ties—some in suits but most in blue blazers with slacks—clustered on the steps to Low Library. They'd gathered there in this quintessential college spot to commemorate the evening. Next to them were women in dresses, mostly black and body-fitting, but some in bright-colored gowns. A few held flowers. A passerby might, at a quick glance, think it was prom. But these people were older than high schoolers. Slightly more confident. And there wasn't a proud parent in sight; the only "adults" around were a few faculty colleagues, scurrying home from a Saturday afternoon spent in their offices. The students coupled up and took their photos together. No one kissed. But some bodies were clearly more comfortable nestled together than others. Sometimes a small group formed around the *Alma Mater* statue. Through the crowd there were plenty of smiles, some nervous but most in excited anticipation of the formal they were about to attend. The men had bought tickets to a boat ride around Manhattan for $70 each. The purchase covered a meal and an open bar. Most had purchased tickets for their dates. The few gay men in the group also took women as dates. They weren't in the closet. It just was what people did. Students really looked forward to these formals. The men clearly reveled in dressing up. Sometimes we saw groups where the men had coordinated their outfits—dark jackets, blue ties, khaki pants, and Ray-Ban Wayfarers. Sunglasses at night are a sure sign of being ready to party. That evening and the next day, Instagram and Facebook would be filled with photos of what unfolded. Some would wake up the next morning and rigorously un-tag themselves in their friends' posts. They didn't want public records of their exploits. Employers might find them, and while they felt they looked pretty good, their drunken escapades weren't always a good look.

There wasn't much notable about this scene, other than how different it was from "normal life." We saw this again and again: how far away "fun" was from "daily life." The thing about a work-hard, party-hard culture is not the line between the two, it's the distance. To get from "work" to "party" takes work. Special clothes. Often lots of alcohol. Exceptional places. Things you're not supposed to be doing. Those sunglasses at night. But what if the differences were shorter? Maybe it wouldn't take such excessive effort to get there.

Plenty of students go to one fraternity party, never to go again. Some never even go to one, or hardly party at all, if by "party" you mean drinking, at the least, and often doing other things like cocaine. For these other students, the distances between the everyday and fun aren't that great. They don't need to get dressed up. They don't need a meal and an open bar. They need a couch and someone else who is psyched to stay up until 4 a.m. playing "Settlers of Catan." Many simply don't have the money to go out. But it's not just that these young people can't afford to party. They have constructed their identities in opposition to college party culture. They would rather talk about what's happening in their Contemporary Civilization class, or what they learned in their Computer Networks course. What is existence anyway? That conversation might be a little easier if stoned. But plenty of students have it sober. "How do you know this couch we're on is real? That we're not just part of the dream of some tick that lives on a back of a wild cat somewhere in the universe? How can we know?" Descartes asked questions like this, after all, admittedly in a slightly more sophisticated way. We hung out with students as they had cereal and milk on Saturday nights, chatting away with one another. These students hooked up, had sex, and experienced assault—though more often in the context of a relationship than a drunken hookup. There were moments of fun that often disrupted sleep, but not the same way a hangover would. And for the most part, these campus escapades were safer than the drunken ones we spent more time observing. As we noted in the introduction, the majority of students do not experience a sexual assault during their time on campus.

LANDSCAPES OF PLEASURE AND LANDSCAPES OF ASSAULT

Among the hundreds of stories we gathered about college student sexual experiences, Austin's story about an evening with his girlfriend was one of the sweetest. During the summer after his junior year, he was living in a great summer sublet in Long Island City, and his roommate had left to see family for the Fourth of July weekend. His girlfriend, who worked near City Hall, had stopped in Little Italy to pick up the fixings for a cheese and charcuterie plate. The night before, he'd stashed a bottle of sparkling wine in the fridge. They were planning to drink it while watching the fireworks from his roof. The sublet had many great features, but its air conditioning was not one of them. And so they stripped down to their underwear in the heat, making each other crackers with a sliver of cheese or salami, talking, and sipping prosecco. Austin described the evening as growing "progressively sillier and sexier." They made out, and then he went down on her while she stood in the kitchen, leaning back against the counter. When she orgasmed, gripping the countertop, she didn't have to worry about those thin dorm walls. He loved how loud she was. Then they had some of the Manchego cheese, with tiny bits of date jam. They made their way into the bedroom. He put on a condom and she got on top of him. She rode him for a bit, came, and then they turned over so he could be on top; she came again, and then he pulled out, removed the condom, and came on her stomach. They snuggled for a little while. As she dozed, he got up to wash some more grapes and slice more dried sausage, and he brought her a little plate. They spent the night there, curled up together. They were fine with having missed the fireworks.

It wasn't just the delightful sex that made this such a powerful story in Austin's memory. It was the whole scene. Having the apartment to themselves meant that they could slowly build to sex while they ate and drank and talked. Away from the dorms, they didn't have to worry about being overheard by friends. The heat led easily to savoring a cheese plate while semi-naked, and summer also brought a lack of homework or anything to do other than being together. What stands out in Austin's narrative is the care—for his girlfriend's pleasure, but also about his girlfriend as a person, and her care for him. They'd met freshman fall, and started dating at the end of that year, so by that evening they'd passed the two-year mark. They were a little buzzed, but weren't drunk. The prosecco was just part of a loose, joyous, steamy evening.

We see hints in Austin's life story of what made him so sensitive to his partner's pleasure, and so comfortable joking about sex that they had developed an elaborate series of nicknames for the variety of orgasms she experienced. Austin never felt like the type of guy that girls just walk up to and want to hook up with. His all-boys school in Pennsylvania hadn't offered many opportunities to hone his verbal "game"—skill at talking with women in ways that seductively conveyed sexual interest. By his own assessment, girls at parties were more likely to be put off by his scrawny build than they were to be attracted to his warm smile. The only women with whom he'd spent any appreciable amount of time before college were his mom, his three older sisters, and his many women cousins. Austin credited having strong women in his life as a counterbalance to his male-dominated school culture, and the basis of his respect for women.

Like a lot of his peers, Austin had turned to porn to learn about sex in high school—but his search for answers also led him to erotic fiction, where he learned to think about sex as something more than just "getting my nut and falling asleep."[31] Austin laughed when recalling everything he didn't learn from his high school's "sexual diseases class." The class didn't succeed in scaring him away from having sex before marriage, nor did the photos of pustulant genitalia answer his questions about sex: what people actually do, what it feels like, how to be good at it. He hated that he was a virgin when he started college, and yet the fall of freshman year he had passed up a chance to have sex for the first time—even though a girl had clearly indicated that she was ready to take things to the next level. He recalled his internal struggle, "I'm an idiot, I'm missing a chance to get my dick sucked." But he experienced the woman as a really negative person and he knew that he was going to break up with her; it felt wrong to have sex opportunistically. He recalled thinking, "Everybody's gonna be angry at me, there's always consequences." Even after he lost his virginity, his few random hookups left him feeling bad about himself. On spring break in Cabo San Lucas, he got drunk and had sex with a girl he met at a club. "Did I need to do that? Having sex with someone you care about is a lot better."

It had taken Austin several years to grow into who he was when we interviewed him. The Austin who was so attentive to his girlfriend on the Fourth of July hardly seemed like the Austin in this story from freshman orientation.

> My roommate was hooking up with this girl, sex and everything. So they made me sleep in her roommate's place. The first night, she was really drunk, and they were just like, "Oh go over there." And I didn't know what to do so I just lay down next to her and she was like "Oh I just threw up, like, I don't want to do anything," but I kind of just laid next to her for a bit and kind of rubbed her body for a bit. I definitely grabbed her boob, but then I felt weird about it, because I was also drunk, and then I slept in the other bed. And then the next time I saw her because they continued hooking up I went back and we talked for, like, two or three hours about bullshit. We actually got along pretty well, and like, it was never bad, it never felt like it was wholly a bad thing, but I definitely felt bad about it. I shouldn't have done that. But I was definitely happy that I had slept in the other bed. Glad I did that. I stopped and was like "Uh, this isn't it." She didn't seem like she was hating it, but she didn't seem like she was loving it. Okay, she probably didn't give affirmative or negative consent. This is a gray area. And I was just like "Okay, this is weird, this is a bad idea." I don't know, it wasn't one of my best moments.

When we asked him how he would categorize the event, he said, "Not something I would do again." When we asked him if it was a "hookup," he was definitive. "No, because we didn't make out. I don't know what to categorize it as. Just kind of shitty." As the interview continued, we asked Austin to share more about his definition of sexual assault and, in light of that, to reflect on what had happened. "I know the definition of sexual assault, like any kind of nonconsensual sexual action, so yes . . . that would probably be considered sexual assault."

By now, Austin was near tears. He distinguished between rape and assault. "Well, rape in terms of vaginal rape. And sexual assault being, like, a lot of, like, bad touching. Which is I guess what I did. But umm. But also, like. Yeah damn. Well, fuck me, right? Yeah."

He looked crushed, as if he'd just realized something terrible about himself.

The assault that Austin told us he committed during orientation week was typical of many campus sexual assault incidents: he and the woman were both drunk, it was not reported, they maintained a social relationship afterwards but never discussed what happened, and in fact the interview seemed to have been the first moment that Austin considered that it was assault. Austin was desperate to accrue sexual experience, anxious about being behind his peers. Intoxication clouded his judgment. People know that being drunk is associated with an increased risk of being assaulted, but less remarked upon are the ways in which heavy drinking raises the risk of assaulting someone. An opportunity presented itself, set in motion by the community norm that part of being a good friend is going along with being shuffled into a virtual stranger's bedroom, or having a virtual stranger shuffled into yours. We don't know how the woman in Austin's story experienced what happened. But we do know how Austin felt, after he began thinking about what he'd done. It's hard to think about Austin as a sociopath or a predator. Did he commit assault? In our view, yes. Is he a terrible person? In our view, no.

Austin knew about affirmative consent; this didn't stop him from doing what he did. What eventually stopped him? His sex education had instructed him to fear sex, but provided no guidance about how to have sex in ways that were healthy and respectful. Maybe it was what he'd gotten from reading erotic fiction—thinking about sex as something other than just "getting his nut"—or maybe it was his broader feeling that the way you treat people matters, that "there's always consequences." Or maybe it was just the fact that he wasn't that tiny bit drunker, so he paid attention when his conscience called out to him: "this is weird, this is a bad idea."

There's a lot that can be said about this. But the role of alcohol in clouding both his judgment and the woman's own capacity to express herself is inescapable. Just over half of those who reported being assaulted in the SHIFT survey identified the "method of perpetration" as "incapacitation."[32] That pretty much means that the person who was assaulted was drunk. This doesn't make the assault their fault, but it does reflect an important reality. We need to grapple with the role of alcohol in the college landscape, particularly because, in our view, it doesn't just put people at risk of being assaulted: it also puts people, like Austin, at risk of committing assault.

3

THE TOXIC CAMPUS BREW

"I DON'T HAVE A DRINKING PROBLEM. I'M JUST A FUCKING COLLEGE STUDENT."

It's the fall of 2015, the first full day of orientation. After years of meticulously planned afternoons, late nights, and bleary-eyed mornings doing assignments for every AP class they could cram into their schedules, or long hours at McDonald's to help their family make rent, or summers of internships and weekends at band practice, tutoring, or varsity sports, and then months of essay writing, test taking, and hand-wringing, these new freshmen were in—at college, away from their parents, in the big city. For many, the focus of anticipation was on what they had deferred—or not been allowed to do—while they were working so hard to get in: "getting drunk and getting laid." Lots of students party really hard during orientation. Many move on fairly quickly, finding friends or other social activities, but for some, it's the beginning of four years of frequent binge drinking. Columbia is not the only campus where students joke that there's no such thing as an alcoholic until after graduation.

Nick, a senior from Ohio, reflected on that week. "One of the guys bought some beer and I walked across College Walk with like a twelve-pack of Bud Lite. . . . 'This is so cool, this is sick. [I'm not even] 21, you know?'" Nick was written up for drinking by his RA several times over the course of the freshman fall. "I had to, like, go to speak to advisors and stuff like, 'Do you have a problem?' Like, 'Do you have a drinking problem you wanna talk about?' I'm like, no, I'm just a fucking college student."

Freshman fall is both exciting and socially painful. Students are homesick, or feeling bad about how relieved they are to be away from home, or both. They are scared that everyone is smarter than they are. They're nervous that everyone is more experienced. Drinking together can break the ice—providing the courage necessary to walk into a party of strangers, jump out onto the dance floor, or flirt with a possible hookup. Not everyone drinks; some students cope by going for a run, visiting a museum, or engaging in religious observance.[1] But a lot of students drink a lot, and their binge drinking intersects with the campus landscape; some Americans even celebrate this kind of drinking as a part of the normal college experience. The stress young people experience factors in, but stress is a justification as much as a cause.

Students arriving on campus have to manufacture an entire social world. Making friends and finding your people are central to the college project. For students new to campus and unsure where their college paths will take them, a big, loud party with some red Solo cups holds a distinct lure in those early anxiety-filled evenings. The contents of that cup promise to dull students' worries about meeting new people and offer a shortcut to building friendships with them.[2] Drunkenness and college are also tightly coupled in the American social imaginary. Before Jennifer's older son left for college, the family settled in for a long-weekend movie binge of college-themed films, culled from lists of "best college movies" and Facebook friends' suggestions. But after following *Animal House* with *Old School*, *Back to School*, and *Revenge of the Nerds*, Jennifer shut down the film festival. It was not fun; it was a master class in binge drinking.

As much as some students don't really want to drink, we were surprised to find that unless activities and groups explicitly reject alcohol, even student activity groups that might not stand out as being structured around drinking frequently cement group bonds by incorporating alcohol into their social events. During the fall semester, drinking provides a common set of challenges and experiences that students can share. As on a scavenger hunt, students work collaboratively to solve a series of problems regarding money or fake IDs or party locations or bars where the bouncers card loosely if at all.[3]

On the opening days of the school year we sat outside bars and watched as bouncers let in large groups of freshmen, some of whom looked like they were high school sophomores or juniors.[4] Students were thrilled to have "gotten in" to the local Irish bar for a classic orientation week scene: drunkenly making out with relative strangers, enveloped by the smells of bodies sweaty from the late August heat, feet sliding on a floor slick with spilled drinks and poorly cleaned-up vomit. If that sounds disgusting, it was. But the first-year students we talked to described it as fun—escaping home, breaking the rules, awkwardly discovering the body of another person, creating stories they could revel in hours, days, or even years later. Students form deep friendships, and sometimes even find true love, while caring for their drunk friends—getting them to drink water, or go for a walk, holding their hair while they vomit, or watching to make sure they don't aspirate vomit while passed out. Assuming that no permanent damage is sustained, the frequently absurd, occasionally life-threatening, hazily remembered and very intense experiences of drunk young people become shared jokes: mistakenly peeing in the closet when too drunk to notice it's not the bathroom, or standing in rumpled formal clothes outside a bar as the rain begins to fall, arguing about whether a friend—stumbling but still conscious—needs an ambulance, or just a taxi home followed by water and ibuprofen.

An ambulance is always parked on College Walk, the main pedestrian path through campus, where Nick so proudly walked with his twelve-pack of Bud Lite. Mostly the ambulances serve students who are exceptionally drunk or on some drug, or who are injured while intoxicated. Were this a housing project rather than an Ivy League campus, we can imagine the outrage at the necessity for such a thing, or the criticism of how that ambulance was facilitating degeneracy by lessening the consequences for bad behavior. But there is no outrage here. This is privilege: students don't have to go far or wait very long for help, and if the Columbia ambulance takes them to an emergency room, the ride is free (although the ER visit, notably, is not). There are lots of reasons why young people who attend college drink more than their out-of-college peers, engaging in a riskier behavior and breaking the law at considerably higher rates.[5] Their privilege gives them some license to break the rules.[6] And for the most part, the law gives them a pass.

No one wants to get "cava'd"—taken away by the university ambulance corps (formerly, Columbia Area Volunteer Ambulance), but this service is an important option and is provided at no cost. Good Samaritan policies encourage students who may themselves have been drinking while underage or using illegal drugs to intervene to help a friend who seems in danger. While the ambulance ride may by free, the ER bill that follows can be well over $1,000.[7] And if the Columbia ambulance is busy, students pay for the ride as well. As much as young people are legally adults, their parents typically find out at this point. An out-of-network ambulance ride and IV drip is a rounding error for some family budgets and a month's rent for others. Because a well-meaning intervention can result in disciplinary action at school, or financial troubles at home, the students who are most likely to drink are the ones who can afford it—not just the alcohol itself, but the risks that go with it.[8]

SOCIAL RISKS

Both of us remember our own college drinking. Shamus's junior year was particularly alcohol-filled. He had to take a bit of a break from drinking after he'd danced in a fountain, passed out in some bushes, and woke up with a horrific hangover and an even worse cold. Jennifer dutifully slurped down the contents of a Solo cup with a goldfish in it as she stood in a basement during orientation week. Thankfully, she doesn't remember the feeling of the goldfish sliding down her throat.

She thought swallowing a goldfish was what you did at college. After all, her dad had done it as well.

But drinking-related mortality is not limited to goldfish. The CDC fact sheet that Jennifer made her older son read after a sheepish call from the emergency room in the winter of *his* freshman year notes that in the United States six people die every day from binge drinking, about three-quarters of them men. Binge drinking is defined for women as four or more drinks in two hours and for men as five or more drinks.[9] In one large national study, about a third of college students reported at least one episode of five or more drinks in the past two weeks.[10] The SHIFT survey found similar rates among Columbia students.[11] Nationally, the students who binge drink are more likely to be white men from the most privileged backgrounds. This doesn't just apply to students; wealthier men in general drink more.[12] Students from this demographic are the ones most likely to have seen their own fathers drink heavily, and to associate heavy drinking with a normal transition to adulthood.

Those concerned about how young people drink today perhaps don't realize that the average eighteen-year-old today drinks less and is less likely to use illicit drugs than one who came of age in the 1970s.[13] Policies and programs have had a measurable impact on substance use among high-school-aged youth, so that students begin college today with less experience drinking than their parents likely have had. But during college, students do a lot of "catching up"—and by the time they graduate they're drinking about the same amount as previous generations.

We could compare students not just to their parents, but to their grandparents, at least for those whose grandparents also attended college. In 1959 two deans at UCLA wrote, "Think of college and you think of flaming youth; thinking of flaming youth and you think of liquor and sex."[14] They go on to cite the heavy drinking, decades before, of F. Scott Fitzgerald's few years at college, noting that his "preoccupation with drink is second only to his preoccupation with sex," before bemoaning similar dispositions in other college students. Studies dating back to the 1950s noted the impact of alcohol on "male aggression" in dating-courtship relations.[15] However, we would be wrong to imagine that since this kind of excessive drinking has been going on for so long, there's nothing we can do about it. We've made great strides in addressing smoking, sexism, racism, and homophobia in the last generation—all of which were far more tolerated a generation ago. We have good models for how to make inroads into the problems of alcohol abuse.[16]

Why do people act in ways that seem dangerous, stupid, or both? The concept of *social risk*—the good (social) reasons we have for doing things that are bad for us, or for not doing things that would benefit our health—helps explain why people engage in behaviors with detrimental consequences, act in ways that seem illogical, or fail to take actions that could protect them.[17] The idea of a social risk highlights one way that peers, organizational environments, and the broader culture shape actions that feel like individual choices. People engage in sex that can have health consequences—for example, forgoing condoms as a demonstration of trust—in part because sex isn't a health behavior, but rather, a social behavior, laden with all kinds of meaning and influenced by our peers, our pasts, and our institutions.[18] Other parts of everyday life are no different; people smoke, drink, eat too much, don't exercise, and subject themselves to enormous amounts of stress. We are not health-maximizing beings; instead, we often prioritize all kinds of social goals over our personal and collective health.

Social risk helps us make sense of why people drink so excessively when they hate how terrible they feel the next day, when they do things they regret or can't even remember, and when other parts of their lives that are valuable to them are negatively affected by their drinking. The drunk sex that happens after a party may be dangerous insofar as it puts students at risk of all kinds of things, including sexual assault—either being assaulted or committing assault. But in college, where party drinking is a major way people socialize, it also may feel like the best strategy to meet potential sexual partners, make new friends, or create meaningful experiences with existing ones.

Students on the same campus experience different social risks in relation to drinking. Forgoing the purchase of a fake ID can mean missing out on socializing with the "right" people, on being able to go wherever those people go. But for others, the social risks of getting that ID feel greater. For example, for people of color, the far higher likelihood of incarceration and the dangers of an encounter with a police officer at a traffic stop are well documented. And for many men, who cannot imagine themselves being sexually assaulted, and who haven't thought about how drinking might make them more likely to commit assault, the conversation about assault and drinking feels irrelevant. Race, class, gender, and sexuality intertwine with institutional structures, peer networks, and cultural frameworks to produce different orientations to what, socially, is a risk. In the context of drinking, the stress of college, sexual shame, the legal drinking age, and the cultural and structural legacy of elite institutions of higher education as places for white men to come of age, all intertwine to shape campus drinking.

When Nick asserted that he was "just a fucking college student," he was drawing on a deep history of American residential higher education as providing a place where "flaming youth" safely toggle between living the life of the mind and being the life of the party. Campuses have grown ever more diverse; thus there are more and more students for whom the social risks of drinking exceed the risks of not drinking. Yet heterosexual, white, wealthy male students still wield enormous social power, because they control scarce social space, and because they can more easily enjoy the undeniable social benefits of heavy drinking—the bonding, the fun, the stress relief, the easy access to casual sex—without worrying so much about being assaulted, or arrested, or the cost of the bill from an ambulance ride. Our point is not that college drinking is the fault of wealthy white men. It's that histories of advantage and specific kinds of masculinity have produced a particular drinking environment—an environment that intersects with the contextually specific rationale behind the heavy partying that is so typical of freshman fall. Which is exactly the period, sometimes referred to as the "red zone," that college students are most likely to experience sexual assault.[19]

"MAN, I JUST WANT SOME ROSÉ WINE OR SOMETHING . . . SOMETHING EASY AND GIRLY."

Today's college freshmen were almost all born well over a decade after Congress's passage of the 1984 Uniform Drinking Age Act, requiring states to raise the legal drinking age to 21 to qualify for receipt of federal highway funds. From a population health point of view, this is an unmitigated success, estimated to have saved half a million teenage lives.[20] Yet today's college students still drink, and enter a context in which institutional liability has pushed drinking out of campus pubs, lounges, and hallways, and behind closed doors and in dark corners (although it is worth noting that there is substantial variation in campus drinking environments, which include traditions and school culture as well as the demographic makeup of the student population, policies or laws at the institutional, community, and state level, and the enforcement of those laws).[21] An unintended consequence of laws to reduce alcohol-related harms is that the easiest path to some crazy orientation-week story is to venture into spaces controlled by older students—usually men.

Freshmen arrive at college already familiar with age-based social stratification. Differences in institutional knowledge, maturity, self-confidence, and friendships deepened through time and shared experience further disadvantage younger students, with these structural inequalities amplified by the control of space on campus. Almost all traditional-aged Columbia and Barnard undergraduates live in student housing, and an unexamined fact of college life is that juniors and seniors have access to better space—either suites with a shared living room and single bedrooms, or apartment-style living. This is a critical aspect of the geography of partying on campus, promoted by the different kind of monitoring to which juniors and seniors are subject. Since seniors are often 21 or older, there is little push to enforce minimum legal drinking age laws in their dorms. Incoming students walk into a situation in which two precious sources of social currency—alcohol and space to party without getting in trouble—are unequally allocated by class year. Such stratification systems are taken for granted, with questions rarely raised about why policies provide better spaces for people who are more "senior," even in the face of evidence that such policies may create considerable harms.

Like Prohibition, laws making 21 the legal age to buy alcohol have led to a series of social work-arounds. Institutions incur liability should they fail to enforce the law, with the result that underage students cannot drink openly in the spaces that they control—their dorm lounges, the small shared kitchens in the freshmen and sophomore dorms, or even cinder-block hallways. But students can get away with drinking in their dorm rooms if they do not to disturb their neighbors or otherwise attract an RA's attention. If they do, students under 21—typically freshman and sophomores—can get "written up," as Nick was, for drinking with friends in a space they control. The take-home lessons are: don't crank the music up, and drink quickly. In this context, pregaming—drinking rapidly with a few friends before going out to a bar—is often done in the form of a drinking game, but it follows a robust logic of efficiency. Students save on the unit price; shots from a "handle" of vodka, purchased by a friend with a fake ID or an upperclassman, cost a fraction of what students would pay for a vodka soda at a local bar. They also avoid the social price. Parties get packed quickly, and as they do, students often have to run the gauntlet to gain admission. Fraternities, by rule, are not allowed to serve hard liquor. If you're a man, getting in is tough, as brothers tend to limit access to men who are not a part of the house (in part to keep the gender ratio to their advantage). If you're a woman and you don't want to drink cheap beer, you have to subject yourself to the evaluation of some fraternity brother, who will decide whether you are cute enough to get a shot of vodka. Pregaming enables students to consume alcohol when, where, and with whom they please.

Rich kids swagger onto this landscape, and wealthy, white freshmen are the ones most likely to arrive on campus with a fake ID. Cecile, a willowy sorority girl from Atlanta, recalled deciding in ninth grade that she wanted to run with the party crowd. They got their fakes as a group, buying them from kids at a different high school. The racial codes of her description made us cringe. The fakes were good because they got them from people who knew what they were doing; she said, somewhat unbelievably to us, that they "also sold cocaine and guns"—she paused to laugh, "Like, who the hell were those kids?" Once she and her high school friends got their IDs, they quickly developed a strategy for where to use them: go to where the poor people were. "You just like go to a more sketch neighborhood and walk into a liquor store." Without needing a paying job of her own, before she even started college Cecile had money to buy liquor, and a "good fake." She was well dressed, with money to spend and the resources to avoid trouble—an ideal patron for a bar or club, except of course for the fact that she was underage. Parents sometimes paid attention to credit card bills. But rich kids had plenty of work-arounds, including ways to get the cash they needed to buy drugs. Charge dinner with a friend on Mom and Dad's card and have your friend pay you back in cash. Mom and Dad probably wouldn't notice that dinner was twice as expensive as it should have been; you can rely on assumptions about how expensive New York is. It was a hustle many wealthy students had learned in high school.

Two decades ago women like Cecile would have entered a campus landscape filled with people like her—wealthy and white, and, in Columbia's case, mostly male. Columbia today is less than 50% white, with a sizable number of students from low-income backgrounds; nearly one in five undergraduates are the first in their families to go to college.[22] Students like Cecile don't totally rule, in part because there are now plenty of students from the "sketch" neighborhoods she referenced. As a white student, Cecile complained, there are certain things you can't talk about—race particularly. It just gets you into trouble. And so for the most part, you learn to be quiet and keep your thoughts to yourself. Most of these rich students also learn fairly quickly not to flaunt their privilege.

The cultural and social traces of higher education's historical role as a coming-of-age setting for white men linger in the social organization of campus drinking. Part of this involves the physical institutions—Princeton has its eating clubs; until just a few years ago Harvard had its finals clubs; and lots of schools have fraternities—where upperclassmen who are frequently white and wealthy control high-value space and access to alcohol. Drunken college high jinks are a core element of the cultural imagination of the American ruling class. Norman, explaining why a friend of his from Germany drank so heavily during his first weeks at school, pointed to Bluto of *Animal House* fame, and said that Franz was "just trying to go out there and be, like, college."

Two basic principles define the relationship between institutions of higher education and fraternities: liability and loyalty. In terms of liability, who is, or should be, held responsible for hazing, sexual assaults, or harms related to binge drinking that are tied to Greek life? In terms of loyalty, how much can or should schools do to regulate, or even shut down, such social institutions, to which alumni may feel an intense devotion, and to which some current students are equally devoted? But there's a third set of questions that might be asked, about how these quasi-independent institutions can, in the aggregate, work against institutional commitments to diversity and inclusion—not necessarily through any intention on the part of the members themselves, but solely by being places that reproduce wealthy men's control over (party) space.

WHITENESS, MASCULINITY, WEALTH, AND POWER

Colleges and universities across the nation are struggling, in ways large and small, with their histories as predominantly white institutions—the names on buildings and statues, the financial legacy of endowments that began with profits from America's original sin of slavery.[23] The drinking culture is not generally flagged as part of this, but our work suggests that the shift to diversity and inclusion requires addressing the dominance of white cultural practices.[24] Although there is not a massive literature on institutional characteristics and levels of binge drinking, it is well established that students at historically Black colleges and

universities—HBCUs—drink less.[25] Some of this, no doubt, is because
Black Americans are surveilled far more aggressively, punished disproportionately for their transgressions, and subject to potentially lethal
force when policed. Students at historically white colleges and universities experience none of these biases, and are, in critical ways, freed up
to drink more.[26] Even within institutions that are more racially mixed,
research going back at least to the 1980s has shown that Black students
drink less than white students.[27] And Greek letter organizations, often
flagged as institutional sources for the reproduction of binge drinking,
are actually only associated with higher rates of binge drinking when
they are white men's Greek letter organizations.[28]

We noted that the Mexican independence party to celebrate "el
Grito," hosted by Latina women students, took place in a fraternity.
Going back at least to Peggy Reeves Sanday's *Fraternity Gang Rape*,
work on masculinity and campus sexual assault has examined fraternities as the embodiment of toxic masculinity.[29] Frequent and egregious
examples keep this narrative alive. But our position is more nuanced.
As others have also noted, fraternities are not all the same; in addition
to the racial and ethnic diversity of some fraternities even on historically white campuses, some are actively involved in intentionally trying
to remake masculinity, while others seem primarily focused on managing liability.[30]

Critically, at Columbia there's at least as much variation in prestige
between fraternities as there is between men who are involved in Greek
life and those who are not. The same is true of athletics.[31] Students we
asked almost all reproduced the same list of the "best" fraternities and
sororities, and the "hottest" men's teams, where "best" and "hottest"
mean the most exclusive, with members who are supposedly the most
attractive, with the highest value as sexual partners. There was also a
high degree of concurrence about the "worst" fraternities. From the
point of view of the broader campus culture, the problem is not that
fraternities offer a highly valued mechanism to foster connections with
peers (and alumni); it's that they reproduce an unequal allocation of

access to space, alcohol, and a specific vision of college fun. The Latino men, in handing over their house to women for the "el Grito" party, suggested just how malleable that inequality could be.

There is Greek life that is actually the opposite of boozy; it's officially dry. Sororities can't even serve alcohol at their events; some can't even have alcohol in their houses at all. That isn't an informal practice; it's a national rule to which chapters must adhere. This further concentrates the power of distributing alcohol in the hands of wealthy men in historically white institutions—and here we are talking about fraternities, not universities. It's not that Black, Asian, and other students don't drink, because many of them do—although notably less so in spaces that they control—but college binge drinking is a white man's cultural practice that other students emulate, in order to embody the white masculinity of "the college experience. The SHIFT survey found gender and racial-ethnic patterns of binge drinking at Columbia similar to national ones, with men, non-Hispanic whites, and Hispanics engaging in binge drinking at significantly higher rates than other students.[32] Girls in high school are increasingly likely to drink excessively, closing some of the difference between how girls drink and how boys drink. There are many reasons for this, but we think that part of this is a vision of "equality" that means acting like the guys.

At 9 a.m. on the Saturday morning of homecoming, one of the year's biggest drinking days, the university-assigned and -employed party monitors came in to inspect a fraternity and make sure it was following regulations—no serving booze other than beer, no kegs, food and non-alcoholic drink available, no nuisance noise. A monitor went through her checklist ritual with the fraternity's "compliance officer"—a junior who was assigned this important leadership position. Was there soda available? Yes. How about food? Five different brothers pointed to the bagels. How loud would the music be? "Party level." The brothers demonstrated. One of the party monitors joked, "Aw, c'mon y'all, this is not party volume, I would not come to your party." Everyone laughed, and they turned the volume up more. The second monitor located the required soda.

There was no acknowledgment of the fact that many of the fraternity members—all wearing logo-printed tank tops and Bermuda shorts despite the fall chill—were already drunk. There were no open cans of beers in sight. No one asked, in part because that alcohol was hidden away. Meanwhile, the guys were fiddling with their phones. Typical enough for college students. But they weren't just texting friends about meeting up to go to the game. They were making "party arrangements." This meant scoring whatever remaining drugs they needed. Maybe some pot. But mostly cocaine. An upstairs closet already held nine boxes of vodka. Boxes, not bottles. One of the brothers slyly but proudly showed this to us after the university staff member had left. She wouldn't be back. She'd done her job.

Murray and Cooper, two of the fraternity brothers, headed out into the chilly morning rain, still festively attired in Bermudas and tank tops, warmed by their buzz from the morning's shots and their adrenaline about the day to come. As they walked over to the local liquor store they knew would sell to them, they planned their purchase. Both were rich, or at least their families were. Theirs is a kind of masculinity that might be called more "metro" than "macho."[33] Murray said to Cooper, "Man, I just want some rosé wine or something, my stomach's kind of fucked, so I just want something easy and girly." Cooper emphatically agreed, hoping they could get a particular brand of "classy" boxed wine—"This is a party, man! But I just spent like a grand on coke this month, I'm out of money. And the problem with that boxed wine is, it is just gone." Murray suggested that Cooper get some and just keep it in his room, but Cooper retorted, "Man, the point of boxed wine is to get the party lit! You can't hoard it." In the end Cooper bought two magnums of the least expensive sauvignon blanc. Girls were more likely to drink white wine. Murray got a larger stash of his own. Cooper and Murray were providers for the party. With some portion of their spending money that remained after the thousand dollars spent on cocaine (in our estimate, not an exaggeration), Murray and Cooper demonstrated their "success" as men. Only some students have the means and ability "to make the party lit." This, of course, puts them at risk for supplying things that are illegal; their privilege comes with an entitlement that promotes dangerous risk-taking.

These men cared about being good hosts, but reveled in their mastery of the space. Control of the physical space in a fraternity house is not just about who gets in the front door—the brothers make it known, sometimes less than subtly, that it is literally their home. Chilling upstairs after the liquor store run, Murray needed to pee. He walked out of his bedroom and up to the first door down the hall. He knocked, heard a female voice, and walked to the second door, where the same thing happened. Frustrated, he leaned his back up against the door, bent one leg, and started kicking the door as hard as he could with his heel. It sounded like he was about to kick the door down. The female voice inside let out a shout of surprise. Two women emerged, flustered, from one of the bathrooms. Turning to us, he explained, "I care about my brothers, but these other people, like, I don't care about you, you're in my way."

Later, back in his bedroom with the door closed again, Murray wanted to talk about a woman he'd just kicked out of his room—not the one in the bathroom, but another one, earlier that day. There was something important he wanted to share with us, and he felt she couldn't be there to hear it. She was, he told us,

> really sexy and really fratty. She's great. Like she can hang around with me and guys and I can get drunk and she'll sit on their laps and the guys are like "Whoa, Murray doesn't care," 'cause we're past that shit, man. And we were in this groove last year where, like, we'd have sex, I'd wake up at six for practice, get back, she'd make me breakfast, we'd have sex, I'd go back to sleep and see her in the evening. It was great.

Clearly, one of the things he valued most about her was her willingness not to disrupt his masculine social circle.

Fraternity men have expanded their social circles to include not just women (if they are sufficiently "fratty") but other types of men who were previously not welcome. Murray asked one research assistant, Alex, about himself. Alex shared that he was married to an Israeli man. Murray was quick to try to prove to Alex that he was not homophobic:

> Aww, that's cool man . . . Dude, I wish I was gay and could just like date a man. I don't think that men are smarter than women, but I do believe that men are more emotionally grounded than women. Like, I'd love to just be able to be a gay dude and chill with a guy and like watch sports and play Xbox and fuck. That'd be a chill relationship.

Alex—not a big Xbox player or sports fan, but a great ethnographer—wisely nodded and said little. Murray continued:

> And like, some of the brothers here are gay. But they're such chill fratty dudes who like sports and play Xbox. I think that when you're in a homophobic place people get pushed into this spot where they need to build a community so they get all fay and faggy, but in New York, it's fine and these bros can just be themselves and be chill bros and not all faggy. I fucking hate the liberal social justice warriors on this campus, but ironically, now I know all these Black guys and gay bros who are super chill and normal. Am I like offending you?

Alex said he was not offended. "Yeah, man," Murray concluded, "you're chill."

There were a series of oppositions here: chill, fratty, and normal on one side; fay, faggy, and social justice warriors on the other. But gay people—and even, Murray emphasized, Black people—could be on his side of that line, as long as they were, in the judgment of people like him, "chill" and "normal."[34]

Malachi, who was a junior when we interviewed him, spoke of Columbia's whiteness throughout his conversation. He shared his regret at having joined a white fraternity rather than a Black one, in part because in his telling, students drank more at white parties and danced more at Black ones. He criticized what he felt was the fundamental whiteness of the school's core curriculum, and was concerned about his elevated vulnerability to accusations of sexual assault because of the "stigma of being a Black male." For him, the safest strategy was to not drink at all. Carl, a Black senior and varsity athlete who we frequently saw surrounded by adoring women and envious-looking men, eschewed alcohol as part of rejecting the whiteness of that college experience. "I'm really just not interested in, like, living someone else's college experience."

There is plenty of drinking that happens outside of the fraternity context and historically white spaces. At the campus center for Jewish student life we saw religiously observant students drenched in sweat and dancing wildly—separated into single-sex groups—in celebration of Simchat Torah, a holiday traditionally accompanied by intense revelry. After a party hosted by the Black Students Organization, we stood near a public safety office in the student center and watched as two men helped a third stagger into the bathroom to vomit; the officer looked at us and shook her head. We also sat through a few beloved "wine-nights": intimate (and, to students, adult-feeling) dinners where students who have found their people and aged into having a suitable space would gather to drink and cook.[35]

This chapter has focused on one very particular kind of drinking— the socially patterned toxic campus brew. It rarely occurs to privileged white men that they could be sexually assaulted, and few have had prevention education that emphasizes how heavy drinking significantly increases their risk of assaulting someone else. This embodied practice of privilege has an unintentional negative impact on the broader social collective. It spreads outward in two ways: culturally through a kind

of symbolic domination, where drunken hijinks come to be seen as a
key route to the essential college experience, and structurally, through
their unequal access to the resources necessary to host, as well as the
resources to cushion the blow of whatever might happen while blackout
drunk. Which, a lot of times, is sex, and sometimes, sexually assault.

"LIKE, SLEEP OVER IF YOU WANT, BUT THAT'S GONNA BE THE END OF IT."

Nearly six feet tall, with blue eyes, curly blond hair, and a little stubble,
Norman was the very picture of the self-possessed undergraduate. As
he spoke it became clear that he'd made himself at home on the campus
both his parents had attended. He repeatedly described himself as "fortunate," in the way that rich people do—"fortunate" that he didn't have
to take the cost of college into account when deciding where to go, "fortunate" that his small private school helped him find an unpaid internship in a vaccine research lab when he was just sixteen, "fortunate" that
his mother raised him bilingual, so that he could chat in Spanish with
the guys in the liquor store on 125th Street. In his telling, this made it so
much easier for him to buy liquor (he also had a good fake ID).

Norman described Columbia's "really serious work-hard, play-hard
culture. Like people go out and they'll be, like, all right, got an A on my
exam, time to go out and just get, like, blackout." He was critical of it.
"It can be fun, and it can be good to spend time with your friends, but
I also think it's super unhealthy . . . the going out with the expectation
of relieving all of your stress by just getting, like, insanely smashed." But
what he took to be the "Columbia culture" and the norm was actually
his own experience as a wealthy white man. Students told us, noncha-
lantly, of heading to Butler Library on Friday after dinner, bags filled
with their laptops, notes, and a water bottle. They'd set an alarm for
11:30 p.m., open their water bottle, and start drinking. They weren't
hydrating. For the next thirty minutes they'd finish up their work and
drink four or five shots' worth of liquor so they weren't too far "behind"

their friends when they showed up at a party just after midnight, when the library closed. There's an intentionality to this kind of drinking, through which students get out of work mode and into party mode; it is an almost baroque imitation of the after-work drink.

Conversations about sexual assault on college campuses frequently point to the substantial research on alcohol as a source of vulnerability— as if raising students' awareness of the dangers of combining alcohol and sex would deter them from doing so.[36] But what goes unacknowledged is that young adults don't get drunk and just happen to have sex. *They frequently get drunk in order to have sex.* The mystery here is not the persistence of drunk sex among students; rather, it is the persistent exoticization, among adults, of students' recreational drinking and sex, especially considering their own well-accepted practice of drinking to have sex. If adults reflect critically and honestly on their own sexual behavior and history, how different does it look? This is particularly true for wealthier, white Americans.[37]

When asked if he drinks or uses substances before a sexual encounter, Norman responded with a clipped "no." But, perhaps noting our surprise, he expanded: "Like, going out and getting drinks beforehand, but not in like preparation for a sexual encounter. Just more as a social thing." He then added, with a sort of bizarre quantification, that he was "probably like twenty-five percent funnier" when drunk. To Norman, the risks of drunk sex felt primarily reputational. "I have definitely hooked up with girls and regretted it on my end." He dimly recalls one night freshman year that began with many rounds of shots; by the time he got to the party he was very drunk. Mischa, who was in his core curriculum section, had been flirting with him, but he was not interested in her; in fact, he described her as "like a three-day-old pizza . . . if you're really that hungry, like, you might microwave and eat it, right? But like, then it's not gonna be that satisfying." And yet, he went back to her room with her and they had sex. He was emphatic, albeit circuitous, in his claim that it was "definitely not something that was not consensual." He regretted having sex with her even as it was happening. "I was just like, 'I don't think you're smart at all, like you're someone I just don't want to spend time with. . . . ' She was definitely not as attractive as most of the girls around . . . the boxes just, like, weren't checked as far as what I would normally want." Yet what he regretted was not the bad sex. He had lowered his standards to have sex Mischa. His friends later made fun of him for it, because she wasn't, in their view, hot. The consequences for his social standing seemed to be his primary regret.

The Centers for Disease Control has stopped using the word "accident" to describe firearm injuries: an accident is something that could not have been predicted or prevented. Instead, the CDC uses the term "unintentional injuries." The United States chooses not to regulate weapons, and consequently has a gun death rate that far exceeds every other developed country in the world—nearly ten times as many deaths per capita as our Canadian neighbors and almost thirty times as many deaths as Denmark.[38] Other countries have effectively used laws and policies to prevent firearm-related deaths. So these deaths can't, in good faith, be called "accidents." Similarly, there might be an element of unpredictability to any particular incident of drunk sex, but there is a clear overall social patterning. As Norman might say, getting drunk, hanging out with friends, and then maybe also hooking up with someone, checks off a lot of boxes. (And hopefully it is not something to compare later to three-day-old pizza.) Chelsea, in one of the all-women focus groups, shared sharply ambivalent feelings about this: "It's so challenging to meet people organically on this campus. . . . I would argue that the only times I've had flirtatious interactions with men [have] been intoxicated. I actually like genuinely hate it"—at which point Shamus broke in to ask, "You mean you're intoxicated or they're intoxicated?"

Both. Or . . . I don't know. I'm not ashamed of this actually. Part of joining the sorority was to meet boys. I just don't know how to meet them. Like, where are they? So being thrown into a fraternity basement where everyone is drinking or, you know, they rent out a bar. Everyone's drinking. The interactions I'm gonna have with people who I want to get to know more or I think are cute are gonna be shaped by how much I've been drinking or—and then also, you know, if we're both intoxicated and we're talking, then the culture that I've experienced so far has not been let's see each other again soon. It's come back to my room tonight. Like, sleep over if you want, but that's gonna be the end of it.

Drinking is a big part of white heterosexual students' strategies to accrue sexual experience. But we found that across racial and ethnic groups, sexual orientation, and gender identity, drinking to have sex is central to many students' early-college projects. It is fairly common; analysis of SHIFT survey data showed that two-thirds of sexually active students who had had sex in the prior three months reported some substance use prior to or during sex.[39]

Rowan, an aspiring neurosurgeon, was hazy on many details of one orientation-week hookup; in fact, she slept with a guy without being one hundred percent sure of his name, although she did remember stopping to buy cookies on the way back to his room—but the thrill of recounting it was evident, as she described telling her newfound friends about this adventure as something that was "very college, very what you do in college." Students talked about how being drunk dulls the awkwardness of hookups, like Novocain before dental work. Margot noted that she "only has the courage to hook up when drunk," and Jeanette talked about drinking in anticipation of hooking up "because it would, like, blur my memory a little bit, I would just be more relaxed about it. . . . I didn't want to remember awkwardness. . . . It was appealing that I could get really drunk and not necessarily be super self-conscious."

Stress and sexual shame are at the heart of a lot of why drunk sex is so common. Scholars have shown that being drunk produces vulnerability to sexual assault, and individuals, communities, and organizations have taken note.[40] One response, common during sexual assault prevention programming, is to convey to young people that they can't consent to sex if they're drunk—that consent, as a legal standard, cannot be given if one person is intoxicated. That may be somewhat true, except that many students (and likely many of our readers) have been drunk and had sex to which they agreed and did not regret. The coupling of alcohol and sex means that for those students who do drink as part of their anticipation for meeting a sexual partner, prevention messages that discourage drunk sex are effectively like saying, "Don't have sex." Moving the needle on drunk sex isn't going to be easy. But moving the needle on some of the underlying causes may be more feasible, and may have additional benefits.

On a tour of one of the dorms we stopped in the basement lounge, looking at the boardroom-like table and whiteboard, to ask what was the most fun thing that he recalled happening there. Our student guide answered, "Um, probably the puppies—when they bring in the therapy dogs during exam time." Everyone loves the puppies, and evidence suggests that they provide real benefits to students—but what does it say about the environment of college today that it requires that degree of stress mitigation?[41]

There are parts of college that are hard in ways that are not modifiable, nor should they be: demanding academics, the developmental challenges of growing up, the college project of figuring out who you are and what you want to do. But there are modifiable sources of stress. Schools can't change the labor market, but they can improve career services; for students without a family friend to get them an internship, the summer job race begins in September, and requires sending out hundreds of resumes to find a position. Leaving behind family and friends can be hard. But schools can do more to address the social and emotional needs that are part of that transition. It's not just a question of what happens during orientation week; schools with the resources to do so can consider how campus social geographies, including both identity group–specific spaces and public spaces that facilitate social interaction, shape students' experiences.

While schools have had little impact in reducing drunk sex by warning students of its dangers in relation to sexual assault, there are at least two precursors of drunk sex that may be more modifiable: sexual shame and difficulties in forming new attachments. Sexual shame is socially produced, reflecting the shame about one's own body produced by porn as a primary source of sexual information and the impact all of those "not under my roof" messages that deny young people's sexual citizenship.[42] Sex with people one doesn't know well reflects the power of hooking up as an ideal, a way to "be college," but it also reveals the role that peer networks and extracurriculars play as substitute families. If it were easier to make friends throughout one's time at college, students might be more willing to risk an emotional entanglement with someone they already know and like. There are ways to build a social environment in which it is less likely that students experience the need to drink heavily to get themselves over that bar where they feel like they can just "let go" and have sex. If sex didn't feel so scary in the first place, students might not need to get so drunk to quash their fears and shame. And so another way into the question of drunk sex is to look at sex more generally: how campus sexual geographies shape it, what students' sexual projects are, the social risks they juggle in realizing those projects, and the moments in which they see, or fail to recognize, each other's sexual citizenship.

4

WHAT IS SEX FOR?

"IT'S THEIR SPACE TOO. AND WE ALREADY AGREED TO NO SEX."

Vera, a young Black woman from Colorado, recalled the sex education at her arts-oriented magnet school as "kind of like, don't do it, you can catch STIs, and make babies accidentally." When her fellow high-schoolers talked about sex, the focus was on judgment rather than information: "There would be rumors going around, she's a—I don't know, insert pejorative word here." Vera was clear both about her ultimate sexual project—"a nice, long-term relationship"—and about the interim plan: "I don't think that's going to happen any time soon, so maybe now, kind of friends with benefits." She sought a partner who was "funny, intelligent, considerate, affectionate, intelligent—and curly hair." The intelligent part was clearly important to her—she mentioned it twice—but she was agnostic about race, other than to note that white guys "don't see me as somebody who's maybe a potential suitor." For gender, she said "male probably," but only because "guys are the default." Her mom's advice about sexual activity was brief but clear: "Just don't do it"—modified slightly with a parting message before Vera left for college: "If you need birth control I'm not going to judge you."

Vera did indeed need birth control. She'd found enough information online to know that she wanted to get on the pill as soon as she got to college; in her words, "I wasn't very sexually active" in high school, but for college "I figured I might as well be prepared." To locate prospective "friends with benefits," she turned to Tinder, an app that people use to match with prospective partners. Her fellow Barnard students were emphatically nonjudgmental about sexual behavior—but early freshman year she and her roommates had "agreed no sex [in the dorm room] . . . just because it would be really hard to coordinate with three other people, and we all have different hours, and it doesn't seem fair to kick three people out at one time. I feel like it would be unfair to kick somebody out while they're studying so I can have sex." She laughed, recalling how her roommates, who she described as "pretty open," told her that she was "getting the most action of any of them." And yet their agreement required that that action had to happen elsewhere. As she explained, "I don't know when I'm going to be alone, and like I said, my roommates are in there studying or listening to music. I don't say, hey, can you leave, I want to have sex. It's kind of rude because it's their space too. . . . So it's kind of a protective thing."

The agreement among roommates not to have sex in their shared space certainly helps with interpersonal harmony. And yet it also produces vulnerability—think back to Charisma, who was far from campus, deep in Brooklyn, when the guy whose apartment she was in started pressing her to do more than make out. The geographic context—the actual spaces through which students move, where they meet, and where they have sex—intersect with their goals and values to shape sexual interactions, creating the possibility for fun, exciting sex, but also structuring opportunities for bad things to happen.

The story Boutros reluctantly shared about being sexually assaulted by a woman he barely knew, while he was very drunk and in a strange city, underlines the spatial dimension of vulnerability. But the way Boutros handled this in his own room was markedly different, reflecting both his gender and his robust sense of his own sexual citizenship. Unlike his American peers, who "just find it incredibly difficult to talk to a girl unless they've had alcohol," Boutros was perfectly comfortable with sober sex. He saw this discomfort as related to Americans' sexual illiteracy and the shame produced by those "just don't do it" messages. He recounted, with incredulity, his freshman-year girlfriend's near-complete lack of understanding of the risks of pregnancy and sexually transmitted diseases. "How is this girl—how do you not know this? Like, for example, she thought you could just pull out and it would be fine. And I'm like, that's obviously not true."

Boutros was forthright with his freshman roommate in claiming space to have sex. At 5:00 p.m. one Monday afternoon, he texted his roommate: " 'Give me forty minutes.' . . . We've got, like, a good code, we've got a good relationship." When asked if he had waited for a response, he laughed. The failure to wait was why he wanted to tell the story. There he was in their double room with his girlfriend:

> fooling around . . . just, like, kissing and maybe a bit of fingering. . . . Clothes are off—yeah, well, actually no, we're both in underwear. And then I take her bra off. Take her clothes off. Take her underwear off, I take my pants off, put on a condom, and then, I don't know, we're just having sex in the bed. We start having sex like missionary, I guess, and then switch to cowgirl. And then I fell off the bed, because our beds are so small.

He laughed.

> And so we started doing it just, like, standing by the bed. And then I look over and sit on the chair. And she sits on top of me. That was good. And then—my desk is full of stuff, it had like a laptop on it and some books. My roommate's desk was completely empty. So we ended up having sex on his desk. And then he knocks! He's like, "Hey, Boutros, I just need to come in really quickly, I need to grab my bag."

Boutros laughed again, telling the story.

And I grabbed the handle—"There's no—don't come in right now."
He's like, "Why?" and it's like, "Um, I'm on your desk." And he's
like, "Fuck." So that was funny.

Boutros was laughing throughout, as he recounted this story of the close
quarters and the challenges of negotiating sex in a way that frequently
involves at least one other person.

The space is not just a backdrop—it is almost a third character in the
sexual scene. The frantic freshman minuet of finding space to have sex
reflects how much more likely first-years are to be in shared bedrooms,
as well as the high stakes of offending a roommate. If a hookup goes
sour, students can "ghost" a sexual partner, particular someone on the
fringes of or outside their social circle, but they have to make it through
the whole year with their roommate. Dorm room furniture all but forces
two people—regardless of whether they just want to make out or even
chat—to sit on a bed if they're going to sit together. And although college beds are multipurpose—study space, snack stop, facetime with
parents—there's no denying that a bed has a strong sexual component.
The almost tidal flow of students in and out of each other's bedrooms
is a defining element of residential higher education. Dorm life is a
fundamental sexual assault opportunity structure. (Social scientists use
the term *opportunity structure* to refer to socially organized and unequal
allocation of opportunities. The original use was in relation to criminal
behavior, but it has been applied to life transitions such as marriage or
finding a job, and more recently to extramarital sexual relations.)[1]

For this generation of digital natives, the online world is a real and
vital dimension of that sexual landscape, with a porous line between
digitally mediated social interactions and those that happen in person. We saw students sitting at a lunch table laughing as one scrolled
through profiles; they collectively assessed the suitability of prospective
hookups. In one interview, a student chuckled in recounting how easily she'd "fact-checked" a guy's assertion that he went to Cornell when
in fact he was a student at the City College of New York ("not that

I'd have cared"). "Suitability" is typically assessed in terms of whether or not someone is in your broader social group. A friend of a friend is the ideal social distance: pre-screened for social acceptability, but still far enough from their primary peers so if things go wrong it won't be socially disruptive.

We heard plenty of stories about students who'd met boyfriends or girlfriends on Tinder or another one of the digital platforms. Apps aren't just for sex; they help organize and categorize partners. Who is also gay? Who is available? Who is looking for fun, and who is willing to say they're looking for something more? Not all students use apps, and the uses are quite varied; several had met long-term girlfriends or boyfriends online, while one student proudly recounted having had sex with 73 men he met on Grindr—as a freshman. Students flirt through their phones. Octavia whipped out her phone in the interview, and started scrolling through, showing pictures that the guy she was hooking up with had sent her:

> Like, he'll send me this at bedtime, right? That's flirty—like, he's topless, and making a smirking face, and I'll be like, "Can I join?" You get the point. Um, or this, oh my god, look, look how hot he looks, holy shit. Oh my god. Or like this—that's flirty—like, they're all flirty. [*She scrolls further.*] Oh, like this, "when I'm giving it to you good." Like, okay, so "Can I come over, so you can give it to me good?"

When the number of suitable prospective partners on campus feels particularly small—for some students of color, or queer students, or students with very specific sexual desires—apps expand the pool.

Early in our research, a colleague at the cross-university council of faculty who do research on gender and sexuality challenged the framing of SHIFT's broad focus on " 'sexual assault and sexual health,' " suggesting that "healthy sex" might not be the best placeholder for whatever one might label the sex that is not assault. There was lots of sex that wasn't assault that wasn't necessarily "healthy." The next week we asked our Undergraduate Advisory Board, a group of students that we consulted with every Monday morning about our research (we explain their role fully in the Appendix A), to articulate for us all the different ways to categorize a sexual interaction that wasn't assault. Over the course of an intense two hours, they listed dozens of categories. Whether power inequalities are present. Whether the sex was drunk sex. They mentioned sober sex, which they called "serious sex," but also noted that for students who don't drink or do drugs, all sex is sober sex. And then there was relationship sex, which included makeup sex, hot relationship sex, relationship sex that is as exciting as going to the store for a quart of milk, and sex when one person is a survivor of assault, with all of the challenges that that can bring. There's "phone" sex (usually using video). The list went on and on.

But underlying that diversity of encounters are five sexual projects: becoming a skilled sexual partner, seeking pleasure, connecting with another person emotionally, defining oneself, and impressing others—all while managing a complex set of social opportunities and risks. Examining students' sexual projects reveals the internal logic of behaviors that may otherwise seem mysterious, a little scary, or downright cruel. Sex is not the opposite of sexual assault, in part because the same contexts and even very similar sequences of interactions define both experiences.

Students have a word for this—they describe some sex as being "rapey." Initially we found this disturbing. Calling something rapey, with a raised eyebrow, seemed to be joking about something that was not funny; we wanted, and still want, a bright line between "rape" and "sex." But the words that students use are a window into their world. When students talked about sex as "rapey," part of what they were indicating was that they were having sex that they were unwilling to name "assault" but that they recognized as having a lot of similarities to assault. And when students talk about other things as rapey—whether it's a 1980s classic teen movie like "Sixteen Candles," with a scene that borders on date rape; a Disney movie scene, such as the song sung by Gaston in "Beauty and the Beast," where he claims he'll make Belle his wife, regardless of her objections; or an old jazz standard such as "Baby it's Cold Outside," where a man tries to not let a woman leave a party, even as she insists she wants to—what they are flagging is a shift in cultural sensibilities that is part of the emerging contemporary collective acknowledgment of sexual assault as a social problem.

"I WAS JUST SO SELF-CONSCIOUS . . . I DIDN'T WANNA BE BAD."

There are plenty of virgins on campus: one in five men who took the SHIFT survey reported not having had sex ever, as did one in five gender-nonconforming students, and one in three women. And yet students who start college without having had penetrative intercourse often feel that they're behind and need to catch up.[2] There's a complex set of motivations packed into this.[3] Many see casual sex as a fundamental part of the college experience—a core way to "be college." But others feel shame at sexual inexperience, as well as fear that a lack of sexual experience will render them inept as sexual partners when they do eventually have sex. For the most part, these students are disciplined, hard workers. They've drilled with SAT flashcards, spent hundreds of hours practicing the violin, gone off-book for the lead in the school play after only a couple of weeks, or perfected their free throws by taking thousands of shots. Many approach sex as a skill rather than as a form of interpersonal interaction. This way of thinking makes it a personal achievement in which partners are interchangeable.

Irene described what sounded like an awful encounter, the sole goal of which was to lose her virginity or, as she put it, "get it over with."[4] It was nearly exam time, freshman fall, and she was walking back from an evening chem lab. Another freshman fell into step with her along College Walk. She dimly recognized him because he lived on the floor across from her, and they chatted. He wanted to go back to her room with her. She thought to herself, "I might as well get it done with." They made out for a while on her bed, but since her roommate was sleeping in the same bedroom, she didn't want to have sex there. He said he'd go get a condom, and they met in the bathroom down the hall. She pulled her pants down, he picked her up, and they began to have intercourse, standing in the shower stall. She was not physically excited, not lubricated at all, and it hurt. He apologized in response to her evident discomfort and yet continued thrusting, saying that next time would be better. But there was no next time. After he pulled out and saw blood on the condom, he realized she'd been a virgin. Irene's roommates heard her come back into the suite. She sat on her bed, quietly weeping. They gathered around her to talk. Looking back on that moment, she described him as "a nasty person." She never spoke with him again.

We have no reason to think of what happened to Irene as an assault. But it was, unquestionably, an interaction that left her feeling bad. The sex that students have to accumulate experience, or to demonstrate that they can be modern people, highlights one risk built into impersonal sex: not caring if the other person has a bad experience, sexually or otherwise. One young woman, Kathleen, told us about a man with whom she'd been in an ongoing hookup for months. He'd generally text her, or she'd text him, some time before midnight. "You up?" "Sure." "Can I come by?" She'd respond with a thumbs-up, or a funny GIF. He'd regularly sleep over; even in a twin bed, it was nice to have someone to cuddle with on cold winter nights. Students called the late fall "cuffing season"—that time when, as it started to get cold, it was helpful to lock down a potential partner for the winter: to cuff them. Cuffing is distinct from relationships, which entail both more time and more emotional risk. Several students described relationships to us as "like an extra three-credit class,"—a class that they hesitated to sign up for, fearing the time commitment, or being hurt, or hurting someone else. In Kathleen's case, the cuffing of this man didn't last. He crossed the line when he started opening up emotionally by telling her how sad he felt about his grandmother's recent death. She was definitely "dtf" (down to fuck), and even to snuggle. But sadness? She hadn't signed up for that. And so she asked him to leave. Kathleen had every "right" to. If she didn't want him there, he shouldn't be there. What is troubling about this is not that these two are "hooking up" outside of a relationship context. Rather, Irene exhibited an intentional lack of care for her partner's humanity; she wasn't alone in doing so.

Sometimes students are more sensitive to each other's cues during encounters. Simon described what had happened with Jordan, a sophomore he met at a party during orientation week, as uncomfortable and embarrassing. After the party, they texted a bit, and then met up in person a couple of days later. They sat on the Low Library steps in the late summer night, talking and making out a little bit. That part was fun. Another night, Jordan took him out for ramen. Eventually Simon confessed to Jordan that he was a virgin, and they made plans to meet in Simon's room. While there, they started making out. Simon told us that Jordan made the first move: without saying anything, he started taking off Simon's clothes, and his own. Once his shirt was off, Simon began to feel nervous—so nervous, in fact, that he told Jordan he was going to vomit, grabbed his shirt, and ran to the bathroom. Jordan followed to make sure he was okay. They returned to Simon's room and Jordan started taking off his clothes again, but Simon stopped him, saying, "'No, I'm not ready for this, right now.'" Jordan asked if he was sure he didn't want to do anything, and Simon said yes. Jordan left, and they didn't see each other again.

> I felt really embarrassed, because it was, like, "I don't even know how this works." I was so uncomfortable in the situation, because I had had no experience. And I don't know where the fear was coming from, but I just, I just was really uncomfortable. It was really embarrassing, because, you know, he's older and seems to know exactly what to do, and I'm just this young freshman who is too nervous to even have fun. I just felt completely embarrassed by it, and that's why I didn't talk to him again, because I was just, like, "I don't want that kind of, I don't want that to happen again." I was just so self-conscious of my own lack of experience, that I

didn't wanna be bad, and I didn't wanna show inadequacy. That was a lot of the nervousness.

It wasn't just nerves. He didn't know Jordan, he wasn't that interested in getting to know him better, and the shallowness of the physical interaction made him feel bad. Simon has grown to be more comfortable with a sexual project that combines sex and intimacy. He described that it felt like a kind of revelation—which he then justified in terms of his conservative Christian upbringing—to admit to himself that he did not want to have sex with someone he did not know or care about.[5] A lot of students feel this way, but then some look around and see their peers having sex with people they don't know well, and feel like they need to get with the program. Up their number, get some stories to tell. The normalization of sex outside of committed exclusive relationships makes students who are uncomfortable with that—which seems to us like most students—doubt themselves. They feel out of step with the times. It's not that hookup culture is intrinsically bad or good, but it exercises power as an ideal form for what young people "should" be doing or should want.[6]

"DON'T WORRY, I'VE HAD A LOT WORSE."

Physical pleasure is a prominent sexual project. Guys sometimes describe it as "getting my nut." Men's "nut" is taken for granted as a goal of sexual interactions. We heard plenty of stories in which the flow of sexual pleasure ran in one direction: from women to men. Few seemed to question this as a logic of heterosexual interaction—a hand job in the library stacks, a blow job a girl gives her guy friend one time when they are drunk, a hookup set in motion when a girl decides that she feels bad for a guy who hasn't had sex in seven months. At least some of the campus orgasm gap reflects heterosexual interactions in which men don't even try to pleasure women.[7] These one-sided hookups reinforce the stereotype of women as desireless sources of sexual gratification.

Imagine if two friends meet routinely for a meal where only one eats and the other one always cooks. Inattentiveness to the sexual pleasure of one party is, in part, an erasure of their social equivalence. To a nontrivial degree, the basis of society is reciprocity.[8] And yet heterosexual encounters often lack such reciprocity, denying women's equivalent standing to men, and invalidating their sexual citizenship. Consensual encounters of this nature are a training ground for sexual assault, schooling young people to accept as normal sexual interactions in which a guy's pleasure is the only outcome that matters.

Boutros ascribed his girlfriend's low expectations for sex to the same inadequate sex education from which she'd gleaned that withdrawal would be effective for pregnancy and STD prevention. But they also reflected her prior experience. He recounted the first time they had sex, "I was like, 'sorry, that was awful.' And she was like, 'no, don't worry, I've had a lot worse.' And when it—when it got good she was like, okay, yeah, no, this is not what I'm used to, which was nice, I guess, it was a bit of an ego boost for me."

Men sometimes talk about women's sexual pleasure in a way that seems more a question of prowess than of care, but Boutros—like Austin—seemed genuinely committed to his partner's enjoyment. Boutros responded to the question about what is important to him about sex by saying, "for them to be into it. . . . like, if they're not into it, it's pointless. Really, what's the point of having sex if both parties aren't enjoying it?" Boutros's girlfriend was being kind in not affirming that their first sex together was "awful." He was emphatic that mutual sexual pleasure was the whole point of sex. And while she was pleased with this development, it seems that she never considered that pleasurable sex was something she could expect. To get a sense of how his girlfriend might have experienced the "sex on the desk" that he found so amusing, we asked him, "Did you orgasm? Did she orgasm?" "Yes, I was—I don't know about her, she got really wet, which I normally take as a good thing. When I asked her, she said yeah, but like all girls say 'yeah.'" Boutros was one of the more attentive men we talked with, and seemed genuinely concerned that his girlfriend experience pleasure. And yet he wasn't sure about the orgasm—after all, "all girls say yeah."

"I THINK I'M FALLING IN LOVE WITH YOU."

Sexual projects can also skew toward emotional intimacy. When we asked students to tell us about their best sexual experience in college, the stories they chose to share frequently signaled a longing for physical intimacy as an expression of care. These stories also revealed students' fears—not just of rejection, but of creating disruption among their friends. Zoey, a bisexual sophomore from Massachusetts, met Dennis while working at the radio station. They were just friends—he already had a girlfriend—but she was starting to "catch feelings" for him. The phrase "catch feelings" was common among students, framing intimate feelings as out of students' control, or even potentially undesirable; they were more like a cold, which she "caught" but could not direct. Zoey wasn't sure about being with someone she was so close to. She was afraid it wouldn't work out and then she'd have nothing—no friend and no boyfriend. One day Dennis told Zoey he wanted to share an incredible view with her, and so they rode the subway down to 34th Street, pushed through the crowded sidewalks, and waited on line to get to the Empire State Building's observation deck. Pulling Zoey close to him as the sun set, Dennis told her that he'd broken up with his girlfriend and said, "I think I'm falling in love with you." He kissed the top of her head and stepped away. He seemed overcome. She pulled him back to her and they kissed, surrounded by strangers. Zoey said it was one of the sweetest experiences she'd ever had.

These "first kiss" stories sometimes had an almost cinematic element; John, for example, recounted walking his (now) girlfriend back to her dorm after her sorority's crush party: where sorority members explicitly invite their crushes to an event. While the fact that he went as her date to a crush party might seem like a fairly clear declaration of interest in being more than friends, the date had been arranged by her sorority "big," so he did not know if she really liked him. His intentions were clear, at least to him. At the end of the evening, as he walked her home, down the freshman dorm's wide cinder-block hallway to her door, their pace slowed. He was hoping she'd do something to indicate interest, but nothing happened. He told her he had a great time, and gave her an awkward pat on the shoulder. He turned to leave. She called out, "Hey, wait." He whipped back around, and reached for her. Their lips touched. They didn't have sex for months. But what John recalled so distinctly as the best sexual moment of his time in college was that turning point, when they shifted to being more than just friends.

"I DON'T THINK I SHOULD GIVE YOU MY NUMBER."

Sex also offers a route to self-definition. Doug described himself as a "baby gay," and was very explicit about how Columbia's New York location and historically LGBT-friendly campus provided him with an opportunity to come into his own as a gay man.[9] His parents had tried to prepare him to launch as a self-determining sexual adult; they talked with him directly about taking care of himself physically and about their own values regarding sex and relationships, encouraging him to limit sex to people he cared about. But though he'd come out to them before leaving for college, they never spoke directly to him about what it meant to him to be a young gay man. To his mind, that meant acquiring a lot of sexual experience. He proudly described how intentionally he had managed this, seeking out HIV pre-exposure prophylaxis (PrEP, which all but eliminates the risk of contracting HIV) and regularly getting tested for STIs. For sex, he'd open Grindr on his phone, chat briefly with someone, and arrange to meet in his dorm room, texting his roommate to say that he "needs the room."

Students use these intentional assignations to test out gendered sexual identities. Justine, an engineer, came out as bisexual before college. But having never explored sex with women, she asked one of her female friends if they could hook up so she could try it out. On occasion they'd get together, hang out, and have oral sex. Justine's descriptions sounded like she wasn't really interested in her friend other than her social proximity and her sexuality; her partner was a placeholder for all women.

There are elements of sexual projects that are not about whether students are heterosexual, lesbian, gay, bisexual, cisgender, transgender, or queer. Rather, they're about being particular types of men or women. Esme (whose experience of being assaulted by a stranger was described in Chapter 1) had grown up watching the television show *Girls*. It played a powerful role in forming her sexual values. Her college sexual project has a clear narrative arc: she wanted to make out with a lot of random guys, lose her virginity, and then settle into a committed relationship. During the fall of her junior year, Esme was out at her favorite bar with a friend when two guys came in. She'd already hooked up with one of them, and the other, James, she knew from a class. Esme and James "vibed," she recalls, and spent several hours drinking, talking, and making out—first at that bar, then at another. They were both seeing other people—and Esme's semi-steady boyfriend was actually James's friend—so the whole episode felt "a little wrong." To her, that made it all that much hotter. He invited her back to his place nearby, saying that she could sleep on his couch. She went along, knowing that sex was still very much on the table. When they arrived, she said she didn't actually want to sleep on couch, and James admitted he didn't want her to either. Esme described the rest of the night—her best sexual experience at college, as she recalled it—as "solid sex," twice, followed by spending the night cuddling. What made it so fun? The recklessness—"it was not supposed to happen"; in fact, it was "generally destructive for both of us." She remembered his "crazy nice" apartment and, laughing, how she declined to give him her number the next morning as she left. "The reason I love it so much, or like, really like the experience, is because I felt ice cold, being like, 'No, I don't think I should give you my number . . . even though the sex was really good. I'm sure I'll see you around.'" His pierced scrotum and fully tattooed arms provided lots of colorful details to share with her friends the next day.

Esme had arrived at college with a well-developed sense of her own sexual citizenship—fostered by her parents, who had always comfortably answered her questions about sex and relationships. Her recounting of this story—first to her friends, but then also later in her interview with us—illustrates the complexity of even something as seemingly obvious as sexual pleasure; her delight in the story is not just the "solid sex," but also the pleasure in seeing herself as a certain type of person—someone who could be "ice cold" in charting her own sexual future. What doesn't appear in her story is her boyfriend; she was so unphased by the consequences of her actions for their relationship that she only noted them in the interview after we prompted her. Some may find Esme's story to be emblematic of modern women's sexual agency, while others may read it as cruel, coarse, or inconsiderate.

Octavia, similarly, was all about being a cool girl. Medium height, biracial, with startling green eyes and long, wavy hair, she had a steady supply of attention from guys. The threesomes that she had had a couple of times were not, for her, about being bisexual; she knows that guys find it a huge turn-on, and she wants to be the girl who is "down for anything." But sexual projects that are not intrinsically relational—those with a focus on one's own pleasure, for example, or a single-minded quest to accumulate experience—pave the way for sex in which the other person figures more as a sex toy than as an equivalent human being.

Not having sex can be a form of asserting one's identity as well. Students' sexual projects can be a demonstration of their religious identities—sometimes in ways that are about the relationship itself, and sometimes in ways that seem to have little to do with the other person. Diego, who was active in one of the campus's many Christian student groups, was not a virgin, and he wanted to have vaginal intercourse with his current girlfriend. He liked her a lot, and felt that it would deepen their connection, as it had in his past relationships. But she didn't want to, and he was okay with that. His sexual project was secondary to his life project of finding a partner he loved and respected, and who was interested in marriage.

Mateo, a third-year student in General Studies and a devout Christian, had trained himself to look only at women's eyes when he was talking with them, to keep himself from having lustful thoughts while gazing at their bodies. In the past, sex was "kind of his drug." Before college, and before finding God, he had worked in a gym, where he would frequently meet women; his goal then had been to have sex with as many women "out of his league" as he could—frequently in his truck in the gym's parking lot. But since his religious conversion, he avoided sex altogether. His sexual project was all about his religious identity.

Religiously engaged students, particularly those from groups large enough to provide their own dating pools and offer ongoing social infrastructure, enjoy what many other students on campus lack: a social organization with an explicit and ongoing conversation that frames sexual projects in relation to community values. There are Barnard students whose identities are bound to a sexual project that delays intercourse until marriage; this is part of a broader commitment to a life well lived. Among these are the seniors whose doors are decorated by their peers to mark an engagement—rare nationally in this age group, but not uncommon among the modern Orthodox who are part of the campus's vibrant Jewish life. For other religiously engaged students, the picture is less rosy: there are far more women than men, producing very intense gendered power disparities. Some religious traditions communicate about sexual projects in ways that do not fully develop a sense of sexual citizenship, or morally regulate sexual behavior in ways that that produces private guilt or public shame; these too can generate considerable harms.[10] Particularly for queer students, some forms of religious life offer more anguish than social support.[11]

"SHE SORTA FORCED ME INTO IT A LITTLE BIT."

Accumulating experience does more than alleviate anxiety; it also provides stories to share with friends, sometimes to bond with them, sometimes to jockey for status. Steve's story started out sounding very much like the story of someone being assaulted, and then pivoted as he realized that even if the young woman had basically forced him into a sexual experience, she also freed him from what he saw as the stain of sexual inexperience. It began when he was out with his friends at one of the neighborhood bars, celebrating the end of finals after the fall semester of his freshman year. He was pretty drunk, and had tried cocaine for the first time that night. He started talking to a group of women at the bar, and one of them suggested that they go back to his room. Prior to this, Steve had had no sexual experience.

> She sorta forced me into it a little bit. She was, like, "Can we go to your room?" And I was just, like, didn't know what to say, and so I was, like, "All right, let's, let's go!" It's not like I had planned or wanted to do it really. The thing is it's not something I wanted to do, really, like, I wasn't particularly attracted to her or anything. I didn't know how to say no, I guess. Or I just, I guess part of it was, like, I kinda just wanted to get it over with, you know.

They went to his dorm room and sat on the bed talking for a few minutes. He then told this woman that he had never even kissed anyone. He said that he was afraid, and didn't know what to do. She turned and started kissing him. He didn't pull away. He fingered her, and then they both performed oral sex on each other. After that, she said they should not have penetrative sex (he suggests that this was because she didn't want to take his virginity). When they were finished, she asked if he wanted to cuddle. He declined, saying that he wanted to go back out to meet up with his friends. He was excited to tell them about what had happened.

> My whole life I was, for whatever reason, just, like scared of being sexually intimate with someone. I used to always be scared of things that I didn't know how to do. I was afraid of being bad, I guess. I was pretty happy, 'cause I kinda just realized like, "Why

am I so afraid? Like . . . this is ridiculous. I'm holding myself back,"
you know? I was just really happy.

Steve's fear of "being bad" paralleled the language that Simon had used.
Steve was clear that he had not sought out the sexual interaction, and
his description of it was mechanistic, with little discussion of pleasure,
but once it was over he felt an intense relief. His virginity was no longer
a "thing." Now he could talk about the experience with his friends—
which was more a discussion of his own feelings and his having finally
"done it"; it didn't have anything to do with this particular woman herself. Steve seemed fine that she "kinda forced" him into this experience,
since it got him over the hurdle of his fear. Other students told us of
getting their first time over with by finding another virgin during orientation week, and deliberately arranging to have sex so that they could
each go on their way with their college sex lives, not having to worry
about their first time anymore. This reflected a kind of college project
defined more by what people did not want than by what they wanted.
"Negative" college projects—to know that you didn't want to be a virgin,
that you didn't want to be bad at sex, that you didn't want to be seen as
inexperienced, or too experienced—often seemed easier to vocalize, or
at least more common than positive ones. A more positively articulated
project was often elusive. Simon and Steve both knew what they didn't
want. But neither of them recounted getting any adult guidance about
what they should want. Simon managed to figure it out for himself and
seemed to be doing fine. Steve was still struggling, driven largely by
that urge that led him to run out of bed and back to the bar after his
first time, an urge to see what his friends thought, more than what he
wanted or valued.[12]

IT'S DEFINITELY MORE ABOUT TELLING YOUR FRIENDS.

Diana's shaved head and monochrome dress gave her the air of a pen-
itent. A junior, she described herself as "previously heterosexual, cur-

rently asexual." But in her freshman fall, sex was a way of racking up achievements. She'd fallen in with a group of super-wealthy women, who would "blow like $5,000 a month on brunch." Mystified, we asked how you spend that much money on brunch. Apparently, it requires drinking a lot of champagne. It may also require a good bit of exaggeration. Regardless, she struggled to pay her part of those brunch tabs, running quickly through her earnings from working at an amusement park the summer before college.

The main Sunday brunch activity was to pass around your phone, showing the Facebook profile photos of men you'd "gotten with" the week before. That competition was the only upside of an experience that she described as "gross." She'd been at a party in one of the senior dorms, just her and two other freshman women and a bunch of men who were athletes, all on the same team. She and her friends had each done a couple of shots before going over there, and they had some of the joint that the guys were passing around when they arrived. Her friends went to another room in the suite, to continue to smoke. Soon after they left, the situation changed quickly:

> There was, like, an unheard signal, and all the guys left except me and this really hot guy. You know, I just feel like it was this, like, alpha shit. Like, he was the best one, so they were gonna, like, let him have sex with me. I mean, it was just really kind of messed up. At the same time, I was like, "Well, like, we're obviously gonna have sex now." And so he closed the door and didn't even say anything. He just started taking my clothes off. You know, I was, like—I was okay with it.

Diana performed oral sex on him; he didn't reciprocate. According to Diana, "He didn't even pretend to think about my satisfaction. We just had sex, and then he handed my clothes back to me." She dressed and walked out, only to find that the many of the team members had been standing there, listening in. Diana felt used. But the using was mutual, even if the pleasure was not. This experience—senior, athlete, hot guy—scored some rare bragging rights at brunch. "I had a good chip in this case." To characterize this sex as impersonal—as one quite reasonably might—is to miss the most important point. It solidified social relations, but not between the two people having intercourse—rather, between each participant and their respective friends.

Diana's brunch triumph has a backstory related to her sexual projects, which included both a specific, performative social identity—she wanted to be a bad girl—and the development of sexual skills. In high school, she had wanted to be "good at sex." She was very explicit about what she was looking for and was, in her own words, "very efficient" about finding it: she "swiped right" on men on dating and hookup apps who listed their ages as between 18 and 30 ("swiping right" means that the app tells these men that you're interested in them, provided they also swipe right for you). She told them up front that she didn't want to have intercourse. She had rules: no guys who sent dick pics, and only those who could string together an intelligent sentence. If they were decent guys, she'd hook up with them. Looking back, Diana is thankful she was never able to bring herself to have intercourse with them, and that none of them forced the issue.[13]

As the end of high school neared, Diana became increasingly annoyed that she was still a virgin. She was a planner. There was little romantic or even sexual about her plan. She started dating her first boyfriend with "losing my virginity" as almost the sole goal. When we sat down to chat with her four years after the fact, looking back on her relationship, the word she chose to describe how she treated her boyfriend was "abusive." After she'd gotten what she wanted, she cheated on him—intentionally choosing his archenemy. Her boyfriend was crushed; Diana didn't care.

Most students have an exaggerated sense of how much sex others are having; few know that this generation is having less sex than those a generation ago. There's a competitive quality among some peer groups about each member's sexual standing, where groups seek to advance their own status, but also compete with one another about who is, by

some collectively agreed-upon metric, winning. The people they're having sex with are not the prize, they're the pawns in the game. Under-
neath this is no small amount of fear—of not keeping up, or of leading
the pack "too much," or maybe even of being ridiculous. For Diana,
that moment of passing her phone around at brunch outweighed the
unpleasantness of the night before.[14]

For high-status men, this competition can take the form of seeing
how many freshman girls, and which ones, they can have sex with in
the early weeks of the fall semester. The summer before college, Murray
and his high school friends looked over the Facebook pages for each
guy's future classmates, publicly making the list of which "cuties" they'd
have sex with. Reflecting back on having had sex with all three of his
designated choices during the first couple weeks of his freshman fall, he
made clear that the thrill was the competition, more than the sex itself.
"It's definitely more about hooking up with hot girls and telling your
friends about it than like any real sexual thing. 'Cause like everyone can
get laid." He continued, making clear that the audience that mattered
for these achievements was not "broader Columbia, just sort of within
your friends."[15]

Peers figure powerfully in determining whether an experience
advances one's sexual projects. During orientation week, for example,
Pratish and a girl he'd just met, Jolie, thought it would be fun to hook
up in the stacks of the East Asian Studies library. Through a staircase,
past the vaulted ceilings, stained glass windows, and long oak tables
of the library's majestic main reading room, lie several floors of stacks,
connected by metal staircases. It is rarely crowded, and was empty that
night in the middle of the week before Labor Day weekend. They made
out a bit, and then Jolie gave Pratish a hand job. In the moment, and
at first afterwards, Pratish was delighted: "It was actually really funny.
And to me, it's, like, such a funny story. And, like, I—I enjoy that, like,
that was a funny experience and I definitely don't regret it, and that was,
like, a fun time." Afterwards, though, things got awkward. Jolie told a
couple of her friends, and word made its way back to Pratish's friends,

who made fun of him because she was not "their stereotypical pretty girl." Pratish was clearly defensive about this; he maintained that she was funny and that they'd had fun together. But it turned out to be embarrassing for him. He may have enjoyed Jolie, but his friends mocked him for it. This influenced his future sexual decisions, as well as how he felt about hist time with Jolie.

The axis along which peers evaluate a sexual interaction is brutally clear—does the person raise your status, or lower it? The "risks" of sex to which students are most attentive are not pregnancy or STIs, which can mostly be managed with morning-after pills and antibiotics. The social risks feel far more pressing. In students' recounting of episodes of sex that stand out in their memories, we see them most attentive to such social factors: the partner's broadly perceived attractiveness, and their peers' responses, and what the sex will mean for their social standing. Such risks are more salient even than whether the interaction was physically pleasurable. The pleasure of sex that most students seem ultimately concerned with is its social pleasure, or status enhancement.

"I FEEL SHITTY IF I'M JUST HAVING SEX WITH MACAULEY AND HE'S NOT MY BOYFRIEND."

In residential college life, friend groups and fellow student activity members become substitute family. That's a good thing. These chosen families are students' most important source of support and emotional well-being. The consequence, though, can often be perverse. Students frequently told us that relationships with sexual partners probably wouldn't last. They would fall apart over summer, or after graduation, or because one person was leaving for study abroad, or even during the school year when there was just so much else they had to do. Students can be reluctant to begin a relationship within a friendship group. The chaos or fracture that a breakup can cause within a tight-knit group of friends makes dating within your group of close friends feel too risky. The possibility of losing your chosen family, or disrupting the dynamic within an extracurricular group, just isn't worth it. The terms "floor-cest" or "hall-cest" to denote having sex with someone on your floor or hall conveys the intensity of the proscription against sex within one's immediate social group. The potential awkwardness outweighs the rare but enormously valued potential outcome of finding love that fits within your life. And so students turn to those on the fringes of, or even out-side, their friendship network. What at first glance seems like reckless behavior—looking for sex with people who are acquaintances rather than friends—is actually a hedge against the risk of losing one's great-est source of support. Students often avoid intimacy with those with whom they have the most in common, or people they already really like. Instead, risk aversion presses them to take a shot among the relatively unknown. And because it can feel awkward to get naked with someone you don't really know, students who hook up hoping that it will turn into a relationship are frequently drunk. Yes, parties are both places to drink and places to meet prospective partners, but the drinking also serves as a kind of emotional anesthesia; recall Margot, who shared that she "only has the courage to hook up when drunk."

It's not just embarrassment—there is a broader set of social risks that students are managing. Apps to connect with prospective sexual partners intersect with the sexual project of accruing experience, offer-ing a way to catch up for students who feel that their "number" is too low. Digitally mediated sex is efficient. If a student meets someone at a party, it's impossible to tell if they're available or already partnered, straight or gay. This could lead to a whole wasted hour at a party—when social time feels very scarce. Swiping right or seeing that they're single skips all these steps, connecting students directly to available and interested prospective partners. It offers emotional safety as well as effi-ciency, getting students past that first possible rejection. Despite being all about the cool-girl pose, Octavia was disarmingly honest about her fear of rejection. There were two ways that Tinder figured in her current ongoing hookup. First, it had helped move things to the next level. As she recounted,

It's hard to meet new people at Columbia. People are very cliquey—you go to a bar, and everybody's already in their own groups, and it's hard to know for sure if someone is attracted to you. For example, Macauley and I, we knew each other . . . but because we matched on Tinder, that gave us a reason to talk, and that gave a confirmation that we were both attracted to each other. Versus, like, if I just meet a guy at a bar and talk to him, he could just be being polite. . . . If you match with someone online, that's like, one hundred percent they're interested.

Octavia's reliance on apps ebbed and flowed, depending on "the month, and what new people I'm juggling, and what old people I'm juggling." Which led to the question, "Why always the need to pull in new people?" She assessed the situation brutally. "'Cause I get uncomfortable if I don't have a . . . I have to be dating, if I'm single. Because I feel shitty if I'm just having sex with Macauley and he's not my boyfriend. That's, like, not okay with me." She laughed. "I'm just like, 'if you're not gonna wife me up, I'm not gonna be monogamous with you. It's not happening, sorry.'"[16]

She rotated between apps, deleting them in frustration, or because she felt they were too distracting, and then reinstalling them when she needed to be "juggling" more people as she tried to work out the role of sex in her life.

In high school I would use it when I was feeling anxious or feeling lonely . . . and now I use it like, "o my god, I'm stressed and anxious, I just need to have sex." It will make me feel better, it will make me feel less lonely. It will make me feel supported.

Octavia was reflective about this.

It's bad to use sex to feel better. I feel like if you're using a chemical, like sex creates chemicals, dopamine and serotonin . . . I personally think it's bad to use alcohol, drugs if you're feeling shitty, you should be using things when you're in a good state, you shouldn't be using things to make your state better.

She was trying, she said, to "move away from that." Her goal was for sex to be "more to bond with the person I like rather than trying to make myself feel better. Like, I've found a lot of other coping mechanisms when I feel stressed or anxious or lonely, like being out with friends. But I still sometimes, when I feel shitty, want to have sex."[17]

Octavia responded without hesitation when we asked about her aims for her sexual life: "So I right now am really—I really want a boyfriend. I really do, and that's a weird thing to want. It's not a weird thing to want but it's a hard thing to aim for." Octavia had a rich emotional vocabulary and well-developed capacity to reflect on what drove her actions—including a fairly scathing analysis of the way that she used app-based sex as an emotionally protective countermeasure to Macauley's reluctance to "wife her up." Octavia, like most of her peers, struggled with a totally understandable fear of rejection. The disjuncture between Octavia's aspirations for how sex should fit into her life, and her actions, constantly seeking "new people" to juggle, was not unusual; what stuck out about her story was how fearlessly clear-eyed she was in admitting that her resistance to being exclusive with Macauley was a performance of independence.

Octavia was hard on herself. College can be a very lonely time—particularly in the first semesters, when students have left home but have not settled into a groove with new friends and established activities. In this context, for many students, hooking up is to intimacy what instant ramen is to food—not really a long-term substitute, but good enough to kill the craving in the moment. Before students have made friends—real intimate friends, to whom they can confess that they are lonely or homesick or scared—it's easier, and more socially acceptable, to get a little drunk—or in some cases, very drunk—and hook up with a relative stranger. It might be scary, but lying in bed with a friend of a friend at least provides a little human warmth and physical connection. For many students, hookups are a form of "satisficing"—finding something that is good enough (sufficient) and allowing it to satisfy a desire. But satisficing prevents some people from seeking what they actually want. An ongoing hookup might keep the despair and loneliness at bay. But eating those instant noodles also means that you're not going to be hungry for dinner.[18]

Margot, an Asian junior, shook her head in frustration, talking about how hookup culture kept people from going out on dates: "Like, at Columbia, or at college in general, relationships start from hooking up instead of the traditional, ask someone out, take you on a date kind of thing." So when she hooks up, "it's like, in the back of my mind, I'm hoping for something more." A striking element of that "something more" that so many students seek is just how low the bar is. They say they are looking for a guy who is "not a creep." Someone, as Oona said, who asks you some "sweet questions," or as Guy said, who "wants to talk after sex," or as Winona said, "will just say hi to you when they see you the next day."[19]

Jay, a young bisexual man whose parents are from India, was clear that his sexual project was really just physical pleasure. He described an encounter with Mostafa, with whom he'd connected on Grindr. They were in Mostafa's apartment, and before Mostafa penetrated Jay, he paused and asked if it was okay. Jay noted that appreciatively, distinguishing it from some people who are "a bit more aggressive" and just turn you over, taking conversations previously conducted over Grindr as consent for all activities.[20]

Across a whole range of sexual projects, what consistently separated interactions that verged on or constituted assault from those that did not was this moment of recognition about the other person's equivalent humanity. That doesn't mean that sex for pleasure, or skills-building, or to impress one's friends, leads automatically to assault. But these sexual projects, because they have so little to do with the other person, lay the groundwork for assault. They are contexts that lend themselves easily to impersonal sex. We're not against hookups or casual sex per se. We're concerned about it in a context where people (mostly women and queer students) lack clarity about their own sexual citizenship, and where many (mostly, but certainly not only, men) also fail to recognize equivalent citizenship in the person they are with.

Early in our fieldwork, we asked students a question that we thought was really important—"What is sex for?" Most students couldn't answer it. We got a lot of "um, making babies," and some blank looks. Eventually we scrapped the question in favor of other ways of eliciting students' sexual projects. Except for those students whose grounding and ongoing participation in religious life offered a framework for them to think about sexual interactions in relation to morality, or those students whose parents took an active role in having a conversations about what sex was for, most students have to figure out the sexual projects question on their own. They have grown to physical maturity surrounded by a cacophony of messages about sex: fear-based messages about the dangers of sex; incitements in popular culture to act and do and achieve; an internet filled with pornography; but often very little else in the way of conversations. They'd been told time and again what not to do— don't get pregnant, don't get a girl pregnant, don't get HIV, and now, don't assault anyone, and be careful about getting assaulted. They are unbound by conventions of gender; pressed to consume; stressed, lonely, and insecure.

But what should sex mean? Recall Simon nearly vomiting from nerves, trying to force himself to live out what he thought should be his fantasy of sex with a hunky sophomore, and then figuring out for himself that he really was not comfortable having sex with someone he didn't know. And so even "normal sex" includes a lot of struggle; young people are confused, and sometimes unkind or even cruel, as they seek to figure it out. When they arrive on campus, the big message that they get is about consent. For a lot of them, this is like starting with calculus when they've never had arithmetic.

5

CONSENT

"LET'S BE REAL: YOU'RE HERE, SO YOU WANT THIS."

Sloan cut an arresting figure—almost six feet tall, with cropped auburn hair and a pierced tongue. She sat down to our third (and final) interview with a coffee cup in her hand. She had three term papers to write that day, she explained, and so wanted to start caffeinating. As we spoke, she fiddled with the cup's cardboard sleeve. She rolled it into a tube, then unfurled it and folded it into a tiny square. She folded the cardboard accordion-style, and set it on the table to watch it unfurl as she spoke. Her eyes welled up periodically, but she didn't reach for a tissue until we pulled one from the box and laid it on top. Sloan had emailed us asking to be interviewed, and she wanted to tell her whole story. Like many students with whom we spoke, she seemed to experience our conversations as cathartic. She also conveyed that telling her story felt like a social responsibility, a way to help make a better future. Her busy hands—and, to be sure, the tears—communicated distress, and yet she laughed on her way out the door. Getting paid to talk about herself for six hours had been "a dream come true." When she laughed, her dimples showed.[1]

Early in her first interview it was clear that one meeting would not be enough, and so those six hours were spread out over three interviews:

she described four assaults altogether, three of them before she set foot on campus. She mentioned the assault at Columbia somewhat offhand-edly during the second interview.

> There was this guy who I had hooked up with drunk once—over, like, winter break or something—and then I had to crash in his room over the summer after freshman year, I forget why. And I woke up and he had his hand in my pants, and I was, like, I'm leaving, thank you. And I left, and I never talked to him about it.

Reflecting on what he might have been thinking in that moment, Sloan highlighted the disjuncture between what people know about consent, and what they actually do:

> I mean, I honestly just think that he thought that because I was staying over in his apartment, it was consent to get involved in something even though I was asleep. Which I think was fairly com-mon, that people were kind of like—"I know definitely what con-sent is, but let's be real, you're here, so you want this, obviously." Which is horrifying, right, but unbelievably common. It's shock-ing to me how often physical presence is consent in people's eyes. Which is just so stupid, but so common. . . . Not just in men. I mean, women too have absolutely done the thing where, you know, you're there with somebody who is very inebriated and should not be messed with and they are like, "Yeah, but you're here, so like, you kind of want this."

We often think of consensual sex as the opposite of assault. But sometimes people say "yes" because they are coerced. And people often consent to sex that they really enjoy and want without ever saying "yes."[2] In this chapter we describe how students practice consent, and exam-ine what shapes those practices. There is an awful lot of consensual sex happening that is, as students say, "kind of rapey," or hurtful, or not very enjoyable for one person, or sometimes even for both. The point is not to be the pleasure police. After all, people can consent to sex, and even want to have sex that isn't that pleasurable physically, because they want to comfort a partner or reaffirm a relationship or have a new kind of experience.[3] And pleasure can have lots of meanings, from physical, to emotionally satisfying, to achieving some desirable goal, like acquiring status or a new experience.

Some students do practice affirmative consent, but many others use a range of social cues to make sense of whether or not a sexual encounter was consensual or nonconsensual. They use space as a shorthand for consent in ways that highlight how campus sexual geography shapes what students do and how they understand it. Students frequently assume that someone else choosing to be alone in a room with them signifies consent. In dark basements, crowded parties, and bars where the din makes conversation impossible, students frequently touch each other's bodies without seeking, much less securing, consent. This touching would be much more recognizable as problematic in the library reading room, or on the campus lawn, or in a classroom.

During the time of our fieldwork, a series of highly publicized cases involving accusations of sexual assault had just recently rocked the campus. Consequently, students were acutely attuned to the importance of consent, and had received many messages about school policy wherein consent was the bright line marking the difference between sexual assault and sex. Men, as a performance of decency and to demonstrate their desirable masculinity, had even begun to talk publicly and loudly about the importance of consent and their commitment to it. In the interviews, to minimize social desirability bias—the fact that research subjects often tell you what they know to be socially desirable, rather than what they actually do—we therefore deliberately asked students to describe a sexual experience in minute detail before asking any questions about consent. Surprisingly, almost no student brought up consent in their initial descriptions of a sexual encounter. Interview subjects were taken aback when they realized, upon being asked to recount their stories a second time, but this time to be explicit about how consent worked, that affirmative consent was not a defining characteristic of their sexual encounters. Some even realized they may not have gotten consent within past sexual interactions—interactions which, until the moment of the interview, they had thought of as consensual.

Many students have absorbed the knowledge about the legal standard of affirmative consent, but this knowledge may not affect their behavior. Their words suggest a kind of cognitive dissonance, as they describe their own consent practices, which they know to be suboptimal. Heterosexual students overwhelmingly operate within an implicit framework in which men are the ones who move the sexual ball down to the field, and women are the blockers.[4] For most of the heterosexual women we spoke to, their response to this dissonance rarely goes beyond bemusement. But for most heterosexual men, the fear of doing consent wrong and unintentionally assaulting someone is deeply held and part of their everyday experience of sex. Some men have socially specific reasons—racial inequality, but also physical unattractiveness or less social desirability as partners—to fear that their consent practices are more likely to be judged as falling short. It's not how they have sex or do consent, but instead who they are that makes sexual contact "unwanted." This is part of what we mean by consent being socially produced. And it's more than space and time—sexual geographies—that form the social shorthand for consent. Peers play a crucial role in consent—defining appropriate partners, setting up consensual sexual interactions, processing sexual experiences and helping those involved categorize them as hilarious, sketchy, gross, rapey, or assault.

Our analysis of consent lays the groundwork for the remainder of our argument about how the campus context produces sexual assault. It also points to the urgency of rendering visible and helping students critique the power dynamics at play in sex, which are about gender but also about race, year in school, and other forms of privilege—or precariousness. And it shows how consent is much more than a verbal transaction between two individuals: what students bring to that moment, in terms of what can be safely taken for granted and whose job it is to be sure that the sex is consensual, is inseparable from their broader college stories. Sexual geography, sexual citizenship, and sexual projects help us see the dense network of power relations present when a hot senior guy sporting a shirt with a logo from his team, fraternity, or summer finance job invites a first-generation, first-year, sexually inexperienced freshman back to his room with a soaring view over Manhattan.[5]

"I DON'T WANT TO HAVE SEX WITH SOMEONE WHO MAYBE REGRETS IT IN THE MORNING."

One of the biggest challenges for Sloan in navigating consent is one shared by many students, but wealthier white students in particular. It's not that she and her peers don't know about consent, and the problems of consent when drinking. As we've seen, drunk sex is so much a part of the landscape they navigate that knowledge alone—or even the experience of being assaulted—may not change their actual behavior.[6] As Sloan said:

> I mean I've actually had the conversation with a lot of my female friends where they are like, man, I got assaulted, and I started thinking, there have absolutely been situations where I did not get sufficient consent from people that I was sleeping with. . . . Friends of mine who are survivors, who got really into discussing what consent looks like, and realized that there were times that they absolutely had not received it. And not so much situations in which they violently force themselves on people, but situations where they were, like, that person was not sober enough to consent to what happened, and, like, nobody's feelings were hurt afterwards. . . . Being, like, well, we both probably want it, "It's a Hollywood movie, we don't need to talk about, everybody's happy," is a very dangerous thing to let slide. And everybody does, especially freshman year of college. Especially in groups where

you just get drunk to hook up. . . . Like, you don't have to feel like you were assaulted every time you have sex when you're incredibly drunk and couldn't really legally consent, but letting stuff like that happen means that the stuff where people really do get hurt, and where it's really not okay and where people really are severely harmed . . . you don't know how the person's going to respond to the fact that they've done this thing that they couldn't consent to. Or that this thing has been done to them. Sometimes it's totally fine. And sometimes it's really not.

Sloan's own consent practices reflected her social commitment to "self-protection, but also protection of the other person. . . . Like, I'm not going to go out and sexually assault people, but I also don't want to have sex with someone who maybe regrets it in the morning, or wasn't super interested, or doesn't know how they feel." For her, that means trying not to have sex while she's drunk. Except that she still has a fair amount of drunk sex. She had done her hardest partying in high school, and so her orientation week stories were about taking care of peers who partied a little too hard for the first time. But her wide-ranging narrative made clear that drinking was such an integral part of socializing for her that a more attainable goal was having an initial conversation about consent "entirely sober."

She recounted the story of one guy she met on Tinder. She'd been chatting for a couple of weeks with him, and he "seemed like a sane person." She laughed again as she explained that that meant that he "probably did not have a bag of dead cats under his bed." Their first in-person meet-up included some "delightful reciprocated oral sex. . . . I was like, oh, this is nice, this is exciting, you are a champion of the female orgasm." Then we asked her to reflect back on how consent had worked in that interaction. She responded:

We had a very clear conversation before we got drunk. I was like, "Hey, so you're attractive, we've had a lot of conversations, and realistically, I'm probably going to sleep with you tonight. If you're down with that." He was like "Cool, yes, me too." I really don't like to be drunk the first time I sleep with someone. And I'm very blunt. Mostly because I've had a lot of nonconsensual sex. And so at a certain point you're just, like, let's just everybody be clear here. Get this out of the way. Because I don't fuck with that anymore. But also, I've just found that you have better sex if you're open.

She was a little drunk when that "delightfully reciprocated oral sex" took place. A lot of students told us that sober sex was "serious sex"— meaning it typically happened in relationship contexts. And sometimes people avoid this kind of sex because it can convey a seriousness that young people aren't ready for yet, or aren't ready to convey.[7]

Sloan's comments underline how deeply rooted her consent practices are in her life story. She's learned that "you have better sex if you're open"; she's made it part of her sexual project to be clear about knowing what feels good to her, and wanting her partner to know that too. Talking about sex is part of her broader sexual project of structuring sexual interactions so that her preferences and desires, and her partner's, are made explicit. Sloan's practices reflect her identity as a survivor who has decided that she "doesn't fuck with" vague consent practices. She is a bisexual woman whose critical thinking on gender and sexuality helps her to identify her own boundaries, and to think in a nuanced way about the boundaries of others. She is also a child of privilege who knew dozens of other freshmen from having rowed on her high school's crew team—and whose operative assumption, in social interactions, is that she should be heard.Aubrey, a Latina from the West Coast who is the first in her family to attend college, was keenly aware of how her background differed from Sloan's. Although her family's southwestern roots may have predated Sloan's ancestors' Mayflower-era arrival, she felt like an immigrant in the urban Northeast. Class president, straight-A student, and captain of her debate team, Aubrey was a high achiever in high school, and yet still she recalled being taken aback freshman year by people like Sloan—"people who've gone to private school, who know

Latin and Greek literature." She shook her long curls and laughed, recalling her bemusement, upon arriving, at seeing guys wearing "Vineyard
Vines and pastel shorts and Sperry's. I'm like, 'What the fuck is this? If
you wore this in California, people would make fun of you.'" Like Sloan,
she had experienced intimate partner violence before coming to campus,
in her case seeking a restraining order on a boyfriend who had threatened to shoot her and fired his gun at her pet bird to show that he was
not joking. Aubrey had been through a lot on her way to the Ivy League.

Like Sloan, she understood consent spatially: "If I didn't feel comfortable with what was going to happen, I wouldn't put myself in a situation
where I think this person's trying to have sex with me, and I'm going to
be alone with them, like, there'd be no one to support me or save me
if something happened. . . . So if I am sitting on their bed with them, I
kind of know that's where it's going to go." But just being in bed with
someone, Aubrey is clear, does not obligate her to have sex. One night,
she was in bed with a rugby player she'd been hooking up with for some
time. They'd already had sex once, but in his drunken state he "was continuing to try to have sex" and either not noticing or not caring about
her unresponsiveness. "I was just over it, and so I was just like, 'No, I
don't want to have sex with you.' Like, I actually said those words." She
did not typically "say those words"; ordinarily, she conveyed consent "by
going with them to a private place, and as the night continues, by taking
off my clothes myself."[8] When we asked her how consent works, Aubrey
was emphatic—"I've never done it if I didn't want to"—but also began
to reflect on her own practices.

> Also I haven't asked them, I just kind of assume, which is bad on
> my part. . . . Now that I look back at all the instances I've hooked
> up with someone, I've never asked, or considered if they were
> granting consent, I just assumed that they initiated it, so if I recip-
> rocated, then they were okay with it. . . . But I feel like I haven't
> really thought about consent as much as I should have.

The rugby player's drunk pushiness to have sex a second time, his obliviousness to her lack of interest, and her description that she actually had to state out loud "No, I don't want to have sex with you" illustrate how, for many students, explicit verbal articulation of sexual desires—not just that you want to have sex, but what you want to do—is the exception rather than the rule. This rugby player wasn't, as Aubrey tells it, a "bad guy." He just thought that if he wanted sex a second time that night it was cool. He was somewhat drunk, and likely less able to read how she was feeling—either that, or he didn't care to and figured he could power through. He stopped when Aubrey was clear about her "no."

In both the focus groups and individual interviews, we found that students had absorbed the information provided by the university about what constituted consent. They knew that affirmative consent, under New York State law, means an explicit indication of a desire to have sex, and not just the absence of a "no."[9] And yet, as Sloan made clear, "It's shocking to me how often physical presence is consent in people's eyes." Her words—as a student who'd experienced multiple assaults, and who worked hard to hold herself and her peers to a higher standard—remind us how important it is to look at how students actually navigate consent, rather than how we wish they'd do it. The words also underline just how cognizant many students are of that gap between ideal and actual. And it's not just that they're aware of that gap—they actively question affirmative consent's emphasis on explicit verbal agreement. As one woman put it:

> I think it's also weird to be like, every time you have sex, "Hey, do you wanna have sex?" or like, "Are you all right with this?" . . . 'cause I think that sex is a natural thing, and to have to ask for consent every single time would be sort of weird, and make it almost seem not so natural, almost seem forced.

Or, in the words of another,

I almost never have a sexual experience where it's like, "Do you want to have sex?" and then the other person is like, "Yes." . . . I guess it's more communicated in body language, or physical action, like, if someone pulls away, or something.

The students we spoke with rarely use direct language to elicit or grant consent.[10] Rather, they use a variety of strategies to navigate sexual encounters that they experience as consensual. These include indirect language like "Do you want to go back to my room?" or "Do you want to get out of here?" They text to meet up for sex, but don't mention that word: sex. Even the most explicit language—"Should I get a condom?"—avoids explicit mention of sex itself. And then there's the classic text, "U up?" In four characters, students check whether someone's awake, imply an interest in sex, and inquire as to the other person's willingness.

Strategies other than explicit talk help assess and evaluate consent.[11] Some students pay careful attention to whether kisses are enthusiastically reciprocated, if a person pulls away or pulls in closer, or if they are unresponsive. They listen for moans and other sounds expressing pleasure. It's not that students never talk during sex. Most, though certainly not all, do listen for "no." In some contexts, neither women nor men feel entitled to say "no." And yet sometimes they have no such discomfort. The most definitive examples of clarity communicating sexual boundaries involve the anus. Several heterosexual men recounted emphatic rejection of their women partner's attempts at anal touching. Similarly, one woman, in response to her boyfriend's desire to go there, unmistakably communicated that she didn't consent to what he was trying to do when she exclaimed, "Whoa there, buddy!"

Sometimes students were in no state to really know or be able to act on what they wanted. And most frequently this is because they were drunk; frequently their partner was too.[12] In the interviews, students dutifully recounted their strategies for assessing if another person was too intoxicated to give consent, and most clearly understood that there is a level of drunkenness in which sex is not okay:

> If, like, the other person is just, like, so inebriated, so drunk, that they can't walk straight and you can't have a proper conversation with them. Then yeah, you shouldn't—probably shouldn't—have sex, or you shouldn't even, like, hook up.

But strategies for avoiding dangerous drunk sex tend to focus on the most extreme physical manifestations of intoxication—not having sex if they are too drunk to sustain an erection or if they are literally vomiting at that specific moment. Students aware that a person can be blackout drunk and yet seem able to speak and walk give themselves moral cover, recounting incidents of drunk sex, by describing themselves or the other person as "brownout" drunk.

What we saw in talking to young people and in seeing them interact at bars, clubs, suites, and parties was that many rely upon tacit signals and contextual knowledge, using touch, sight, and hearing, rather than waiting for positive verbal affirmation, to ascertain a partner's desires. This shouldn't be shocking to most of us. Critically, students consider these to be ways to indicate their own consent: not saying "no"; agreeing to meet up somewhere; going back to someone's room with them; taking off their own or a partner's clothes; or writhing, moaning, or pulling the person closer. These were all ways that students described consenting to a sexual advance.[13] Consent is important to students, and they think about it a lot. But their behavior generally falls far short of the increasingly adopted standard of affirmative consent. And given how frequently students encounter unwanted and nonconsensual sexual touching, which was the most frequently experienced form of sexual assault in the SHIFT survey, it is noteworthy that when students do reflect on consent, they focus almost entirely on securing consent for intercourse.[14]

"GUYS ASK YOU FOR CONSENT, RIGHT?"

Cheong's short-sleeved polo shirt, which showed off his well-defined arm muscles, was neatly tucked into his khaki pants. Crisp white sneakers and very short hair completed the picture of someone who cared about the impression he made—further conveyed by his mentioning that he'd stopped smoking when he started college because, unlike people in in Hong Kong, his home, "Americans don't smoke." His story illustrates how students' sexual projects frequently shift from impressing their friends and accumulating experience to finding intimacy during the college years. But it also shows how men's uncritical acceptance of a gendered sexual script where their job is to pursue sex and women's job is to convey agreement or not renders them susceptible to sexually assaulting someone. Cheong navigates intimate relationships now with same intentionality he exhibits in his dress. He admits that "over the years, my concept of dating and intimacy has changed. Right now, I've been looking for an emotional connection. Before that's established I wouldn't get into anything physical. I would much rather have a good conversation with someone, getting to know someone, than engaging in physical behavior just to satisfy my desires . . . I think more in terms of the long run."

Like a lot of the men we interviewed, Cheong is a bit of a romantic. When asked about his best sexual experience, he spoke about the care and thoughtfulness that went into producing a moment of intimacy, rather than the physical satisfaction of the sex itself. First, he invited a young woman he'd been seeing on a swan boat ride in Central Park, followed by a picnic; on the top layer of the picnic basket he'd lugged along were a dozen roses and a card, asking her formally to be his girlfriend. Later that day was the first time they had sex—which he was surprised to learn was her first time ever having intercourse. "I was, like, 'Let me know how you feel, do you want me to continue, or if you feel pain, let me know . . . ' It was really hard at first, because she had never done anything like that, so it was painful . . . so we went really slowly."

Cheong cared about being an attentive sexual partner; when asked what he worries about when having sex, he responded: "not being able to pleasure my partner as much as I would like."

He assessed his early attractions and interactions as "very superficial." Looking back on his very first sexual encounter, he smiled: "I had my first kiss in high school. It was a triple dare. I was stupid." He described seeking out his first sexual experience while he was away on a school trip. He said of one young woman, "My friends thought she was attractive so that rubbed off on me and I just started talking to her. . . . I don't think I genuinely liked her as a person, I don't think I knew enough about her to actually be fond of her." The desire in those initial sexual encounters was to impress his friends. Even his first girlfriend at Columbia was someone selected by his "big" in his fraternity: "We have a banquet every year and I didn't have a date, I wasn't going to bring anyone." Cheong stopped, and then repeated himself, making clear just how much this was driven by his fraternity mentor. "I wasn't going to ask anyone but he wanted me to bring this girl."

Cheong's shift to a focus on "the long run," to wanting sex in the context of a relationship of mutual care, emerged against the backdrop of several distinctly unpleasant experiences. One involved disentangling himself from an ongoing hookup in a way that, upon reflection, he felt was unnecessarily cruel. There was another hookup he regretted—not because of anything he did, but because he realized he did not like sharing his bed with a stranger, so much so that he lied about having a stomachache, and left his own bed to go curl up and sleep alone on his suite's couch. Cheong grew into a sexual project that links emotional and physical intimacy; his story provides glimpses into how sexual interactions that cause distress—things that he has done, and things done to him—have led him to think more deeply about the kinds of sexual interactions that he values. Like a lot of the men with whom we spoke, he seemed kind. But it's important to realize that kindness, and the moral desirability of a sexual project focused on intimacy, are not a guarantee that an assault won't occur.

Cheong thought securing consent was a man's job, which trapped him in a framework that placed him at risk for making unwelcome advances and left him without a language to fully consider being the object of women's unwelcome advances. He was typical of the hetero-sexual men we interviewed, thinking that his job in a sexual interac-tion was to make an advance and a woman's corresponding role was to be the sexual gatekeeper. Within this framework of gendered sexual agency, interpreting a woman's lack of resistance as consent makes per-fect sense. And so with his high school girlfriend, as well as the women he'd been with at Columbia, he was emphatic that consent did not require a verbal exchange:

> You can see that she's reciprocating, then I would move on to the next step. . . . Like if she's willing to take off her clothes, like if she touches me certain ways, to me, those are nonverbal cues that tell you that you can move forward. I don't think I've ever asked, "Can I have sex with you?" 'cause that would be pretty awkward, but it's pretty obvious that it was consensual.

Cheong is not alone in seeing it as his job to act, and his partner's to resist or to acquiesce: "It's like when, for example, I'm removing her clothes and she doesn't stop me, then to me, that's consent." But when asked how he conveys consent, he says, "I'm the one that takes the initiative most of the time, so consent is on her side." "Sexual scripts" denote shared ideas about how a sexual scene is supposed to unfold. Cheong described this "slow process" with his girlfriend eventually leading to intercourse, but without there ever being an actual conver-sation about it: "making out first, and then moving on to, like, I don't know, second base, whatever that is, and then finally, after a period of time, we tried [sex]."[15] In his view, this was the "real" way people manage consent. When we asked Karen, whose experience of being assaulted we recounted in the first chapter, how she got consent from the men she'd had sex with, she paused and said, "It's implied consent, I think. . . . I don't think I have ever asked for consent." Then she turned the conversation around, asking us, "I think guys ask you for consent, right?"[16]

Michelle Fine's classic 1988 article about high school sex education described the "missing discourse of desire"—the ways that an earlier generation of programming was grounded in (and reproduced) the assumption that sex is something that boys want, but not girls.[17] In heterosexual students' consent practices, this discourse of desire is still missing; sexual interactions reflect the widely shared and largely unexamined assumption that men seek sex and women grant access.[18] Heterosexual students in our study frequently either laughed or were a little taken aback when asked how women sought or ascertained men's consent. And consent education frequently misses an opportunity to challenge this gendered responsibility for consent, using scenarios with gender-neutral names and pronouns out of a desire to be inclusive to LGBT, queer, and gender-nonconforming experiences. Unquestionably, that inclusivity is vital, yet it should not come at the cost of critical discussions about gendered sexual agency, power, and the gendered practice of consent. These conversations are the first step toward undoing the equation of masculinity with sexual agency.

Women can be charitable in evaluating men's struggle with how to move things to the next level. Rosa was distraught throughout the course of her interview; she nervously agreed when we offered her a cup of coffee, then dropped it when we handed it to her. Her eyes welled up as she mopped frantically at the coffee, beaded up on the rug. But our research team had seen her out and about, and she was generally like that—high strung and a little sad. She was recovering from an eating disorder, and not on speaking terms with her father. Freshman year was not off to a good start. So Rosa did not want to make a big deal of what happened that Saturday, several weeks before she was interviewed, when she went back to a guy's room with him. They had been in the library, and he suggested that they pick up the handle of vodka in his fridge so they could go drink in her room with her suite mates. It had been a hard week, and what he proposed seemed like it could be fun. She bent down to get the vodka out of his minifridge, and as she turned back around he "swooped down" and stuck his tongue down her throat. She said, "Like, whoa, buddy, sorry but not sorry, I was not expecting this." He stopped, she reported—"he 'got it'" that she was not interested. Yet in the ensuing weeks he followed her around at parties and texted her daily. "I don't want to, like, put him down as a person just because of that, he didn't rape me, he just thought that I was down to do something I was not down to do." But her concerns about him grew: "I don't think he's totally healthy the way he's going about trying to have sex, he's kind of—being kind of forceful."

An analysis of the SHIFT ethnographic data led by Matthew Chin examined the how consent was intimately tied up with different notions of time, noting differences in student practices depending on the time of year (some events, like the big spring party "Bacchanal," are particularly sexualized), the amount of time people are in a relationship, the time of day, and the ways in which students and their peers interpret events before, during, and after the sexual encounter to make sense of consent.[19] The young man in Rosa's story may have read her willingness to go back to his room as an indication of sexual interest, or understood the room late on a Saturday night to be a sexual space in a way that it would not be if she were stopping by Tuesday morning to compare notes from their Humanities class. He may have read the signals really incorrectly, or just literally not have been able to imagine any other way to produce a sexual scene than to just go for it and see if she said no. He was a freshman, too—awkward, perhaps without a lot of experience, still trying to find his "game." Those are explanations, of course, not justifications. As parents tell young children who hit when they are angry instead of talking, or who grab toys they want instead of asking, he needed to learn to use his words, or at the very least get more explicit positive feedback from her before putting his mouth on hers—particularly since, moments before, she was not longingly looking into his eyes, but instead, had her back to him.

One young woman said that the man she has sex with "always asks." But she was startled to realize, in response to our question, that she'd never asked in return. Another woman said that eliciting consent from her boyfriend had occurred to her but "he thinks it's dumb that I ask." Young men also point to the inconceivability of men's consent: "No one's ever asked me, like, let's kiss now. Like, that's weird." In heterosexual couples, almost no one imagines that men don't want it. This places great demands upon women to be capable of sexual management, and potentially blames them for being ineffective in this social task if they are assaulted. It also invalidates moments where men don't want sex.[20] Most heterosexual students approach sexual encounters with this implicit understanding about the gendered unilateral responsibility for consent. At best, such a script normalizes men's sexual aggression. At worst, it lays the groundwork for sexual assault.

"I DON'T LIKE MEDIOCRE."

For students who use their words, that comfort with talking about sex reflects a sexual project focused on pleasure and emotional intimacy, coupled with an expansive understanding of one's own sexual citizenship. Lydia, born in Taiwan and educated at an elite English-language boarding school in Southeast Asia, is into kink. She describes herself as "switchy"—comfortable playing both submissive and dominant roles—so that "the best sex that I've had is usually when those roles just, like, transition seamlessly, one into the other." We asked her to recount a specific interaction, and she paused:

> With my most recent ex-boyfriend, I think our sex was really good on an erotic level because I use my words a lot, and I'm very picky with my words and so is he. . . . The second time we hooked up

after we broke up . . . we did a little bit of switchy—like, switchy power play, but during the middle, we just stopped and I was, like, you're really beautiful. And he said, "I don't—I don't—" I was, like, "You don't believe me, do you?" And he was, like, "It's kinda hard to." So we just spent the next 20 minutes, like—I spent ten minutes just running my hands down his body and telling him, "You're really beautiful, I really like this part of your body because of this," and then he did the same for me. And it's just the seamless interrelation of both intimacy and of, I guess, passion, erotic sex that I really like.

Lydia evaluated her own practices as meeting the spirit of affirmative consent:

Saying consent is implied sounds really, really terrible because then it's, like, that's not really affirming the consent. But I think that, after having established a lot of boundaries within our relationship itself I guess we didn't really have to ask each other if this was okay or if this was okay, we were largely doing things that we've done before. So even though it wasn't in a relationship, neither of us felt like it was necessary to explicitly ask, um, "is this okay" unless it's something we haven't done before. And I usually tend to gauge the reaction based on nonverbal, body language cues. For example, if I'm doing something, I say "Does this feel good, is this okay, tell me if it doesn't." And I think that when you already have an established level of trust, that that person will tell you if it's not comfortable. For example, I move my hand down their body, it's, like, "Is this okay?" Or, "Does this feel good, is there anything else you would like for me to do?" I'm usually quite responsive, and my partner usually tends to ask as well if he's doing something new. For example, does this feel good. I'll be, like, yes. I think body language is very important for both of us, so things like moans, squirming, arching of the body. I think they're very easy signs to tell. Usually if they're not responding with enthusiasm, I'm just, like, okay, I have to change something up because I don't—I don't like mediocre.

Lydia was describing her general approach to sex—what she usually does, how she usually listens, how she "changes something up" if her partner is not responding with enthusiasm. And she contrasted that with a specific sexual interaction where the standard of verbal affirmation was met, but nonetheless the encounter was something she would not choose to repeat. The prior summer, she had had sex with one of her close male friends. They'd talked about sex before, comparing notes, and she knew that he found it a real turn-on to have his head massaged. So she made her move: "It's like a proposition. I knew that about him beforehand, it was pretty obvious." But she describes the actual sex as unsatisfying: "He says, like, can I fuck you, I was, like, okay, yes. Then that's the extent of the way that consent would work. But, I mean, personally it wasn't too satisfying. I mean, it was good, but because we didn't talk about, okay, so this is what I like to do and this is the erotic kind of things that turn me on."

Lydia's exceptional ease in talking about sex—not just with her partners, but in the interview itself—reflected her underlying comfort with sex itself.[21] When we asked her "What is sex for?" she answered immediately, indicating that it was a question she'd previously considered:

Actually, it's been shifting for a while because when I first started having sex, it turns out I was pretty good at pleasing other people, but, despite having done a lot of research into it, I don't really know what people can do to please me. So for me, at university, it's increasingly important for me to be in a relationship where it's very much sexually mutual. . . and maybe it's only because, my first couple boyfriends were both virgins, so they didn't really know what they were doing, and I knew a little bit more than they did just because I would look it up on the internet. And so that left me feeling like, you know, this is great, this is really fun—but what can make it better? So I guess maybe that's my goal. I mean, obviously I love to please my partner, but I'm also very interested in seeing what I like and what they can do to make me feel good.

Lydia's life before college may not seem to be predictive of her expansive sense of her own sexual citizenship, or of her evolving sexual project. Her first introduction to information of any kind about sex, when she was about ten, was leafing through a magazine in the dentist's office and coming upon a description of sexual assault. In sixth grade, her mother's response to learning that sex education would be taught in her school was "Okay, you can go, but don't think about it." Lydia described herself as curious about sex, not discouraged by two middle-school years of "abstinence-only education where it's, like, it is bad, don't do it, that is the red zone, do not let people touch you in the red zone." Then in her third year of middle school, "it suddenly changed. We got this really cool sex educator—this group of university students who present situations in which things like consent would come up." But largely she is self-taught, in a process that is ongoing and supported by the internet: "I'd look up websites like Scarlet Teen just to see what—see what it's like. People around me were, like, oh my gosh, sex is so gross, but for me, I'm just, like, no, it seems interesting. I wanna know more." Lydia lauded the generally "sex-positive" climate of the university—"you have organizations that will hand out condoms, so I think people get the message that sex is okay"—but also noted that existing resources may not reach those who need them the most; in her experience,

> people who are likely to go seek out resources regarding sex are people who already know quite a bit and who have a pretty positive idea of sex. And I feel not everybody comes in with the same amount of knowledge, not just of sex and the physiology, but also of consent and of how to make it pleasurable and fun. Maybe it

would be weird to have a workshop. How to Have Sex 101 treats everybody like a kindergartner. But at the same time, it would be nice to have a baseline.

"I'M GONNA MAKE THE LOUDEST SCENE. I'M GONNA SHAME YOU": QUEERING CONSENT

It would be a mistake to talk about "the experience" of LGBTQ students, because there is not one singular experience; the experiences of cisgender gay men, for example, can be as different from transgender gay men as they are from cisgender heterosexual men. As we analyzed how LGBTQ students practiced consent, we began to see new possibilities for interventions, and new ways to understand why assaults were happening. In part, these insights emerged because of a puzzle we encountered as we dug into our data. As we've noted, research (including our own) has found that LGBTQ students experience far higher rates of assault than heterosexuals and those within the gender binary. Yet when we interviewed this diverse population, we also found that their consent practices generally (although not universally) were much closer to the ideal of affirmative consent. How could it be that people who were more likely to practice affirmative consent were also more likely to experience assault?[22]

One of our first realizations was that for LGBTQ students, the experience of sexual assault is not limited to sexual situations. It is true more generally, of course, that sexual assaults also occur in nonsexual situations, but we heard many stories of assault experienced by LGBTQ students in heterosexual contexts, where they were hoping to socialize and were not looking for sex. It wasn't that they were necessarily targeted by straight people, but instead, that what heterosexuals experienced as "normal" sexual activity, LGBTQ students experienced, and were more willing to label, as assault.

This pattern was clearest among queer women of color, like Michaela, who described a freshman-year fraternity party. She wasn't there to meet men or women. These parties are a big part of the social scene, and she simply wanted to share in her floormates' experience. What she experienced, however, was something quite different.

> It was just like people are grabbing you, touching you, extremely drunk, loud, screaming, and . . . it's an aggressive atmosphere. . . . And [men are] telling people to drink more when they obviously shouldn't be . . . telling women to drink more. I was there with a girlfriend and I was felt up ten different ways. . . . Women would have drinks spilled on them, or someone would say, "Take off your shirt!" or something. It's egregious and it's laughed off because "Ha, ha, Charlie was drunk," . . . but it's very on the edge of like just playing and violent . . . When people grab me I'm like, "Okay, so you grabbed the wrong person 'cause I'm gonna make the loudest scene. I'm gonna shame you, I'm gonna make sure you remember that like this is not what you need to do." Usually they're like, "Oh, oh, I'm sorry." I'm like, "Sorry about what?" And it becomes this like thing, the situation that grabs the attention of other people, and in nearly all the cases they felt embarrassed and be like, "Ugh. Bye." And I'm just like, "Oh, I ruined the experience for you? Great. That's what you did to me. Um, hope you enjoy your party now 'cause everyone knows what you did. . . ." It's just, it's like, it's frustrating not to be able to say no.

What stands out is not the uniqueness of being grabbed in a party space packed with people, but instead, Michaela's refusal to accept this as "normal." We offer here a partial explanation of the high rates of assault found among LGBTQ students, which is their greater willingness to label what heterosexual students (women in particular) experience as "normal" as "nonconsensual." The high rates of assault among LGBTQ people may in part reflect their refusal to accept heterosexual students' normalization of sexual aggression. Most LGBTQ students arrive on campus having experienced a lifetime of verbal erasure; misgendering, assumptions about heterosexuality, and a social context in which at every turn—the locker room, the bathroom, the prom—they are forced to navigate a world that fails to recognize them for who they are. So it's understandable that they would be a little quicker to denounce assaults that their peers, sheltered in the gender binary and by heterosexuality, are more willing to endure.

When it came to consent, we also saw significant differences among the practices of LGBTQ students. For some kinds of sex, gay men's consent practices were similar to their heterosexual peers. Major, a white gay man, echoed themes that we heard from straight men, who typically thought of consent as happening through informal rather than explicit communication. When asked about his consent practices, Major told us that it was "much more kind of like body language of—you know, you can tell when someone's, if someone's okay with something or if they feel very uncomfortable with it." Yet such implicit consent had limits. Major noted that this kind of "body language" consent did not extend to all sexual practices, particularly when he and his partner had anal sex, "Especially during actual anal penetration and all, I think that that [consent]'s usually something that um—there's a lot of checking like, you know, 'Are you okay? . . . ' Yeah, I just think that's part of the deal and even—actually I would even say if it's not the first few times but like any time I'm doing that [anal sex] with someone, [there] is usually a lot of checking, like. 'Is this okay?'"

Some of this was practical—negotiating who would be the "top" and who would "bottom," or, making sure that the person bottoming wasn't concerned about their anal cavity having fecal matter. But it also had to do with not wanting to cause a partner physical pain. Jacob, an Asian bisexual man, reflected on the kindness of the first man with whom he had anal sex. "It kind of hurt. I bottomed, and so of course I hurt in the beginning. But he was understanding, and so eventually it was pleasurable. . . ." As we listened to stories like this, it became clear that the lack of sexual scripts and prescribed modes of interacting meant that consent often had to be more intentional. In part this reflects the lack of cultural representations of sexual intimacy for these students; only in the past decade, and very tentatively, have mainstream American films and television shows begun to depict lesbian, gay, or bisexual adolescent romance. And even those generally shy away from characters that do not fit neatly into the gender binary. There are sex education curricula that are LGBTQ-inclusive, but every single queer or trans student we talked to said the sex education they received was "not applicable" to their sex lives. The unintended consequences of this denial of their sexual citizenship is that, for trans and queer students in particular, affirmative consent becomes the framework for their improvisation. As one gender-queer student described their first sexual experience with their current partner, "Yeah, it was like, 'I'm not sure what's going on here, but—' I was like, 'I'm not even sure what I'm supposed to be doing' . . . 'cause we knew that we hadn't had sex—like a same-sex relationship before. . . . So I was like, 'I don't know but we can try.'" Explicit communication was an almost necessary feature of sexual interactions.

We didn't find evidence that this was driven by identity; instead, the particular experiences of having sex really mattered. So bisexual and queer-identifying women who only had experienced heterosexual sexual contact tended to describe their consent practices in ways that were very similar to heterosexual women. But those who had had non-heteronormative sex, like Clarice, a bisexual woman we interviewed, described fundamentally different consent practices.

Clarice noted that when she had sex with other bisexual women, or lesbians or queer people, she had to talk to them about what they wanted. "It's not gonna be like butch/femme or anything . . . it's just a little bit blurry." And once she started engaging in these kinds of discussions with her partners—not relying on gendered sexual scripts—her sexual practices with cisgender men also began to change.

In one encounter . . . he was really vague. He was like, "Oh, is it cool if I take my shirt off?" and I was like, "Do you wanna have sex?" *[Laughs]* I was just like, "I don't like really vagueness with sex" . . . and he was like, "Yeah." 'Cause I personally think when you're really direct, it spurs self-confidence when someone says, "Yes, I'm attracted to you. I want to have sex with you." That's great, and so that's how I view it, and so whether—if I was asking for consent, I would say "Do you wanna have sex?"

This provides some evidence that practicing consent matters. Actions aren't just the result of deliberate decisions; they are shaped by habits that we rely and fall back upon.[23] In analyzing queer experiences, we began to see important things about the heterosexual experience, particularly the ways in which heterosexual sexual scripts may create habits of consent that rely considerably on nonverbal communication. But for those who can't rely on such scripts—who have gay, lesbian, or queer sex that requires them to communicate desire in more explicit terms—such habits are either never developed, or may become unsettled. We found that this would spill over into how bisexual and queer people had heterosexual sex. Learning about consent is not enough; it's something people have to experience and practice. These insights are critical for potential interventions that seek to promote affirmative consent.

"I REALLY REALLY REALLY REALLY WORRY ABOUT THAT."

Sloan never worried about belonging at Columbia; she answered the questions about the transition to college by talking about how easy it was for her, given her previous schooling, and the fact that her parents both went to college, as did everyone else in her family. For other students, regardless of what they might have known or not known about sex, their consent practices reflected their feelings of precariousness at college—not so much whether they had a right to have sex as whether they had a right to be at Columbia at all.[24] Malachi, a Black student and a senior, talked about the hard academic adjustment to Columbia and how lucky he felt to be there. Throughout the story of his time at

Columbia, he repeatedly conveyed a feeling of being on the margins, of teachers who "make snarky comments" about student athletes, of a core curriculum that lacks "representation of different minority groups," of finding the academic adjustment grueling: "Even being pretty near the top of class in high school . . . when I got here, I would take something that was beginner level, like calc for example, and I sat in there and it was like, 'I know nothing.' And this was apparently stuff that everybody else around me learned in high school." And yet he reveled in what he saw as a "once-in-a-lifetime opportunity . . . to get this level of education": "People here are geniuses. . . . It was the best part of being here, hearing all this stuff that I've never heard before—how are we the same age and you know all this stuff that I never even knew existed?" Freshman fall he considered leaving (something he never told his parents), but ultimately he talked himself out of it. This was his big break, being in the Ivy League, "and I feel like a lot of people who may be a lot smarter than I am didn't get that break. So I just felt bad, like I took somebody's spot getting in here, and then I'm going to give it up?"

Part of his settling-in process involved finding spaces where he'd be welcome and supported; he found the church that was most like the one he'd grown up in, and made some friends through the church. Malachi would have preferred to join a Black fraternity, but when he was a freshman there wasn't one on campus, and so he rushed the fraternity that had "the people I got along with most, because they were more laid back and not always drunk and stuff." Finding his way also involved leaving spaces where he didn't feel welcome.[25] He recounts transferring out of a class "because the professor literally said when we walked in, 'Oh, you're football players, this is going to be a *great* semester' [*said mockingly*]. And I was like, 'Yeah, I'm not staying in this class at all.'" And he did what he could to make the spaces he was in better. Freshman fall, there was conflict in the room next door, where a "really wealthy, obnoxious kid," who would be so drunk every Saturday night that "it would be not even ten o'clock yet and this guy was throwing up in the bathroom," shared a room with a "really quiet, computer science guy." When Computer Sci-

ence Kid went home to visit his family in Long Island, Wealthy Obnoxious Kid "would let people come into the room and sleep on his bed and
use his stuff." And so eventually Malachi and his roommate "were like,
this is dumb. We told him, 'If you do it again, one, we're going to tell the
guy. And two, we're going to have problems.' And we were bigger, so we
did kind of intimidate him. But I mean, it was for a good reason." Like
many other (although not all) Black college students and students from
less wealthy backgrounds, he didn't start drinking until he was 21. He
didn't have a fake ID, knew that acquiring one was against the law, and
was not willing to risk the consequences of an unnecessary encounter
with law enforcement. Getting really drunk wasn't a part of his college
project, and it wasn't something he grew up thinking was an essential
part of the college experience.

Malachi's consent practices revealed that unlike other students he
didn't believe himself to be entitled to other people's bodies. But they
also revealed a sense of being on thin ice, always.[26] Drunk hookups—
"you meet them that night, and then have sex with them that night"—
are "completely a no" for him. With the few hookups he had before he
met the girl he was then dating, "whenever we were about to get to that
point, I always personally asked, like, 'You sure you want to do this?'
I always asked that question, just for my personal satisfaction. . . . I
always just feel that it's good to make sure that they want to have it."
He explains this in relation to "the entire stigma of being a Black male.
And I know that a lot of times, if situations were to happen, then if one
person says something, that I did something, even if I know it's not true,
because I'm Black they're probably going to believe them, like if it was a
white girl, or if it was somebody that just wasn't Black. I never had that
concern with Black women."

Carl, another Black senior, echoed Malachi's caution about the racialized risk of false accusations, with an additional layer of sadness and fear
that reminds us just how much many students are managing. He doesn't
drink, and was so careful about what others thought of him that he
spent a good fifteen minutes with us after the formal interview ended,

probing for how his answers compared with his peers'.[27] Even during the interview, he stopped repeatedly to ask how his answers measured up. When we asked why he didn't drink, he parroted back the question, laughing: "People ask, 'Why don't you drink? Why don't you drink? Is it for athletics?' I'm like, no. 'Is it for religion?' I'm like, no":

> There are two answers. There's my political, easy, so I don't have to talk about it too much, bullshit answer. I mean, it's like a real answer, but the easy answer is I always want to be accountable for the person I'm being. I never want to be in a room and say it was the alcohol. The guy you get in this place is the same guy you get in the classroom or at the party.

This seemed practiced: not quite false, but not quite true. He resumed.

> The honest answer is that my dad died when I was six, and I don't really know what kind of guy he wanted me to be. And I think that in all my actions, I'm trying to be worthy of his memory. I genuinely don't know if he wanted me to be a Columbia Lion, or a football player, or a politics major, but I do these things with the hope that it lives up to some essence of worthiness.

Carl was measuring himself by the memory of his father, but what drove him was not just personal; he felt the weight of representation as well—the responsibility to be "the talented tenth."[28] "I think being on this campus, in a place that has not always been welcoming or home to Black people—people of color, really—I think you spit in the face of convention every day you are here and continuing to thrive."

Carl had caught our attention as he moved through the crowd at a Black Students Organization party; many women followed him with their eyes. He was handsome, and clearly desired. He admitted, "Uh, I go on a lot of dates." And he described himself, as others might see him, as a guy who is "someone who's always sober but having more fun than you"—but that is also a meticulously curated self, which he described as rejecting the "Clarence Thomas future" that Columbia made possible for him, "to fall into this category of transcending your Blackness." He admitted that the perception of his public commitment to only dating Black women gave him a certain social advantage, signaling to these women that they were not competing with "Becky, who they'll never be in a million years," that "I value my Blackness, but I also value the Blackness in you." He segued from the subject of interracial dating to the question of his own legacy—to how odd it feels, knowing that just by graduating from Columbia, he had positively affected the life chances of an entirely imaginary, as yet unconceived child. He recalled his grandparents, who "used to pick cotton. . . . That's all their parents knew. . . . I am the product of a lot of people's work. . . . I am here only by the grace of God." His Columbia education was the product of generations of striving. "I really try to conceptualize myself as one part of a larger story." Wealthier students occasionally expressed gratitude for all that their families had provided, but reflected less on themselves as part of a "larger story." For Carl, that larger story is reflected in his everyday social choices, including his preferred party spaces: "I really like spaces that are sort of tailored to dancing, and especially Black people, because drinking is not the event."

Carl's consent practices—like Malachi's, Rosa's, and Sloan's—are inseparable from his broader college story. An explicit dimension of this is about alcohol and risk "because I don't have to think about, like, okay, is she drunk right now?. . . . So if she's been here for two hours it means that, like, whatever decision she's making, it's because she really wants to hang out with me." We stopped him: "Is that a risk you're really concerned about?," to which he responded, "Yeah, I really really really really worry about that." Four "reallys." He continued: "Consent matters so much, like, it really does matter and I would hate for a second for you to not, A, enjoy yourself, so like we're gonna focus on you tonight, or that B, um, for you to have any regrets, like, for you to think even twice about this interaction." Carl noted that "I have a lot to lose as a man," and his consent practices reflect that fear: "I have girls say to me, like, 'Please stop asking so many questions,' and, like, that's great but even then I'm, like, 'No no no, that doesn't work for me.' You say—it doesn't matter what you say in this moment, it doesn't really matter, when you leave this room, in twenty-four hours, you could say something very different. And I don't control the narrative."

Carl told a story that gave a sense of just how fearful he was. A girl he met at a party asked if she could go back to his room with him. He said okay, but "suspected she might not be as sober as possible." So he walked around with her for forty-five minutes, and then once they went up to his room, they sat and talked for another forty-five minutes. And then,

> She still wanted to hang out and then we hooked up, but afterwards I recorded her saying—she didn't know this, because New York is a "one-party" state—but I recorded "Okay, like, you enjoyed yourself, you had a good time, this was fun, you were okay with this," and she went "Yeah, it was great," and that—this is like really fucked up, because I was like, that helped me, just really allowed me to feel a lot more comfortable the moment she left, I at least had some evidence for my own conscience.

It was astonishing to us just how prepared he was for this moment. He knew New York's "one-party" rules on recording conversations—that he didn't need her permission. Clearly he'd done his homework. Think about that: the kind of fear, concern, and deliberation that would lead a student to look up the rules for recording conversations.

The fear was not limited to Black men; almost every young man we spoke with, regardless of race, revealed an earnest desire to do consent right, and a real concern about doing it wrong. Of course men are scared: they learn that they are responsible for eliciting consent, and such consent can't happen when people are drunk, and doesn't count unless it's explicitly verbally affirmed. It makes sense that prevention messages target men, as they're the ones committing the vast majority of assaults, and yet emphasizing men's responsibility, absent a broader critical conversation about gender and power, inadvertently casts them as the sexual aggressors and women as the blockers. Men know that when two drunk people have sex, it's somehow supposed to be their responsibility that no one gets harmed. And yet many heterosexual students—especially drunk white ones—do not verbally communicate consent.

Why is drunk heterosexual assault the man's "fault"? If both parties are too drunk to consent, why do we typically view the man as responsible when an assault occurs? The underlying reason is that the person who causes harm is the person responsible. In this sense, drunk assault is not that different from most other sexual assaults—one person thinks they're having a sexual encounter, and the other person experiences that encounter as assault. The responsibility lies with the person who causes, rather than experiences, the harm, whether they're drunk or sober. Men are more likely to cause harm during heterosexual sex, in part because of greater power, and in part because of sexual scripts. While men don't always have more power within sexual encounters, social arrangements produce heterosexual dyads in which men tend to be older and control space, and to have been socialized to be attentive to their own sexual desires. They are also often larger and physically stronger. On top of that, gendered sexual scripts teach men to do their "gendered job" by trying to advance sexual contact. In drunken scenarios, doing this job puts them at risk of committing assault, because they're the ones advancing their agenda, in a context where they don't have their full cognitive capacity, where the other person may not have the capacity to fully express how they're feeling, and where men who think of themselves as good people and not assaulters may not recognize the power disparities that make it hard for women to voice their wishes.

Research suggests that men massively overestimate the frequency with which false accusations are made, but that fear is an important part of men's lived experience of consent on campus.[29] And in a context where accusations of sexual assault can, as both men and women told us, "ruin your life," the fear is understandable. This intense fear of the consequences of doing consent wrong represents the emergence of a shared understanding that consensual sex is important. Fear might signal a desire to do better, but it is not a prevention approach. Engaging competently in consensual sex requires both articulating that as a goal—which most of the students we spoke with had done—and then building the skills to do so.

We cannot know what the man who put his hand down Sloan's pants while she was asleep was thinking—but it seems unlikely that he would have done that if he'd come upon her asleep in the library, rather than on his couch. Sexual geography is part of what produces vulnerability. Since a great deal of sex happens in dorm rooms, students who feel unable to ask or are not interested in asking interpret being in a sexualized space as consent to sex of some kind. Sexual projects shape the kind of sex that students seek out, and the way that they see their partners—as a warm body, the next number, or a person they care about. The heavy reliance on acutely gendered sexual scripts among heterosexual students—even those with intimacy-oriented sexual projects—lends credence to the notion that a woman's consent can consist of not saying no. For some students, the fact that all of this is navigated while they are intoxicated adds to the fundamental impossibility of clearly communicating with one another; the whole point of getting drunk is to blow off steam and do stupid things that you might not feel comfortable doing if you weren't drunk. Demanding that both parties secure consent isn't to "de-gender" consent, in part because sex still happens within a set of power relations which are often gendered. Men don't always have more power than women, not all sex is heterosexual, and there's lots of power that isn't about gender. "Mutual consent" doesn't seek to pretend that power doesn't exist; in fact, it requires its recognition.

Undergirding all of this is sexual citizenship: the recognition of one's own right to sexual self-determination, and an equivalent right in others. The feeling of a right to say yes, to desire sex, is fundamental to being meaningfully able to say no. Consent as a verbal transaction between two individuals is meaningless when either individual arrives at a sexual interaction with deep, culturally imposed limits on their beliefs about having the right to others access to their bodies; or when a student's language or understanding of sex is so impoverished that they don't even know what they want. Many young people—men and women both—had come of age in contexts that failed to promote their development as sexual citizens, or as people with respect for the citizenship of others. Examples include the aside, in an undergraduate's story about having sex, that she felt that it would have been rude to say no, or, as we heard frequently, a woman giving a man a blow job "just to get out of there," when she does not want to have penile-vaginal intercourse, or perhaps even spend more time with a man.

Sex that isn't assault, but that involves treating the other person like an object, or is characterized by a mutual acceptance of a one-way flow of pleasure, trains young people to overlook other's sexual citizenship. This isn't assault, but it helps pave the way, culturally and interpersonally, for assault. But to see this even more starkly, we turn to the accounts of people who, either by their own admission or in the eyes of others, have committed assaults.

6

ACTS OF ENTITLEMENT, SELF-ABSORPTION, AND VIOLENCE

"SPOILER ALERT: I'M THE ONE THAT CROSSES BOUNDARIES HERE."

Those who commit sexual assault are commonly depicted as immoral, calculating men. While men commit the vast majority of assaults, we found that perpetration took many forms. For example, Diana, who we met in Chapter 4 as part of a fancy "brunch crowd," is an unlikely image of someone who commits sexual assault. But her story, like all the others in this chapter, offers an apt starting point for our examination of the experiences and thoughts of those who either by their own admission, or in our evaluation, committed an assault. She had been a "nerdy, smart kid" in middle school and much of high school. She told us she hadn't been popular or particularly happy with herself back then. As for many students we spoke with, college wasn't just a chance to move out from under her parents' watchful eye. It was a chance to reinvent herself, leaving behind her "shitty behavior" to her high school boyfriend, and deliberately transforming her body, her look, and her personality.

But Diana's adjustment wasn't a smooth one. She spent most of ori-entation week drunk, and had sex with several men she barely remem-bered. She didn't exactly regret this, but it was hardly the new beginning she anticipated. One guy told her he was twenty-one and the cousin of a fellow Columbia student. As they spent more time together, Diana realized that he was twenty-six and had no relationship to campus. He wasn't a "bad guy," Diana told us, but he was clearly comfortable lying to her to get what he wanted.

During these early months at school, Diana's sexual project was about self: who she was, and how she fit into a peer group. She seemed clear about one part of her own sexual citizenship—her right to explore, to seek out sexual experiences that made her feel the way she wanted to feel. But less present in her mind was the fact that the people she was having sex with were also people. As described in Chapter 4, she and her friends treated sex as a sport—or, like so many things at Columbia, a competition. That achievement-oriented sexual project, combined with a lack of attention to other people's sexual citizenship, rendered her vulnerable—both to being assaulted, and to committing assault.

Midway through freshman year, deciding that the brunch crowd were not really her people, she found a new community of friends, reveling in her status as the most sexually experienced in the group. On one occasion, her role in the group as expert led to giving two of them, a man and a woman, kissing tips. It felt necessary to demonstrate. "Oh, I'll teach you how to kiss, too," she said to the woman. "Like, I'm just such a good kisser." Diana chalked up her confidence to, in part, being very drunk and stoned. She remembers stumbling and slurring her speech.

The man she had "taught" to kiss was sober. Shortly after giving him instruction, the alcohol hit her hard. She felt ill and laid down. He proceeded to get a banana, and "started dangling it in my mouth and, you know, saying, 'It's just, you're, like, sucking a dick. Like, wow, this is so fun to watch.' I was kind of just, like, too drunk to understand it at all." The woman she had kissed stopped it, afraid that Diana would choke.

I, like, woke up the next day feeling like, "That was, like, really gross," and definitely, like, again like I didn't really think of it as, like, he did something wrong. Looking back on it, it basically fits the definition of crossing someone's sexual boundaries without their consent . . . putting something in my mouth in this very sexual way. Um, and we've never discussed it. . . .

This incident was an unwanted nonconsensual sexual interaction, but Diana didn't consider what happened to her an assault. Thinking back, she recognizes it as "technically" an assault, but it's not how she experienced it.

As freshman year progressed, Diana became increasingly close with a man who identified as gay. As in many of her earlier relationships, sexuality was a terrain of play and performance. They shocked themselves—and, they hoped, others—by making out in public while drunk or stoned at parties. It was all just fun—until they were alone, without an audience. In his room one night after another evening of partying, they found themselves making out. They almost had intercourse, Diana thinks, but she stopped the encounter. She had her period, and while she would not have been that worried about something like this with a man who had had sex with a woman before, she was concerned how her friend might experience it as his first time having intercourse with a woman. They slept in bed together, but did not have sex.

The next morning Diana was thrilled by the idea that maybe his sexual identity wasn't an impediment to her desires. Over breakfast he said to her, "I think I'm moving down the Kinsey Scale for you." It was the sexiest line she'd ever heard.

That week Diana couldn't concentrate on her work. She barely slept. She was obsessed. She wanted to be the girl he turned straight for.

"It was kind of this, like, conquest-like, thing, which I think is unhealthy and, like, bad." Diana told us. "And, spoiler alert: I'm the one that crosses boundaries in this situation." At this moment, three things collide: the clarity of her sexual project, which is to feel desired—so desired that she could "turn someone straight"; her assurance about her own sexual citizenship, the notion that yes, she should have the right to realize her sexual projects: and the lack of consideration for other people's sexual citizenship. Diana's achievement-oriented sexual project also made her vulnerable to committing assault. All those times that she treated other people like objects—they were doing the same with her. But not this time.

Diana reflected, when we interviewed her, on how her single-minded focus on the thrill of her capacity to "turn him straight" made her inattentive to what her friend might have wanted—her sexual project made his desires invisible.[1] But she was accustomed to being the object of someone else's desire, not to acting as the agent in a sexual encounter, and was unsure how to proceed.[2] So she went to an expert: she called a man.

Diana's ex-boyfriend recommended what she described as the "frog-in-hot-water" approach—slowly advancing the heat of the encounter, to the point where someone ends up doing something to which they would never initially have agreed.[3] The analogy is as apt as it is disturbing. With a clear goal in mind, Diana developed a plan to "push the ladder to sex."

Her execution was clumsy; after all, she wasn't used to playing this role. She invited her gay friend over to hang out. They were sober. As soon as he settled in she told him, "We're going to have sex."

"I'm actually gay."

She changed the conversation, and after a long period of getting comfortable again, suggested that they just hang out in their underwear. He agreed, and she again raised the issue of sex.

"I still don't know," he replied.

She wished she had said, "Okay. Let's put our clothes back on and go take a walk and get some ice cream or something."

But she didn't. She was blindly focused on getting what she wanted.

He kissed her first. Diana knew something wasn't quite right; it felt really awkward. She started taking off his clothes.

"I don't want to," he said.

Diana cut him off. "Oh, you don't have to." She thought he meant he didn't want to go down on her. "To this day I don't know if he was about to say, 'I don't want to have sex with you.'"

Diana performed oral sex on him. As she guided him to penetrative sex she said, "Are you ready for this moment in your life?"

"Yeah . . ."

Diana asked him a couple times, "Are you okay with this?"

"Mm-hmmm . . . yeah." Her successful extraction of a verbal agreement to sex underlines the limits of a focus on affirmative consent.[4]

When they were done, Diana asked him to sleep over. He left to sleep in his own bed. She felt something was wrong. But when she woke the next morning, she bragged to her friends, "I have the power to turn gay guys straight!"

When she next saw him, he told her, "That was good sex, but I don't really want to have an ongoing sexual relationship with you because I actually am gay."

About a month later, Diana was frustrated that they weren't spending as much time together as they used to. To express her anger, she brought up the issue of his leading her on, saying that he'd had sex with her and then abandoned her.

"I didn't want to have sex," he replied.

It didn't sink in at first. But a day later Diana was distraught. "Am I, like, a rapist?" she thought.

She texted him immediately. "You gotta come over here. We gotta talk. Did I assault you. Like, did I rape you?"

Diana said, "He had to, like, calm me down, 'cause I was so upset. And we had a lot of other conversations about it. He basically said, 'You didn't assault me. But I didn't want to have sex.'"

Diana suddenly experienced their encounter in an entirely new light. She didn't have the power to turn gay men straight. He didn't move down the Kinsey scale—she'd dragged him down it.[5] She knew she'd "gotten a 'yeah'" from him. And she was emphatic: "I think of myself as very concerned about consent, I did at that time as well. And the fact that I could still, basically, violate someone, even thinking about consent the whole time, was also really shocking. . . . It makes me think, like, what I had been taught about consent was just very basically, 'you need to get a yes.' And I got a yes." But now, looking back, she understood that the "yeah" was meaningless if there was something coercive about it.[6] He insisted he was fine, emotionally. But Diana's life changed.

In the following months, Diana again reinvented herself. As she told us her stories, she admitted, "I guess weed really features in a lot of my stories of my life, but I do not smoke weed anymore." She cut her hair. She hasn't had sex since, and is not pursuing it. At the time of our interview she identified as "currently asexual, previously heterosexual." She partly blamed her previous engagement with femininity.

> I was really upset with the traditional trappings of femininity. I was basically just getting tired of being that sort of person, and femininity sort of seemed to me like this powerless position all of a sudden. And I was also still really upset about what had happened, you know, because I just was really, really angry at myself and worried about what the whole thing meant. Femininity just seemed very dangerous. So then I was basically like, "I want to work on my gender identity," 'cause I felt pretty strongly masculine. . . . A lot of times that's a classic sign of realizing you're trans, just struggling with your gender identity. But it sort of never got to that point for me. I just had this phase, and then I sort of settled into . . . not really presenting as hyper-feminine anymore.

The realization that she might have harmed someone she cared about left her feeling that the only path to recovering a moral self was to reject both femininity and sexuality. What had felt modern, brave, and cool, enabling her to win at the brunch competition, she suddenly experienced as self-absorbed and unkind. There is a gendered dimension to her transformation—she only confronted the limits of treating other people like objects when she moved out of the sexual gatekeeper role. Her high school entanglements and that "gross" freshman year experience with the hot senior, who dismissed her after sex by handing her her clothes, were both grounded in an achievement-oriented sexual project and a disregard for men's self-determination. But none of those interactions, framed as they were within the heterosexual logic of men being the ones who advance a sexual interaction, had spurred her to think she might need to care about her partner's sexual citizenship.

> In therapy what I really wanted to talk about was my unhealthy tendency to get obsessed with people. Partly because I felt like that's what had led me to really ignore the warning signs of consent—[I'm] looking back on all my relationships and thinking, "Was I like that? Like, have I done this before? You know, is my behavior intrinsically sort of angled to put pressure on people?"

In therapy Diana found connections between overlooking "the warning signs of consent" and her more general patterns of human interaction. This wasn't just cognitive work, learning the rules of the road; it was a project of self-reconstruction that involved reimagining her approach to human relations. Not all students who assaulted others were so self-aware.

"I PUT ON A TIE. SO I KNEW I WAS GOING TO HAVE SEX."

The moral opprobrium in the language and ideas used to talk about sexual assault make it impossible to imagine that those who commit it could be our sons and daughters, or our friends and peers. We picture some evil stranger, a distinct kind of person: a perpetrator. The term calls attention to what's wrong with them—a deep flaw in personality, or attitudes, or some other individual trait—rather than what might be awry with "us"—our communities, our relationships, our actions. It suggests that the task is to protect ourselves from a predator, the same way we would against, say, a lion. Which is to say against something that isn't human. This is a convenient way to think about perpetration. But it's also dangerously incomplete.

We suggest thinking of *perpetration*—an act that people sometimes commit—rather than *perpetrator*—a stable identity that someone might inhabit.[7] A lot is known about the characteristics of those who sexually assault others.[8] A paper led by Kate Walsh, using the SHIFT survey, echoes and advances that work by showing that on this campus, having been the victim of assault in the last year, believing in and relying on nonverbal consent strategies, binge drinking, having depression symptoms, and having committed assaults before college, were all predictive of committing assault.[9]

There's considerable unrealized potential in prevention work that goes beyond the "good guy/predator" dichotomy. We heard many assault stories in which students thought they were just telling us about an interesting or weird sexual experience they had. Not only were they not trying to commit an assault, they did not recognize how what they were doing could be seen that way. We're not arguing that those who harm others should be held blameless or that sexual assault is never intentional. But focusing only on character flaws and individual responsibility distracts from opportunities to prevent assaults that reflect a lack of consideration of the other person's sexual citizenship, rather than a deliberate erasure of it. And, to be fair, we are social scientists; our purpose in this book is to look at how institutions and social structures, rather than individual psyches, contribute to sexual assault.

From the students who were assaulted, we heard plenty of stories that sounded like predation—someone deliberately creating circumstances in which to sexually assault someone, either by force or intoxication or both (think about Esme's or Lupe's experiences). We also heard stories in which one person clearly articulated not wanting sex and was ignored (think Luci and Steve: she said no, and he said, "It's okay"). A student who sees campus as a hunting ground in which to find other students to rape would have been unlikely to sit down with us to talk about their strategies, motives, and desires. None of the twelve stories of assault told from the perspective of the assaulter are like that. Rather, they depict behavior that is harmful, but hard to read as evil. This chapter represents the perspectives of a very particular subset of people who commit sexual assault. These are voices that are rarely heard at all, but they are worth listening to.

Eddie was from a well-to-do family in Chicago. A tennis player, he was handsome and had always been popular. He had never really talked much with his parents about sex or drugs or drinking. As long as he did well in school and at sports, and didn't create a scandal, they basically had a "don't ask, don't tell" policy. One Saturday night back in high school, he was drinking with friends at someone's house. Their parents were away for the weekend. He knew that one of the girls there liked him, but he wasn't particularly attracted to her. Both drunk, eventually they started making out. They wandered down into the finished basement, away from everyone else, and began to fumble beneath each other's clothes. As Eddie tells it, she started to give him a hand job. But he wasn't into it, and so eventually he just got up and went back upstairs to the party. About an hour later a group of women came up to him, yelling.

"What the fuck, Eddie! You left her passed out, naked, on the couch down there!"

Eddie said they "basically accused me of rape." He didn't know what to say. But he figured a safe bet was to just keep hanging out with her. As her friends saw her cuddled up with Eddie on the couch, they figured nothing bad could have happened. So they dropped it.

Once at Columbia, Eddie cut back a little on the drinking because it got in the way of athletics and academics, and sometimes got him into situations he regretted later on, but otherwise didn't change much. By junior year he had been "seeing" Wendy for a bit: this basically meant they'd met at a few parties, hung out, and had sex a couple times. A member of a popular sorority, she invited him to her sorority formal, a clear sign that she liked him. Eddie was proud to be picked by a woman from a prestigious sorority; it was a positive sign of his social position on campus. He felt that accepting the invite came with an obligation, one that had little to do with how he felt.

"I put on a tie. So I knew I was going to have sex."

Eddie recounted that he had intentionally not gone "all out" at the formal, because of a looming early-morning practice the next day as well as his decision to drink less in general. His date was a different story. She threw back shots at the Mexican restaurant that was the group's first stop. Then they headed to a club for the actual formal. Eddie told us he purposefully didn't show his fake ID to get wristbanded; he didn't want to be able to drink. His date continued to drink heavily. At 1 a.m., with a practice the next morning starting at 6, he told her he was going home. She said she'd go back with him. He really wanted to go home alone so he could sleep. He felt it would be rude to have the cab pull up to her sorority and ask her to jump out, but if he walked her inside the cab would leave and then he'd have to walk home in the pouring rain. He told the driver to go to his dorm. As they got out of the car she wrapped her arms around him—in part to flirt, but also because she couldn't really stand on her own. As Eddie described it, "She comes up to my room with me." He didn't really want her to. Sharing a twin bed with her meant he would get even less sleep. But he didn't tell her how he felt. "I didn't make an effort to prevent this."

He found the sex unpleasant. The condom broke. And she was in and out of consciousness. She told him she wasn't on birth control. They had sex a second time, that time without a condom. He was upset, because she was there all night and he couldn't really sleep. And he was really concerned about practice the next day: he hadn't been playing well and was worried that his coach might demote him to a lower-ranked position on the team. He made it through, though, and after practice, went to the pharmacy to get Plan B—a morning-after birth control. He went by the sorority and gave it to her. Their interactions weren't the greatest afterwards. Eddie's read was that Wendy was upset that he didn't keep seeing her. A part of the same small social circle, within a year they had "patched things up." They never had a conversation, but she didn't seem angry anymore. We interviewed Wendy as well, but she never mentioned this night. She did share a story of being assaulted before college (which was fairly common; one in five students in the SHIFT survey had experienced some form of pre-college assault), which seems to suggest she was willing to talk about experiences she thought of as assault.

As Eddie described it, she had been drifting in and out of consciousness—blackout drunk—as he had sex with her. He seemed sincere in his belief that there was a social debt: that taking a woman out for a formal "required" that they have sex. She'd asked him out, and had been interested in him for some time. He felt obliged to deliver. The fact that Eddie even sat down with us to talk about his experiences, describing this encounter as "weird," but certainly not as an assault, underlines our point about the continuum of assaulters stretching from intentional predators to people too wrapped up in their own desires, insecurities, goals, or social obligations to hear what the other person is saying or notice what state they are in. Eddie was typical of many people we spoke to who genuinely did not understand that they might be committing assault. Having sex (or sexual contact) with women who were blackout drunk but (perhaps in his imagination) really into him was a pattern he seemed not to recognize. It was just part of his sex life.

During data collection, we had a clinician on call in case a team member needed help figuring out whether to triage a distraught participant to care. The concern was that a student who had been assaulted might become intensely distressed during an interview. This happened, but the more typical response among those recounting assault experiences was, "It was good to finally talk about it." Even Fran, who recounted supporting her high school cocaine habit by giving blow jobs to married men, thanked us, saying that she hoped her story would press parents to look beyond their children's grades and field hockey scores as measures of whether they were doing okay. She gathered up her coat, threw her backpack over one shoulder, and strolled out. Jennifer, who had interviewed Fran, walked slowly up Amsterdam Avenue in tears. She had to make a call for support. For herself.

But there was a third group for whom very powerful feelings surfaced during the interviews: those who realized they'd committed assault.

Diana was deeply shaken when she considered how her actions may have been experienced by her friend. Think about Austin's recounting of that moment freshman year, when he got in bed with a girl and touched her breasts. "Well, fuck me," he said to us, tears welling up in his eyes. There were times when we heard experiences unquestionably as assaults, but the person who told these stories—like Eddie—never gave any indication that they viewed it this way. But others, either in the moment of the interview or some time before it, did. And they were crushed. For some of the men, we suspect the response is bound to fear—imagining that their life could forever be "ruined" because of what they did. But there is more to it. Most people want to be seen as desirable—to imagine that others are genuinely attracted to them and that they are good at sex. They don't want to think of themselves as people whose sexual exploits are produced by coercion rather than desire. They have been taught the importance of consent. Many students belong to groups that have explicitly set community standards regarding consent—from athletic teams to fraternities to the band and the debate team. And the university is striving to develop these cultural norms as well. Students have mostly gotten the twin messages that assault is bad and that an accusation of assault will, as students put it, "ruin your life."

Our point is not to make those who commit assault look like victims, or suggest that they have no responsibility. Rather, we argue that while the vilification of "perpetrators" may have helped achieve important political ends, creating widespread social support for the recognition and prevention of sexual assault, it has also narrowed understanding. It's been decades since the finding first emerged that many campus sexual assaults are committed by a friend or intimate partner, and yet those assaulters have largely remained shadowy caricatures.[10] They haven't fully been integrated into the broader understanding of why assaults happen or what we should do about them. Thus we provide some details from the family and educational backstory of those who sexually assault others. These details are part of the story of what leads to campus sexual assault.

"I WISH I HAD BEEN IN AN ENVIRONMENT WHERE TALKING ABOUT SEX WAS EASIER."

Elliot was a smart but awkward teen who grew up in a financially comfortable, stable household. His mother stopped working when he was born, and his father worked long hours but made it a point to come home every evening for family dinner. Their wealthy, conservative Michigan neighborhood had good schools. Few of his high school classmates drank, and fewer still did drugs. Being sexually active didn't make you a "cool kid." Elliot's peers didn't focus much on accruing sexual experience; they were more driven by their families to launch their careers.

The major lesson about sexuality that Elliot learned from his parents was not to talk about it: "Sexuality wasn't necessarily stigmatized in my family, but it wasn't open." From school, he took away two lessons, both focused on the bad things that happen after sex: "If you have sex you might get pregnant" and "This is what happens if you have STDs." Elliot struggled with anxiety, and his early sexual experiences featured little pleasure, joy, or intimate connection; he recounted them mostly as experiences to power through. As his high school years passed he became fixated on his virginity—the desire to lose it, coupled with the fear that maybe preserving it might be a better choice. When he was a junior dating a senior, she prodded him to talk about what he wanted sexually, what she wanted, and what they might do together. Her openness made him think that maybe he was making too big of a deal about sex. Finally, one day his girlfriend said to him, "Hey, you want to get this over with, like, have your first time and, like, move on?" He answered, "Yeah, like, fine. Why not?"

She took charge of the situation, bringing him back to her family's house one weekend when her parents were out of town. As he remembered:

> She was pretty much, like, large and in charge . . . I was too nervous to help her take her shirt off and stuff like that. So she just

did it all and was telling me what to do, like, "Get undressed." I was nervous, but excited obviously. I was very comfortable with what was going on, so I didn't really mind. I just kind of let it happen.

Otherwise articulate, Elliot struggled to describe his sexual experiences, stumbling as he spoke, and falling back frequently on the words "awkward" and "uncomfortable."[11]

In senior year Elliot recreated his own virginity loss experience, except that this time he was the one who "did it all." His new girlfriend had never had intercourse, and wanted to. Like Elliot, she suffered from extreme anxiety. He figured if they talked about it, she'd become overwhelmed by her own anxiety. So one day, while getting undressed on the couch, Elliot leaned back and said to her, "I'm going to get a condom." He continued: "That was the point that I expected her to be, like, either, 'No,' or just, like, continue on." She was dead silent. Elliot could tell she was nervous. As they began to have intercourse, she gave no sign it was a pleasurable experience. But she also didn't indicate that it was bad. Elliot expected that she'd feel able to ask him to stop if she wanted to. "She was very independent, self-aware, and easily the most successful, driven person that I knew in my life." Then she did say something. Elliot recounted that she "kind of asked him to stop because it was painful for her." So he pulled out.

She showered and Elliot accompanied her home. It was an awkward, silent ride. Growing up in a community where people didn't talk about sex, neither of them knew what to say. As they continued to date, the sex got better. Years later, home on break, they ran into each other at a party. Both drunk, they laughed, reminiscing at how terrible her first time was. When we talked to him, after Elliot had been through so much more, we asked him if he regretted anything about these early sexual experiences.

In retrospect, I don't really regret any of it. I wish I had been in an environment where talking about sex was easier, because even largely to this day, I'm not even that comfortable talking to the rest of my family about it. I kind of have it in my mind that they knew what was going on with my sex life, but nobody was going to address it. Even with friends, though, it was not super open. Nobody ever talked about the actual act of sex or anything like that. It was more gossiping about who was having sex with whom.

Elliot had accrued more sexual experience by the time got to Columbia, but little in the way of sexual vocabulary. He continued to feel anxious, and started to experience depression. Eventually he saw a doctor and began medication; it helped, but the day-to-day was still hard.[12] He found a student group where he felt like he belonged, and was excited to be in a new, more open sexual environment. Like many of his peers, his sex life involved a lot of alcohol, and not that much emotional intimacy. One night, for example, after drunk sex with a woman he barely knew, he asked her if she wanted to stay over. "People do that?!?" she laughed.

Layered on top of the silence and fear were sexual interactions that taught him to separate intimacy from sex. In his freshman year there was a woman he really liked, but she wasn't interested in any kind of relationship. Still, their physical connection developed, and they hooked up for several months before drifting apart. It was a lonely year for Elliot; the Model UN, which had been so important to him in high school, wasn't nearly as meaningful in college. He felt surrounded by others who were sure of their paths after college, already on the hunt for internships.[13] He got mono, missed a major conference, and faced his teammates' ire. That, on top of his mediocre grades and his feeling that everyone else was doing college better than he was, made him feel that summer couldn't come soon enough.

The following December, Katie walked into the dorm's common room, where Elliot sat studying for finals. Elliot later learned that she'd taken some Clonazepam, a tranquilizer prescribed to treat seizures and panic attacks, and had been drinking. Katie found the Clonazepam helped make her "chill," something hard to achieve during finals week.

Katie complained to Elliot that since breaking up with her ex—someone Elliot knew well from Model UN—she hadn't had sex. And she talked about loneliness in a way that resonated with Elliot. He asked her if she wanted to have sex with him. She said no.

They continued to talk. Elliot was sober, and suggested they go for a walk together in the unseasonably warm night. They'd lived on the same hall now for a semester but had never really spoken. In the early hours of the morning they strolled around campus and through the Morningside Heights neighborhood, talking about the things that were so frustrating about college, and their lives. Feeling they were now connecting, Elliot again asked Katie if she wanted to have sex. She said no.

It was just an hour or two before dawn when they finally returned to the dorm common room, where they continued to chat. One last time, Elliot asked if she wanted to have sex. She agreed. At nearly 5 a.m., with their roommates fast asleep, they couldn't use either of their rooms. Katie went to her room, got some lubricant, and met Elliot back in the common room. They closed the blinds, had sex, and then each went to back to their own rooms, across the hall from one another, to sleep.

A few days later a mutual friend came to see Elliot. Katie was concerned about what happened. She didn't want people to know she'd had sex with Elliot, given how close Elliot was to her ex. The friend told Elliot that Katie was concerned about the "social consequences." Elliot was focused on finals, and it hadn't occurred to him to tell others about what had happened with Katie. He blew it off, didn't reach out to Katie, and went home, ready for a break.

Early in the spring semester Elliot received an ominous email, summoning him to the Gender-based misconduct office. Katie had reported their incident as an assault. Months later, after the investigation was completed, Elliot was called in to meet with his dean. He'd been found guilty. She had repeatedly said "no." She had been drinking, and was on a drug that further impaired her. He had worn her down, extracting a yes that she did not want to give, that she was not capable of giving.

As Elliot tells it, the experience was catastrophic for his identity—he had never imagined himself to be the kind of person who would assault someone. His depression worsened. He considered suicide. When he returned to campus after his suspension, he felt—and was treated—like a pariah. His old friends wouldn't speak to him. "Nobody even acknowledged me." Katie's friends saw him heading to a bar one evening, and screamed at him: "Rapist!!!" The experience forced him to grow as a person. As he recounted, "I was admittedly kind of terrible to other people sometimes: just mean or not accepting. So, looking back, I have turned it into a positive experience for myself. I am now just, like, a kind, gentle person I think as a result."

The first time he had sex after being found responsible for committing assault, Elliot had a severe panic attack. Before sex, he'd told the woman what had happened with Katie and about the school's decision. She reassured him that the sex they were about to have was consensual. But still, as soon as the sex was over he locked himself in the shower to have a private place to cry. Today he has rules for himself. One of them is telling his partners what happened. "I can't have a physical relationship with somebody without explaining that to them. It's almost unfair to that person. It explains to them a lot of the anxieties on my end." Women have been open to him, mostly, even after he's told them what happened. He requires a lot of reassurance before they have sex, that they are not "going to in any way use sex against me. Because I mean obviously at this point, all it takes is one person to turn around and say, 'Elliot also raped me,' for me to just go to prison, at least in my mind."

He says he'd never have a one-night stand again. "That would cause me too much anxiety." It's not the emotional connection Elliot needs; it's trust. And yet Elliot continues to have drunk sex. With his current girlfriend he would "drink and party with her friends and stuff. I would stay with her in her dorm room and we would have sex, and, like, me being drunk and having sex, and her being drunk and having sex, that freaked me out because then it becomes, like, 'Is this actually consensual?' and so that question is always in my head." In fact, he told us that while drunk, he's had sex with his girlfriend that he didn't want.

She probably had no idea of, like, the state that I was in. I woke up and I was like, "Let's not do that next time. That was not a good choice on either of our parts. I mean I was so drunk that it wasn't enjoyable." She felt way worse than I intended to make her feel about it, because like I said, I felt in no way abused or taken advantage of. I just know that it was probably not worth it.

Still, he couldn't think of this, in any way, as rape—even though his girlfriend had sex with him that he didn't want, while he was too drunk to consent. Elliot didn't feel harmed. He also felt, and clearly expressed, that he didn't want it to happen again. Elliot turned the experience of being found responsible for committing assault into something "positive" in part by developing a broader sexual vocabulary, and reflecting more deeply about his own sexual experiences.

I think there should be another term. Not so much that I think that, like, date rape or something like that isn't rape, but I think there's culturally such a connotation with rape and physical violence, that it conjures up the wrong image of what consent is meant to be. I think in coining another term—and I'm sure a feminist will point out how this is entirely wrong of me were I to bring it up, but that's okay—in coining another term, you could kind of take the wrong connotation away from it [physical violence] and start to break down what consent actually is in the context of alcohol, drugs, and all of these altered states of mind and stuff. I woke up and I didn't feel like I was abused or raped, or violated. I wasn't. And yet I think there are people who look at it and be like yes, you were raped and she should go to jail for that. Or she should be punished in some way for it, but I don't think that accomplishes anything. I think it was much more useful for myself and for her to be like "Hey, that wasn't consent. I don't hold this against you but don't do that." But at the end of the day, like, not giving consent is not giving consent.

Many of the assaults we describe feature students who were not inter-personally skilled and who had sex with people they didn't know well, sometimes when they were very far from sober. Some people might judge sex under those conditions to be wrong, coarsening, or exploitative. Our point is different: the body is a social canvas, and when people do things with their bodies, these experiences are a training ground for what feels normal. Years ago, doing fieldwork in rural Mexico, Jennifer taught her young sons to kiss strangers hello—an act at which they initially recoiled in horror—in order to conform to local expectations about good man-ners. In a few months, through a combination of stern glances, some gentle shaming, and positive social reinforcement for good behavior, they dutifully began to offer up their cheeks, experiencing as normal what had previously disgusted them. (In subsequent years, there's been an active discussion of those type of forced kisses as a crucial teachable moment about consent and boundaries.) In an analogous way, a lot of the sex that students have with people they do not know well socializes them, in an intimate and embodied way, to regard noncommunicative, largely narcissistic encounters as consensual sex. Although there are certainly assaults that look very different from consensual interactions, for Diane, Elliot, and many other students, consensual sex is often char-acterized by limited communication and even less intimacy.[14] And so, disturbingly, the experiences they had that were consensual often look very similar to those that were not. This is why being accused of assault can be so confusing. Previous sexual experiences, consensual though they may have been, set the stage for subsequent assaults, in large part because the main question they asked was, "what do I want?" in a con-text where no one—parent, teacher, mentor—had ever talked to them about what sex was for, or taught them to also ask the other person, "What do *you* want?"

Diana and her friend talked about what happened. Elliot didn't listen to Katie, when he kept trying to convince her to have sex after she'd repeatedly said no; and he didn't listen to her later, when he blew it off when her friend came by to convey that she wanted to talk about it.

Later, having been sensitized about nonconsensual sex by the consequences of his actions, Elliot was able to say to his girlfriend, "Hey, that wasn't consent. I don't hold this against you but don't do that." For better or worse, consent doesn't just happen in the moment. It is something that people process over time. The problems of communication are not just in the moment of sex, but also in the temporal arch before and after. Remembering that the assaults in these two stories represent a very particular subset, those grounded in entitlement and self-absorption rather than an intentional violation of another's boundaries, what we frequently saw was a fundamental problem with communication around sex: before, during, and after.[15]

"IT GOT TO THE POINT WHERE SHE DIDN'T FEEL COMFORTABLE WITH IT, BUT SHE DIDN'T SAY ANYTHING ABOUT IT."

Martin's story illustrates the risks created when young people's curiosity about sex is sated only by pornography, untempered by family conversations about values and relationships or school-based sex education. What happened went unreported, and he did not label it assault. Maybe it wasn't an assault. But based on his narrative, the other person felt uncomfortable during the interaction and, for a reason we cannot know, also felt unable to say so. Leaving aside the sex part, it sounds scary to be choked harder than desired by a much larger person and to feel unable to stop what was happening.

The story came out in fragments, over the course of several rather disturbing interviews. Martin could not remember receiving any sex education at all in the wealthy but very rural Idaho community in which he'd grown up. He was emphatic—not only had he never spoken with anyone in his family about sex, but he would never want to: "My sex life is my sex life. I don't ask—I have no interest in knowing what my parents do, I have no interest in knowing what my brother or sister does . . . because of all the people I'd want to talk about sex with, do I really want to talk with people like my mom and dad and siblings about it?"

More than two dozen US college campuses feature BDSM clubs or student interest groups, and it's important not to confuse BDSM itself with assault. For example, Lydia, who was into kink (her story appears in Chapter 5), was among the most scrupulous and intentional sexual actors we met. She expressed a well-developed sense of her own and others' sexual citizenship, a meticulous and pleasure-oriented approach to sexual communication, and deep fluency in the erotics of consent.[16]

Martin's interest in BDSM was more of a private thing. The students at the campus club did not feel like his people. His ample BDSM knowledge, primarily from watching porn, extended to specific actors and their specialties. But in at least one instance, his self-taught sexual skills, combined with his insistence on negotiating the terms of a sexual encounter in advance, led to a "complicated" experience. When asked if he'd ever reflected back on a sexual experience and felt that something nonconsensual had happened, Martin said "I did, one time, actually have something like this, where a week after something happened with a girl, she was like, 'So, I wasn't actually feeling this way.' And I mean actually that got me a little mad."

> So, she was there, and we were starting to do stuff. . . . What she had explained to me—she liked to be defiant . . . which gets the person more aggressive. But she kept being defiant, to the point of, she never said anything, and so it got to the point where she didn't feel comfortable with it, but she didn't say anything about it.

We asked how he would have known the difference between a performance of defiance as part of a sexual scene and someone's actual objection to what was going on.

> So when I say defiant, I mean, in a very teasing way. So it's like, you tell her something, and she says she's not going to. It's more like, "I'm not going to do this, you have to do this . . ." There was no change in her tone of voice and stuff like that. . . . It was said in

a very teasing-y way, and she kept using that same voice, instead of a much more serious "no, don't do this." There wasn't a shift in her attitude.

Martin was distressed, recounting what happened after, when she texted him. "She said she wasn't comfortable in the moment, and I was just like, 'I really don't know what I could've done there, in that situation, 'cause you weren't doing something very key to the whole aspect." Martin provided a little more detail:

> it was kind of ridiculous because she got mad but—well, no. . . . So apparently, I was at one point choking her really hard . . . but she never said anything throughout the whole thing, she just kept egging me on for some reason. . . . She never said anything like, "Don't do that," it was more, it was always just like more teasing essentially. . . . She was not articulating—like she was not being how you should be when you are being submissive, on account of it requires a lot of communication. . . . She said it was too rough afterwards, like through text. I was like, "You never said anything . . ." and she was like, "I was afraid to." And I was like, "No." I was like, "What?" I didn't really understand that well . . . because she was saying she didn't like—she thought I was being too rough and stuff, but she didn't say anything during. I'm just, like, I don't know what you want me to do with this.

Martin met that woman through an app, but to focus on the digitally mediated element of their connection is to miss that these were two complete strangers engaged in a complex sexual interaction, each seeking his or her own physical gratification, without having established even a safe word, much less an in-person understanding of the other's communication styles and sexual preferences. Martin had absorbed the campus messaging around consent to the extent that he always negotiated it up front, discussing through the app what he was into, what the other person wanted, and what was not on the table.[17] As he lived out his fantasy of finding the perfect submissive to his dominant, his acceptance of a temporal separation between consent and sex—not just agreeing to sex, but planning it—was just a more extreme version of how many students "do" consent, where consent involves agreeing to go back to someone's room. Once in that room they pretty much assume that consent has happened. Being in a scene scripted around overpowering his partner posed real challenges for his capacity to notice her discomfort. Learning about sex from porn is like learning how to drive by watching automobile ads in which professional drivers do stunts. But those car ads warn, "Professional driver on closed course. Do not attempt"; with porn, there's no warning label.[18]

WORKING HIS WAY THROUGH THE LIST

We've met Tim before. He's wealthy, attractive, and determined to be known as a man who provides the party. He drinks copiously, often in combination with marijuana or cocaine. He was the man in Chapter 2 who told us the story of being assaulted, and being upset that he couldn't report it because since he was drunk, the woman could just turn the story around on him and he'd be the one to get into trouble. Tim started his freshman year with a boldness verging on arrogance. He had a credit card, with the bill paid by his family every month, no questions asked, and a fake ID he'd secured months before arriving on campus. Early in orientation week, he bought some handles of vodka and threw a party in his room, inviting his teammates, and some women he had gone to high school with and others he deemed attractive, including one woman ranked high on his list of "Facebook cuties." Tim recounted how they did shot after shot—nothing out of the ordinary for him. The Facebook Cutie leaned over and asked him if he wanted to go back to her room. Tim nodded to one of his teammates as they left his party.

Things escalated quickly. Soon they were naked, but she didn't have a condom, and she wanted him to use one. Tim dashed back to his room to get one. He flashed the condom as he left the room—the victor, going to claim his prize. The party-goers who had stayed, continuing to drink the booze he'd procured, cheered him on. Her door was locked, but when she heard him outside she let him in. Tim quickly undressed. As he was putting on the condom, he saw her reach for her phone and type a single word:

"Help."

She'd sent the message to a group text that included several women Tim knew from high school. They were just a floor away, at his party. Tim quickly threw his clothes on and went to talk to them. He hadn't done anything! he exclaimed. They hadn't even had sex yet! She'd asked him to get a condom! She was drunk. Crazy, even. Tim insisted that these women come back with him to her room to convince her that she didn't need any help. When they arrived at her room she was naked, jumping up and down, laughing and largely incoherent. They all left.

We don't know why she texted "Help" to her friends, and why she couldn't say something to Tim at that moment. We have his story. He told us that the next day she started flirting with him again. He was upset, and determined "never to go there" because she'd implied he had done something wrong, that he was going to rape her. For a while he avoided her. Several months later they had sex.

This story is unclear. It was likely also unclear to Tim, and to this woman, given how much they had had to drink. But what is clear is that this woman was incapable of consent. At face value, Tim's narrative—her erratic behavior, her incoherent babbling and laughing, their heavy drinking—conveys incapacity. So clearly, they shouldn't have had sex, right? But we can also see why Tim wouldn't think of it as an assault. She'd asked him to get a condom. It doesn't meet the "affirmative consent" standard that appears in an increasing number of state laws, but it is a pretty common way for students to signal consent.[19]

Yet when someone who is out-of-their-mind drunk asks for keys to the car so they can drive home, we don't give them those keys. We don't say to ourselves, "Yes, this is what they really want to do." Instead, we think, "Wow. This person is in no condition to make this decision right now. And I'm not going to facilitate it, even if it means I pass up a potentially delightful ride home. And now I have to wait more than an hour for the next bus." It may seem condescending. It may compromise the other person's agency, refusing to give them what they're asking for. But there are plenty of situations where we say to ourselves, "This person may say they want this, but they're really too incapacitated to make that decision." Why should sex be any different?

While we often think of alcohol as creating risks for victimization, what became clear to us was how much it created risks of perpetration. A vital conclusion of our work is that students should be attentive to how much they are drinking because being drunk means having hugely compromised judgment. They might assault someone.[20] And that doesn't just apply to men.

"IT MADE ME WANT TO BE MORE AWARE OF THE STUFF THAT I DO WHEN I'M DRUNK."

Cheong, the khaki-clad, no-longer-smoking student from Hong Kong whose swan boat excursion with his girlfriend appears in Chapter 5, asserted that his approach to consent—"I get to know a person sufficiently long enough and also, I don't move that quickly"—enabled him to engage in sex without forcing a partner. And he initially responded "not really" to the question about whether he'd ever had a sexual or intimate encounter that, in retrospect, might not have been fully consensual. But then he recounted two incidents in which his advances had been unwelcome. Both were the form of assault—unwanted sexual touching—that was most prevalent among the students that SHIFT researchers surveyed.[21] In the first—which he brought up twice during the relatively short interview, suggesting that he found it relevant to our examination of sexual assault—he "stole a kiss" from the girl who eventually became his girlfriend. They were out at a jazz club for the evening during one of their early dates, and "She was taken aback. She was like, 'Oh, I don't want that.'"

Another time, a woman with whom he later became friends described to him something he'd done at a party—something he did not even remember. "She said that I was pretty drunk, and that as she walked in, I slapped her on the butt." Cheong laughed nervously at this point. "I don't remember anything like that happening." When we asked him how he felt about it, he said he was "really taken aback, really shocked that I would do something like that, 'cause it's not something"—more nervous laughter—"I can imagine myself carrying out." He said that when she told him, he was "apologetic," and when we asked him if he would describe what happened as sexual assault, he did not hesitate: "Yes, I would say so." We asked if he told anyone. More laughter, this time lighter. "I mean, I still joke about it with her, but we don't go telling people that I slapped someone." But it was a learning experience: "It made me want to be more aware of the stuff that I do when I'm drunk, just so I don't do anything stupid that I might regret or that might offend someone, 'cause I wouldn't like my butt to be grabbed by some random stranger."

For Cheong, the experience of being touched in a way that made him uncomfortable was part of his emerging understanding about the need to be respectful of women. One night out at a bar downtown, he described a girl as "overly affectionate" with him, to the extent that—he laughed as he shared the memory—he was "running away from her" all night, as she repeatedly hugged him and kissed him on the cheek. "That made me uncomfortable because I did not see her that way and I'm not usually touchy with girls." He was uneasy—both about the interaction and the decision to confront her. As they walked to the library the next day to prepare for the econ review session, he shared with her that he wasn't crazy about what had happened. She'd been so drunk, she didn't actually remember. It was even more awkward because he had to spell it out. She was apologetic, and said that it was also kind of ironic, because "she's had it happen to her on several occasions. . . . Guys tend to be pretty aggressive, so it is something she's come to expect but not a situation that she would like to be in."[22]

Cheong was very reflective about sex, trying to be considerate of other people, and to learn from his experiences, and yet those two incidents of unwanted sexual touching, combined with the fact that the first time he and girlfriend had sex they had never discussed that she was a virgin, points to the problems of a script in which men's job is to move the ball down the field. This analogy frames sex as a game people play against an opponent. It's not playing with a partner; it's scoring against them. The implication is that there are winners and losers. But what if we changed this script to think less about offense and defense—about trying to "steal a kiss"—and more about being on the same team, where a win for both people requires conversation about which plays sound good?[23]

III

Our introduction to the campus landscape raised the larger question about what is required to prepare students to interact respectfully across many forms of social difference. Queer students talked about how much work they had to do to teach others how to respect them. We heard parallel stories from racial and ethnic minority students. The amount of emotional labor that it took to educate their peers about simple principles of respect was exhausting. That work's cognitive and emotional burden created differences in how these students felt about their college experience. Recognizing others' sexual citizenship, like their broader citizenship, takes effort, feedback, and practice. And yet young people have been left to figure it out for themselves—with the primary responsibility of educating students about how not to harm others shouldered by those who are disproportionately the objects of violence, and often the most precariously positioned.[24]

The silences around sex produce harms—harms that cannot be addressed by adding fear-based messages about campus sexual assault to the "risk-avoidance" sex education that has left this generation of youth so underprepared for navigating sexual intimacy. Bringing sex out of the closet can't just be volunteer work by those who are having "weird" experiences, or who label what happens as assault. There are lots of reasons why people don't want to report their experiences of assault. But one of them is that victims are concerned about the person who assaulted them. That person may be a friend, a part of their community, someone who has been decent before. Institutions might consider, at the discretion of those who are assaulted, a process of "no-fault reporting," as exists on many campuses for alcohol abuse.[25] If someone has been drinking too much and is at risk to themselves, students can let a resident advisor know, so that their friend gets counseling.[26] If the framework is predators on the prowl, there's no reason to give sanctuary to assaulters. But victims often want recognition and repair, not revenge. And those who assault others often think about what they're doing as having sex, not assaulting someone. What if, then, we found ways to convey to people how others were experiencing sex with them? That it wasn't okay? What if this communication could occur in ways where those who were assaulted didn't have to be worried about "ruining the life" of another person, perhaps one they cared about? That would transfer the work of educating young people back to parents and caregivers, to religious communities for those who are a part of them, and to adequately trained and institutionally supported teachers and campus health promotion services. This would be far better than what we're doing now: leaving it to the victim to decide whether to do the emotional and practical work of talking through what happened and why it wasn't okay with the person who assaulted them, or with whom they had that "rapey" encounter.[27] It certainly would be better than demanding that they don't just educate that person, but enter into an adversarial process *against* them.

We began this chapter with Diana for a reason: to remind readers that men aren't the only people who commit assault. A lot of attention has been paid to the ideas of a campus "rape culture" and the "toxic

masculinity" that produces sexual violence. We don't deny the power
of these ideas. But there are a lot of assaults for which those concepts
provide insufficient explanatory power; the SHIFT survey showed that
nearly one in six men experienced assault by senior year and, as we've
noted, the highest rates of assault are found among LGBTQ students.[28]
Assaults of men and of LGBTQ students require a different accounting
of campus power relations. Doubtless, Eddie's cluelessness about the
potential toll of having sex with women for whom he does not particularly care feels toxic—or at minimum, excessively self-involved. But let's
return to Diana one last time. She was working with her therapist on
her tendency to treat others as objects to be consumed along the path
to her own self-realization. Where were the adults in her life, teaching
her to treat other people as humans rather than objects?[29] The question
is not what's wrong with Diana, or Eddie, or Elliot, or Tim; they are
products of communities and institutions that see "triumph" in having
sex with a girl from a list of Facebook cuties, and of families and peers
like Elliot's, who actively maintain silence about all things sexual. Eddie
learned somewhere to think of sex as an obligatory form of reciproca-
tion. Martin's only tutor in navigating intimacy was pornography. What
kind of ecologies have we created that make these kinds of projects seem
reasonable? How are we raising young people—enormously successful
ones who have learned other lessons so well—that they are allowed to
ignore the humanity—the citizenship—of those with whom they share
some of their most intimate moments?

7

THE POWER OF THE GROUP

"I GUESS THEY MADE AN 'IRISH EXIT.' "

Jillian was having a fun night with a dozen friends and acquaintances, sprawled in the living room of the large suite in East Campus, a building that housed mostly seniors, with views over Harlem, twinkling lights stretching to the East River and beyond. The music was on but not so loud that they couldn't talk. The harsh overhead neon lights were off, and a string of Christmas lights somehow attached to the ceiling washed the room in a warm glow. They passed around a magnum of red wine and plastic cups. Considering she was a junior, Jillian had terrible housing: she shared a relatively small room with a friend, without any common space to gather a larger group. This was the kind of night she often longed for—where she could sit around with a group of people, some she knew, some she didn't, and just talk. The awkward, smelly, loud fraternity parties were part of a past she didn't regret but was glad to have left behind.

Jillian got up to go to the bathroom, and when she came back she sat down next to a man she didn't really know. They moved in the same circles and he seemed interesting. Even though there are over 9,000 undergraduates on campus, getting to know someone new was a relatively rare opportunity.[1] Bobby, a senior, lived in a single off the hallway that led to the suite they were in. Both history majors, they had taken some of the same classes. They talked about professors they'd enjoyed and others who seemed underprepared for class or slow to respond to email. Conversation flowed easily. It might have been the wine, but they weren't drinking that much; mostly, it was being with someone easy to talk to, in a place that was comfortable, away from the daily stresses. As both Jillian and Bobby reached the bottom of their cups, she thought she'd pour one last glass of wine and then maybe they'd go out to the local bar to meet up with a larger group. But when she looked up from their conversation to see where the wine was, she noticed something startling: she and Bobby were alone in the dimly lit room.

The situation had changed. She looked across at Bobby, surprised, and he smiled. "I guess they made an 'Irish exit,'" Bobby joked—everyone had left, somewhat oddly, without saying goodbye. Nothing happened that evening. Bobby noticed Jillian's awkwardness and they headed out to find their friends elsewhere. But Jillian took home an important lesson, one she felt was important to talk with us about: casual drinks with friends could shift into a far more intimate context, through no action on her part. It was clearly a setup; why else would her friends have left without saying anything to her? Maybe it was spontaneous—they saw her and Bobby engrossed in conversation and decided to slip away to give them privacy. Maybe it was more deliberate—perhaps Bobby asked his friends to help him out by giving him an opportunity to be alone with Jillian. They were, after all, just a door away from his room. What Jillian was certain of was that this sexual opportunity emerged not because she had made it happen, but because her friends had.

We're not suggesting something terrible happened to Jillian. She wasn't suggesting it either. Her friends, intentionally or not, had set up a sexual situation. Jillian felt like something had been sprung upon her. It would have been nice if someone had asked. Jillian's story shows how sexual geography (Bobby's room was right there) intertwines with how peers produce sexual opportunities, in ways where her own sexual self-determination was not necessarily taken into account.

Readers may think of and experience sex as an extremely personal affair, defined by intimacy between people. Yet we saw in this situation exactly what decades of social scientific research on sexuality indicates: sex is a social activity, with peers working to produce sexual experiences for one another.[2] The socializing that leads up to sex usually involves friends, roommates, or fellow members of a team, hall, religious group, student organization, or club. These groups of students often quite intentionally create sexual opportunities for their members, defining desirable partners and producing sexual situations. But in creating such situations, they also create the conditions for assault. Assaults happen frequently within preexisting peer groups, who play a part in interpreting and labeling what has happened, and shaping the aftermath.

"YOU'VE BEEN RAPED," HE TOLD HER.

Rebecca was hoping for a fun time. It was Friday night, near the end of the semester, and she'd had a long week. She sent a text to her friends to see who was up for hanging out. They knew what "hang out" meant—meet up, get drunk, head to a neighborhood bar, and maybe "get with" someone. By her own assessment Rebecca drank a lot, and so did her friends. That evening, before heading to the bar, Rebecca and her friends pregamed, meanwhile catching up with each other in a way that would be impossible in a crowded space with music blaring.[3] Once they were sufficiently drunk, and it was late enough that they knew others would also be at their bar of choice, they headed out together. Rebecca didn't meet anyone, but she wasn't really trying to. Her friends didn't have much luck either. It was a typical night. The group danced, talked, and mostly drank more and more.

At closing time Rebecca was very drunk, as were her friends. Someone expressed concern about whether she could make it back home safely, but luckily two of her male friends lived in the building next door to her. They walked her down the steep set of stairs from the bar to the street and said that they'd make sure she made it home safely. This she remembers. She also remembers passing in and out of consciousness as these friends took turns having sex with her. She woke up alone in her room the next morning, hazy, headachy, profoundly hung over. Something felt wrong about what happened. She went to talk to Jed, a member of her friend group who had been there that evening. He assured her that it wasn't a big deal, that she was overreacting, and that she was very flirty at the bar, dancing and kissing her friends. This wasn't that out of the ordinary. Neither was hooking up within their friend group. Confused and late for a meeting of a student group for which she was on the executive board, she left her dorm and started to walk across campus. On her way she called to check in with Shepherd, a friend who wasn't part of that same crew, to tell him about her night. He was horrified. He insisted that she immediately go to the hospital. "You've been raped," he told her. Rebecca still wasn't sure how to think about what happened. But on Shepherd's urging she agreed to go to the local hospital to get a sexual assault forensic exam. As she lay in her hospital bed she was visited by Jed. Shepherd had called him, worried about Rebecca and outraged about what had happened. Jed told Rebecca what he'd also told Shepherd: she really had it all wrong. It wasn't rape. Did she really want to ruin their friends' lives?

Rebecca's horrific story is both typical and atypical. This was the only assault involving multiple assailants that we heard about in our interviews. But Rebecca's concerns about her relationship with Jed, and with Shepherd, and even Jed and Shepherd's relationship with each other, are fundamental to understanding the suffering involved in this experience. It wasn't just the assault, awful as that was. Reporting would have meant risking the loss of her whole social world. Who would Rebecca have relied upon, if her community fell apart over this incident? These aren't trivial concerns. And for most assaults, they're inescapable. Anyone who questions the very low rates of formal reporting for campus sexual assault should know that reporting is also very low for sibling sex abuse—and when students come to campus, their peers feel to them like family.[4]

It was hard for us initially to understand Rebecca's reluctance to label her friends taking turns having sex with her as she went in and out of consciousness as assault—just as we struggled to grasp why another student who told us her story would endure years in a student organization, spending a great deal of time around the man who had raped her and the people who worked to set up that situation (though certainly they thought they were setting up a fun encounter of sex, and not a rape).[5] The social networks that these young adults stitch together in college are transitional kinship networks. They help students separate from their families, but they do more than that; they're sources of identity, access to social spaces where students feel at home, and networks that give them information on everything from what's happening this weekend to jobs—not just how to apply, but, through networks of alums, how to find jobs.[6] And crucially, in a time of sexual discovery and assertion, networks of college friends help young people hook up.

It is hardly a radical notion that communities actively shape people's sexual lives. Families often try to weigh in on how they feel about potential partners.[7] States make rules about the kinds of sex that are and are not allowed.[8] Most of the institutions in our communities play a role in organizing and regulating sexual activity. Churches, synagogues, and mosques almost all articulate "acceptable" sexual relations, and serve as places where those with the same beliefs and background can come together to meet one another in the hope of forming a union. Any young person who has ever been encouraged by a parent to participate in a religious youth group knows that from the parent's point of view, the group offers more than religious education; parents hope their child will meet someone there, someone they would be happy to welcome home for the holidays. Religious institutions use what power they have—blessing sexual unions in marriage, for example—to organize sex in a way that reflects the community's shared values.

Friends often work very hard, and very purposefully, to create sexual opportunities for one another. We even have names for the social roles of those whose job it is to arrange sexual relations—the matchmaker and the wingman, for example.[9] There's also a term for someone who blocks sexual opportunities: the cockblocker. Ask couples how they met and those stories will almost always involve friends. Event "dating" or "hookup" apps have not fully sidelined peer networks; many students limit their searches to friends of friends, or "research" the people they match with online to see who they know in common. We often only come to see a partnership as serious when the person is introduced to friends and family.

Understanding how our peers and social networks influence our sexual lives thus provides an opportunity to think about how they might also be mobilized to help create healthy rather than harmful sexual experiences. Student life involves peer networks and hundreds of student organizations—the Korean Students Association, Christian Fellowship, the Gaming Society, even a BDSM club. These groups play a crucial and almost entirely unrecognized role in campus sexual assault through creating opportunities for sex and, the morning after, meeting up to make sense of such experiences.

In Chapter 4 we met Octavia, who bemoaned Macauley's reluctance to "wife her up." Late one night, Octavia texted her friends to say, "You're not gonna believe whose bed I'm in right now? Google his name! He's so hot!" As we've seen, she wasn't alone in thinking about her sexual life as a kind of conquest, with her friends' assessments a crucial element in each conquest's value. Not all students share this orientation, but unquestionably those who demonstrate it are not all men. Remember Rowan, the aspiring neurosurgeon, and the orientation week hookup, described in Chapter 3, which she talked about as "very college"? Sex isn't only (or even primarily) about pleasure, nor is it necessarily private. When people view sex as a kind of conquest, one of the conditions of that conquest is that others hear about and acknowledge your success. To no small degree, this approach fits perfectly within the achievement-oriented lives of Ivy League students. But its roots are far deeper, and more universal. Intimacy is a form of individual expression, but it's also a way to convey that identity to others: giving a sense of worth on the sexual marketplace, and ranking compared to others.[10]

Consider the phrase "She's out of your league." The concept of "leagues" flags what scholars call "status hierarchies."[11] Groups of people—because of their attractiveness, social position, family wealth, and their race—are "above" or "below" others. American movies often play with this idea—the surprising moment when the captain of the football team chooses to go to the end-of-year dance not with the head cheerleader, but instead the "new girl" who people didn't think was in his "league." The implication is that we don't just date (or hook up) with someone because we want to—we choose that person because we are supposed to. Recall Cheong, whose girlfriend was chosen for him by his older fraternity brother, as part of the rush process. His brother wasn't hazing him—he was helping him. Or remember Murray and the "Facebook cuties"—that was a moment of making a concrete plan to carry over his high status in high school (he was surrounded by those friends), reproduced through his assurance that he'd succeed in working his way through the list (which, as it turns out, he largely did). Beyond what we individually want, the social patterning of what's desirable weighs heavily upon us.[12]

Understanding sexuality, then, requires putting individual desires in dialogue with what's socially desirable. That means that others—particularly those who are relevant to us—loom large in our intimate lives. Sexual projects are, to no small degree, status projects. Groups have an interest in ensuring that members maintain standards.[13] Acts that are socially undesirable can impact the status of all the group members. Norman was emphatic that his unfortunate hookup was not assault. What he regretted was both that the woman, like "three-day-old pizza," didn't "check the boxes" for him, and that his friends roasted him for having been with her. The power of the group can even curdle pleasure; in the case of Pratish's library hand job—which he both enjoyed physically and thought was a good story to tell socially—the experience lost all luster when he told his friends, because the girl was not their type.

The fact that groups organize sexual opportunities for their members isn't good or bad; it just is. There's certainly been some recognition of how peer groups form sexual assault opportunity structures—that is after all what the vast literature on campus Greek life and sexual assault is about: how organized groups of men in institutional settings create conditions that make assaults more likely to happen.[14] But what has received less attention is that peer groups of all kinds—both peer networks and formal student organizations—play a more general role in producing and interpreting campus sexual assault. Groups construct the contexts for meeting sexual partners: they produce situations (such as parties), use space (for example, by arranging an event on or off campus), and organize people (group members and those they should meet). So groups, as well as individuals, have sexual projects tied to group solidarity and prestige. Groups, like individuals, use sex to jockey for status.

Joaquín was a senior at what most students identified as the "it" fraternity (even if they noted this begrudgingly or contemptuously). Handsome, captain of the golf team, and dedicated to his schoolwork, he had lined up an enviable future in a financial firm. He was popular and respected by his peers. We sat with him on a massive, overstuffed dark couch on the first floor of his fraternity house. Chairs were strewn about the old brownstone, which had few remaining interior architectural details. Wafting up from the basement was the yeasty smell of cheap beer. When he showed us around the basement, the floor was disconcertingly sticky. From the upper levels, we caught an occasional whiff of a locker-room odor, a mixture of sweat and spray deodorant. Joaquín could see our reactions to the place and was slightly embarrassed, but this was also his home on campus, where he could be himself among his "brothers." And despite the smells and stickiness, we could see why Joaquín loved his house. It was his. Pictures of brothers adorned the walls. As we sat there, men walked in and out. Some were a bit shocked and worried to see their sociology professor sitting there. But it was noon on a Tuesday. No one was up to anything terribly interesting, much less illegal or embarrassing. As they talked with one another, the casual way in which they dropped their stuff in the common area conveyed something powerful: this was home; they could leave their bags packed with laptops and school notes out in the open. This wouldn't happen just anywhere on campus.

We asked Joaquín about what seemed to define these houses. His answer wasn't quite what we were imagining. He knew what we were looking for—descriptions of raucous "keggers" and drunken escapades. Sure, those happened (although not with kegs, as they'd been banned on campus), and our research team had spent a fair amount of time in fraternity basements observing these kinds of parties. They'd even been in this particular basement before, as well as in suites on East Campus with sweaty bodies jammed in so close that the dancing was more like a single organism moving about than individuals swaying to the music. For the most part, what our team saw at these parties was uninteresting, because they were almost exactly what we expected. Young people had been drinking. Their party antics seemed like reenactments of scenes from movies. They were having the "college experience" many students wanted, and though the experience seemed "wild," the script seemed to have been written long ago.

It was the mixers rather than these drunken basement affairs that Joaquín felt defined his fraternity—smaller, more intimate gatherings with a select group of women, and no outside men invited. Joaquín described the care with which the brothers prepared for the event. They scrubbed the place from top to bottom. They bought wine instead of cheap light beer, and splurged on ice. They didn't pregame, and no one did shots at the party. The aim wasn't to have a drunken good time, it was to meet someone: that in itself was a different kind of good time. The most important part of this event was making sure that the "right" women came. The brothers invited women from a similarly high-status sorority—there were two they typically paired with. The men and women put on carefully chosen outfits, nothing too formal but nothing too casual either. The music was "chill," and they stood around, drank a bit, and talked. Men and women might exchange phone numbers, but no couples walked upstairs together to hook up. At Columbia there are more women in sororities than men in fraternities. In this particular fraternity all the men were straight—something a bit unusual, as a lot of fraternities had openly gay members.[15] At their mixers fraternity men, like all heterosexual men, had more options for potential partners. This is in part because of a sex ratio where 60% of the campus are women; sororities, as a consequence, had more members than fraternities. This imbalance gave men power.[16] Exiting a relationship is easier if you're likely to have many more options. But there's more to this power than just numbers. As men aged and acquired status, more women were "available" to them. Senior men could date, or hook up with, a freshman as easily as they could a senior. But for women, the accrual of status had the opposite effect. Few senior women ever hooked up with a freshman. For men, status often yields more power, but for women, as their status grows, their sexual options can dwindle.

Participants valued these fraternity-sorority mixers because they offered the "right" kinds of partners. The groups prepared and showed up in full force to facilitate connections. This conveyed a lot to both the men and the women. Each person was deemed appropriate as a future partner by virtue of association with the group. Each was, in part, protected by that group. And both groups were protective of their relationships to one another. Joaquín thought of these events fondly because two and a half years ago he'd met his girlfriend at one of them. They picked each other, no doubt, but within the clearly circumscribed contours of what had been arranged. Their organizations created a context where consent is not absolutely predetermined but certainly made more likely by defining desirable sexual partners.

Of course, groups like fraternities not only facilitate such happy sexual unions as Joaquín's with his girlfriend, they also facilitate sexual assault—both rape and unwanted touching at parties. To be clear: the

SHIFT survey didn't find significantly higher rates of assault at fraternities, but it did find that fraternity members were more likely to be assaulted than men who were not part of fraternities.[17] The research regarding perpetration by fraternity members is mixed, and there are challenges to research on perpetration, in no small part because sexual assault prevention has made those who perpetrate less likely to talk about it. Both the analysis of SHIFT survey data led by Kate Walsh and our observations and interviews suggest what many other researchers have found: fraternities aren't safe places, but they're not much more dangerous than anywhere else.[18]

"I WAS SO DUMB TO GO THERE IN THE FIRST PLACE."

Freshmen face the twin challenges of finding a place to meet people, and gaining access to alcohol to make it more fun (and less stressful) to do so; this often drives them to fraternities and parties hosted by juniors and seniors, which provide both alcohol and crowds.[19] Spaces controlled by upperclassmen are a major source of alcohol, particularly in the earliest months of school. This is also the time when students are mostly likely to be sexually assaulted. Part of the "problem" with fraternities may well be that they are all-male spaces centered around a culture of excessive drinking. But another part of the problem, as we've noted before, could be the rule that sororities can't serve alcohol, and laws and policies that push curious freshmen, including those inexperienced with alcohol and sex, into these spaces.[20]

Fraternities can serve alcohol in part because of their quasi-independence. But concern over excessive drinking has produced widely varying campus-specific rules. At Columbia, those include "no hard alcohol" and no kegs at parties. As depicted in Chapter 3, university representatives come by the day of parties and confirm that only beer is present in the areas where the party will be held. Fraternities assign a "compliance officer" or "risk officer" to make sure the rules are respected; students are serious about not losing their house, or their charter as members of a national fraternity. This means the hard alcohol is mostly hidden—moved from public spaces to private spaces. Many fraternity men live in their houses, above the party spaces on the first floor and basement. Those who don't live there spend time in their fellow brothers' rooms—retreating from the chaos and noise, or to do lines of cocaine or smoke weed, or just to hang out. The "no hard alcohol" policy has an unintended consequence of moving people—not infrequently women—from public spaces downstairs to private spaces away from others, if they are invited. Such asks are particularly attractive to women who (like most people) don't enjoy warm cheap beer, and who may want to escape the chaos of the party, perhaps to do other drugs, or simply to get a break. The vast majority of the time what happens in these spaces, whether legal or not, is consensual and fun. But not always.

Octavia was thrilled when she got the invitation to hang out Saturday night at one of the most prestigious fraternities on campus. She hadn't previously needed an invite to get in the door, but receiving one conveyed that she'd been noticed. When they host parties, fraternities have one member work the door—often to keep out other men, but also to regulate the kinds of women they want inside. "Oh, I'm cool!" Octavia thought to herself, upon opening her personal invitation to the party. "I'm getting invited to ABK! I'm just a freshman, and I got an invite to ABK! That's so cool."

Octavia couldn't believe her further luck when she was asked to go hang out upstairs. There she was, doing shots with some of the hottest guys on campus. She felt special, chosen. She wasn't some random freshman no one knew. She was with the in-crowd. Everything was fine until it wasn't. As if on cue, all the guys except one got up to leave. They wanted to go back down to the party, they said. The only man still sitting, a senior, told Octavia to stay for one more drink. It was similar to what had happened to Jillian, but Octavia definitely felt it had been planned. She wanted to leave with the group but felt pressured to stay. It would be rude to leave. She might not be invited again, ruining her chances of being able to hang out with the cool guys. She decided to stay for one more drink. The man started kissing her; she didn't really mind but she wasn't really into it. Then he forcefully removed her clothes and raped her.

Octavia never reported what happened. "I was embarrassed because I was so dumb to go there in the first place and not realize that I was only going there to have sex with this guy. . . . I felt so dumb for not knowing why I was invited." She blamed herself. She felt she couldn't reasonably say something against a senior from ABK. They were powerful, respected, the "coolest" on campus.[21] Her story didn't have a chance against them. The brothers who left Octavia alone almost certainly did not know that she would be raped, or they may have found it unimaginable that she would be anything other than thrilled to have sex with one of them. They did, however, facilitate her going up to a senior's room, have some shots, and then depart en masse, turning this social situation into a distinctly more sexual one. It may have been a sexual situation, but for Octavia it wasn't sex; it was rape. The group acted to set up this situation, and then its reputation influenced Octavia's own behavior. They didn't do anything to silence her—possibly because even the guy who raped her might still think of what happened as sex, not rape. But they didn't need to do anything: the power disparity acted for them.

Some frats have reputations for being "rapey"—for being places where you need to be on your guard. The word is an important signpost in students' symbolic universe—and, critically, one that sometimes points to relative social prestige, rather than actual risk of assault. Fraternity members we interviewed expressed extreme worry over this kind of reputation, because even if they're not the one committing rape, the association creates a stigma. As one brother told us,

> In a fraternity you have to be especially careful because it's so easy for anyone to jump to the "fraternity guy rapist" assumption. And

not only do I not want to rape anyone, but if I did it affects everyone I'm associated with!

A reputation for being rapey can be very sticky. A sorority member we
talked to described one of the low-status fraternities on campus: "You
hear weird stuff coming out of there. They're just weird guys. I wouldn't
go there. They guys are all pushy and stuff. I mean, they're always trying
to prey on little freshman girls and stuff."

We followed up on this, looking into the reputation and the reality
of this lower-status fraternity, which we will call PDQ. We spent time
there, and talked to members of the house. The responses were fairly
consistent: passionate denial, and bemoaning the struggles the fraternity had with its image. It seemed not to matter what PDQ did, and no
matter how they responded, they just couldn't shake their reputation.
One brother was so animated about this it was hard to keep up with
his torrent of words—

Someone posted on social media that a woman was raped at our
house. I freaked out. Like, did I join the wrong frat? Who are these
people I'm in with? Did I make the wrong decision? I had made
the drinks and was handing them out that night with my friend!
I looked into it, and talked to all the guys, and no one did that! I
make all the drinks, and I make them kind of weak, just because
I don't want someone to get drunk fast and feel that and think
they got roofied. Our brothers would rather not get laid than to
do that. I mean, I know they're not getting a lot of sex, but they
wouldn't do that.

High-status frats like the one where Octavia was raped tend not to
have reputations for being rapey. One of the ways—at least at Columbia, but also increasingly elsewhere—that a male-dominated or all-
male organization gets to be "high-status" is to brand itself as feminist,
or at least gender-egalitarian.[22] Many fraternities have gay members,

demonstrating their opposition to homophobia and heteronormativity.[23] However, we learned of instances of assault in both the high- and low-status frats. Being high-status makes a fraternity's members sexually desirable—or at least socially desirable for sex. This can make it a far greater challenge to report or talk about sex as "unwanted." Sometimes it is even hard for someone who is assaulted to perceive the sex as unwanted—they are weighing the unpleasantness of the experience against the lure of recounting having been with a prized social object. High status provides men with some protection against allegations of sexual assault, because it's harder for others to imagine that sex with such men could be unwanted. This leads to a disturbing conclusion: the reputation of the group may help protect its members from accountability.

Again and again, we saw how explicit and conscientious group members were toward protecting or improving their status. We heard high-status groups call lower-status groups "rapey," "pushy," "sexist," or "creeps," to publicly affirm that they were none of those things. Groups use their reputations to preserve their status and to dominate other groups lower in the hierarchy. We saw this dynamic very markedly with fraternities and athletic teams, and much less so with identity-based groups, organized religious life, or other kinds of extracurriculars. It's possible that high-status people and groups are actually less likely to commit assault—that is, that their status reflects actual behavior that is more socially desirable, and that conversely the rape stigma attached to lower-status groups reflects actual behavior, not relative social prestige. It also could be the case that being high-status means that when people commit assault, they're less likely to be reported, and if a reported is made, the accuser is less likely to be believed. Or, as we believe, a combination of all of those things is likely true. In Octavia's case, her rapist was aided by his group affiliation in a number of ways, from his brothers getting up to leave so he could be alone with Octavia, to his group's power and desirability, which contributed to Octavia's self-blame for and silence about what happened.

"I JUST WORRY THAT HANGING OUT WITH HIM SENDS SOME SORT OF SIGNAL."

Jed's pressuring of Rebecca to interpret her experience with their mutual friends was an extreme instance of the interpretive work that students do for one another. For the most part, we saw young people deeply engaged in caring for one another—and both our ethnographic work and SHIFT's survey showed that most students felt supported by their friends.[24] The interpretive work done by peers often had the friend in mind, but friends also experienced important secondary pressures. Peer groups and formal organizations work to manage their reputation. Organizations certainly did not always protect their members; some, in fact, expelled those whose behaviors were unacceptable. But motivated both by a commitment to their organization and by self-interest (because the reputation of the organization impacts its members), the general push we saw both in networks of peers and in formal student organizations was to avoid labeling sex as nonconsensual. We didn't interview Jed, and so we can't know what his motive was. But from the way that students talk about managing these situations, there may be reasons behind the frequent "downgrading"—labeling incidents as gross, sketchy, or even rapey rather than actually calling them assault— that are not entirely nefarious. Often it seemed like the primary motivation was to maintain harmony within a friendship community. The result is disturbing, prioritizing social harmony over recognizing and remediating harm. Peers and organizations shape consent not just by structuring sexual opportunities—they also do it through interpretive work and social pressure.[25]

In Chapter 6 we recounted the time Tim was cheered on by his peers when he went back to his room to grab a condom, only to have the woman he was with text "Help" when he returned to her. But let's also recall what happened next: Tim went back to his group, bringing the women he knew from high school to convince this woman she didn't need help, that she had it all wrong. These women, at least as Tim related, saw that she was hysterically laughing, happy to see them, and clearly completely out of her head. They served as witnesses. Nothing bad had happened. That Tim could mobilize pre-college connections to get him out of a complicated situation is just one of the myriad ways in which privilege protects.[26]

We can read this witnessing as malicious, and it may well have been. But in protecting their friends, people are also protecting the idea that their community is a good one; that the people with whom they're close are morally upstanding; that the world they've built around themselves and by which they've defined themselves is to be admired, or maybe even envied. Except for Jed's friends (and we only have second-hand knowledge of his behavior), we didn't see any examples of people explicitly trying to "protect rapists." Instead, we saw and heard about students working to maintain the view of their group as an upstanding, valuable, moral community, and of themselves and those around them as good people. Sometimes the consequence was—inadvertent in our view— protecting people who had committed assault.[27]

Bystander programs that train students to spot and interrupt unwanted sexual advances and seek to promote campus conversations about respectful relationships are one of the few interventions with a demonstrable impact on reducing campus sexual assault.[28] In our analysis of how students act as bystanders, led by Alexander Wamboldt, we saw bystander interventions have had unintended impacts, and that students act as bystanders in ways that sometimes protect the status of group members.[29] Students, almost exclusively men, intervened for reasons of liability, reputation, and moral commitments.

The legal boundaries between Greek life and campus life are disputed, but the quasi-independence of fraternities enables underage members of the university to access alcohol and have a "college experience." Young men in fraternities that we spoke to recognize this, and we understood why they perceived this situation as an offloading of liability. National structures of Greek life explicitly instruct young men to intervene in problem behavior, in part because it's wrong, and in part because brothers could be held personally liable for things that happen in their house. As one fraternity president told us, "We have to be super careful because we have really no insurance if anything happens. So we always have to be very meticulous about how things happen." Many fraternities have a "risk management officer" whose job it is to make sure that things like death from drinking or assault don't happen at their events. No insurance, after all, will protect students from that.

Whether or not they were in fraternities, the men we talked to worried about being associated with "rapey" people. Students routinely exchange information with one another about people or places to avoid. After hearing one of these conversations, a man expressed some degree of pity, but not so much that he wanted to be around the man who used to be his friend. "He's a fucking pariah. As shitty as it sounds, I don't fucking want to be seen sitting with him at the dining hall because then you're like friends with the rapist, you know? It could fuck up your life too!" Readers might think to themselves, "Good! If we just severely punish these people and make them total social pariahs, then people will stop!" But criminologists have shown that extreme punishments are one of the least effective tools at our disposal to deter behavior.[30]

In addition to being motivated by concerns about liability and reputation, most men we spoke to had moral commitments to being good people.[31] Removing potential "sexual offenders" from a group is both a performance of one's moral nature and an expression of a genuine commitment to sexual violence prevention. The president of a student group proudly told us how he intervened when, at one of their events, a man kept asking a woman out, not taking "no" for an answer, not understanding her avoidance as a polite way to ask him to move on. But he also noted that he needed to be ever vigilant. At that same event, a woman had been groped. His pride shifted to despair. "The fact that it can happen under the radar like that is scary. I mean I saw this one thing and I was able to stop it! But I couldn't stop that other really bad thing. It's just sad."

Peer networks and formal student organizations provide sexual assault prevention opportunities, but the same social pressures regarding reputation, and the same genuine intentions to care for one another, also create sexual opportunities, sexual assault opportunities, and missed opportunities for intervention. Sometimes students interpret the bystander approach to mean that they should keep an eye out for "predators," when in fact they would be better served by looking at their friends. They don't always know how to intervene. We saw students talk to friends and peers when they behaved badly. But more frequently we saw people just remove the problem person, using physical force if necessary. One strategy when a peer was seen as being too sexually aggressive was to get the person high so that they would, in the words of one man, "fall asleep or get chill and calm down, or . . . just get the spins and start puking." Presumably after puking, they'd be less likely to sexually assault someone.

Though "bystander intervention" is presented to students in trainings wherein stopping sexual assault is regarded as everyone's job, we saw it almost exclusively undertaken by men who acted virtuously, in their view, by protecting women from other men's sexual aggression. There's an obvious heteronormative limitation to this, and feminists have reasonably critiqued a kind of neo-Victorian erasure of women's sexual agency, framing women as objects in need of protection.[32] When men noticed that women were excessively drunk, we observed their tendency to intervene by removing these women from the space where they were in control. This could have been a way of "helping," but it also was a way to avoid the consequences if a woman was later assaulted or had some other terrible experience because of her drunkenness. Such intervention could take the form of walking a woman home, bringing her to a private room where she'd be "safe" from potentially predatory men, or finding her friends and telling them to "get her out of here." Yet as we've seen, getting walked home or being brought to a private space doesn't necessarily protect women from being assaulted.

As for men who were being "creepy," the intervention depended largely on whether or not those men were a part of the group or organization. Men worked hard not to embarrass a friend publicly or raise broader awareness of the problem behavior. During one of our observations, we saw a group of men notice that one of their friends was getting a little too pushy with a woman sitting next to him at the bar. His friend employed a distraction strategy. He put his arm around the offending group member and said to him, "Hey man, we need another person for this game of beer pong," nodding at the woman as he walked his compatriot away. The "smoke him up" strategy was also fairly common, particularly at parties held on campus. And sometimes men just tried to defuse the situation by edging into the conversation and pivoting it in a different direction. One man in a prestigious fraternity, who rather immodestly told us he was "very renowned for being the kind of noble shit kind of guy," described the subtler, educational method used for his brothers. "There's guys . . . that come off too strong to some girls in our fraternity just because they're younger kids that don't exactly know how to talk to girls. And we try to help them. Be like, 'You need to chill a little bit more.'" His "noble shit" was very different for guys who are not fraternity members; his goal was then to get the offender off the property as soon as possible. Men who used this method would get together and decide to "kick the guy out." If he didn't go, they weren't against using force. The strategy was pretty direct, "Grab the guy in a headlock and remove him!"

These various strategies have unintended, and sometimes adverse, individual and social consequences. One woman we spent a lot of time with talked about avoiding a "known rapey man" who lived on her hall, even though she thought he was, "like, okay." When we asked her how he was a "known rapey guy" she told us that they'd lived in the same dorm freshman year and he'd been dramatically asked to leave a party where he was "kinda an uninvited guest" because of how he was acting. The reputation stuck, and she wasn't about to do anything to make it less sticky. "I just worry that hanging out with him sends some sort of signal. Like if I hang out with him [it] says to other people that he's trustworthy." We opened this chapter talking about how group dynamics were intimately tied to status hierarchies. Grabbing a guy in a head-lock and throwing him out of the party serves multiple purposes. It potentially interrupts bad behavior. It protects a group's reputation. It helps men establish themselves as "noble shit" guys, while imposing a difficult-to-shake polluted identity on the man kicked out. This poten-tially facilitates the "noble shit" men's access to sexual partners by defin-ing them, in contrast, as good and not rapey.

Of course, it could be that some men have fewer social connections because of their behavior, that the campus whisper network is con-veying some accurate information. But we didn't find a lot of evidence for this. We heard about assaults that occurred immediately after the victim and the person who assaulted them had been in a public space where others were around; these friends could have acted as bystanders but did not because they assumed mutual sexual desire. Students have gotten the message that they should intervene to stop nonconsensual sexual encounters, but often those encounters begin with some degree of interest. And more importantly, students' strongest impulses are typ-ically to try to be "wingmen" or "matchmakers." They're often drinking, in spaces where verbal communication is difficult—music is blaring, in a tiny space crammed with people.

Gendered sexual scripts, and the consequent idea that only women need protection, leave men at risk. Students who saw drunk men being groped and plied with alcohol mostly shrugged it off, even laughed about it later. Men's inability to consent wasn't really a question; the sexual script that men always want sex made it hard to think through what an intervention would look like. Tim told us how his friends saw a woman plying him with drinks, and simply figured he was on the path to getting lucky. They didn't want to get in the way.

Rebecca was raped by the men who walked her to her room. Her story isn't unique. Samantha told us about a friend who "helped" her one night when she was too drunk to get home. Her narrative is frag-mented, perhaps like her memory. But also it suggests a struggle to make sense of it.

I think he was a really good guy. He saw that I was sick and said to me, "Let's get you home." And so I—I got home. I was fine. I was just—I didn't really remember if anything happened. In retrospect I don't think that we had sex. But I was worried and that week I got mono and my period stopped so I was super worried that we'd had sex. I took a pregnancy test. But no, I was just like really sick. But yeah, no, that was really scary.

She's still not sure what happened, much less how to think about. They remain friends. We are not writing in opposition to bystander interventions; rather, the examples of how students deploy these ideas underlines the need for programming that does more to help them think critically about status and power on their own campus. Moreover, there is a distinction between reactive and proactive approaches to bystander interventions; *reactive* ones train students to interrupt assaultive interactions as they are in process, while *proactive* approaches seek to promote broader critical conversations about respectful interactions.[33] Given the fundamental role of formal and informal student groups in shaping campus sex, and the earnest desire of many groups to both reputationally and actually be spaces that discourage assaults, there is enormous potential in the proactive approach. It's hard to know what to say about instances in which a person offers to get someone very safely home, only to then assault them, other than to remember that there is a point at which social analysis cannot explain individual bad behavior.

We have noted how designating some men as rapey has become a way for groups to claim a dominant social position, and to dominate other groups of men. Men in particular work to minimize their friends' sexual aggression and highlight the aggression of other, unaffiliated men. This is, to no small degree, because of the increased stigma associated with sexual aggression. Men with control over space and powerful allies can use this stigma to augment their position by ostracizing others—and in so doing, to inoculate themselves, to a degree, from assault accusations. The public shaming of men who are socially vulnerable and the protection of men who are institutionally established augments the power of the already powerful. It also produces a distorted sense of the risks within the campus landscape.[34]

The power of the group can operate even for assaults that take place without any witnesses. Jaylene, who considered herself artsy, was drawn to Columbia in part for its New York location. Her wealthy family didn't blink at shelling out large sums of money for a purely social extracurricular activity, and so she joined the Epicurean Society, which frequented restaurants around the city and gave her a chance to meet other students (all of whom were similarly wealthy). Spring semester freshman year she started "crushing hard" on one of the upperclassmen running the program. She had to say something. She trudged through the snow to his room. But then, overwhelmed, she abruptly left to go to a party, trying to "destress." Having composed herself, she returned to his room and declared her feelings. He responded by reaching for her hand, then asking her to kiss him "to see if there's a spark." Jaylene's only intention had been to have a conversation about her feelings—to see if he was also "catching feelings" for her—but she consented to the kiss. After all, she liked him. They moved to the bed and kept kissing, but things started "escalating sexually." Because they were friends, they had talked about sex before, and so she was surprised when he asked her to give him a blow job. Jaylene had specifically told him in the past that it was something that she would never do because she did not feel comfortable doing it. She kept trying to have the conversation, but he kept kissing her and asking for a blow job. Eventually he wore her down. Looking back, she felt he had manipulated her. They talked about it later and he admitted that he took advantage of her. No one was with them there in his single room; but the group was still present. She ended up doing things she didn't want to in part because she feared losing a connection to a group that had become part of her identity.

Peer groups are a fundamental element of the social production of campus sexual assault, but in ways that go far beyond what Octavia experienced that night her freshman year. These group-level influences cannot be eliminated, but can perhaps be harnessed, by understanding how groups create risks for their members and for others, by attending to how much (or how little) control groups exercise over their members, and by thinking about how selection processes may amplify rather than challenge the abusive tendencies of some members. Groups themselves aren't the problem; but particular ways of forming and running groups can be a big problem. Whatever the type of student group—Hillel, the Black Students Organization, Columbia Queer Alliance, one of the many South Asian cultural groups, or any of the hundreds of identity and activity groups that constitute the social landscape—associational life is a central part of people's college projects. These are where students feel at home. They are their family. Joaquín's sense of security among his fraternity brothers was as touching to us as it was important to him. There is enormous potential in organizing group-level conversations that encourage students to clarify their sexual projects; to claim their own sexual citizenship and recognize that of others, including students who are not members of their group; and to understand how the dimensions of campus sexual geography under student control produce conditions of vulnerability. This potential exists because these groups, as it turns out, don't only create the conditions in which assaults occur; they also play a crucial role in the aftermath.

8

THE AFTERMATH

"I DIDN'T WANT TO BE 'THAT GIRL.'"

The Poetry Society was Maureen's home on campus. Early in her freshman year she'd struggled to find her place, but in November she attended her first meeting and knew she had finally met her people. The group met weekly, and once a month they went out for drinks at a neighborhood bar after the meeting. It was typically a relaxed affair. Halfway into her sophomore year Maureen left the bar with a senior from the society. They'd been flirting with each other for a while. Neither was drunk. She was excited to go back to his room and make out. She wanted a little human contact, not to have sex. He raped her. Maureen continued to attend their weekly meetings, including the social hour at the bar where she'd connected with the man who raped her. She saw him at these events. She never told anyone what had happened.

Davis was out one night for some heavy drinking with the fencing team. A woman he'd repeatedly told he wasn't interested kept buying him shots and eventually took him home to have sex. When he told his friends the next morning they laughed, saying that it had been obvious that she was trying to get him drunk so he'd go home with her. Several shared that they'd had the same experience with her; it was almost a rite of passage, and served as the basis for some kind of solidarity. Davis felt a little "weird" about it, but joined in their laughter.

Chase was raped by a fellow member of a tight-knit queer community. Chase tried to "work within a social justice framework," gathering together peers to confront the person who raped them. Things went awry, and a community that had been a home on campus for so many quickly turned into one where people felt they had to pick sides.

Cindy, by her own report, had been drinking "way too much," when she accompanied a man she knew casually back to his apartment, where he raped her. She reported her experience to police, as she felt she was supposed to. She later characterized this as "one of the worst decisions" of her life, referring not to what led up to the assault but instead to involving the police.

Adam never talked to his boyfriend about how pushy and forceful he was about sex, even after his boyfriend came home one evening after a long night of drinking and "basically raped" him. He was otherwise happy in the relationship and didn't want to get his boyfriend into trouble.

Stephanie was depressed and felt alone. Her relationship seemed to be the only thing holding her life together. She had no sexual drive, and so the frequency of their sexual relations had dwindled. Her partner threated to break up with her, saying to her, "Why are we in a relationship if we're never going to have sex?" Stephanie lay there, enduring sex she didn't want, to keep the relationship alive. Her depression worsened as the relationship crumbled.

The story of Karen's rape in the park by her ex-boyfriend appears in Chapter 1. She told us the story in part because she knew there was something wrong about what had happened. She didn't want sex. She even exclaimed "no" several times. But she also found it physically pleasurable. She used that pleasure, and the fact that she still cared about her ex, to minimize what had happened. She laughed when she described the experience to us. In our estimation, she seemed to be dealing with what happened and did not seem to be hugely affected by it.

After assaulting her friend, Diana, who we introduced in Chapters 4 and 6, stopped having sex altogether. Her previously very active sex life was gone; now she identifies as asexual.

We heard stories about other students who, after being assaulted, were so traumatized that they ended up dropping out of school. The ambition they'd organized so much of their life around—going to college—was no longer bearable. So our narrative may not fully capture the experiences of those whose trauma was the most severe.[1]

In the first chapter we outlined just how varied the experiences of assault are. This chapter bookends those stories of assault by emphasizing just how varied the aftermath is.[2] What we consider as the aftermath of assault includes the decisions whether or not to label an event as an assault, to tell someone, and to make a formal report; and the community-level experiences of carrying each other's burdens and navigating a sexual landscape that is filled with survivors of assault. Across dozens of stories of trauma, resilience, and recovery, there were some striking social regularities.

How could Maureen possibly go back to the Poetry Society, knowing she would likely continue to encounter the man who raped her? Why did people remain in relationships defined, in no small part, by intimate partner (sexual) violence? How could people have sex with a hookup who'd previously assaulted them? If assaults are so traumatic, why does it take some people so long to talk to others about them, and why do some never talk about them at all? For those of us who haven't experienced assault—and even some of us who have—this doesn't seem to make any sense. The gap between the imagined aftermath of sexual assault and the actual experience leads some to doubt those who tell their stories. The concept of a "social risk"—which was introduced in the third chapter to explain the cultural rationales and social goals that shape drunk sex—helps us understand these actions. It foregrounds what is at stake in labeling an experience "assault," telling one's friends, and reporting the experience to school or public authorities.[3]

Part of managing the aftermath of an assault is an individual choice or deliberation. But social risks can also be relational or institutional. By this we mean how peers and organizations influence how the person who was assaulted thinks and feels. Think of Rebecca, from the previous chapter, who was raped by two friends who had offered to walk her home when she was very drunk. Her other friend intervened while she was waiting in the hospital to get a rape kit exam. He insisted that her interpretation of what happened was "all wrong." Understanding the aftermath of an assault means not just understanding "what happened"; it requires understanding how experiences are made meaningful. Friends work together to process and label experiences that are difficult to understand. An individual's feelings for the person who assaulted them, as well as their understanding of themselves as someone who may have sought out a sexual encounter with that person, also shape the aftermath.[4] The conceptual resources they have—what they have been taught about sex and sexual assault—matter, as does what they have learned about what happens when someone makes a formal report to the school or the police.[5] Those who don't believe that the adjudication process will produce a just outcome are unlikely to pursue it. People who have been assaulted weigh the costs and benefits of reporting, and are particularly cognizant of the time and effort reporting their experiences will entail. They ask if it is worth the effort, given what they see as the likely outcome: that they will not get the recognition or resolution they seek. In the aftermath of an assault, people experience feeling unheard as a kind of revictimization, and avoiding that is one reason that many decide not to proceed with reporting.

In recounting her story of rape, and explaining why she refused to think about what happened that way, Felicity told us, "I didn't want to be 'that girl.'" "That girl," for her, is the girl who was raped. Because then maybe other people wouldn't want to date her, or have sex with her, or they'd just avoid her. "That girl" is the girl who was out of control at a party and because of it got into a bad situation. "That girl" is the girl who wasn't sexually in control of her life. "That girl" is the girl who "ruined" her friend's life. "That girl" is the girl who wasn't the assured, capable-of-anything, roll-with-the-punches modern woman all women should be, leaning in to her twenty-first-century sexual freedom and deftly managing all the risks that entails. "That girl" doesn't have a name, and is only known because she was raped, or because she said she was.[6]

After being assaulted, not thinking about the experience as assault can feel protective. It allows them to help maintain their current understanding of themselves and their identity. It gives them more options— imagined or real—for the future. They can even think about themselves in moral terms. They turned the other cheek. They are capable of forgiveness and compassion. They are not defined by that scary, disempowering word: "victim." Being a "survivor" can be an empowering response for those who choose it, a way to draw on one's suffering to reduce stigma and to push for social change. But we found that many students did not want to be so publicly defined. And when it was their friend or partner who raped them, their own identity wasn't the only thing at stake. Naming an encounter an "assault," or worse, a "rape," has consequences for the other person, and potentially also for the shared friend group or student activity. Is it really fair to label that friend a "rapist," especially if you believe the label will "ruin their life"? The landscape that students who have been assaulted face is filled with social risks—for their friendships, for the organizations they call "home," for their future, and even for the person who assaulted them.

"I JUST WANT TO FEEL LIKE IT DIDN'T AFFECT ME."

In one of our very first interviews we talked to a freshman, Kate, who had been raped in the opening weeks of school. When we asked her about it, she rejected the label of assault. Yes, the sex had been "nonconsensual" (in her own words). No, she didn't want it. Yes, she had said to her partner she did not want to have sex. But she was emphatic: it was not "assault." She could see that we were having a hard time processing this. And so she explained, "'Unwanted sex' is, like, the scariest thing." Kate was a commanding young woman. She seemed fully possessed of herself. Some of this, no doubt, was a performance, but a convincing one. She wanted to view herself as ever-capable of realizing her desires. She was unwilling to admit to herself or to anyone else that she was subject to the power and the will of another. Kate rejected the label assault. "I didn't want to give him the power to be able to say that he did that to me. I just want to feel like it didn't affect me."

Over time, grounded in our broader commitment to understanding the socially shaped reasons that students act in ways that might seem initially puzzling, we came to understand that Kate did not lack awareness about what constitutes sexual assault. Her response was, instead, a partial consequence of the success in raising awareness about campus sexual assault as a public problem. Consciousness-raising by activists and scholars has done enormous good, transforming the private experience of some students into a public problem about which there is widespread concern.[7] But to lift the profile of an issue that was ignored for so long, activists have had to raise their voices louder and louder. One strategy has been to frame assault as "the worst thing ever." For some students who are assaulted, it is—leading to depression, isolation, and even suicide. But others do not experience it that way. And still others may have those experiences, but don't want to, and so they will themselves to think about what happened as anything but assault.

On and off campus, people who are assaulted are questioned, vilified, or ostracized.[8] Some don't see themselves captured by the typical assumptions of what a victim looks like, because they're men, or because they weren't drunk, or because the person who assaulted them is their partner, not a predator. Some blame themselves for being in a situation because they wanted sex, feeling that such wanting necessarily comes with risks and harms. Being a "survivor" can transform the experience of being a victim of assault into a more positive social identity, but one that is in tension with other prospective identities, thereby making some sexual and life projects more or less possible.

Elsie went to a bar, got very drunk, and went back to the room of a friend she had previously hooked up with. When she woke up, her pants were on backwards. What could have happened? Who took her pants off and put them back on? Something felt so off about it. Elsie wondered if her friend had a part in this. But why? What was he covering up? She never spoke to him about it, or to anyone else. Talking to us was the first time she'd told her story. She had been too drunk to remember what happened. She didn't know if she consented, or even if they had had sex. As she tried to make sense of it, voicing her experience, her thoughts kept swirling. "It, like, doesn't—I don't think that necessarily means that we had sex but I also don't think. . . . But I also do think that it sucks. I really don't remember. It sucks. . . ." Elsie paused, looking away. And then she came out and said it. "Not, like—only upsetting in that I should do better, you know? I'm upset with myself."

Elsie was typical in thinking that what happened had been partly her fault. Students shared guilt and shame about putting themselves "in that situation"—whether that meant being at a particular kind of party, having too much to drink, being too flirtatious, or not recognizing the "reasonable" or "expected" consequences of their actions. Again and again, in the aftermath students who are assaulted question themselves.[9]

Camden, a Black man from the Midwest, told us about a party he had gone to freshman year. It was fun. He was drunk. And for a while he thought this is what college was all about. Then the woman he was dancing with, a senior, grabbed his crotch. He was shocked and not really sure what to do. He moved away a bit, but then two other women did the same thing, in rapid sequence. He wondered, were they her friends? He didn't stick around to find out. After having his genitals repeatedly grabbed by women, he quickly left the party, overcome by embarrassment. Even two years later his eyes seemed to well up a bit thinking about it. The events met the definition of sexual assault—unwanted and nonconsensual sexual touching—but he did not define them that way. "I would have said no to them if they'd have asked," he recounted. But he also felt like he should have known better. "This is how people interact; this is how people get down" in college.[10] We read a racial element into Camden's story—one he did not raise himself. The bodies of Black students seemed to be touched with alarming frequency, viewed as objects to be played with and commented on.[11] Like Elsie, Camden had not told anyone about what had happened before he talked to us about it. But this kind of silence was not common.

Analysis of the SHIFT survey found that 81% of students who experienced "sexual contact without their consent or agreement," regardless of whether or not they thought of it as assault, talked to their friends about what happened.[12] Jemma went to talk to her friend Chantal soon after she had an "experience" with their mutual friend Derrick. She kept wondering if she was "irrationally upset" about what had happened. Chantal, she hoped, would give her some perspective. Jemma had been drinking—that much she remembers. She doesn't think Derrick was anywhere near as drunk as she was. She doesn't remember exactly how they got back to her room, though she's pretty sure she invited him. She went in and out of consciousness as they had sex. She remembers bits of it. Her next definitive memory was waking up, alone and naked in her bed. A couple of days later she texted Derrick to see if he wanted to go down to Times Square and get same-day tickets for a Broadway show; it was something they'd been talking about doing for a while. She also asked him what had happened that night, telling him she didn't really remember. "He was kind of like, 'Oh, we kind of like hooked up and had sex,' and I was like, 'All right . . . ' I was just kind of upset, I guess, or kinda like, I was like, 'Well, it's kind of a little slimy, I mean, a little bit.'"

Chantal assured Jemma that she had reason to be upset, that she wasn't being irrational. This provided some comfort. Jemma was pretty sure she'd invited Derrick to her room, and had been flirty. But she also was unnerved by the fact that she had been so drunk, and that it never occurred to him to check in with her after she texted him she didn't remember what happened. He never asked, "Are you okay? Should we talk about this?" In the end, Jemma was glad Chantal affirmed her experiences. She ended up going to a Broadway show with Derrick, but things weren't ever the same again. Her entire life felt unsettled. She had trouble concentrating in class and maintaining friendships. She wondered what she'd done wrong. She questioned her capacity to evaluate people, and whether her friends truly respected her. How could Derrick be so cavalier about this? He knew they'd had sex when she was black-out drunk. Thinking back on it, it was so much more than the sex that bothered her. Everything was up in the air. "I felt pretty shitty about life. . . ."

Concerns about social failure and personal shame prevent most people from doing anything more than telling a close friend about what happened. Jemma experienced both of these—doubting her capacity to judge people's true character, and fearing that a person she had thought of as her friend fundamentally did not respect her. Another woman with whom we spoke, who had been assaulted several times, was fearful that making a formal report would put her reputation as a "with it" woman at risk. Reporting, she told us, "involves way too many people. It means a ton of people that I could see on a regular basis would know." She didn't want the potential consequences for the person who raped her on her conscience, much less have to deal with an investigation, where she'd have to counter his narrative, and where her friends, who had been with them before the assault happened, would be called in to testify. They'd have to pick sides. She was mad about what happened, but subscribed to the commonly held belief that if she said something, she'd "ruin his life." She didn't think it was worth it—particularly because she anticipated that their mutual friends would hold her partially responsible; she was a big drinker, after all, and she held herself partially accountable because of it.

Reports of assault require investigations. Investigations require witnesses. Friends are typically called in, as they are often present before the assault. Yet for people who have experienced assault, this is exactly what they do not want: for other people to know. Recall Kara from Chapter 1, who was assaulted her freshman year by a relative stranger as she slept in her bed. Her explanation about why she did not want to make a formal report was focused entirely on her relationship with her roommate. There had been so much tension. Things were starting to work out a little better. She was finally feeling more comfortable coming back to her own room. But it was a fragile truce. If she said something, she figured, her roommate "would just hate me even more and be even more horrible to me." In that moment, avoiding conflict with her roommate was more important than setting in motion a process to discipline the stranger who had taken advantage of her while she was drunk, pushing her head down to give him a blow job.

An analysis of SHIFT survey data found that 75% of victims knew their assailant. But they didn't just know them socially—in the questions about the most significant incident of assault they had experienced, over 30% of students chose to describe something akin to intimate partner violence, raising challenges to labeling and reporting that go beyond preserving a friendship group.[13] Those intimate-partner sexual assaults, as Louisa Gilbert's analysis of SHIFT survey data showed, are more likely to be carried out by force, and less likely to take place under conditions of intoxication.[14] The person assaulted is silenced from within by the acute shame that those in an abusive relationship often feel, but also by external pressure, of an experience that does not conform to predominant narratives about campus sexual assault. Refusing to think about what happened as an assault—even when the student has chosen to describe events in an interview about assault—helps preserve the identity of the person with whom the student has, or has had, a relationship. Recall Karen (Chapter 1), pushed back against a rock and raped in the park by her ex, who then dragged her to the ground as she said "no." She justified his actions by reasoning that he probably thought of her "no" as about the place they were having sex (maybe the rock was uncomfortable?), rather than the sex itself. He was, to her, still a good guy. Some cognitive and emotional work was required to continue to think of him in this way: trying not to think about what happened at all, and when she did recall it, avoiding the label of "rape" for the "sex" to which she had explicitly and repeatedly objected. We see something similar in Adam, a gay man who was extremely critical of what he viewed as a culture of casual sex among gay men. He was so happy to have found a boyfriend. He did not have to be on the market anymore, to deal with men who said they wanted a relationship just to get him into bed, and then ghost him. Sure, his boyfriend was super forceful when he wanted sex. He even came back to Adam's room one night and, in Adam's words, "basically raped" him. Adam was completely sober at the time. He tried to stop it. But he never reported what happened, or even spoke to his boyfriend about it. He didn't want to put his relationship at risk or get his boyfriend in trouble. He told some friends, in vague terms, about what was going on, but he didn't want them to hate his boyfriend.

Both Adam's and Karen's stories highlight another consequence of thinking of assault as something committed by bad people, rather than by people who do bad things. Neither Adam nor Karen could imagine imposing the perpetrator identity on someone they were so close to, maybe even in love with. What would it say, after all, to be the kind of person who fell in love with, or enjoyed a relationship with, a rapist? It could pollute and even destroy fond memories and meaningful shared experiences. It could mean giving up a relationship that was one of the most important parts of your life, and even a core part of your identity. It could mean thinking of yourself as someone with poor judgment.

Sometimes people were emphatic in asserting that they did not experience what happened as traumatic. This was particularly true of men. Tim and Boutrous, introduced in Chapter 1, said as much, but there were also women who said their experience had not harmed them.

Beatrice was playing beer pong with some friends. After a couple of rounds, Alexei invited her back to his place to drink some more and smoke a joint. She ended up vomiting all over his room. She was mortified, but so out of it that she couldn't even help as Alexei did his best to clean up. Beatrice recalled passing out on his bed. Later—

she's not exactly sure when—she was awakened by Alexei's kisses, and his attempts to have sex with her. Still totally out of it, she nonetheless clearly recalls saying "no." But as Alexei persisted in his sexual advances she decided to "get it over with" and help him orgasm. She fell asleep again, and when she woke up early the next morning, she rushed home, filled with embarrassment and confusion. Beatrice wondered: why would he want to have sex with her after she vomited everywhere? Wasn't that just gross? Who would want to kiss after that? She hadn't even brushed her teeth. Alexei tried to follow up with her, asking to hang out again, but Beatrice avoided him. She told us the reason she avoided him was that she was too mortified about having thrown up. "I was almost disgusted myself and it was like the—for me, it was the most awful moment. Like it was the most mortifying moment ever. . . . Like, I was more mortified. Like, my immediate reaction was, oh, my god: I'm so embarrassed. Rather than, oh, my god, he, like, practically sexually assaulted me." Beatrice told her story to one other person: a friend who was adamant that Beatrice had been assaulted, and that she should report what happened. But this interpretation didn't sit well with Beatrice. She firmly told us that she did not feel "traumatized by it." She continues to tell the story to friends, but, admittedly, omits crucial details. "Like, I've told people the story of, like, how I threw up over this guy's room. . . . But I didn't tell anyone else more detail than that . . . just that I threw up over this guy's room and then this guy tries to ask me out later." Beatrice had decided to help Alexei "finish." But his kissing her and trying to have sex with her when she was passed out is a textbook definition of assault. So too is persisting after she'd said "no." Beatrice made a choice not to think of it this way, to reject her friend's label.

We are not mental health professionals and we were not doing clinical research; we can't know if this refusal to label was effectively self-protective or if it inadvertently amplified the harm of the assault.[15] Our focus is the social landscape. The vast majority of the students who shared with us their experiences of being assaulted described suffering, particularly those who had never spoken to anyone about what had happened. We heard of suicidal thoughts, of grades collapsing, of deep depression. We were concerned about the extremely detached way that some of the students told us about what they'd experienced. There were real horror stories. But we nonetheless stop well short of saying that people like Boutros, Tim, Beatrice, Adam, or Karen are living a lie. They are living the truth they want to live.

Students who don't want to call what happened to them "rape" or "sexual assault" are unlikely to seek out services at places designated to help them, like a "rape crisis center." We're not arguing for the need to rename these centers—such names are symbolically important. But for those who don't think of what happened as "rape" and don't feel like they're in "crisis," then finding places of support, staffed by people who have the necessary expertise to help, can be a significant challenge. This can prevent many from getting the help they need.

It also has consequences for prevention. People like Alexei are unlikely to be told that they're committing assaults. Alexei was "lucky" in that Beatrice rejected her friend's interpretation and did not report her experience. Alexei may view the nonconsensual sex he had with her as "normal." He's playing a game of roulette, perhaps without even knowing it: while Beatrice told us she didn't experience her encounter with Alexei as particularly harmful, the stories we heard suggest that plenty of others would have felt differently.

It's helpful to think of this within our ecological framework.[16] We saw students making decisions because of worries of losing their friends, of not identifying the "right" way, of imposing a polluted identity on a current or former loved one, of being seen as "that girl" or "that guy," of being perceived as naïve, inexperienced, or ridiculous. Rather than pressure people to report their experiences, or to embrace the identity of a survivor, we might organize our communities in ways that help those who have experienced an assault to put themselves more firmly in the center of their decision making. There's no right way to experience the aftermath of a sexual assault; a first principle in supporting those who have been assaulted is not to impose even more upon those who have already borne so much.

"DEALING WITH PUBLIC SAFETY? DEALING WITH THE POLICE? THAT WOULD JUST ADD TOO MUCH TO MY PLATE."

Heterosexual men have their own challenges in making sense of what happens to them. Their victimization is often hard for others to see, or imagine. In Chapter 1 we described Tim's drifting in and out of con-sciousness as, in his words, a woman "sat on my face." He was clear in labeling it an assault and adamant that he couldn't talk about it or report it.[17] He'd been very drunk, and his memory was cloudy at best. But what would happen if he reported his experience? "All she has to say is, 'He was drunk, he doesn't remember, he raped me,' right?" Tim felt that the gendered scripts in which men were always assumed to want sex, combined with what he perceived to be a double standard when it came to drunkenness, would work against him. If he admitted to being drunk and having sex, he'd basically be admitting to having commit-ted a rape. Tim had talked about his experience with a counselor and was okay about it now. But it still bothered him that he felt he couldn't report what happened to him because he was a man.

Tim has good reasons to understand his experience this way. But reporting is hard for almost everyone.[18] A question everyone who has been assaulted seems to ask themselves—and, in many cases, their peers—is, in our language, "What kind of projects are available to me after this?" They are concerned about their life projects, their college projects, and their sexual projects. Within a university setting young people have academic and career goals, identity goals, and extracurric-ular interests. They're also part of formal student organizations that are meaningful to them, and whose reputations are at stake. Students talked to us about their already stressful lives, how little time they had, and how they often felt barely able to stay afloat.[19] Adding one more thing was just too much. With their many other commitments and activities, as well as their already taxed emotional capacity, most decided that they'd be better off allocating their energy to other goals, ones that might actually result in something positive and advantageous in the long run, ones where they had more control over the outcome. As one young woman put it decisively, "Dealing with public safety? Dealing with the police? That would just add too much to my plate." For most students, their primary concerns in the aftermath of an assault are not to mount a moral crusade or see it as an opportunity for political activism. Our students were consummate rational actors, submerging these painful and upsetting experiences, along with many others, to optimize their time in college and to avoid the time and emotional costs of having a more public conversation about what had happened to them. The low probability of being able to successfully get what they wanted out of the reporting process was particularly important in students' calculations. Campus inequalities played a big part in this.

Tanique was on "full aid." In her sophomore year she was assaulted by someone she described as a "big man on campus." He was rich. When his parents showed up on campus, they were frequently greeted by senior administrators. And beyond his economic and institutional power, he had social power. He was "hot." People liked him. His big smile, sharp clothes, and air of a confidence that lacked arrogance made him someone everyone wanted to be around. When he expressed sexual interest in her, Tanique was excited, even giddy. But after he sexually assaulted her, she came to see his power as something far different than sexiness. She told us she just couldn't afford the personal investment in presenting her side against him. Why put in the effort? His high social status meant that other students weren't likely to say much against him in an investigation. Even with Columbia's guaranteed provision of an attorney-advisor at no cost to students who cannot afford to hire their own, she imagined the kind of high-powered New York lawyers he could hire—to say nothing of his family's long-running connections to the school. Tanique figured that even if she put everything she had into holding him accountable, he would have more, and the power imbalance would lead to her losing.[20]

The diversification of the student body has made for more representative and learning-rich environments, but also more unequal ones. The rich have gotten far richer, making these inequalities that much more extreme. Students see that. They live with it every day. Some wealthier students, unhappy with their lottery number for picking their dorm room, have their parents buy them an apartment near campus—or even better, in the "cooler" parts of town. If they can afford that, students like Tanique reason, think of everything else they can afford: lawyers to defend them, investigators to dig up dirt. It just wasn't worth it to Tanique. She was beginning to feel at home at Columbia before she was assaulted. But that had all changed. Her grades had slipped and it was hard to motivate herself to try or care. What had been her opportunity to "make it" had become more of a jail sentence; a little more than a year and she'd be out of here. She couldn't wait.

"SOMEONE CAN LITERALLY GET A LAWYER AND ARGUE AGAINST MY EXPERIENCES."

What happened when people actually did have contact with authorities—security, police, or the central office responsible for investigating and evaluating cases? Sadly, the answer was: not much that was good for the person who reported.[21] Our study was conducted on one campus, but we don't believe that Columbia is any worse than any other school. Moreover, the study design was likely to elicit responses from those who were most dissatisfied with their experience, whose "having a story to tell" provided a way to share ire toward the university itself. Those who reported, found justice, and were satisfied with the experience may simply have been too busy, or not seen a need to participate in our study.

Before turning to the experiences of those we did hear from, we think it's important to look at these processes from the perspective of investigating bodies, according them the same respect we've tried to give everyone with whom we spoke. As researchers our job is not to impose our viewpoints onto people, but instead to try to understand and convey their point of view. This doesn't mean we stand outside of judgment, or that we don't make arguments about what we think is happening. But our task is to make sense of why people and organizations do what they do.

Those who are accused have rights. The rates of false accusation are incredibly low; the estimates within the scholarly literature float around one in twenty.[22] But they're not zero. And so investigators ask victims to tell their story. These are not just any investigators. In response to complaints about students being questioned by faculty or deans untrained in the area of sexual assault, Columbia has hired former sex crimes investigators, trained in trauma-informed interviewing. They get the story directly from the person who reported, known as the complainant; then they ask the respondent to tell their story; and then they ask the complainant again, because the stories don't usually line up perfectly. The person who reported their experience of being assaulted is likely to feel like they're being doubted.[23] They have to go over details again and again. They have to deal with new details that they didn't mention the first time around. Third parties are brought in. And then there are more questions. Memories are often hazy.[24] Observers aren't exactly reliable. And the process drags on. Our legal system uses what scholars call an adversarial process. This is not an accident; it was designed so that the parties involved argue before a neutral evaluator, each seeking to advance their own interest. There's little about the process that pushes both parties toward a shared understanding. Instead, people are forced to advocate. It is contentious by design. And when the stakes include getting expelled, or being suspended and then returning to face the label of "rapist" or "predator" as a "fucking social pariah" (or, for the person filing the complaint, being called a "psycho" or a "liar"), the process becomes even more adversarial.

Experiences of trauma can impact memories and narratives.[25] People who have experienced trauma rarely provide consistent accounts of what they have experienced; they often do not recall critical details. We saw this ourselves when we did two or three interviews with students who had experienced multiple sexual assaults. New details emerged. Others dropped out of the account. And ours was a low-stakes context—not a highly stressful one where students have to advocate for their position against someone else's, and are being questioned repeatedly about "what happened" when sometimes their memories are fragmented. It's a nearly unendurable for the students who report having been assaulted.[26] But it's also nearly impossible for investigators. The steps required to help those harmed get what they need—which typically involves affirming their experience—run directly counter to the legal procedures of "blind" justice. And coming to a decision about what happened is no simpler. If one person says, emphatically, "It didn't happen that way," the investigators have to listen. In an adversarial process where the stakes are high, the accused will almost certainly take that position. There's no easy path through an investigation to a conclusion. This is part of why our emphasis is not on adjudication.

One woman put it succinctly: "One, it's ridiculous that it's an investigative process because that means that someone can literally get a lawyer and argue against my experiences. Two, it's traumatic." In the last two chapters we wrote about Rebecca, who was raped by two friends who offered to walk her home. She reported what happened to her to the university office that managed investigations and student discipline, to the Office of Gender Based Misconduct, and to the local police. During the university investigation, her friends were brought in, including Jed, who continued to maintain that she had not been assaulted, even though his only evidence was what the two men had told him. Both of the accused had admitted that they had had sex with Rebecca, but maintained that she was a willing, even eager participant. They denied that she was going in and out of consciousness. It all became too much, and Rebecca wanted it to end. The police did not pursue a full investigation; they determined that there wasn't enough to indict, especially as

Rebecca didn't cooperate with them. Rebecca did not want to be part of Columbia's investigation either, especially as it dragged on far more slowly than she wished, but she was told that the university investigation would continue with or without her. This is understandable, of course, since the university would want to address a situation where a student had reported being raped. But while it was in the interest of the university to continue, Rebecca's attitude was more fatalistic:

> Every step of the way, I've been like, "Oh, I wish I wasn't doing this. But, like, I have to be." There's no alternative 'cause . . . I can't just pretend it didn't happen. That's unrealistic. So, I was like, "I have to deal with it no matter what, and the process really sucks, but, like, it's the only thing that they have. So, I just have to do it."

She did experience some benefits to reporting; both she and one of the accused men were student athletes, and the university coordinated her team's travel so she didn't have to be on the same bus with his team. But the constant questions weighed upon her. She felt like she had to justify her drinking as something other than "out of control." Her friends felt that they had to pick sides, and so the social network that should have been a source of support was collapsing around her. She felt unable to participate fully in student life because her assailants were still on campus. It was relentless. At the time of our interview the outcome of the university investigation had yet to be determined, but Rebecca claimed she didn't care what it was. The whole experience had just made things worse. The aftermath was worse, Rebecca told us, than the rapes. She had lost many of her friends, her sense of herself, her connection to her school, and at times, her will to keep going.

Rebecca was like a lot of students, whose primary complaint was that no one listened to what they wanted. Their voice wasn't heard. The first violation of their autonomy was the assault. And then they went through an adjudication process where their voice was challenged. Even if they wanted it to stop, it didn't. This felt like a second violation.[27]

Other than Rebecca, only one other person we spoke to reported what happened to the police. This should give a sense of how rarely that happens. The police are informed of reported assaults on campus, but victims rarely cooperate. The one woman who did explained why, in her opinion, the police are even worse.[28]

We mentioned Cindy's story in the opening of this chapter. She was raped off campus by someone who didn't attend Columbia. She immediately labeled her experience as a rape, told friends and family, went to the hospital for medical care and a rape kit exam, and filed a police report. She did so without hesitation. "This is what you're supposed to do," she told us. Cindy felt compelled by a duty to community and to the justice that the police could provide. But instead, she found the police not only unhelpful, but coercive. The detectives assigned to her case wanted her to call her assailant in an attempt to get him to incriminate himself as they listened in on the call. She didn't want to; she didn't want any contact, real or pretend, with him. The whole thing felt "gross." She said they put enormous pressure on her. She held firm. She said she told the police officer, " 'No. I'm not doing it.' But the officer was just, like, pressuring me over and over and over again." It was over a year later when she spoke with us. She now understands why so many people don't want to go to the police, or report to anyone. "Now I understand because my first instinct was, 'go to the police; that makes sense.' " But after what she experienced, she described the aftermath in two simple words: "It's horrible."

Students' experiences of assault, like their practices of consent, can't be removed from their broader experiences in life. Assaults can amplify other frequent experiences of not being heard, respected, listened to, or considered. Such experiences are not limited to women, LGBTQ students, students of color, and students from working-class backgrounds, but they are more common among those groups. And reporting, at times, augmented the feeling that no one listened, or that your experiences were not respected. We saw the positive cultural ripple effects of a sustained public conversation about sexual assault on campus, of survivors coming forward, and of clear institutional messages that non-consensual sex is not acceptable. These effects were stronger for women than for men, whose experiences of being assaulted are still often illegible to peers. Still, most students drew upon their peers to collectively mull over and label their experience.[29] Rebecca didn't know how to make sense of what had happened to her. And her friends worked hard to interpret the event for her. For the vast majority of students we spoke to, the aftermath involves collective interpretation, with pressures typically toward keeping the peace rather than raising the alarm.

But there's an important yet under-discussed consequence to all this work that peers do: the community burden of assault. Friends carry each other's burdens, and it is a heavy weight. People work to minimize the effects assaults have on their college and sexual projects. As Claude Mellins's analysis of SHIFT survey data shows, more than one in three women and one in six men on campus were assaulted by senior year; on average, those who are assaulted are assaulted two or three times; and 80% of students who are assaulted tell at least someone; the stories of assault thus touch almost every corner of the university community.[30] We noticed the impact of this in our fieldwork. Students realized that their friends might be too exhausted to be willing or able to help process their experiences and the aftermath. After she was assaulted, Jeannie sought out her best friend to talk. But the conversation quickly turned to her friend's far more violent experience of being raped—which Jeannie hadn't even known about. She was glad her friend could finally tell her about what happened, but it resulted in putting her own story, and her own processing of what happened to her, on hold. "I told one of my female friends and she just, like, had a war story. She had a story that was, like, a more violent story. And she just kind of missed mine because hers was worse. I felt, like, less able to, like, I don't know. . . ."

This sheds new light on the most common reason students had for not reporting what happened to them: it didn't seem important enough. After hearing other students' "war stories," young people may minimize their own experiences. We found that some friend groups had become so emotionally oversaturated that individuals in those groups did not feel comfortable talking about their own experiences anymore. As we concluded our conversation with Jeannie she said, "I stopped talking to my female friends about it because they just, like, all had their own stuff going on. . . . And it didn't seem important to them." When pressed, it wasn't that she thought her friends didn't care about her. Their capacity to care had been maxed out. When Jeannie left the interview, she, like so many subjects, seemed relieved. She had finally had the chance to talk to someone.

"IT'S STILL A STRUGGLE TO GET THROUGH THAT ROUGH PLACE."

Diana, the woman who assaulted her gay best friend, who had that weird experience with the guy sticking a banana in her mouth, and who was summarily handed her clothes after that freshman-year "alpha male shit," stopped having sex after she began to reflect on her actions as a sex partner. But she's incredibly rare—both in her capacity to reflect on her behavior, and in opting to stop having sex entirely. In fact, since those who are assaulted tend to be victimized many times, there's plenty of evidence that they continue to enter into sexual situations.[31] This also means that many people on campus also manage and experience sex with survivors.[32]

In most instances, of course, people don't know that their sexual partner is also a survivor. In Chapter 6, which dealt with the perspectives of people who assault, we met Elliot. After being found responsible for committing assault, he told his potential sexual partners about it. We suspect this is relatively rare—both for those who have been accused and for survivors. We never heard a story of someone saying to a hookup or a date, "Before we do this I need you to know that I was raped last year." It's not like survivors want to relive their trauma before a consensual sexual encounter. But as relationships progress, partners talk about their past experiences. And in small communities, rumors about past experiences spread.

Fran, whose story we recounted in Chapter 1, was raped in ninth grade and was now a few years into sobriety. She spoke about the inti-

macy she developed with her boyfriend: "I had to learn how to have sex
and not, like, disassociate myself completely. That was really hard, but
he was someone I could be honest with, like, 'I have a hard time being
intimate with guys.' And he gets that, and we have been able to work
on it together." But that was inseparable from his being sober too, and
the fact that this was different than any other relationship she'd ever had
with a man. "This was the first time I was ever honest with guys about,
just even what's going on, or even if I had a bad day." Her sponsor in
AA had prodded her: " 'Okay, like, what kind of woman do you wanna
be? Let's, like, grow into that.' " Fran continued, saying, "That in itself
has been really healing, sexually too, 'cause now I enjoy having sex, and
I don't feel pressured to do it." As she told her story, we heard her talk
about finally claiming of her sexual citizenship.

> When I was first in that relationship, I'd always pressure myself, in
> my head, "I need to have sex to please him, otherwise he'll leave
> me," whatever, 'cause I was so used to thinking that. And then
> when I found out, oh, it's okay to be like, "No, I don't wanna have
> sex tonight" and he's totally loving and supportive of that, and
> it's like, wow—I had never done that before . . . so much of my
> life and decisions, before that, it was just like, "oh this is the only
> option" . . . So figuring out that "oh, I can actually do what I wanna
> do, especially in a relationship with a guy," and actually viewing
> my partner as someone equal to me, rather than either me trying
> to control them, or me trying to get something from them . . . like,
> actually viewing them honestly as another human being who—my
> actions affect him. Like, that was totally novel to me, literally I
> thought men did not have feelings, and I could not hurt them.

For Fran, as a survivor of sexual assault and someone healing from substance use disorder, learning to have sex as a choice was part of seeing
herself as self-determining, but also seeing a man as "honestly another
human being."

Jaffe looked like a native Coloradan—slouchy knit beanie, hiking boots, and plaid shirt. Active in citywide social justice movements, his initial response to an invitation to be interviewed was to voice suspicion about what a study funded by the university would want from him, or whether his comments would even be listened to. Once in the interview, though, he was thoughtful and reflective, talking about his interest in learning "why social change happens and how to bring . . . decoloniza- tion." He'd recently become a vegetarian, on principle: "It didn't make sense to me to eat another conscious being without its consent and just based on my own group membership in this species, this is the same sort of mentality that, you know, colonizers used, it's the same type of men- tality that makes violence against other people." His intentionality in his diet reflected a certain consistency in his awareness of the impacts of his actions on the world around him. He wasn't the only student who shared with us what it was like to navigate sex with a survivor, but his story stood out both for the concern he expressed for his girlfriend's physical and emotional experience, as well as for his honesty about his own distress.

He met his girlfriend at one of the bike racks outside of Lerner Hall. The rack was so crowded that their bike pedals had gotten stuck in each other's wheels. Each rushing to get somewhere, they had to stop and shift all the bikes one by one—all of course still locked to the rack— so that they could untangle their two. He'd put his helmet on already when she blurted out, "Can I get your number?" and whipped out her phone. Shortly thereafter, as Jaffe tells it, they "got coffee and watched a movie together and eventually . . . started hooking up, we were in her bed and it was getting intense and so I reached for her belt. And she said, 'No.' And so I stopped. She said she just wasn't ready yet, and so we stopped." He continued:

> To be honest, the first few times weren't great . . . it took her a while to get into it. She had had some very bad sexual experiences before that, so it was hard for her to get into it. . . . She told me she had never orgasmed before having sex with me, it was hard for

her to even think that sex is about her pleasure. . . . That's been a process, but it's been a lot better, it just takes communication, and at times we would have to stop, but if she ever felt uncomfortable about it, I told her she could tell me and then we would stop.

The transcript runs on for several pages as he describes the care with which he makes space for her to articulate what she wants: "It's been like this often, even today, we'll just ask each other, do you want to? Or, like, I want you, do you want me? And then just go from there. Sometimes you just feel it and there's not as much verbal communication. . . . There have been times where we've had to stop, but it's always been, like, we are both open to communicating before, during, and after." Asked for an example of how it actually works, in the moment where they stop, he lays out in greater depth some of what she's managing:

> Like I said, my girlfriend has a lot of—has had a lot of really bad sexual experiences before, and so sometimes she will get flashbacks because she has post-traumatic stress disorder. In those instances, she sometimes becomes very upset during sex. One time, she even started crying. And we'll stop and be like "Hey, what's up? What are you thinking right now? What are you feeling?" And we'll talk about it. This actually happened recently over the break. And I said, "Hey, you know, this really upset me as well. Maybe we should stop for a little bit." But in the end she didn't want to stop. . . . In some ways she feels like she doesn't want her PTSD and her previous experience to get in the way of our relationship. And I want to give her space to work that out. But if she feels like she's ready, then, that's okay with me as well. But yeah, like I said, it's still a struggle to get through that rough place.

For all his intentional self-reflection, our conversations with Jaffe accentuated that people are a bundle of contradictions. When asked if he'd had any sexual interactions that he regretted, he told a story where at the very end he admitted that the sex was not fully consensual. His whole telling of the story was halting, full of turns and corrections. In the end, he was insistent that what mattered is that he did not feel hurt:

> I was just hanging out with some friends. There was this girl who my other friend was into and I—I thought she was cute but I didn't really know her. She messaged me on Facebook once. And we had, like, a very brief conversation. I had seen her around but I'd never really talked to her. And so we're just chilling. We got some wine, and we literally started drinking and we were chilling on my friend's bed and then just all of a sudden she was—her face was on my face and she was just making out with me. And I was like, I should—this is I guess what I want. Like, I would be down for this. It wasn't like—but I didn't even have time to think about, and I didn't want her emotionally, necessarily, because there was no time for that to develop. And it was also just weird because my friends were there and they were like, um, okay?

We asked, "Like, in the same room?" And he answered emphatically, "Yeah, like on the same bed!" And then he continued:

> And then yeah, it was really weird. She just took me down to her room and she got a condom and we did it. And yeah, it was really weird the next day, as you might imagine . . . I just left. She really didn't want me to leave, but I was, like, I don't know what just happened, I needed some time to think about it. And she stole my shirt and she still has it. [*He pauses, and laughs.*] "Yeah, I just left. We didn't really talk about it, and I think she defriended me on Facebook. Like I said, my friends were there, so they knew it had happened. . . . I guess my friend who was in the group was upset about it, but it's whatever.

When asked how he felt about it, his answer was revealing:

Uh, it's fine. It's been a while—I don't—I, I feel fine about it and I don't feel hurt. I hope she doesn't harbor hard feelings about it, but if I felt anything, she brought that on me and I—before I could think about it and I didn't—like that was the only instance I would probably say I felt like I wasn't fully giving my consent while it was happening, but . . . it felt weird, but I don't feel hurt or anything.

His experience encapsulates so much of what we are trying to illustrate. There's such a stark contrast between his attentiveness to the real and ongoing harm that his girlfriend experienced as a result of her own "very bad sexual experiences" and his assessment of his own experience of being relatively unscathed by having been pressed and rushed into sex he did not choose. We see how friends are affected, and how one of his primary concerns in this sexual interaction—both before and after—was the impact it would have on his circle of friends. The notion of men's responsibility for sex is so ingrained that even in describing a situation in which the young woman was clearly the one who propelled the interaction forward, he feels compelled to note that he "hopes she doesn't harbor hard feelings" and that "if anything, she brought that on him"—as if even in being coerced someone still could hold him responsible for what happened.

In the aftermath of an assault, students who are assaulted struggle with their identity. Being a victim, they imagine rightly or wrongly, can close off some doors and make certain futures more difficult. Many want to be heard, to have what happened be recognized, and to get the help they need. But they also want to go on with their "normal" life and try as much as possible to preserve their former self. Their friendships are both more important and more fragile than ever—this is the moment they need the most support, and yet stories of assaults have the potential to fracture friend groups. Social continuation often wins out over social rupture. Sometimes silences emerge because friendship communities are just too overburdened. But maintaining one's life, college, and sexual projects aren't the only concern. How people experience the aftermath of assault is fundamentally tied to how they imagine their reaction and their conceptualization of what happened, will influence their identity.

An analysis of the SHIFT survey data led by Shamus and Aaron Sarvet found that 57% of students who described an assault indicated that it affected their life in some way. respondents reported that being assaulted didn't really affect their lives.[33] We use the word "victim" sparingly, referring more commonly to the "person who was assaulted" to describe what activists call "survivor" in part because "survivor" transforms victimhood into an identity—one that many do not want to embrace. This suggests the utility of moving away from an understanding of assault organized around identity categories such as "survivor" or "perpetrator" and toward categories of experiences.[34] About twenty years ago, HIV researchers and activists began using the phrase "men who have sex with men" instead of the category "gay men."[35] Their reason was simple: many men who have sex with men don't identify as gay, and so won't be reached effectively by talking about the risks of HIV among "gay men" or among men who engage in "gay sex." Similarly, people might not talk about or even think of what happened to them as "assault" or define themselves as "survivors." Instead of pushing them to do so, we need to think about how we can use language and an understanding of their experience that helps them get the assistance they need.

For all victims we spoke with, regardless of how they labeled their experience, there was so much self-blame. They drank too much. They were naïve. They didn't protest or fight back. One widespread and well-meaning impulse upon hearing people blame themselves is to tell them not to. But that is an invalidating response; when people blame themselves, they are giving us valuable information about what they experience as the social failures that lay behind their vulnerabilities. When victims talk about their excessive drinking, that's important to hear because it can reflect challenges with addiction, or it could be related to mental health struggles—to sadness, or depression.[36] Yet in other instances, excessive drinking is about an intense discomfort with sexuality. Such discomfort is socially produced, and thus potentially modifiable. Victims aren't at fault. But the reasons they blame themselves point to critical opportunities to transform the sexual landscape. A major element of that transformation involves addressing the power disparities among students—both those shaped by campus life, and those with much deeper roots.

9

GENDER AND BEYOND

SHE SAID, "NO, DON'T." HE RESPONDED, "IT'S OKAY."

We return to the beginning, with lessons amassed through the previous chapters. Recall Luci, who in the opening weeks of freshman year was raped by a senior in his bedroom. She was a virgin at the time. She'd met Scott, the man who raped her, at a bar. He invited her back to his fraternity to have a bit more to drink, and to experience the fun of a college party. Luci enjoyed making out with Scott in his room—until he began to push things too far. He took her pants off, and started to put his penis inside her. Luci exclaimed, "No, don't." He responded, "It's okay." After it was over, and he discovered that she had likely been a virgin (something she denied to him), he recruited a friend, a senior woman, to walk Luci home. As Luci told it, it was pretty clear that he'd preyed on her, and she'd heard that he's done the same with others.

We cannot make sense of what happened to Luci without thinking about gender inequality—socially organized unequal relations between women and men.[1] But there's a great deal that we miss if we view it through a lens of gender as the sole power disparity. Scott's predatory behavior was amplified by his control over the space, by his capacity to mobilize others to gaslight Luci into thinking of it as consensual, by Luci's newness on campus, and by his access to additional alcohol.

This is a dense set of resources that come together for upperclassmen—usually men, but in some instances women. As survivors frequently do, Luci partly blamed herself, but her self-blame is itself a social product. Understanding how social forces produce situations in which assaults are likely to occur does not mean we shouldn't hold assaulters responsible. Our point is not to let Scott say, "Society made me rape her." After all, we heard a lot of stories that started exactly like this one, but ended differently.

Daria met Rob at a party hosted by seniors in their East Campus suite. They each had several cups of whatever weird punch was on offer; looking back, Daria describes herself as pretty drunk. Rob walked her to her dorm and came upstairs with her. Once they were in her room he put his arms around her, kissing her and unbuttoning her shirt. She kissed him back, but wasn't really into it, so she told him that she just wanted to go to sleep and that he should leave. He asked for her number, concerned because she was so drunk. He texted her the next morning to see how she was feeling, they met for coffee, and as the months wore on, they became friends.

Most students do not to rape each other. Part of the reasons is all the teaching institutions have been doing about consent; that is the moment when things can run off the rails. But consent itself is never the whole story. Some assaults happen through verbal coercion in which one person has in effect extracted verbal consent from the other. A more complex, and complete, accounting of power relations points to how we might remake the rails, rather than focusing just on those moments when people run off them. This requires understanding what (other than moral bankruptcy or an imperfect grasp of the rules of consent) shapes the outcome of that moment.[2] Consider, for example, the difference between Daria being in her own room, asking Rob to leave, and Luci, in Scott's room on the third floor of the fraternity.

Most stories do not feature predatory seniors in fraternity houses. Research on campus sexual assault has largely looked at gendered power by examining heterosexual couples and men's single-sex organizations like fraternities.[3] Power is frequently approached as if located solely at the interpersonal or institutional levels and consisting only of one axis of stratification—gender, read as heterosexual cisgender men's power over heterosexual cisgender women. Even the name used for this problem in policy circles—gender-based violence—emphasizes a singular lens. Without question, the preponderance of campus sexual assaults are committed by men and experienced by women, and it is critical to look at men's exertions of power over women, both interpersonally and institutionally. But even in assaults that fit that narrative, individuals are situated along multiple hierarchies—yes, gender, but also race, socioeconomic status, sexual identity, sexual experience, adjustment to college, access to material resources, and peer networks.[4] Still other forms of power, such as age, control over space, and relative sobriety, are more situational.

Our approach to power and assault must help us understand the elevated vulnerability faced by LGBTQ students and the less numerous instances in which heterosexual men are sexually assaulted by women.[5] Different types of assault are produced by different kinds of power dynamics. A better accounting of power relations in campus sexual assault must go beyond a singular focus on gender in two ways: it must be more intersectional, and it must acknowledge the social fluidity of power—that there are forms of power where, situationally, the same person could be on either side of the equation.[6]

"HE CAME ALL THIS WAY TO SEE ME"

Cindy was assaulted for the first time in the fall of her freshman year. Her perfectly straight hair was pulled back into a classic sorority girl ponytail, and she curled her long legs up onto the chair during the interview as the words poured out. She had been sexually assaulted three separate times, so we arranged for a follow-up interview, to give her a chance to unpack and reflect on those stories. The spring of her freshman year she had been rejected from her top-choice sorority, and was worried that her dream of a particular kind of college experience was slipping from her grasp, so being invited to a party hosted by juniors and seniors was a step toward one of her goals of being a never-say-no kind of person. She and her friends got decked out for the night; Cindy donned a crop top and a spandex skirt, secure in the knowledge that she could look sexy and liberated while still benefiting from the protection of her female peers.

She was raped that night by a junior she met at the party. She didn't stay long, but he got her number and his texts kept coming over the course of the evening, as she and her friends moved to a party on East Campus, out to the bars, and back to her dorm. She wasn't really sure if she was interested, but when she asked a friend if she should go hang out with him, her friend's "Why not?" resonated with her "never say never" aspiration and drowned out her reservations. Still, she was still leaning toward just ignoring him. Her phone had died, which seemed to make the decision for her, since she stopped getting his texts. But when she got back to her dorm, there he was, waiting for her in the lobby. She felt that he "came all this way" and so agreed to go back to his dorm with him, although she did not want to fool around with him.

Once there, her discomfort grew. She plugged in her phone, and tried to derail the situation by asking for a tour of his dorm. He dutifully if impatiently walked her around the kitchen, living areas, ending their short stroll back at his room. She texted a friend to see if the party they'd left was still going on, hoping for a pretext to leave. Then he began to undress her. She protested, not wanting to have sex, and clearly telling him so. She pleaded with him that she was a virgin and a freshman. He asked her if she had a boyfriend. She continued to tell him to stop. He held her down and penetrated her. Much bigger than she was, he used his physical power, but—as with Luci's story—the forms of power at work in this interaction extended far beyond the physical. They were in his single room, that recurring privilege of junior and senior housing, where she was more vulnerable than in her suite at the freshman dorms. The power of the group also figures here: having just been rejected by a sorority, she was that much more primed to go along when her friend told her that yes, she should go hang out with him that night, that she should "enjoy her life." And in the background were the complex demands of "doing gender" correctly as a young woman, which to her meant both being agreeable—she reasoned that she had obligations to him because he walked across campus and was waiting for her (the walk took about five minutes)—and demonstrating an "up for anything," sexually adventurous idealized self.

Without question, some assaults—like Luci's—happen in the context of men's single-sex social organizations, where control over space and control over alcohol are amplified by the prestige of the institution. Recall how Scott asked a female friend of his to walk Luci home—that was for his well-being, not for hers. But other similarities between Luci's assault and Cindy's are instructive: the age differences between them and the men who assaulted them are not that great—just two or three years. But such small differences are socially consequential because of the enormous differences in social resources that students accrue over time. In college as in high school, age becomes a stand-in for social power, access to desirable space, knowledge of the rules, self-confidence, legal access to alcohol, and stronger peer networks.

If it is the goal of ethnography to make the familiar strange, then one point here is to lead our readers to think critically about gendered age differences in sexual partnerships. The pairing of first-year women with upperclassmen represents a situation in which class year arguably brings as many power disparities as gender does.

"I ENDED UP HAVING THIS MARKER OF PROMISCUITY, HAVING THIS MARKER OF BEING A WHORE."

Liliana shook her head, her curls bouncing, as she recounted a relationship that she described as "maybe the most confusing thing for me to even parse out now"—even with two years' distance. When she first mentioned the relationship, she ascribed their frequent and very acrid conflict—what she called their "choking collisions"—to the fact that they came "from very different backgrounds," suggesting that having met him on Tinder "should maybe have been the first warning sign." Complex power disparities, including different levels of sexual experience, operated in the background of this story of relationship violence. Liliana told us of ongoing verbal abuse from her boyfriend, who belonged to a "niche at Columbia that I did not fit in with at all, and knew that I didn't. . . . they're pretty anti-feminist . . . they called me a 'feminazi,' they called me a bitch. These are my boyfriend's best friends."[7] Liliana looked back with the shame so characteristic of people who have been in abusive relationships: "I'm so embarrassed of that period. It just doesn't reflect any of the values that I hold. . . . I stood up for myself, but not to the extent that I should have, necessarily."[8] She explains it in part as being a first-year student without a lot of perspective: "I think it was just me as a woman engineer, not knowing many guys at school, and just feeling sort of like, I guess this is what Columbia men are like—I guess this is what dating is like."[9] When asked why she stayed in the relationship for eight months, she paused—for long enough that we checked to see if she was okay. Then she continued:

> Yeah, I'm trying to think. It's a good question. The best answer I can give, which is extremely personal is that—so I wasn't sexually experienced really before I started dating him. . . . He was the third person I had ever had sex with, and he was—I don't know how sexually experienced he was, but far more than I was. I would say quadruple the experience I had, around.

As she continued to recount the story of their relationship, it became clear that it wasn't just the disparity in their experience. Liliana was very precise in her language:

> He performed oral sex on me and had a cold sore, HSV-1, and transmitted HSV-1 to me genitally, which is obviously every girl's

nightmare, especially a girl who doesn't have sexual experience. That was beyond traumatizing, because I had had no sexual experience, and I think I felt like my sexual opportunities were over. . . .

She paused.

I sound so overdramatic. It devastated and destroyed me. I considered taking a medical leave from school. I was like, "All right, I'm never getting married, I'm never having kids." It was pretty early on, and I knew that the relationship was total shit by that point, total shit. And I was like, "Oh my god, I've ruined my entire life." I felt like my life was over . . . I said, "Okay, I guess I'm gonna be alone for the rest of my life unless I stay with this kid, who I don't like, who doesn't treat me well, whose friends hate me, who all my family and friends think is totally bad" . . . I guess the blunt way to say it is I hadn't had any opportunity to be young, and it's over. I told my mom. Obviously got a gynecologist. Did all the things you would do. Went on medication so that I would never transmit it to anyone else. But I was like, "Oh my god, how did this happen to me?" 'Cause I had only had protected sex. I was never taught, in my entire progressive education, never was I ever taught that you use a dental dam when getting oral sex. I hated myself for it. I felt like, "Okay, you blew it, you blew college." And I felt I couldn't have kids.

We rarely interrupted a student to correct erroneous information. We also strove to present ourselves as nonjudgmental, and avoided interjecting in ways that suggested there were things we wanted to hear or things that were true or false. Our goal was create a space for young people to tell their stories. But with Liliana, we couldn't help ourselves. We interrupted her, saying gently, "None of these things are true."[10] And she shook her head again, "Yeah, I know none of them are true. I think I'm just very critical of myself, and I'd always sort of known I was making a mistake. So then, to have that mistake confirmed, through a message from the universe—I felt, I had made a massive, massive mistake and that my opportunities in college were over." She talked to her mom, who was "so understanding, just so chill." Liliana then made clear the full range of social factors at play—not just the disparities in their sexual experience, but her feeling of vulnerability because of her belief that having a viral STD scuttled not just her college social project but her life project. Liliana had a very powerful commitment to a particular sexual project, one that strongly influenced her identity. In describing this project she hedged, simultaneously deploying and critiquing tropes of gendered sexuality:

> In a socially loaded way, I had always sort of been like, "It's good that I have waited, it's good that I haven't had casual sex." . . . You know, in a way that's totally socially determined and based on these standards of female virginity and purity and innocence and whatever . . . I had avoided those things because I felt they were socially not desirable—just to end up with being totally screwed over and having this marker of promiscuity, having this marker of being a whore—I didn't know how to reconcile that with my identity of not having much sexual experience compared to my peers . . .

Having shared that part of her story, she explained that "that is mostly why I stayed in the relationship with him." Liliana understood her boyfriend's behavior as a reflection of his social background. His working-class upbringing, she reasoned, had been difficult. Verbal abuse was just part of how his family operated. To be sure, there were other students whose cross-class relationships did not devolve into searing verbal abuse. She described the mix of legal, economic, and health-related crises that her boyfriend's family was facing. Without having observed the interpersonal or group dynamics ourselves, it is hard to know how that would have translated into his treating her as if she were "worthless" and his friends calling her "like, feminazi, she's so ugly, she's such a, you know, cunt." But there are some important clues.

Liliana's boyfriend was at the bottom of the campus pecking order. A white "kid," as she called him, from a working-class background, he and his friends were part of a team that wasn't respected. The prestige of athletics at Columbia is highly class-based. Crew—a sport championed at places like Oxford, Harvard, and elite boarding schools—was at the top of the heap, followed closely by other "rich people sports" like tennis, squash, and sailing. His team, by contrast, was subject to widespread social disparagement.[11] His body looked like one prepared for physical battle, but Liliana admitted that there was something "attractive" about it. He'd grown up in a context where saying things like "that's retarded" or "that's so gay" were part of everyday parlance. At Columbia, this marked him a bigot and a homophobe. His politics were more conservative than most students; in the campus context, he may have felt that that put him on the margins. In our analysis, he and other men were responding to a feeling of being symbolically dominated by higher status men by challenging the things they felt put them at the bottom of the status hierarchy.[12] This included feminism, but also what they read as a "political correctness" that pretended to insist upon being socially open, but sought to silence and shame men like them for their opinions and experiences.

None of this justifies abusive behavior, but it helps us understand it. Gendered power relations on campus encompass relationships between men and between women, as well as among men and women. Gendered prestige structures advantage some men (and women) over others. As we've argued, groups of men at the bottom of the hierarchy are perceived as socially undesirable, and often described as "rapey." At Columbia, more powerful men present themselves as "modern," suggesting that they're feminists and welcoming of gay people; they use their social power against men at the bottom of the hierarchy, suggesting that they're somehow the opposite.[13] This social domination helps produce gendered sexual violence in two ways. First, sexual contact with men who are seen as less desirable is more likely to be perceived and labeled as "unwanted." Second, lower-status men challenge their domination in part by challenging the very principles of the hierarchy that dominates them. They may not be sexist or homophobic or racist, but some resist their domination by embracing misogynistic, homophobic, or racist violence and language.

Liliana's boyfriend and his peers expressed all kinds of things that were socially undesirable. We didn't just hear about this from her; we heard about them from others, and saw them during our fieldwork. They called women "bitches" and used the word "fag." They railed against feminism and expressed political attitudes viewed by many of their peers as contemptible. Their low social position is both a result of these attitudes and actions and a response to the dominant mores and norms that seek to keep them at the bottom of the campus social hierarchy. Such attitudes put them at risk of committing sexual assault. And as we saw in the previous chapter, this masculine hierarchy also protects more dominant men, whose social desirability as sexual partners makes encounters with them more likely to be viewed as wanted, and thus consensual. This shows another way in which students' focus on status in finding sexual partners is part of the context that produces vulnerability to sexual assault; the heavy emphasis on a potential partner's social desirability can drown out the question of the student's actual interest in that person. Remember Gwen (Chapter 1), in bed with that senior her roommates had encouraged her to date, having doubts about trying to "force something" that she wasn't feeling.

Understanding power, then, means thinking about how people's association with particular groups or institutions places them in positions that are more dominant or more dominated within a prestige structure, and how such positions enable certain kinds of behaviors and attitudes, or at least make them more likely. What Liliana experienced is sometimes referred to as "relationship violence." But that focuses attention only on the relationship between the person acting abusively and the person who is the target of that bad behavior; our interpretation of Liliana's story points to the many other relationships that produced that violence, including those between her ex-boyfriend and his teammates and between the team and the rest of campus.

"HE WAS 'FACEBOOK FAMOUS.' "

Settling into school is thrilling, stressful, and, sadly, dangerous. For students it is a high-stakes moment: an extended process through which they decide which extracurriculars to pursue, and then frequently compete for entry into them. They can reinvent themselves from high school, and set themselves upon the college project they've planned, which for many includes a particular sexual project. Scholars call these first few months of freshman year the "red zone"—that period of increased vulnerability to sexual assault.[14] The "red zone" may be the period of greatest risk, but that is socially produced, not inevitable. We need to better understand the social processes that produce this temporally elevated vulnerability, in the hopes of imagining how to transform those processes.

Marla, who we interviewed as a junior, experienced multiple sexual assaults in her years on campus—primarily instances in which men had intercourse with her while she was too drunk to consent. As a teenager growing up in Tennessee, Marla was subject to a fairly relentless barrage of (quite possibly well-intentioned) shaming from her mother, whose insistence on baggy and modest clothing left Marla feeling simultaneously unattractive and as if the world were full of sexual danger. During New Student Orientation she began to experience a sexual power she found thrilling: "It was like, yeah, I can kind of, like, see who I want to make out with at a party and/or hookup with at a party and I'll do that. Like, I just . . . make eye contact and then it will happen." As a junior, she could look back and reflect critically on her freshman experiences seeking men's attention as a way to affirm that she was sexy and desirable; in the moment, however, self-doubt about her desirability rendered her acutely vulnerable. On the fourth night of orientation, back in her dorm after a round of parties, she received a text from a fellow freshman. But he was not just any freshman—he was a guy who she and her roommate had discussed, even before they got to campus, as "Facebook famous" for being among the hottest guys in the class.[15]

When he texted her "You up?" she agreed to go meet him in a stair-well, thinking that maybe they'd make out. After all, he'd spent the earlier part of the evening trying to chat up another girl; he hadn't put in the time with Marla, so she felt he couldn't expect much more. But he was intending to have sex. They made out, and then he took out a condom and pushed her up against the stairwell wall. Her sexual inexperience and the vulnerability of being drunk, combined with the power he exerted by being such a desirable partner, so clear in his sexual goals and apparently oblivious to the possibility that she might not share them, made the assault almost inevitable. We only have the story from her perspective, so it's hard to know what this man's sexual project was, but it seems safe to say it was not related to expressing feelings of respect for her.

It is the variability in *sexual citizenship*, however, that brings the unequal social terrain into sharper relief. When Scott said to Luci "It's okay," he was speaking to her from a land where her desires literally did not exist, where her claims to bodily autonomy were illegible. Similarly, when the junior who raped Cindy asked if she had a boyfriend, the implication was that another man's claim on her body would be reason to stop, but her protests were not. He might have to respect that man's "rights," but Cindy had no rights to speak of. Heterosexual cisgender encounters show many instances of women having been socialized to question their own sexual citizenship. Cindy's reflection that he had "come all this way" across campus to see her was part of the calculus that drove her to walk back across campus with him even though she wasn't that interested. Some people feel entitled to others' bodies, and others do not feel entitled to their own bodies. This suggests the value of strategies and programs to promote sexual citizenship once students are already in college—a little late, we'd argue, but perhaps not too late.

But it is our third key concept, *sexual geographies*, that most tren-chantly reveals the campus-specific social patterning of power that elicits and produces bad behavior. Spaces create and constrain oppor-tunities. Those opportunities are unequally allocated; again and again, gender and class year come together to impel first-year women into spaces controlled by upperclassmen. Spaces are also a key dimension of institutional power to shape student life. There may be many good reasons for first-year students to have roommates, and at a lot of institutions the only way to arrange that is to put two students in a bedroom.[16] But those shared bedrooms often propel younger women into spaces controlled by older men.

"THAT WAS MY FIRST SEEING OF QUEERNESS."

The experiences of queer and trans students challenge a singular focus on gender and sexual assault in even more fundamental ways.[17] Charlene, a white, genderqueer student, was tall, with a dancer's posture and a warm and engaging smile. Coming from a small town in Minnesota, they didn't have a lot of access to queer community, and so a theater program in St. Paul in the summer after sophomore year of high school was a revelation. They recounted, "I did a musical there, and that was the first time that I encountered gay people—um, more specifically, white gay men who were also doing the show. . . . I was like, oh my god, they're gay, that's cool." They were all older, "so they are automatically cooler; I wanted to be like that, because that was my first seeing of queerness." Charlene described their first sexual experience as "rape." Charlene was drunk and he was sober; the power imbalance also included differences in age and sexual experience. "I had no knowledge of what was going on, and it was also a situation that was very pressurized because of the power dynamic—because of that, I felt like I needed to do it." We see in this experience something particular to LGBTQ young people's lives—the search for connection within a sexual and gender community that is the very first place where they feel seen, where they might have a place, where they belong—and how it intersects with some of the same vulnerabilities in Marla's story— disparities in age, sexual experience, and levels of intoxication.[18] Charlene's vulnerability in that summer theater program is inseparable from the socially produced, but not inevitable, sense of isolation that many queer and trans youth face.

Once at Columbia, Charlene was very involved with, and most at home around, their network of queer students from other schools in the New York area. Sophomore year, they were spending time with Jordan, assigned male at birth and transitioning. Jordan was from a nearby school; they'd study together in Jordan's dorm room, chill, sometimes watch TV. Jordan and Charlene sometimes had sex, but Jordan wanted it a lot more frequently than Charlene did, and would push for physical intimacy in a way that Charlene experienced as hard to say no to. Jordan would make a physical advance and they'd start to kiss. But if Charlene wanted to stop there, Jordan would say things like "You don't love me," "You should want to do this with me," or even, "You don't think I'm beautiful." Charlene knew what it felt like to be unsure of one's appeal; especially during the transition, they really wanted to be a source of support. This ended, more than once, in Charlene giving in: closing the computer, lying back, letting Jordan give them a blow job, and then reciprocating. Totally sober, within a relationship that was important to Charlene, such consent under coercion looks totally different than the kinds of experiences that Luci had. While in some of our examples, people who committed assault clearly "had" power, in the form of resources, strength, status, it's not clear that Jordan had any of these things. But power does not always need to be possessed in order for it to be practiced. Jordan was able to exercise power by playing into Charlene's vulnerability to emotional manipulation. Power isn't just about maleness, or whiteness, or heterosexuality. The distinction between having and exercising power isn't just academic; it has important implications for interventions. Just because people don't "have" power doesn't mean they can't use power to achieve their goals. The prevention implication is that even those who do not feel that they have access to much social power should still be taught to be attentive to the ways in which they can use power in interpersonal relationships.[19]

It is notable that Charlene's experience happened in Jordan's room.

The impulse of wanting to affirm a partner's identity out of solidarity seems at least one kind of power relation that is specific to queer students.[20] Jordan may have been manipulating Charlene because they knew about this impulse, their feelings of being "unattractive" may have been keenly felt, or it could have been a bit of both. Programming focused on consent, bystander interventions, or the dangers of alcohol do little to avert this type of scenario.

Certainly, queer people also experience intoxicated assaults. Jacqui, a white, genderqueer engineer from a wealthy background, was active in campus social justice work. As the only queer student in their high school, Jacqui was excited to start off orientation week having already connected with another queer student through the class Facebook page. A queer party on their third night on campus seemed like a great place to go with their new friend, and to connect with other similarly identified students on campus. Jacqui hadn't partied much in high school, and was unprepared for how they'd feel after getting high in an upperclassman's room, and doing a couple of shots of vodka back downstairs at the main party. At this point, they felt very out of it: their movements and perceptions were sluggish and lethargic, and they felt "kind of underwater" as they followed a pack, first out to an all-night diner and then back to their new friend's room. Some other queer students were watching tv as Jacqui lay on the bed, drifting in and out of consciousness. The group left Jacqui alone with their new friend. Jacqui tried to leave but couldn't stand unassisted. The new friend guided them back to the bed, then kissed, fondled, and fingered Jacqui. Jacqui did not want this to happen but felt unable to move or to say anything. The new friend tried to get them to reciprocate sex, moving their hand, but Jacqui was way too out of it for that. At this point the new friend said that their mother was coming the next day so Jacqui should leave. Somehow, Jacqui made it to the elevator, and back to their dorm room.

Jacqui experienced this assault as enormously harmful. In high school, they had no fellow queer students to connect with. And yet this first experience with the other queer students on campus went terribly wrong; they weren't sure there would ever be a place they could feel comfortable. The very promise of queer community produced a deep sense of loneliness and harm. Both the factors that led to this experience of assault and Jacqui's subsequent suffering are only apparent through an understanding of the particularities of queer students' experiences. Frequently stigmatized and isolated in high school, they see college as offering a social landscape where they can finally belong. But the relatively claustrophobic social world they face on campus means that negative experiences within the community, even in a city of possibility like New York, can create a context wherein abuses go unchallenged. To walk away would leave queer students with almost nowhere else to call home.

RACE, SEXUAL GEOGRAPHIES, AND ASSAULT

Race as well as gender structures space. At Columbia, socializing spaces and music choices that reflect the tastes and preferences of high-status white students predominate. This drives some students of color to seek partners off campus, away from classmates who might remember their bystander training and who, because of community norms or solidarity, might intervene to help them.[21] Recall Charisma, for example, who felt turned off by the mainstream campus social scene that she saw as fratty white guys who drink too much, have bad taste in music, can't really dance, and go for thin girls with straight hair and thin noses. She was also frustrated by the relatively small numbers of Black men, who she deemed more suitable partners, on the Columbia campus. She was the woman who ended up in the apartment of a man she barely knew in Brooklyn, thinking that they'd just smoke a little pot, chill, and watch television. But instead, he assaulted her. The racialized nature of campus space is also an element of Lupe's story, the person who had nowhere on campus to listen to bachata, their favorite kind of music. Lupe was the one in a midtown bar when a man approached and bought them a drink. The next thing they knew they were being mostly carried

from a taxi into his apartment, where they were raped. The intensity of
the power differential was foregrounded by Lupe's fear for their life; students discussed (and experienced) many awful consequences of assault,
but in no instance did a student talk about fearing that another student
might murder them.

The hypersexualization of students of color is reflected in how persistently they are subjected to unwanted sexual touching. One man we
interviewed speculated that white women's apparent comfort grabbing
his penis at a bar reflected both a racialized lack of respect for his
autonomy and white fantasies of Black penises. Black women expressed
this even more consistently; every single Black woman student with
whom we spoke had experienced unwanted sexual touching on campus.[21] That bears repeating: every single one. This becomes part of an
unseen burden that Black women bear; in the interviews, they noted
it, only to shrug it off as just one more indignity. Building campuses
where Black women feel like equal citizens requires complementing
prevention focused on consent, alcohol, and healthy relationships with
programming grounded in a framework of anti-racism, interpersonal
respect, and the right to physical autonomy.

Drunken campus assaults—the challenges of investigation and
adjudication, the question of how it can be fair to hold one person
responsible when both people were drunk—have dominated the public
conversation. What social scientists call "discourse"—the way people
talk about campus sexual assault, the incidents that receive media attention, and the examples provided in cautionary words from parents or
in prevention programming problems—shapes how people understand
the nature of the problem. That, in turn, can influence the investment
of resources in prevention programming. Remember that the analysis
of SHIFT survey data led by Louisa Gilbert showed that a very substantial proportion of sexual assaults that students experienced did not
take place under conditions of intoxication.[22] As in our discussion of the
historical whiteness of the campus drinking landscape, there's a racial
component to this focus on intoxicated assault: the assumption that

white students' experience is universal. Not surprisingly, given that students of color generally drink less, the Khan and Sarvet SHIFT survey data analysis also found that students of color are more likely to experience assaults resulting from verbal coercion in the context of ongoing intimate partnerships, rather than drunken assaults with a new partner they met at a party.[23]

"THEY WERE JUST SORT OF SKEPTICAL."

Heterosexual men's sexual assaults by women are also rendered invisible by prevailing discourses of gender and power.[24] These stories, some of which we've already shared, are not numerically nearly as common as those of women assaulted by men, nor do they happen at the extremely high rates at which queer and trans students experience assault. Naming this as assault has the immediate practical value of helping men who feel harmed access the resources that they need to heal. But there is also a symbolic and political value to undermining the equation of masculinity and sexuality agency; describing men as the potential objects of someone else's aggression and not just as the agents gives men social permission not to be sexual aggressors and frames sexual assault as something that they have a stake in preventing not just as allies but to protect themselves.[25]

It would be hard to think of a man who embodies hegemonic masculinity more intensely than Rick. He grew up on a farm out west, and joked before the interview began about how useless his cattle-roping skills were in Morningside Heights. Not from a wealthy background, he responded to the ad about SHIFT because he needed the cash. Initially he seemed discomfited by the directness of the questions—leaning back in his chair as if to escape, tapping his hands on his knees and on the table. But he relaxed as the conversation progressed. He waved his hands for emphasis, raised an eyebrow to indicate a joke, and leaned forward, smiling, as he spoke about his ex-girlfriend.

He did not describe what happened that night as an assault. It began, as many of these stories do, on East Campus (where seniors live), out-side a party that had just been shut down. While Rick was standing on the concrete outside the townhouse-style dorms in the wintry chill, Cassidy, who was a friend of a friend, walked over. With their friends they first headed group to one bar, and then to another. Cassidy bought Rick drink after drink throughout the night, pressed herself on him physically, and eventually went with him back to his room, where they had sex. He awoke the next morning filled with misgiving and confu-sion, and asked his friends what happened. The guys confirmed that from the moment they walked into the first bar, Cassidy seemed to be intent on getting him drunk. They didn't think to intervene—as far as they could tell, he was getting lucky. No need for a wingman; he was headed for sex without even having to pay for his drinks, so what was the problem? But his friend Renee had a different take on the interaction, and she raised the whole issue of gender, saying, "If you were a woman, you would be in hell right now." Ultimately, Rick decided it was not an assault, just a gross story.

But not all men who have these experiences shrug them off. Maddox, who we met in Chapter 2—he was the man who didn't want to tell us the name of the bar he and his friends had found—answered interview questions quickly and efficiently. He leaned forward, letting his hair hang over his eyes, or turned his head, avoiding eye contact. Maddox was assaulted—it was unusual to hear a cis-hetero man describe the experience in these terms—at a party freshman year. It was the cast party from a play he'd been in, and everyone was very drunk. The next day he had to piece together what happened.

> I remember being mostly fine and talking to this person, and then I was drinking and drinking, and then I blacked out, and I don't remember anything else that happened except like a few flashes of being in her room. Then I was told what happened [by her room-mate, who had also been at the party] and was sort of uncomfort-able with it. It was bad . . . I had some really good friends that were

a pretty good support network. I had one friend tell me to call the hotline for whatever, whatever it's called here. And I did that, and that was very helpful. The hotline was more just like having an ear to just talk this through . . . I don't know, it was just sort of therapeutic. My parents, it was more negative. I didn't tell my dad for a while afterwards, and then he was sort of like, didn't take it very seriously, didn't understand. And so we just stopped talking about it. My mom I think struggled to understand, but made more of an effort to just sort of, like, be there to comfort me."

"What did they struggle to understand?" we asked.

Just, like, how that can be, or, like, happen to a man, I think. Both my parents struggled to understand that . . . [they thought] that it had to be very physical and very, like, rape, rape, like violent rape, and so they were just sort of skeptical, like, "Oh, how could this have happened." My mom . . . sort of, like, struggled, but came through that to, like, help me. And then my dad just sort of didn't, and so we don't talk about it.

Maddox was one of the few men we interviewed who described himself as asexual; it's possible that this sexual identity provided him with the critical distance from hegemonic masculine sexuality needed to label what happened to him as an assault. If we read an erection as a barometer of desire (as Maddox's father may have), it is impossible to conceive of a man experiencing penetrative sex as assault—unless he is the one being penetrated. If a man is doing the penetrating, how can he also be assaulted?

HOW TO THINK ABOUT POWER

The stories in this chapter hardly exhaust the multiple forms of power that create the conditions in which sexual assaults occur. In our analysis of all the stories we heard, the power disparities related to age, levels of comfort in the campus setting, mastery of the rules of the game, and disparities in social status, intoxication, levels of sexual experience, clarity about sexual projects, race, wealth, and control over space. Sometimes only one major power disparity was at play; other times disparities seemed to layer one upon one another. We heard from one participant about what she thought of as a "near miss" of being assaulted by older, wealthy foreign students whose downtown apartment was a kind of palatial man-cave stocked with booze and cocaine, with Uber XLs shuttling women in and out. The woman who told us this story entered that apartment, felt profoundly uneasy, and left almost immediately.

In thinking about the multidimensionality of power, we are not arguing against the notion that certain fraternities, or sports teams, or any other single-sex men's organization can produce vulnerability to sexual assault. Rather, we are suggesting that it is simplistic to think about the assaults that happen in those contexts as only reflecting gendered power differences. Not all groups are created equal. Where single-sex organizations like fraternities and men's athletic teams differ from, say, band or the debate team or the newspaper, is that women are absent from leadership, creating the possibility for bonding around shared norms of masculine entitlement to other people's bodies. But coed teams and student activity groups create other dynamics of vulnerability, with students working together intensely, sometimes traveling together, and often celebrating wins, or mourning losses, by drinking heavily. The assaults that take place between students in these activity groups, and that go unreported, speak to the power of the group both to organize opportunities for sexual contact and to downgrade instances of assault. Such instances get relabeled as sketchy, weird, or gross sex, in the interest of preserving group harmony, and because of individuals' wish not to lose access to a valued social activity.

Power can be thought of as something people possess, as something they practice, or as something they enjoy because of structural advantage. The first form of power, as a possession, is something someone "has": for example, if they're physically imposing, very attractive, or control substantial social or monetary resources. The second form of power is something that someone "does": for example, if their sexual experience is so considerable that they find it easy to act in sexual situations in ways that help them get what they want. And the third form is a position they occupy that gives them power: being the captain of a team, or on a student organization's leadership board. Power is personal, relational, and institutional.

These forms of power are unquestionably gendered. But other dimensions of social inequality are extremely important; we have highlighted racial and economic inequality, and on the particular vulnerabilities of students who are not heterosexual or are outside the gender binary, but this hardly exhausts the forms of inequality relevant to sexual assault (disability, for example, merits a great deal more attention). Acknowledging power as personal, relational, and institutional, while at the same time keeping an eye on the forms of power that reflect broader social inequalities, is essential.

While no society is without power disparities, our argument is not that the inescapable intertwining of power and sex means that consent is truly impossible, and therefore all sex is rape.[26] That kind of thinking doesn't reflect most people's experience. Moreover, it diminishes the suffering caused by sexual assault to suggest that somehow, it's the same as "normal" or typical sex. It's deterministic, making assault seem inevitable, and enables those who commit assault to abdicate responsibility: that it's society's fault, not theirs. Uncovering sexual assault's deep social roots suggests that sexual assault prevention is inextricable from broader projects of social justice.

We have said little about the agency and choices of those who *don't* commit assault, instances in which an advance was made, consent was not given, and this was respected, or where consent was given, but still not acted upon. But these stories are also important. One Latino man told us of a time he was "hooking up" with a woman. She said "yes" to sex, but he thought she was too drunk to be able to truly consent. And so he stepped back, ending the encounter. His sexual agency was critically important, particularly the agency he exercised in deciding not to have sex that he wanted, out of concern for his partner's state of mind. Another man recounted having sex with his girlfriend, and looking down at her on the bed to see her looking up at the ceiling, expressionless. He stopped. And he had a conversation with her. He implored her to be clearer about her feelings; no matter what they were, he wanted to hear them.

While power differences may be inescapable, schools and the social policies that shape higher education can mitigate asymmetries; this includes policies related to financial aid, student debt, housing, and career services as part of our expansive vision of building a safer environment. But mitigating these asymmetries also includes social sources of vulnerability prior to orientation week: Charlene's "first seeing of queerness" would not have been a first time if her high school had had a gay-straight alliance.[27] And more can be done to raise awareness about power asymmetries that are not modifiable—in particular, to sensitize students to the power of age disparities.

Although power generates privilege, privilege possessed need not be privilege exercised. Some of us have the privilege of clearly defined sexual projects for a host of reasons: we're heterosexual and our project is widely accepted; we came from a community that provided us with information about sex and sexuality; we have family and friends who have affirmed our project. Others do not. A critical part of realizing our sexual projects requires recognizing the privileges we have, in relationship to the power we possess, that we practice, and that institutions bestow upon us. Sexual projects, as we use the concept in this book, is descriptive, highlighting the range of what people want out of sex, or through sex. It is agnostic as to what is right or moral or what people owe each other. The normative dimension of sexual projects is something about which people will disagree, and that is for them to decide. That is also where sexual citizenship comes in; equality is a fundamental element of citizenship. Recognizing everyone's sexual citizenship means checking our privilege, and checking in with each other. Combining attention to sexual projects with the promotion of sexual citizenship and the transformation of sexual geographies suggests a pathway to a world where sexual assault is less common.

FORMING SEXUAL CITIZENS

I f widespread suffering were sufficient to render something visible as a social problem, every day we'd wake up to the same headlines: "One third of world's population still without adequate sanitation facilities" and "Hundreds of millions without safe drinking water." And yet, we do not. Nor does knowledge alone drive policy change. Decades elapsed, for example, between the discovery of the link between smoking and lung cancer and the emergence of policies that led to a decline in tobacco consumption in the United States. And despite widespread access to information about the harmful effects of smoking, there are parts of the globe where tobacco consumption continues to rise.[1]

Issues that have huge consequences can go unnoticed or be ignored. Successfully transforming suffering into a widely recognized problem that engenders a collective response takes work.[2] Consider school-based bullying: in our lifetimes, it has gone from being a part of the childhood landscape—as predictable as the slide and the swing set—to being the focus of legislation, official pronouncements and condemnations, and widespread prevention efforts. This didn't happen because bullying became more common. Individuals and organizations worked to make us see it as a moral failure of our communities, one that we had both the obligation and the capacity to remedy. Thinking of public problems as "socially constructed" sheds light on the processes through which individuals and coalitions draw attention to particular issues in need of action, ascribe responsibility for fixing them, and outline a path or plan to rectify the problem.

While it may seem unimaginable to our younger readers, sexual assault was not always viewed as a problem. In the United States, the Model Penal Code—a set of revisions meant to modernize state penal codes, suggested to the states in the mid-twentieth century and widely adopted—defined rape as something that a man committed against a "female not his wife."[3] This effectively rendered rape impossible within marriage (it also made the rape of men impossible). It was not until the 1970s that states started making laws against marital rape, and not until 1993 that all fifty states had laws that made marital rape a crime.[4] At the time of our writing, in 2019, twelve states still have loopholes to marital rape; in South Carolina, for instance, the incident must be reported within 30 days, and it must involve a weapon, a threat of a weapon, or violence of a "high and aggravated nature."[5] While historically some sexual assaults have been taken seriously, violation of a victim's sexual autonomy has not traditionally been what marshalled public attention. Sexual violence, whether by men against their wives or by white men (slave owners or not) against Black women, has long been used as a tool of racial and gendered domination, and it has rarely been called "assault."[6]

When we set out on this journey together in 2014, the work of creating cultural consensus that campus sexual assault was a problem was near completion. A generation of researchers had toiled to collect and analyze data, many with very little support from their home institutions and sometimes facing active opposition.[7] Impassioned activists, documentary filmmakers, and journalists lifted up the stories of those who experience campus sexual assault. Survivors themselves, refusing to be silenced or shamed, moved their stories from the margins to the center, so that campus sexual assault is now a problem that all American institutions of higher education are required to recognize and address. Elected officials sensed the changing winds, and have proposed a range of legislative responses. The #MeToo movement, surfacing while we were writing this book, signaled an expansion and further solidification of attention to sexual assault as a social problem—not just on campus but at work, in public spaces, and in families.

But having generated social agreement that something is a problem entails addressing another large task: building consensus about the solution. Some problems have clearly identifiable causes, and thus obvious policy targets. Take, for example, lung cancer: it mostly has a single cause (smoking), so a single industry (tobacco manufacturers) can be held responsible. This causal clarity and distinctly defined target helps coalesce organization and action. But campus sexual assault is, as we've shown, not one thing, and across many kinds of assaults, there are a range of causes, and thus no clear institutional enemy toward which animus and energy can be directed. Some have tried to organize around combatting "toxic masculinity" or "rape culture." But these are relatively diffuse targets. Moreover, a singular focus on masculinity ignores assaults committed by women, does not fully capture the unwanted touching to which women of color are persistently subjected, and makes invisible assaults experienced by queer students. Student activists frequently direct their ire toward schools themselves—but as we have shown, while sexual assault is clearly a problem for which schools must be held accountable, it is not at all a problem entirely of their making.

We do not deny the problems of certain expressions of masculinity. But just as explanations that are purely psychological (sociopathic perpetrators) are incomplete, so too are ones that are entirely cultural (toxic masculinity). We are all responsible. Most of us have never committed assault. But all of us have allowed social conditions to persist in which many young people come of age without a language to talk about their sexual desires, overcome with shame, unaccustomed to considering how their relative social power may silence a peer, highly attentive to their personal wants but deaf to those of others, or socialized to feel unable to tell someone "no" or to give a clear and unambiguous "yes." Without question, individuals bear responsibility for their own actions; the exercise of the responsibility to respect others' bodily autonomy can be seen in the many instances in which one person said no or otherwise managed to convey that they were not into what was happening, and the other person noticed and stopped. But the confusion around sexual projects, the lack of clarity about one's own and others' sexual citizenship, and the creation and perpetuation of sexual geographies that intensify power inequalities, these are *our* fault.

As we've already shared in our scientific papers and summed up in the final report that the SHIFT team submitted to Columbia University, there is untapped potential in looking at the many modifiable dimensions of the campus environment, layered together with interventions to influence individual attitudes and beliefs, and teach interpersonal skills.[8] In attributing responsibility for solving the problem of campus sexual assault, we want to expand the conversation. The focus on adjudication has had the advantage of a clear and obvious target: institutions of higher education and their responsibility to get cases right. But there are limits to this approach.

Schools' prevention work should be integrated into their core mission of education, in both skills and critical thinking. The focus of current programing is too narrow, structured primarily around consent education. We believe that the framework we provide—of guiding young people to think about their sexual projects and how they fit into their broader life projects, of thinking about cultivating their own sexual citizenship and asking what it means to recognize something similar in others, and to think critically about geographies of experience and their relationship to power—will have far greater success, with benefits that extend well beyond sexual assault. College is, truthfully, late for these conversations to begin; but given the widespread hesitation to have them earlier, these institutions have a moral obligation to make such discussions a fundamental part of the curriculum.

The recommendations we make are far more provisional than we would like them to be; in large part that's because the evidence base for sexual assault prevention is limited, and what has been found to work is almost entirely focused at the individual and interpersonal level. In the late 1970s and early 1980s the National Center for the Prevention and Control of Rape at the National Institute of Mental Health funded researchers to advance knowledge of sexual assault and how it could be prevented, but those days are long gone.[9] There are no current funding initiatives at the National Institutes of Health specifically to support sexual assault research of any kind, much less campus sexual assault research; the National Institute on Alcohol Abuse and Alcoholism has supported a great deal of investigator-initiated research on alcohol and campus sexual assault, but as we have argued, that is only one piece of the problem. Nor have any major foundations stepped in to fill this gap. Across the whole federal government, the funding available for sexual violence–related research and programs is a fraction of what's available for cancer, coronary artery disease, or HIV, despite the fact that American women's lifetime risk of experiencing sexual violence is higher.[10]

Externalities are costs created by the production, distribution, or consumption of a product that are not taken into account in the product's price. The classic example is a power plant that pollutes the water in the river it's next to, creating a negative externality, borne by the power plant's downstream neighbors. It's worth considering sexual assault as a negative externality, although there's no one for-profit entity that can be held responsible for sexual assault in the same way that we can hold a utility company accountable for the pollution from its power plant. But the alcohol industry makes billions in profits, and sexual assault is an associated negative externality, in part through the perpetuation of a culture of heavy drinking, alongside the promotion of the idea that fun and sexual expression are tightly entwined with drinking. Alcohol taxes could support revenue streams for sexual assault prevention, and specifically for comprehensive school-based sex education. The success of the pornography industry reflects young people's curiosity about sex in a context where schools and homes have chosen silence over education and information. Young people turn to pornography, in part, seeking a kind of sexual education. But they are not learning what they need, and meanwhile, the industry is reaping billions in profits. This industry, too, should be taxed, with revenue used to support actual sex education. Pornography and alcohol consumption do not cause sexual assault, but both industries are enormously profitable and help create the context of vulnerability, and could be held, in part, accountable.

CREATING SAFER SPACES

Educating individuals as a way to address sexual violence is important, but insufficient. At the core of a public health approach is systems thinking, which means considering the broad ecology, placing the individual in the context of their interpersonal relationships, institutional environment, and cultural context. We've argued for a shift away from a focus on consent as a verbal transaction and toward providing opportunities for students to clarify their own sexual projects, and for programming that provides opportunities for young people to reflect critically on how they can enact those sexual projects in a way that is grounded in respect for sexual citizenship—both their own and others'. This would involve reflection on interpersonal and intergroup power dynamics, gendered and otherwise, and skills-building around talking, listening, and interpreting nonverbal cues and body language. It would mean disrupting the gendered scripts that are part of why some interpret "not saying no" as "yes" and why some read an erection or other forms of physical arousal as an indication of consent. It would mean helping students think through how to balance their commitment, as a friend and member of a peer group, to set up sexual situations, and how to, as a friend and member of that same peer group, care for all members of the community. It would be mean expanding social recognition of the types of campus sexual assault—intimate partner violence, unwanted touching, the assaults experienced by queer students and by men—beyond the intoxicated party rape that has dominated the national conversation.

Once it becomes clear how the sexual geography of residential dorms and party spaces is essentially a sexual assault opportunity structure, we can start to imagine what it would look like to design safety into campus life. There would be party spaces controlled by women, queer students, younger students, and students of color. There would be spaces accessible to all students that structure social opportunities, whether for intimate chats or board games, in contexts that are not automatically interpreted as sexual. There would be programming for students who have had confusing or upsetting sexual experiences that do not require them to label an experience as sexual assault, or to report it in ways that would result in punishment of the other person if they did not want that. The survivor identity has, for some students who have experienced sexual assault, been a source of resilience and a way to draw on their own experience to create political change. But for others who do not see themselves that way, institutional messages that communicate more clearly that there is not one right way to feel after being assaulted—or even after having had sex that feels awkward, confusing, hurtful, or diminishing—can help students access the support they need. And if we are correct in our argument that many instances of assault were not interactions in which the assaulter intended to commit an assault, then it is essential to find ways to provide feedback to the assaulter, feedback that says, "The 'sex' you're having with others is a problem. Your partners are finding it less than consensual. You need to think through and work on this. Here's how. . . ."

These transformations should make assaults less likely, but assaults are not going to disappear. As we've shown, students' calculus in relation to reporting is complex, as they balance time, emotional, and reputational costs against a mix of other concerns, including the desires to see bad behavior receive an appropriate institutional response and to keep other people from being harmed.[11] Ideally, students would have the option to seek restorative justice with peers whose behavior they have experienced as harmful.[12] Such an approach places those who have been harmed at the center of generating resolutions, rather than demanding that they advocate for their position. It insists more on an acknowledgment of harm than an insistence on punishment, and includes engaging the entire community in work to make sure the harmful experience doesn't happen again. Instead of a system that demands that two parties be opposed, each advocating for their own interests, this would offer a structured, mediated opportunity for the parties to encounter one another, acknowledge the harm that was caused, and support the process of reintegration into friendship networks or student groups. This would not work or even be desirable for all cases, but it may be helpful for many. Implementation would require acknowledging the opportunity costs to engagement; just as it is powerful to see sexual assault as limiting women's access to equal education, so too must we consider the impact of institutional responses to sexual assault on the time and emotional resources of survivors—whose goal in going to college is to get an education, not teach their peers how to behave.

The key metric, for those students who are assaulted, is not whether they formally report what happened; it's whether they get the help they need to process their experience, continue their studies and resume their lives as best as they are able. Most students' emotional support comes not from psychologists, physicians, deans, or faculty members, but from friends. It is not just those who experience an assault who are survivors, it is the broader community of co-survivors, who can be overwhelmed by supporting a peer in crisis. Institutional responses need to target more than the individual, because the harm experienced goes far beyond that person. This doesn't mean outsourcing all the work to peer groups; it can mean, in fact, the opposite: helping peers understand that they are not mental health professionals, and that they can both be supportive friends and manage their own boundaries. Given the substantial community-level mental health burden that sexual assault places on all students, our communities need to do much more, and think much more systematically, about those students who are supporting their peers after an assault, particularly as overall student mental health continues to worsen.

Such improved processes and responses after an assault has happened are welcome, but as we've argued, ultimately limited. The main goal must be to prevent people from sexually assaulting others. Institutional efforts to work directly with those imagined most likely to assault, student athletes and men engaged in Greek life, conflates organizations that consist of groups of men with a specific kind of (toxic) masculinity. The structures of masculine prestige vary from campus to campus, but at Columbia there was as much variation in social status among fraternities and among athletic teams as there was between athletes and fraternity members and men who participated in neither. The recurrent emphasis on sports and fraternities fails to protect students outside those structures. Without question, many of the most widely discussed sexual assault cases have involved athletes and fraternity members; leaving aside the question of whether rates of perpetration are actually higher in those groups, for which the evidence is mixed and likely institutionally specific, we believe those cases are more readily highlighted because they fit existing explanatory models.

Although pretty much no one (at least no one we spoke with) wants to assault someone, that alone does not prevent assaults. Rather, it simply means that people are often unwilling or unable to see what they have done as an assault. Most campuses have many students, mostly men, who have had sex with others that was unwanted and nonconsensual. When students feel like they've fallen short and want to learn to do better, there needs to be somewhere for them to go for help, a place where reaching out doesn't mean potentially getting kicked out of school. Those who commit assaults should have avenues for repairing the harm they've done to a peer and then learning to do better. For many, that work will involve understanding how heavy drinking puts them at risk of assaulting others. There's a lot we can learn from the recent social policy failures and successes around crime, as well as the feminists critiques of approaches that "protect" women in ways that are carceral.[13] Aggressive incarceration has had some impact on crime—but its effects are often overestimated, and the moral tolls of this policy have been enormous.[14] It's important to make sure people adhere to social norms, and to invest in ways to help them do so. But policing and punishment are not the same thing, and keeping people from harming others doesn't require that we completely ostracize those who do. Criminologists have long argued that we should spend as much time on community organizing as on policing. Concretely, this means creating campuses where students feel enabled to develop their life projects, building a sense of self-efficacy and respecting others, in community spaces that seek to diminish rather than augment power asymmetries. Communities that enable and support "collective efficacy"—understood as social cohesion among members combined with a willingness to intervene on behalf of the social good—are places where people thrive, and where sexual violence is less likely.[15]

FOUR MAJOR OPPORTUNITIES

Building campuses where all students can thrive—indeed, building a world where there is less sexual assault—requires action across four interrelated areas: issues of diversity, power, and inequality; sex and sexual assault; substance use; and mental health. Inequalities between men and women are the form of power inequality that most easily comes to mind, and it is one we must address in a range of ways: from consent and sex education that takes gender seriously, seeking to develop sexual citizenship in women and respect for that citizenship in men, to geographic interventions to address men's unequal control over spaces where alcohol is distributed and parties take place. But as we argued in Chapter 9, power inequalities can produce silence. Sexual assault prevention is necessarily about diversity—including but not limited to gender. Failing to take racial and ethnic diversity as well as gender and sexual identity into account in prevention, for example, means that efforts to protect students from sexual assault at historically white institutions will concentrate on the experiences of those who have historically comprised the majority of the student body. We see this reflected today, where the type of assault that figures most heavily in public conversation about campus sexual assault—the kind where both parties have been drinking at a gathering—is one that is most likely to be experienced by white students.

This is not to say that we should ignore alcohol. It is clearly associated with a certain type of sexual assault, and one that is fairly common. The National Institutes of Alcohol Abuse and Alcoholism's "College Alcohol Intervention Matrix," summarizing the environmental strategies for which there is substantial evidence of impact, points to restrictions on happy hours, bans on Sunday sales, enforcement of the legal drinking age, and increased alcohol taxes as environmental-level strategies for which there is substantial evidence of effectiveness in reducing underage and excessive drinking.[16] As tobacco prevention efforts have found, young people are highly sensitive to pricing changes. And yet, even though we see the value of counting assault as a cost of alcohol consumption, and raising the price accordingly, we worry about possible unintended consequences of doing so. Wealthier students find a way to get their hands on what they want—they find cocaine, for example, despite the fact that it is both illegal and very expensive. Community-level efforts to increase the costs of alcohol may concentrate campus power disparities, even if they reduce overall levels of drinking. And so community-level actions need to be complemented with a harm reduction approach.[17] This means accepting that some substance use will happen, and so institutions should work to it make less dangerous. We tell students not to drink on an empty stomach, but they can't bring a bottle of wine or a six-pack into the dining hall, nor can they easily cook a meal and share it with friends over a drink in a freshman dorm. Respecting young people's autonomy, developing institution-specific approaches to minimize the harms associated with heavy drinking, and focusing on support rather than punishment have been shown to be more effective than simply saying, "This cannot happen, and if it does you will be punished."

Finally, we cannot talk about sexual assault without also thinking about mental health. The associations between sexual assault and mental health are complex, with mental health struggles likely being both a cause and a consequence of assault.[18] As with addressing the spatial landscape of campus, developing harm reduction policies around substance use, and attending to power and inequalities on campus, combatting mental health struggles is critical to addressing sexual violence within our communities. This includes providing individual-level clinical services—for which campuses face an insatiable demand—but also adopting a more preventive approach, attending to the multilevel drivers of mental health challenges, from individual struggles to community burdens to students' anguish about paying for college. Having spaces where students can exercise and play together, training professors to express not just judgment but also care, and maybe even more therapy dogs. Mental health promotion is a fundamental element of sexual assault prevention; that means not just expanding clinical services, but also taking a community-level mental health approach, and examining how adapting the environment can improve well-being.[19]

The way current sexual assault prevention fits into orientation illustrates more concretely the potential of this multisectoral approach that focuses on diversity, substance use, mental health, and sex and sexual assault education. The first year of college—and in particular the first semester—is a time when students need to figure out many things in short order—choose extracurriculars, find friends, test themselves against college-level academic work, start searching for work on campus or a summer job, learn to do their laundry, and regulate their own sleep. This is a hard and stressful time, whether indexed by freshman-year weight gain or by the high rates of mental health disorders among first-year college students.[20] Sexual assault prevention is already firmly integrated into pre-college orientation; indeed, a whole industry has sprung up to provide online pre-matriculation prevention programming, and many schools complement that with mandatory in-person sessions about affirmative consent, sexual assault resources, and mandated reporting. The college student onboarding process typically also includes programming related to substance use, to diversity and power, and to mental health. These are topics that students are actively—and sometimes dangerously—trying to figure out for themselves as part of the transition to college. But what's missing is space for students to make the connections among these four areas. Reimagining orientation as a way to meet students' social and emotional needs, and then considering how to continue to meet them over the course of freshman fall, might mean that some students wouldn't need to drink so much or that others wouldn't find themselves following a senior up a staircase. It is also important to raise upperclassmen's awareness of just how substantial these power disparities feel to first-year students. Freshmen might not be the only people who receive orientation; as students acquire status, they might be educated in the consequences of that acquisition. There are enormous opportunities for prevention work that considers multiple forms of power and inequality. Just as the experience of assault can reflect multiple simultaneous power inequalities, so too should the institutional structures for prevention engage with the full complexity of inequality.

EDUCATING YOUNG PEOPLE: EVERYONE'S JOB

Fifty years ago, more than 40% of schools had a pre-graduation swim test. A handful of schools across the country, Columbia included, still require that students learn to swim (or at least tread water for five minutes) before graduation. But the lifetime risk of drowning in the United States is 1 in 5,732.[21] By way of comparison, the SHIFT paper found that by senior year, 36% of women and 15% of men surveyed had experienced some form of unwanted nonconsensual sexual contact.[22] Twenty percent of women who were seniors, and six percent of men, reported being raped. And an analysis of SHIFT survey data led by John Santelli showed that nearly 20% of students surveyed had experienced unwanted sexual contact before matriculating at college; that same paper showed that students who had been assaulted before college had greater odds of being sexually assaulted after coming to campus.[23] Putting off conversations until college is, simply, too late. Change is not just necessary, but urgent.

Many students who arrive on campus lack the basic skills they need to succeed. This is enormously frustrating to educators. But when a student has been underserved by middle and high school writing programs, we don't just say, "Stop writing bad essays"; we have required courses on freshman writing, and a writing center to which students can be referred for further help and to continually refresh, refine, and develop their ability. These programs help young people express themselves in the ways they want to, leveling the playing field created by enormous differences in pre-college preparation. Sex is a critical life skill—vital for our sense of self and for connecting intimately with others. And yet many students are profoundly underprepared to become sexually active. Schools should consider sex education as a critical part of their educational mission—at the very least providing optional, online, straightforward remedial sex education to the many students who have had limited sex education.

If there's any single target in the United States toward whom activists should direct their ire, we would argue that it's not campus administrators; rather, it's the state and federal elected officials who have failed our young people by allowing so many of them to come of age without having received comprehensive sex education. High-quality sex education can modify the beliefs and attitudes about gender and sexuality associated with a propensity to assault.[24] The analysis of SHIFT data showed that women students who'd received comprehensive sex education before college that included refusal skills training were half as likely to be raped. If there were a vaccine that could prevent half of all campus rapes, and it was only provided to young people in half the school districts in the country and those whose parents could afford a progressive private education, there'd be a national outcry. And yet that is essentially the situation in the United States.

Without question, it makes sense for institutions of higher education, as part of community norm-setting for incoming students, to communicate standards of interpersonal conduct, including respecting other students' sexual citizenship. But that should be a booster, not a first shot; for a lot of students, those sessions about consent are totally insufficient, in part because of the lack of a foundation for these lessons to build upon.

The partisan capture of sex education policy reflects the preferences of politicians, not the public. Across the political spectrum, American parents are strongly and overwhelmingly supportive of the provision of school-based comprehensive sex education.[25] The patchy, imperfect, and worsening landscape of sex education produces vulnerability to sexual assault, and represents an important missed opportunity to prevent it. It's not just about denying young people information; the failure to contest the framing of adolescent sexual behavior as intrinsically bad leaves young people underprepared for what lies ahead. State legislatures can take up this issue, rather than leave it to individual school districts, but the growing divergence in state-level policies related to sexual and reproductive health points to the need for federal standards as well. In a country where life expectancy varies more than twenty years by zip code, in the absence of federal and state action on sex education, what will happen is what typically happens in the United States: wealthy schools and school districts will take up this new knowledge about sex education and sexual assault, with parent-child discussions about sexual citizenship integrated as just one more task in American elites' culture of intensive parenting, and the wealthiest children will be sent off to college better prepared for what lies ahead.[26] Everyone else will continue on just as before, resulting in widening inequalities. Sex education has been our focus here, but ensuring access to affordable, confidential sexual and reproductive health services, provided with sensitivity to the diversity of young people's needs, is another way to recognize and promote sexual citizenship.[27]

As we push to expand access to comprehensive, age-appropriate sex education, leveraging the full power of K–12 education requires exploring schools' "hidden curriculum." School classrooms, playgrounds, bathrooms, lunchrooms, and locker rooms, as well as moments of drama such as prom and homecoming, convey powerful messages about whose bodies are valued, whose voices matter, and what success looks like. In pre-kindergarten, boys learn to chase girls, inculcating early lessons in sexual scripts and heterosexuality. There are just as many if not more opportunities to talk about masculinity, femininity, queerness, and racial inequality in English, social studies, gym, and recess as there are in that one unit of sex ed. Throughout high school, classics from Ovid to Jane Austen provide rich texts for conversations about sex and power from the demure to the dramatic, and Harper Lee reminds readers that race has long been part of the American narrative about sexual assault.

While parents, teachers, and school principals wait for legislators to provide support for comprehensive sex education, there may be opportunities for curricular innovation at the school level.[28] Jennifer's experience as a parent and Shamus's as a high school teacher remind them how little learning goes on in the final semester of high school. This might be a particularly apt time for a school-based version of the film festival Jennifer tried at home before her older son left for college—but repurposed as a critical media studies class, with those college classics mixed in with *School Daze*, *Dear White People*, and other films examining diversity and inclusion in higher education and in communities more broadly, all of which would provide a foil for young people to talk about their own sexual projects and college projects. There is also a rich and growing body of young adult literature about sexual assault, some of it substantially predating the #MeToo era. At the radical edge, we're enthusiastic about porn literacy classes, which seek to teach students to apply their critical thinking skills to their viewing.[29] Though we admit that it's rather naïve to imagine that a nation that has punted on sex education is going to embrace classes that take as a starting point the fact that young people are already frequent consumers of pornography.[30]

Getting schools and the government to do this work will require an enormous mobilization. But in the meantime, there are still concrete things we can do to help our young people. We distinguish between sex education—which schools can do well if provided adequate resources and political support—and sexual socialization, which is the responsibility of families and communities.[31] There is substantial disagreement over the appropriateness of different sexual projects, and especially regarding the expected configuration of sex in relation to emotional connection, mutual monogamy, and even marriage. The charge for families, communities, and religious institutions is to clearly and explicitly communicate a vision of morality around sexual projects—but at the same time to recognize, with some humility, that young people's passage to adulthood inevitably involves making choices for themselves about their bodies in ways that are sometimes troubling and worrisome to those who care for them. We have a collective responsibility to raise children who are comfortable in their bodies and with their sexuality, who are clear enough about their own sexual projects to enact them without having to anesthetize themselves by doing shots, and who—whatever their sexual projects—understand that the people with whom they engage sexually are autonomous and self-determining humans, not objects or sex toys.

A lot of parents and caregivers find talking about sex acutely embarrassing. So let us provide some advice. Start young, using the actual names for body parts. If we were never to say the words elbow or neck, we'd be communicating that there is some secret shame in naming elbows and necks. The same is true with penises and vaginas. Grasp the teachable moments: books, movies, television shows, even memes are full of messages about bodies, respect for others, and the meaning of intimacy. Call out examples of people treating intimate partners with care and recognition. Don't focus so much on "the talk": information about the biology of reproduction. Rather, connect talking about sex to the broader project of teaching children how to interact with other people in a way that is sensitive and kind. And these conversations about sexual projects and sexual citizenship need to acknowledge gender dynamics rather than be generic, and to make space for young people whose sexual identities may still be emerging and whose gender identities may differ from those assigned at birth. Parents and caregivers will get it wrong sometimes, but they have nearly two decades to help right the process. We teach young people to apologize when they step on someone's foot; that same principle is the groundwork for conveying sexual respect. Try not to harm anyone. And if you perhaps might be doing that, stop, apologize, and talk to that person about what happened. Our rules, and our silence, send a powerful message.

It's a parent's right to tell young people, "not under my roof." But they shouldn't fool themselves into thinking that that rule will keep young people from having sex. What it does do is effectively convey a refusal to see them as sexually maturing young adults. Those who are not comfortable letting their high school-aged children's intimate partners sleep over are not, in that one act, producing vulnerability to being sexually assaulted, or making it more likely that their child will assault someone. But parents and caregivers are the most important arbiter of morality for their children. Whatever their values about premarital sex, our point is that those parent-child conversations about the circumstances under which it might be okay to say "yes" to someone are a moment of recognition for young people's sexual citizenship—and thus also a strategy to help prepare them to say "no" authoritatively. These conversations, particularly for a generation who themselves likely grew to adulthood in a family-imposed cone of sexual silence, will not be easy. But it is possible to raise a generation of children where silence will not be so powerful, and where their children may have a chance at a more fulfilling sexual life—one that will help them connect more deeply with their partners.

Of course parents and caregivers could do all this, and their children might still be assaulted, or commit assault. But think back, for a moment, to Esme, who told us, "Thank God it's me." She wasn't glad she was assaulted. She was glad it was her, not one of her friends, because as hard as it was, she knew she could talk to her mom about what happened, and that she'd support her; she wasn't worried about her mom condemning her for not being a virgin. Or recall Liliana's relief that her mom was "just so chill" when she talked to her about her partner giving her an STD. Liliana got the support she needed. Esme was able to weather her experience of assault better than others, and Liliana was able to begin thinking of herself as not permanently damaged and thus not deserving of abuse, because of the work their parents had done to convey that they were willing to talk about it, no matter what "it" was. Families do this all the time with alcohol, telling high school-aged children that they are too young to drink, but at the same time conveying that no matter what the circumstances are, they should reach out and will be received without judgment if they need help getting home safe late at night.

While legislators, schools, and parents all have a role to play in preparing young people to navigate, with understanding and compassion, the transition to being sexually active adults, there are other important institutions and organizations that might do more, or be held to a higher standard, in helping form sexual citizens. Churches, mosques, synagogues—all kinds of religious organizations—have a part to play. Their task of communicating moral frameworks about interpersonal behavior can emphasize doing more good and less harm. Jennifer's own experience teaching sex education at her temple has given her evidence that this is possible. Religious institutions can show young people that religious engagement is not just about holidays and rituals, and not even just about morality: it can be part of leading a meaningful and satisfying life.

The positive role that religious institutions play also comes with a responsibility to avoid harm, and in particular, hate. American LGBTQ youth attempt suicide at three times the rate of their heterosexual peers, and face elevated risks of anxiety, depression, and sexual assault.[32] These are harmful experiences that our communities produce, by conveying lessons of shame about certain kinds of bodies and desires. Scholars think about the experience of these youths as being produced by "structural stigma"—laws, norms, policies, and institutional practices that in combination create hostile conditions in which marginalized youth grow to adulthood.[33] This includes much higher rates of school-

and family-based persecution, violence at the community level, and ostracization from religious and other groups. These experiences are perhaps the clearest illustration of how sexual projects are impossible to realize if social citizenship is compromised. Addressing sexual assault means confronting all kinds of discrimination and harms done to minority populations.

Over the years since we've been working on this project, a lot of people, from many different institutions of higher education, have reached out to us to ask about how to do more, how to do better, how to use evidence-based approaches. Most of what gets tested by research so that it counts as "evidence-based" are what public health calls "interventions"—communication efforts, or small-group teaching, or skills-building sessions, or online education. But our focus has been on the environment, on how sexual geographies shape patterns of vulnerability, and on how institutional policies exacerbate, or at best inadvertently fail to reduce, those vulnerabilities. And so *Sexual Citizens* does not offer one solution; rather, along with some very specific suggestions, it presents a new way of thinking about this problem, one that could generate a score of different intervention studies.

Parents don't hand their kids a set of car keys and say "good luck learning to drive"—and then turn away thinking, "I hope they learn to drive safely, and don't hurt anyone, even if they're doing it drunk."[34] Drunk driving is a rich metaphor for thinking about sexual assault prevention, speaking to the need for a multilevel response: change how people think about the problem, build their skills to do better, and create an environment in which doing better is easier than doing worse. Legislative changes (the drinking age) have combined with the cultural promotion of sober driving as moral behavior and communications campaigns encouraging a specific interpersonal interaction: a discussion about who is the designated driver. Seatbelts and engineering changes have made cars safer to drive, better road design has smoothed dangerous curves, and stepped-up enforcement on holidays and New Year's

Eve has addressed the temporality of danger; in many ways, this is a prototypical success in multilevel prevention. It's striking how much social effort has gone into making driving, but not sex, safe. All of us need to take more responsibility for addressing the lack of sexual citizenship among our young people. And the goal is not only to make sexual assault less likely; it is also to reduce sexual anguish and unkindness.

We end where we began: with a reminder about empathy. Campus sexual assault has been successfully transformed into a public problem that demands a policy response. But this very success has entailed mobilizing a notion of assaulters that leaves out some stories. Yes, there are predators out there, and they need to be confronted. But we can have the biggest impact by addressing the assaults that happen because of sexual projects that only have one's own goals in mind, combined with a lack of attention to other people's sexual citizenship. Most young people, it seems fair to say, do not attain adulthood in geographies of equality, feeling clear about their sexual projects, supported in their own sexual citizenship and recognizing other people's. Our society is failing them. Yet we have charted a new path forward. The challenge is to join together to build communities in which all young people can become fully formed sexual citizens.

ACKNOWLEDGMENTS

Our deepest gratitude is to the young people who shared their stories and their lives with us. Over and over again, students would walk into the interview room, fling down their backpacks, and open their hearts in an astonishing and incredibly generous way. Some of these students also welcomed a member of the SHIFT ethnography team into their daily life—meeting them for boba tea on Broadway, letting them tag along for meals at the dining hall, inviting them upstairs to a room on fraternity row to chill and talk, having them join in at church and brunch, or bringing them along for a night of barhopping. Both during the data collection and after, we felt moved by their struggles, inspired by their resilience, brokenhearted by their grief, and awed by their willingness to share complicated experiences—frequently things they had never told anyone else. We hope we have done justice to their stories and their lives.

From the moment that this book started to take shape, we began compiling in our heads a long list of people to thank. There are four people to whom we owe not just our gratitude but also an acknowledgment that without their efforts, this book would never have come to be at all. First among them is Claude Ann Mellins, who Jennifer drafted into codirecting SHIFT before the project even had funding (or an acronym). She has been an incredible partner in research, and remains a dear friend, bringing an enormous depth of knowledge about mental health, a capacity to match Jennifer worry-for-worry, intense care and empathy for the young people who were the object of our work, and savvy about navigating a scientifically and institutionally complex landscape. Second, Suzanne Goldberg, Executive Vice President for University Life at Columbia, who saw the promise in Jennifer and Claude's initial idea, advocated for SHIFT, and helped create the best possible circumstances for research in our own institution, with substantial institutional and financial support complemented by scientific independence. Leigh Reardon, SHIFT project director extraordinaire, faced a first day at work welcoming hundreds of attendees to SHIFT's public launch—and the chaos never really stopped. We could not have built the airplane while flying it without Leigh's unflappable good humor, zest for multitasking, and spiral-bound notebook. And finally, Alex Wamboldt, in addition to doing brilliant and empathic fieldwork, then stayed on as a SHIFT team member through the data management and writing phases, demonstrating enormous dedication, wry humor, creativity, and resilience.

Matthew Chin, Gloria Diaz, Melissa Donze, and Megan Kordenbruck, the other members of the team who carried out the extended fieldwork, were also extraordinary—holding students' painful stories, enjoying their funny ones, and engaging with this challenging work with rigor and respect. The ethnography was only one component of the much larger SHIFT project, and we are grateful as well to the other members of the SHIFT executive committee (John Santelli and Patrick Wilson) as well as to the full faculty investigator team (Louisa Gilbert, Constance Nathanson, Martie Thompson, Melanie Wall, and Kate Walsh). And while we had a great deal of help over the course of fieldwork from many corners, three others are deserving of particular acknowledgment: Peter Taback, for his steady voice and perspective when we hit bumps in the road; Michael Weisner, for his boundless patience in helping us figure out and maintain a collaborative and secure data-management platform, and Alondra Nelson, for playing academic matchmaker by setting the two of us up to work together.

We feel enduring gratitude for the contributions of SHIFT's Undergraduate Advisory Board (Roberta Barnett, Emma Bogler, Meredith Dubree, Irene Garcia, Corey Hammond, Robert Holland, Morgan Hughes, Trendha Hunter, Sarah Lazarsfeld, Amber Officer-Narvasa, Sidney Perkins, Irin Phatraprasit, Gregory Rempe, Sean Ryan, Stephanie Steinman, Shaakya Vembar, Brendan Walsh, Michela Weihl, Liza Wohlberg, and Nicholas Wolferman). All current undergraduates at the time, they met with us for two hours every Monday morning at 8 a.m. From diverse corners of campus life—from the head of the association of fraternities and sororities, to the head of the militant sexual assault activist group, to students who, by their own account, "kinda did nothing"—these students served as our guides to campus. Spending time with them was one of the great joys of the project, and we are deeply indebted to them for their commitment, advice, and good cheer.

We are grateful as well to the many administrators from divisions across campus who served on SHIFT's institutional advisory board, both for their willingness to act as a sounding board for our initial findings and for their reflections on the policy implications of what we saw. We hope that they continue to find our work useful as they strive to build a campus where all students can thrive. We are particularly thankful to Cristen Kromm, Dean of Undergraduate Student Life, and her entire office, for all their help and insights.

When we began this research, a group of experts generously joined us for a two-day conference, to help us anticipate some challenges and think through our ideas and design. We are grateful for the generosity and guidance of Antonia Abbey, Elizabeth A. Armstrong, Sarah DeGue, Mary Koss, Tal Peretz, Sharyn Potter, Laura Salazar, Martie Thompson, and Mikel Walters. We are indebted to those who generously gave us comments on the fully drafted manuscript—Victoria Banyard, Kathleen Clark, Roger Lehecka, Connie Nathanson, and Adam Reich—as well as to Elizabeth M. Armstrong for incisive comments on Chapters 2 and

9 and to Leslie Kantor for reviewing the conclusion. We did our best to respond to their valuable suggestions. In addition to sharing this work both formally and informally with colleagues at Columbia, we greatly benefited from the feedback we received on this project by giving lectures in other institutions of higher education, including: Carleton College, Haverford College, Hanoi Medical University, Institute for Philosophy in Prague, the Norwegian Center for Violence and Trauma Stress Studies, Princeton University, Rutgers University, Sciences Po, Stanford University's Clayman Institute University of California–Berkeley, Trinity College Dublin, University of Massachusetts–Amherst, University of Oslo, University of Pennsylvania, University of Virginia, University of Waterloo, Uppsala University, SUNY–Stony Brook, Vanderbilt University, Washington State University, and Yale University. We also presented ethnographic findings, and received useful feedback, at scientific meetings of the American Anthropological Association, the Society for Applied Anthropology, and the Population Association of America. Of course, none of those who we consulted along the way bear any responsibility for our failures to fully heed their advice.

We are fortunate to have been able to work with John Glusman and Helen Thomaides at W. W. Norton, with Jodi Beder, the copyeditor of this manuscript, and with our agent, Eric Lupfer at Fletcher and Co. They all worked patiently with us, carefully shepherding our work from proposal to actual book, providing insights and thoughtful feedback along the way.

SHIFT was funded by Columbia University, with special thanks to generous support from the Lavine family. The research benefited from infrastructural support from the Columbia Population Research Center, which is funded by the Eunice Kennedy Shriver National Institute of Child Health and Human Development of the National Institutes of Health, under award number P2CHD058486. The content is solely the responsibility of the authors and does not represent the official views of the National Institutes of Health or of Columbia University.

Along the way the two of us have individually accumulated some debts, primarily to those who have provided moral support during what has been at times an emotionally grueling journey. Jennifer is grateful to her husband John, who did triple duty as a member of the SHIFT scientific team, sex education policy consultant, and captain of the home chicken cacciatore and chili support team; her sons Isaac and Jacob, for their support and willingness to serve as sounding boards for some of the arguments around hooking up; to Kathy Leichter and Jessica Hirsch, for their words of encouragement; and to her parents, David and Ellen Hirsch. Her father did not live to see the book's completion, but he is in her heart always, and she is grateful every day to have her mother by her side. Although this was not the book that she set out to write during her Guggenheim Fellowship—SHIFT both interrupted that project and provided a very different ethnographic context—it enabled her to explore those same questions at the intersection of sexuality and public health. It would be hard to imagine a more tranquil setting than an office overlooking the Woodrow Wilson School fountain, and so enormous thanks are due to Princeton's Center for Health and Well-Being for hosting Jennifer during the 2018–19 academic year, and to Ted Nadeau and Kirsten Thoft for sharing their warm roost on Linden Lane.

Shamus is thankful to those people he spoke to about the project and who offered insights, read the work, and provided the emotional support needed to write this kind of book. Thanks especially to Peter Bearman, Sam Kanson-Benanav, Max Besbris, Mark Bittman, Zach Bruder, Andrew Celli, Sara Christopherson, Nick D'Avella, Matt Desmond, Mustafa Emirbayer, Amy Feldman, Heather Ford, Brendan Gillett, Phil Goff, Mark Gould, Andy Hall, Christine Hall, Laura Hamilton, Mike Hirschfeld, Jonny Hunter, Eric Klinenberg, Jennifer Lena, Sharon Marcus, Tey Meadow, Chris Muller, Alondra Nelson, Cathy O'Neil, Eric Schwartz, Harel Shapira, Patrick Sharkey, Harry Stephenson, Alex Tilney, Rebekah Vaisey, Steve Vaisey, Andrea Voyer, Kate Walbert, Bruce Western, Fred Wherry, and Kate Zaloom. His students, and especially his graduate students, provided endless enthusiasm, inspiration, and support. Trinity College Dublin's Long Room Hub provided a wonderful summer retreat in which to write. Most of all, his parents, Omar, Divya, and Aidan helped make this book possible by reminding him of the joys of being with family.

Finally, to each other. This research has been a struggle and a joy. We—Jennifer and Shamus—didn't know one another before starting this project; today we joke that because of all the time we've spent together researching and writing, we've become almost the same person. We cried a lot together, but we laughed more. That may seem macabre, given the topic, but being able to talk about anything and everything, showing up in the work and for each other with our full selves, made the research not just bearable, but maybe even better. For all our work on designing this research, all our attempts to adhere to the highest standards of rigor, and our drive to develop new theoretical and conceptual frameworks for other scholars to draw upon, it was this more humanistic dynamic that made our research what it was. A guiding feature of this book is empathy; making that part of our research, we feel, made this project possible.

APPENDIX A: METHODOLOGY

The Sexual Health Initiative to Foster Transformation (SHIFT) was funded by Columbia University and formally launched in early 2015, under the joint leadership of Jennifer Hirsch and Claude Ann Mellins. SHIFT's broad goals were "to advance the science of sexual assault prevention and to contribute to building a healthier and safer undergraduate community."[1] Columbia administrators and staff provided institutional input through the research process. However, the SHIFT faculty investigators retained complete scientific independence in terms of study oversight, data access, and decisions about what and when we published. Unlike many faculty who conduct research on sexual assault at their own institution, the SHIFT team benefited from enormous institutional support, including help securing an exemption from mandated reporting. Federal rules require designated university employees to report all instances of gender-based misconduct, defined as sexual harassment, sexual assault, sexual exploitation, stalking, domestic violence, and dating violence. At Columbia, all faculty and staff are designated mandated reporters; without an exemption, the SHIFT team would have been required to make a formal report to the university for each instance of sexual assault we learned about. But as most students chose not to report experiences of assault, this would have rendered SHIFT unable talk to most students about their experiences. Our SHIFT-related mandated reporting exemption enabled us to guarantee confidentiality to students with whom we interacted in our capacity as SHIFT researchers (although not in roles of teaching or administration).

STUDY DESIGN AND COMMUNITY-BASED PARTICIPATORY RESEARCH APPROACH

In addition to the ethnography, SHIFT's overall research design involved two forms of quantitative research: 60-day daily diary study with 427 Columbia undergraduates and a population-based survey, sent out to a representative sample of 2500 Columbia and Barnard undergraduates.[2] The project drew on the tenets of community-based participatory research, including stakeholder engagement both to improve the quality of our research and to help us develop effective recommendations for innovative, institutionally appropriate, evidence-based strategies to reduce sexual violence and promote sexual health at Columbia.[3] Concretely, this meant working with an Institutional Advisory Board, consisting of a group of administrators from Columbia and Barnard responsible for undergraduate safety and well-being; an Undergraduate Advisory Board (UAB); and a Faculty Advisory Board. The UAB comprised of approximately eighteen undergraduates from Columbia and Barnard. They represented a range of different student interest groups, from the head of the leading organization protesting how the University handled sexual assault cases, to captains of athletic teams, members of student government, and those who, by their own account, were relatively disengaged from campus life. They also represented a range of sexual and racial identities, as well as socioeconomic backgrounds and national origins. We met with this diverse group of undergraduates once a week, on Monday mornings, from 8 to 10 a.m., over the course of two years. Members were paid for the time so they didn't have to choose between participating in our group and working a campus job. The UAB also helped us develop strategies to recruit students for the different components of the research, and provided insight into life at Columbia and Barnard. They contributed in important ways to our campus presence as a student-friendly organization that could be trusted. The UAB helped create a campus-wide buzz about the project with activities such as posting flyers, sponsoring study breaks, advertising on Facebook, and sending creative emails. As our UAB was composed of current students, we set clear guidelines about their work with us. Each member signed collectively developed and mutually agreed-upon rules that outlined confidentiality of information shared in our meetings as well as respect for group members' opinions. UAB members were excluded as research subjects and were never presented with any data that would allow them to identify an interviewee or someone we encountered during our fieldwork.

TIME FRAME AND SCOPE OF ETHNOGRAPHIC RESEARCH

Jennifer and Shamus first met in November 2014 to discuss working together on SHIFT. Nine months of pre-fieldwork preparation were spent constructing interview protocols, participant observation guides, and the wide range of research procedures required to do this study. We also hired our staff during this time. Interviews began in late summer 2015; ethnographic observations began shortly thereafter. Research continued through January 2017, spanning one and a half academic years. The team completed 151 in-depth student interviews, 25 student follow-up interviews, 18 key informant interviews, 17 focus groups (of about 10 students each), and about 600 hours of community and participant observations. All of the research procedures, including steps taken to protect the data itself, were reviewed and approved by Columbia's Institutional Review Board (IRB). The three tables in Appendix B contain information on the characteristics of our interview sample and our focus groups, and the spaces and length of time where we made observations.

We began data analysis while still collecting and writing papers from our data starting in 2016. We began writing this book in January 2018 and completed it in summer 2019.

ASSEMBLING OUR RESEARCH TEAM

For the ethnography we hired a diverse staff with master's- and doctoral-level training in both interviewing and participant observation. We provided this staff of five people with additional training in study goals and methods, procedures for the protection of human subjects, and our shared emergency protocol in case a research participant became distressed. In addition to the research expertise of Hirsch and Khan, the ethnographic team collectively had done research on queer communities of color (anthropology), masculinity, power, and relationship violence (anthropology), and trauma and sexual abuse (social work), and had worked on a series of public health research projects on sexual activity within communities of color. Like everyone involved with the SHIFT project, team members adhered to SHIFT's publication policy, which specified the process for proposing and doing the analysis for scientific publications drawing on the SHIFT data. As we prepare this book for publication, seven papers have been published or are scheduled for publication with a SHIFT ethnographic team member as first author, and several others are in development or under review. From the beginning of the research, Jennifer and Shamus made clear to the SHIFT research team that they intended to write a book drawing on the ethnography.

RECRUITMENT OF INTERVIEW AND FOCUS GROUP SUBJECTS

Students were recruited for interviews in six primary ways: (1) by being contacted after they wrote directly to SHIFT requesting to be interviewed, in response to an email sent to all students about the SHIFT survey; (2) through our Undergraduate Advisory Board (UAB), which connected us to student interest groups we wanted to reach, and where we made in-person presentations about our project; (3) using a snowball sample where some interviewees recommended to their friends that they contact the research team; (4) by targeted recruitment of survivors of sexual assault through email that asked students to contact us if they had "a story to tell"; (5) through an on-campus presence in the form of articles in the student paper, flyers, signs, and electronic bulletin boards; and (6) through our participant observation, during which we asked people if they were interested in being interviewed. About half of the students who participated in in-depth interviews were recruited by research staff in this sixth way: through participant observation.

A word of explanation is necessary about that first group of students. The email sent out in the winter of 2016, announcing the upcoming survey, went directly to the entire undergraduate student body at Columbia from SHIFT's (no longer operative) general account, shift@columbia.edu, and was sent to Barnard undergraduates as well. We were somewhat taken aback to receive responses from many individual students, saying that they wanted to participate in a confidential interview because they had a story to tell. We hired another interviewer, Megan Kordenbruck, who had a background in trauma-informed interviewing, to help us respond to these interviews; Megan followed up with each one, and then they were interviewed by a team member of their choice. We were struck by how eager many students were to tell their stories as a way of shaping campus responses to sexual assault. Because of how we picked students to interview, there are likely biases within our sample. We did not interview any students who described intentionally acting in a way that they understood in that same moment as sexual assault; we suspect that those who deliberately act to harm their peers were unlikely to choose to sit down with us for an interview. Students who were assaulted and who were unhappy with their experiences reporting to the university were probably more likely to sit with us than those who were happy with their experiences.

The team tracked various axes of diversity to ensure that the many voices and perspectives of the student population were represented.

Research participants, who were screened to ensure that they were currently enrolled undergraduates at either Columbia or Barnard, also provided demographic information. Students received $35 for participating in the initial in-depth interview; for those for whom subsequent interviews were required to capture the breadth of their experiences, $40 was given for each follow-up interview. Interviews averaged approximately two hours. The SHIFT website featured a photo and brief bio of every member of the ethnographic team, and participants could select who they wanted to interview them. Our team of seven people represented a range of gender identities, sexual orientations, religious backgrounds, racial identities, and personal experiences. Students tended to pick the person who first contacted them as their interviewer. One student expressed regrets about what they had said in their interview; we deleted this interview and did not use it in our analysis.

CONDUCTING OUR INTERVIEWS

Our in-depth interviews were all done in a private office on campus. During these interviews we gathered information on the participant's life before college, including their relationship with their family; their experiences with substance use; their life as an undergraduate; current and past sexual and intimate relationships, with an emphasis on experiences during college; how consent worked within their sexual interactions; nonconsensual sexual experiences; and how the organizational rules and structures at Columbia or Barnard shaped their lives. Our interview started by asking students about how they ended up at Columbia, and continued by asking about their experiences with their family, with substance use, and sex were before coming to college. We then asked about college experiences, before asking subjects to describe a typical sexual experience, a good sexual experience, and a bad one. We never used the word "consent" in these first conversations; instead we simply asked students to describe what happened. Often they would say things like, "Well, you know . . ." so as to avoid more explicit descriptions of how they ended up naked with another person. We would reply with some version of "I'm sorry, but I don't know. I'd like you to tell me, to the degree that you're comfortable." After we heard these descriptions of what happened, we went back over the sequence of events to talk about consent. Students are well versed in the necessity for consent, and had it been in the forefront of their mind when they first described their sexual experiences, they would have likely framed all their encounters relative to consent. After they described the three kinds of encounters we asked them about, we asked them about assault. We didn't ask questions about stalking, revenge porn, sexual harassment, or nonsexual forms of intimate partner violence. We intentionally chose to dig deep on a narrower set of topics focusing on assault rather than to provide a shallower understanding of a wider range of experiences. Several of the students we interviewed had not had many sexual experiences; some had had none at all. These interviews were briefer, but we nonetheless asked questions about their sexual projects. About a quarter of the way through our research we revised the interview questions in light of what was and was not working within the interviews. The interviews were professionally transcribed by a company that had a written agreement with Columbia University to adhere to standards for data protection. For quotes drawn from the interviews, we have removed "ums" and "likes," but otherwise have not altered direct quotations in any way.

FOCUS GROUPS

The focus groups, all moderated by Shamus, touched on topics similar to those of the in-depth interviews, but emphasized how groups of students think about those issues, and general patterns of behavior and shared ideas. Focus groups lasted approximately two hours, and participants received $30. Groups averaged about ten participants each. Students either volunteered to participate by responding to posters placed around campus or to a campus-wide email, or they were directly recruited because they represented or participated in a group of interest. There was little overlap between focus group participants and interview subjects. In addition to groups that included any member of the student body, we constituted groups that were solely comprised of students of a single sex, international students, first-year students, athletes, LGBTQ students, religiously engaged students, racial minority students, and students who were the first in their family to attend college. Our aim was to capture both the general conversation on campus, and those of specific groups or kinds of campus experiences that were of interest to us. Table 2 in Appendix B provides a more detailed account of the focus groups' composition.

KEY INFORMANT INTERVIEWS

Jennifer and the research staff conducted key informant interviews, composed to form two groups. First were administrators, who oversaw specific policies and procedures like housing, alcohol, or orientation that were relevant to our study. The second group were a small number of students who held student leadership positions or served as resident advisors. The goals of those interviews were to understand what administrative actors know or perceive regarding social, academic, and interpersonal student experiences; how administrative actors perceive and describe sexual assault; and what the institutional terrain is, including relevant policies related to alcohol and substance use, and to sexual assault. Students received $35 for the key informant interviews; administrators were not compensated.

PARTICIPANT AND COMMUNITY OBSERVATION

For just over one and half academic years, from September 2015 through January 2017, the team engaged in participant and community observation at various locations both on and off campus. On-campus spaces included Columbia and Barnard dorms, academic buildings, campus community space, athletics spaces, fraternity-sorority life spaces, and dining halls. Off-campus spaces, which were visited by invitation from a student, included bars, restaurants, coffee shops, and public and community spaces around New York City.

Jennifer and Shamus's participant observations were limited to large public events; the experiences and activities that were in some way the most essential to understanding students' lived experience were off-limits to us. Instead, we had to set up structures to transfer both the field notes and the "headnotes" from our research staff to us. We required weekly submission of detailed field notes for all observations and brief write-ups of each week's in-depth interviews. These field notes were submitted each Sunday. Jennifer and Shamus reviewed the notes and met for two hours on Mondays or Tuesdays. On Thursdays we held two-hour meetings with the entire ethnographic team, who also read each other's notes and interview summaries. These weekly meetings provided an opportunity to ask questions, discuss emerging themes, push the staff to follow specific lines of inquiry, and keep tabs on which groups were being included in the research and which were still not adequately covered. It also allowed all members of the research team to discuss their various impressions of the previous week and the project more generally.

From fall 2015 through spring 2017 the authors of this book met for a minimum of six hours a week, and often longer: two with each other, to discuss the field notes and interview summaries; two with the UAB to discuss the design and findings; and two with the ethnographic team as a whole. We also met with the quantitative team regularly. The quantitative team was led by Claude A. Mellins, an expert in adolescent and young adult development, mental health, substance use, and trauma, and included Louisa Gilbert, a professor of social work with expertise in gender-based violence, substance use, and HIV; John Santelli, a pediatrician and expert on adolescents, sexual health, and sexual education (and Jennifer's husband); Melanie Wall, a biostatistician with expertise in public health, epidemiology, and quantitative analysis; Kate Walsh, a psychologist whose research has focused on trauma exposure, particularly sexual assault; and Patrick Wilson, a psychologist with experience studying health disparities, HIV, and the health outcomes of more marginalized populations. We held occasional all-team meetings to share findings with the quantitative and ethnographic teams.

Throughout the book, all of the fieldwork activity is presented in the first-person plural; that is, we talk about students talking "to us" or write about things that "we" saw. In participant observation in public places, interviews with students that Jennifer or Shamus personally conducted, all of the key informant interviews with university administrators, and all of the focus groups, this "we" refers to Jennifer or Shamus, who collected the data directly. In all other instances, "we" refers to the ethnographic research team staff members, with the write-ups based on interview transcripts, interview summaries, field notes, and other documents produced in the course of data condensation and analysis.

PROTOCOL FOR INTERACTING WITH STUDENTS

An essential element of the participant observation was the clearly articulated protocol for identifying ourselves as researchers when interacting with students. Team members always identified themselves as researchers, told students what SHIFT was, advised them that interacting with the researcher was optional, and offered contact information for the lead researchers should the student have questions or concerns. SHIFT researchers were never "under cover." We publicized our project with flyers, emails, and several pieces in the student newspaper, the *Columbia Spectator*. Team members always secured permission from hosts to enter any private student space such as a dorm room or a suite or basement party, and provided information about who students could contact if they had further questions. Jennifer and Shamus did not do any participant observation with students in student-controlled private social spaces such as dorms, student apartments off-campus, and fraternity houses. We are both faculty at Columbia University; it seemed unlikely that we would be able to gather reliable data, and we were conscious of student concerns about having their professors hanging out at parties with them. All of the participant observation with students in student-controlled spaces was conducted by the research staff we hired, who were closer in age to the students and thereby less likely to stand out in such spaces.

DEALING WITH STUDENTS IN CRISIS

Given our topic, we developed a process to identify students we encountered who were in crisis and refer them to services in the hope of getting them the help they needed. This "emergency protocol," drawing on Claude Mellins's research with vulnerable adolescents and young adults, provided our staff with guidelines to assess and appropriately refer students in crisis. As a further safeguard, one of SHIFT's two clinicians—Mellins, who is a clinical psychologist, or John Santelli, who is an adolescent medicine physician—was always on call in case a team member had questions. Over the course of our research, we retrained our team multiple times in our crisis assessment and procedures. Mellins also supported the entire team in managing our own emotional responses to the difficult stories that emerged during the course of our research. At one point or another every member of our team experienced some degree of "vicarious traumatization"—taking on some of the emotional burdens experienced by our interview subjects. Mellins helped all of us, including the authors, manage these experiences.

ON OBSERVING ILLEGAL ACTIVITY

During our research, our team sometimes observed illegal activities, from cocaine use (relatively rare) to underage drinking (fairly common). We developed a protocol to articulate our obligations for intervention: simply put, if someone seemed in acute danger of harming either themselves or others, we had an obligation to intervene. Otherwise, we simply observed. We made clear to our research staff that even if it meant threatening our capacity to do research, we had an obligation to intervene if, say, we saw a man carrying a woman who was all-but-passed-out from a party to some other location. This never happened. But it was necessary, for example, to help get a young woman an ambulance to the emergency room because she was so exceptionally drunk at a downtown club (away from campus). She was also underage—but our concern was her severe incapacitation, not her age. Our researchers never broke the law, nor facilitated any breaking of the law. Our role was not to police behavior, but to observe it. Through our observations, we hoped, we would generate insights that could make experiences of sexual assault less likely. Had we intervened at every illegal act, our observations would have been impossible. We were always transparent with our subjects about what we were doing, and raised with the IRB any ethical concerns that arose during the course of our research; we were always in compliance with what we saw as our ethical obligations, and with the requirements of the IRB.

TEAM MEETINGS

We started every ethnographic team meeting with a mental health check-in. This book contains a lot of painful stories; hearing them directly was emotionally difficult, and talking to one another helped with this burden. Acknowledging and providing each other with support was essential to the team's capacity to do our work. The mental health check-in was also the time to share feelings that research staff suppressed as we strove to maintain a relatively neutral listening stance when students shared stories that generated strong feelings. Taking into account how each member of our staff deliberately crafted a social self, we asked the team members involved in participant observation to write up lengthy notes about who these social selves had been and how they had experienced inhabiting them. These created a written record of how each researcher made deliberate choices regarding self-presentation, and gave us a lens through which to read and consider the interviews that each member of the ethnography team produced. Such reflections were essential to our data analysis.

DATA ANALYSIS

The data from this research consisted of interview transcripts, focus group transcripts, research notes about each interview and focus group (describing the mood and other details that could not be captured in a transcript), field notes, and descriptions of each researcher's "social self." The interview transcripts totaled nearly 20,000 pages; the other materials added thousands more. We analyzed our data in two ways. Two team members coded all information for eleven major themes: socializing, partner selection, relationships, sexual projects, stories of sexual assault, consent, telling someone about sexual assault, mental health experiences, alcohol and substance use, sexual experience (not assault), and other notes. We also constructed many types of secondary documents: for example, extracting all the stories of assault from interviews and analyzing what happened before, during, and after the event. These secondary documents were essential, given the mass of data we had; they also helped us see themes we hadn't coded for. While many qualitative researchers today use coding and analysis software, we do not. Instead, we pored over the transcripts and field notes, writing about them, having conversations about them, and eventually, coming to some kind of understanding. There were major themes we paid attention to because the broad literature guided us to. But there were also themes that emerged over the almost five years of working together, talking about it with one another and our team, and writing up our results. We did not include quotes from every single student we interviewed or interacted with in the book. But the experiences of every single participant shaped the analysis presented here; we have spent hours and hours poring over their transcripts, reading the field notes, reviewing the write-ups produced immediately after each interview.

STUDENT PRIVACY AND IDENTITY

To protect the identity of participants, we took a number of steps beyond the obvious one of not using their real names, including changing critical identifying details such as hometown, family characteristics, physical descriptions, and extracurricular activities. We have gone to particularly great lengths to mask group identities as well. We tried, in selecting alternate descriptions of students' group participation, to pick groups that paralleled the social prestige and meaning of the original group. Anything named as a team is not that team and may not have been an athletic organization at all. Yet we would not transform a member of the football team into a member of the chess club. Football players may be members of the chess club, but the interpretation of the reader for such a replacement would likely generate an inaccurate impression we sought to avoid. Some organizations we made up; we know that there is not an epicurean club.

At the same time, some information we do not change. All the stories of assault remain strictly true to the experiences of students as they described them. Demographic and personal information might be purposefully inaccurate, but the stories hew extremely close to how the events were recounted to us. And if information is analytically important (for example, gender or race), we haven't changed it. The experience of Black men having unique experiences navigating consent are all from Black men. We have not created any "synthetic characters"—combining stories from different people into a single person. However, we have, in a small number of instances, made a single person into different people for purposes of telling different stories unrelated to one another and, in our evaluation, unimportant to one another. Doing so reduced the likelihood that research subjects could be identified by their friends and peers. We believe that most people will be unable to identify themselves, though given the specifics of some of the stories, and the fact that they know they spoke with us, some subjects may suspect that a person in the book is drawn from their story.

In some cases, students who participated in the research struggled to grasp the separation between our roles as professor or class teacher and as researcher. We stressed that all research would remain confidential and that data would be deidentified, coded with research IDs and pseudonyms, not actual names. However, students often missed this distinction. For example, a student in Shamus's class told him that her assignment would be late because of reasons discussed in her recent in-depth interview, which had been conducted by another team member. Shamus had to reiterate that he did not know which of his students participated in the research, and that her name was not associated with her stories. Similarly, we repeatedly had to clarify both with research participants and with the UAB that our team members were not "spies"; we always identified ourselves as researchers when doing observations in both public and private spaces.

Alexander Wamboldt, one of our ethnographic team members, reviewed this manuscript with two tasks: (1) to weigh in on the changes we had made to protect students from identification by their peers, and (2) to verify our representation of every single story, making sure our accounts accurately represented the material in our transcripts and field notes. This second task allowed us to authenticate every account provided in this book. We are deeply indebted to Alex for undertaking this task. Any errors are, of course, our own.

APPENDIX B: TABLES

Table 1: In-depth interview sample characteristics (N=151)

CHARACTERISTIC	N	%
Year in school		
Freshman	26	18%
Sophomore	38	26%
Junior	54	37%
Senior	29	20%
College		
Columbia College	100	68%
Barnard	28	19%
Engineering	14	37%
General Studies	5	3%
Gender		
Female	85	58%
Male	55	37%
Trans Female	1	1%
Genderqueer/Other	6	4%

CHARACTERISTIC	N	%
Race (not mutually exclusive)		
Am. Indian/Alaskan Native	8	5%
Asian	30	20%
Black/African American	28	19%
Hispanic or Latino only	11	7%
More than one race	22	15%
Nat. Hawaiian/Pacific Isl.	3	2%
Other	7	5%
White	73	50%
Sexual identity		
Straight/Heterosexual	107	73%
Gay/Lesbian	8	5%
Bisexual	12	8%
Queer/Asexual/Other	20	14%
How students pay for college		
Pell Grants for low-income students	16	11%
Parents/family only	80	54%
Other (combination of ways)	51	35%

Table 2: Focus group characteristics (N=17)

GROUP CHARACTERISTIC	N
Co-ed	3
Male only	2
Female only	3
Barnard only	1
First-year (freshmen)	2
First-year (freshmen) minority	1
International	1

GROUP CHARACTERISTIC	N
Minority students	1
First-generation college	1
Religiously engaged	1
LGBTQ	1

Table 3: Participant observation hours and locations

LOCATION TYPE	HOURS
Dorm	160.4*
Special-interest house (residential)	9.5
Fraternity/sorority	18.75
Dining hall	8.5
Religious space	19
Ethnic and cultural space	27
Off-campus space—outdoor	54.5
Campus space (including outdoor campus spaces)	185.5*
Off-campus space—indoor	111.25

*Fraternity and sorority events took place in fraternity houses, dorms, and campus spaces.

NOTES

INTRODUCTION: A NEW APPROACH

1. Jennifer S. Hirsch et al., "Transforming the Campus Climate: Advancing Mixed-Methods Research on the Social and Cultural Roots of Sexual Assault on a College Campus," *Voices:* 13, no. 1 (2018): 23–54, https://doi.org/10.1111/voic.12003.
2. Peggy Sanday, *Fraternity Gang Rape: Sex, Brotherhood, and Privilege on Campus* (NYU Press, 2007); Elizabeth A. Armstrong, Laura Hamilton, and Brian Sweeney, "Sexual Assault on Campus: A Multilevel, Integrative Approach to Party Rape," *Social Problems* 53, no. 4 (2006): 483–99, https://doi.org/10.1525/sp.2006.53.4.483.
3. U. Bronfenbrenner, "Toward an Experimental Ecology of Human Development," *American Psychologist* 32, no. 7 (1977): 513–31.
4. Richard H. Thaler and Cass R. Sunstein, *Nudge: Improving Decisions about Health, Wealth, and Happiness*, rev. and expanded ed (New York: Penguin Books, 2009).
5. Jennifer S. Hirsch, "Desire across Borders: Markets, Migration, and Marital HIV Risk in Rural Mexico," *Culture, Health and Sexuality* 17, no. S1 (2015): 20–33, https://doi.org/10.1080/13691058.2014.963681.
6. Claude A. Mellins et al., "Sexual Assault Incidents among College Undergraduates: Prevalence and Factors Associated with Risk," *PLOS ONE* 12, no. 11 (November 8, 2017): e0186471, https://doi.org/10.1371/journal.pone.0186471.
7. Bonnie S. Fisher, Francis T. Cullen, and Michael G. Turner, "The Sexual Victimization of College Women: Research Report" (Washington, DC: Department of Justice, National Inst. of Justice, Bureau of Justice Statistics, 2000), http://eric.ed.gov/?id=ED449712; Lisa Fedina, Jennifer Lynne Holmes, and Bethany L. Backes,

"Campus Sexual Assault: A Systematic Review of Prevalence Research From 2000 to 2015," *Trauma, Violence, and Abuse* 19, no. 1 (January 1, 2018): 76–93, https://doi .org/10.1177/1524838016631129; Christopher P. Krebs et al., "The Campus Sexual Assault Study (CSA) Final Report: Performance Period: January 2005 through December 2007" (Rockville, MD: National Institute of Justice, 2007).

8. Mellins et al., "Sexual Assault Incidents among College Undergraduates."

9. William George Axinn, Maura Elaine Bardos, and Brady Thomas West, "General Population Estimates of the Association between College Experience and the Odds of Forced Intercourse," *Social Science Research* 70 (February 2018): 131–43, https:// doi.org/10.1016/j.ssresearch.2017.10.006; Ann L. Coker et al., "Are Interpersonal Violence Rates Higher among Young Women in College Compared with Those Never Attending College?," *Journal of Interpersonal Violence* 31, no. 8 (May 2016): 1413–29, https://doi.org/10.1177/0886260514567958; Sofi Sinozich and Lynn Langton, "Rape and Sexual Assault among College-Age Females, 1995–2013" (Washington, DC: Bureau of Justice Statistics, U.S. Department of Justice, December 11, 2014), https://www.bjs.gov/index.cfm?ty=pbdetail&iid=5176.

10. Cora Peterson et al., "Lifetime Economic Burden of Rape among U.S. Adults," *American Journal of Preventive Medicine* 52, no. 6 (2017): 691–701, https://doi.org/10 .1016/j.amepre.2016.11.014.

11. Jennifer S. Hirsch et al., eds., *The Secret: Love, Marriage, and HIV* (Nashville: Vanderbilt University Press, 2010); Hirsch, "Desire across Borders."

12. Stephanie Sanders et al., "Misclassification Bias: Diversity in Conceptualisations about Having 'Had Sex,'" *Sexual Health* 7, no. 1 (2010): 31–34.

13. Maggie Jones, "What Teenagers Are Learning from Online Porn," *New York Times*, February 7, 2018, https://www.nytimes.com/2018/02/07/magazine/teenagers-learning -online-porn-literacy-sex-education.html.

14. Daniel Jordan Smith and Benjamin C. Mbakwem, "Antiretroviral Therapy and Reproductive Life Projects: Mitigating the Stigma of AIDS in Nigeria," *Social Science and Medicine* 71, no. 2 (July 2010): 345–52, https://doi.org/10.1016/j.socscimed .2010.04.006.

15. Janet Zollinger Giele and Glen H. Elder, eds., *Methods of Life Course Research: Qualitative and Quantitative Approaches* (Thousand Oaks, CA: Sage Publications, 1998).

16. Steven Epstein and Héctor Carrillo, "Immigrant Sexual Citizenship: Intersectional Templates among Mexican Gay Immigrants to the USA," *Citizenship Studies* 18, no. 3–4 (April 3, 2014): 259–76, https://doi.org/10.1080/13621025.2014.905266; Jessica Fields, *Risky Lessons: Sex Education and Social Inequality* (New Brunswick, NJ: Rutgers University Press, 2008); Diane Richardson, "Constructing Sexual Citizenship: Theorizing Sexual Rights," *Critical Social Policy* 20, no. 1 (February 1, 2000): 105–35, https://doi.org/10.1177/026101830002000105.

17. Karen Benjamin Guzzo, "Trends in Cohabitation Outcomes: Compositional

Changes and Engagement among Never-Married Young Adults," *Journal of Marriage and Family* 76, no. 4 (August 2014): 826–42, https://doi.org/10.1111/jomf.12123.

18. Lawrence B. Finer and Jesse M. Philbin, "Trends in Ages at Key Reproductive Transitions in the United States, 1951–2010," *Women's Health Issues* 24, no. 3 (May 2014): e271–79, https://doi.org/10.1016/j.whi.2014.02.002; Guttmacher Institute, "Adolescent Sexual and Reproductive Health in the United States" (New York: Guttmacher Institute, September 2017), https://www.guttmacher.org/fact-sheet/american-teens-sexual-and-reproductive-health.

19. Guttmacher Institute, "Adolescent Sexual and Reproductive Health in the United States."

20. Lawrence B. Finer, "Trends in Premarital Sex in the United States, 1954–2003," *Public Health Reports* 122, no. 1 (January 2007): 73–78, https://doi.org/10.1177/003335490712200110.

21. Finer and Philbin, "Trends in Ages at Key Reproductive Transitions in the United States, 1951–2010."

22. John S. Santelli et al., "Abstinence-Only-Until-Marriage: An Updated Review of U.S. Policies and Programs and Their Impact," *Journal of Adolescent Health* 61, no. 3 (September 2017): 273–80, https://doi.org/10.1016/j.jadohealth.2017.05.031.

23. Santelli et al., "Abstinence-Only-Until-Marriage."

24. Fields, *Risky Lessons*.

25. Laura Duberstein Lindberg, Isaac Maddow-Zimet, and Heather Boonstra, "Changes in Adolescents' Receipt of Sex Education, 2006–2013," *Journal of Adolescent Health* 58, no. 6 (June 2016): 621–27, https://doi.org/10.1016/j.jadohealth.2016.02.004.

26. Guttmacher Institute, "American Adolescents' Sources of Sexual Health Information" (New York: Guttmacher Institute, December 2017), https://www.guttmacher.org/fact-sheet/facts-american-teens-sources-information-about-sex; Madeline Schneider and Jennifer S. Hirsch, "Comprehensive Sexuality Education as a Primary Prevention Strategy for Sexual Violence Perpetration:," *Trauma, Violence, and Abuse*, May 2, 2018, 1–17, https://doi.org/10.1177/1524838018772855.

27. Lindberg, Maddow-Zimet, and Boonstra, "Changes in Adolescents' Receipt of Sex Education, 2006–2013."

28. Robert J. Sampson, *Great American City: Chicago and the Enduring Neighborhood Effect*. (Chicago: University of Chicago Press, 2011); Hirsch et al., *The Secret*.

29. Jennifer S. Hirsch, *A Courtship after Marriage: Sexuality and Love in Mexican Transnational Families* (Berkeley: University of California Press, 2003); Hirsch et al., *The Secret*; Lynda Johnston and Robyn Longhurst, *Space, Place, and Sex: Geographies of Sexualities* (Lanham: Rowman & Littlefield, 2010).

30. Elizabeth A. Armstrong and Laura T. Hamilton, *Paying for the Party: How College Maintains Inequality* (Cambridge, MA: Harvard University Press, 2013).

31. Kimberle Crenshaw, "Demarginalizing the Intersection of Race and Sex: A Black Feminist Critique of Antidiscrimination Doctrine, Feminist Theory, and Antiracist Politics," *University of Chicago Legal Forum* 1989: 139–67.

32. Gerda Lerner, ed., *Black Women in White America: A Documentary History* (New York: Vintage Books, 1992).

33. Danielle L. McGuire, *At the Dark End of the Street: Black Women, Rape, and Resistance- a New History of the Civil Rights Movement from Rosa Parks to the Rise of Black Power* (New York: Alfred A. Knopf, 2010); The National Museum of African-American History and Culture, "The Scottsboro Boys," 2019, https://nmaahc.si .edu/blog/scottsboro-boys.

34. Combahee River Collective, "Combahee River Collective Statement," in *Home Girls: A Black Feminist Anthology*, ed. Barbara Smith (New York: Kitchen Table— Women of Color Press, 1983), 264–74; McGuire, *At the Dark End of the Street*.

35. Combahee River Collective, "Combahee River Collective Statement."

36. Susan Brownmiller, *Against Our Will: Men, Women, and Rape*, reprinted edition (New York: Ballantine Books, 1993); Megan Gibson, "I Am Woman, Hear Me Roar: Take Back the Night," *Time*, August 12, 2011.

37. Desiree Abu-Odeh, Constance Nathanson, and Shamus Khan, "Bureaucratization of Sex at Columbia and Barnard, 1955 to 1990," *Social Science History*, forthcoming.

38. Sanday, *Fraternity Gang Rape*; Regina Kulik Scully et al., *The Hunting Ground* (Anchor Bay Entertainment, Inc., 2015).

39. Clifford Kirkpatrick and Eugene Kanin, "Male Sex Aggression on a University Campus," *American Sociological Review* 22, no. 1 (February 1957): 52, https://doi .org/10.2307/2088765.

40. Kirkpatrick and Kanin, "Male Sex Aggression on a University Campus"; Mary P. Koss, Christine A. Gidycz, and Nadine Wisniewski, "The Scope of Rape: Incidence and Prevalence of Sexual Aggression and Victimization in a National Sample of Higher Education Students," *Journal of Consulting and Clinical Psychology* 55, no. 2 (1987): 162–70; Robin Warshaw and Mary P. Koss, *I Never Called It Rape: The Ms. Report on Recognizing, Fighting, and Surviving Date and Acquaintance Rape* (New York: Harper/Perennial, 1994).

41. Jody Jessup-Anger, Elise Lopez, and Mary P. Koss, "History of Sexual Violence in Higher Education: History of Sexual Violence in Higher Education," *New Directions for Student Services* 2018, no. 161 (March 2018): 9–19, https://doi.org/10.1002/ ss.20249; Heather M. Karjane, Bonnie Fisher, and Francis T. Cullen, *Sexual Assault on Campus: What Colleges and Universities Are Doing about It* (US Department of Justice, Office of Justice Programs, National Institute of Justice, 2005), https://www .ncjrs.gov/App/abstractdb/AbstractDBDetails.aspx?id=205521.

42. Lori L. Heise, "Violence against Women: An Integrated, Ecological Framework," *Violence against Women* 4, no. 3 (June 1, 1998): 262–90, https://doi.org/10

.1177/1077801298004003002; Rebecca Campbell, Emily Dworkin, and Giannina Cabral, "An Ecological Model of the Impact of Sexual Assault on Women's Mental Health," *Trauma, Violence, and Abuse*, 2009, http://tva.sagepub.com/content/early/20 09/05/10/1524838009334456.short; Erin A. Casey and Taryn P. Lindhorst, "Toward a Multi-Level, Ecological Approach to the Primary Prevention of Sexual Assault: Prevention in Peer and Community Contexts," *Trauma, Violence and Abuse* 10, no. 2 (April 2009): 91–114, https://doi.org/10.1177/1524838009334129.

43. "Jeanne Clery Disclosure of Campus Security Policy and Campus Crime Statistics Act of 1990," 20 U.S.C. § §1092(f) (2018); Title IX, 20 U.S.C. Education Amendments Act of 1972 § §§1681–1688; "Violence Against Women Act of 1993," 42 U.S.C § §13701–14040 (1994).

44. A. Russlynn, "Dear Colleague Letter" (U.S. Department of Education, Office for Civil Rights, April 4, 2011); Celene Reynolds, "The Mobilization of Title IX across U.S. Colleges and Universities, 1994–2014," *Social Problems* 66, no. 2 (May 1, 2019): 245–73, https://doi.org/10.1093/socpro/spy005.

45. Reynolds, "The Mobilization of Title IX across U.S. Colleges and Universities, 1994–2014."

46. Nick Anderson, "At First, 55 Schools Faced Sexual Violence Investigations. Now the List Has Quadrupled," *Washington Post*, January 18, 2017; Juliet Eilperin, "Seeking to End Rape on Campus, White House Launches 'It's On Us,'" *Washington Post*, September 19, 2014, http://www.washingtonpost.com/blogs/post-politics/ wp/2014/09/19/seeking-to-end-rape-on-campus-wh-launches-its-on-us/.

47. Shannen Doherty and Cypress Hill, "Is It Date Rape?," *Saturday Night Live*, season 19 (NBC, October 2, 1993); "Affirmative Consent Laws (Yes Means Yes) State by State," AffirmativeConsent.com, accessed July 17, 2017, http://affirmativeconsent .com/affirmative-consent-laws-state-by-state/.

48. Catharine A. MacKinnon, "Feminism, Marxism, Method, and the State: Toward Feminist Jurisprudence," *Signs: Journal of Women in Culture and Society* 8, no. 4 (July 1983): 635–58, https://doi.org/10.1086/494000.

49. John J. Dilulio, "Fill Churches, Not Jails: Youth Crime and 'Superpredators'" (1996).

50. John D. Foubert, Angela Clark-Taylor, and Andrew F. Wall, "Is Campus Rape Primarily a Serial or One-Time Problem? Evidence From a Multicampus Study," *Violence against Women*, March 18, 2019, 1077780121983382, https://doi.org/10 .1177/1077801219833820.

51. David Cantor et al., "Report on the AAU Campus Climate Survey on Sexual Assault and Sexual Misconduct: Columbia University" (Rockville, MD: The American Association of Universities, September 21, 2015).

52. Amy T. Schalet, *Not under My Roof: Parents, Teens, and the Culture of Sex* (Chicago: University of Chicago Press, 2011).

53. Sharyn J. Potter, "Reducing Sexual Assault on Campus: Lessons From the Move-

ment to Prevent Drunk Driving," *American Journal of Public Health* 106, no. 5 (2016): 822–29.

54. Victoria L. Banyard, Mary M. Moynihan, and Maria T. Crossman, "Reducing Sexual Violence on Campus: The Role of Student Leaders as Empowered Bystanders," *Journal of College Student Development* 50, no. 4 (2009): 446–57; A. Mabry and M. M. Turner, "Do Sexual Assault Bystander Interventions Change Men's Intentions? Applying the Theory of Normative Social Behavior to Predicting Bystander Outcomes," *Journal of Health Communication* 21, no. 3 (2015): 276–92; Sarah DeGue et al., "A Systematic Review of Primary Prevention Strategies for Sexual Violence Perpetration," *Aggression and Violent Behavior* 19 (2014): 346–62.

55. Cantor et al., "Report on the AAU Campus Climate Survey on Sexual Assault and Sexual Misconduct: Columbia University."

56. Hirsch, *A Courtship after Marriage.*

57. Shamus Khan, *Privilege: The Making of an Adolescent Elite at St. Paul's School*, first paperback printing, Princeton Studies in Cultural Sociology (Princeton, NJ: Princeton Univ. Press, 2011).

58. Colin Jerolmack and Shamus Khan, "Talk Is Cheap: Ethnography and the Attitudinal Fallacy," *Sociological Methods and Research* 43, no. 2 (May 1, 2014): 178–209, https://doi.org/10.1177/0049124114523396.

59. Reuven Fenton and Danika Fears, "Columbia Profs Creep out Students by Watching Them Drink for Sex Study," *New York Post*, October 21, 2015, https://nypost.com/2015/10/21/columbia-profs-creeping-out-students-by-watching-them-drink/.

60. Mellins et al., "Sexual Assault Incidents among College Undergraduates."

61. Wick Sloane, "Veterans at Elite Colleges, 2016," *Chronicle of Higher Education*, November 11, 2016, https://www.insidehighered.com/views/2016/11/11/how-many-veterans-do-elite-colleges-enroll-not-enough-essay.

62. Barnard College, "Fact Sheet," 2019, https://barnard.edu/pressroom/fact-sheet; Columbia University, "Class of 2022 Profile," May 1, 2018, https://undergrad.admissions.columbia.edu/classprofile/2022.

63. National Center for Education Statistics, "Fast Facts" (Washington, DC: Institute of Education Sciences, 2018), https://nces.ed.gov/fastfacts/display.asp?id=372.

64. Patrick A. Wilson et al., "Using a Daily Diary Approach to Examine Quality of Sex and the Temporal Ordering of Stressful Events, Substance Use, and Sleep Patterns among College Students," in process.

65. Mellins et al., "Sexual Assault Incidents among College Undergraduates."

CHAPTER 1: SEXUAL ASSAULT

1. Fedina, Holmes, and Backes, "Campus Sexual Assault"; Fisher, Cullen, and Turner, "The Sexual Victimization of College Women."

2. Campbell, Dworkin, and Cabral, "An Ecological Model of the Impact of Sexual Assault on Women's Mental Health"; Janine M. Zweig, Bonnie L. Barber, and Jacquelynne S. Eccles, "Sexual Coercion and Well-Being in Young Adulthood: Comparisons by Gender and College Status," *Journal of Interpersonal Violence* 12, no. 2 (April 1997): 291–308, https://doi.org/10.1177/088626097012002009.

3. Armstrong and Hamilton, *Paying for the Party*; Armstrong, Hamilton, and Sweeney, "Sexual Assault on Campus"; Scott B. Boeringer, "Influences of Fraternity Membership, Athletics, and Male Living Arrangements on Sexual Aggression," *Violence against Women* 2, no. 2 (June 1, 1996): 134–47, https://doi.org/10.1177/1077801296002002002; Kaitlin M. Boyle, "Social Psychological Processes That Facilitate Sexual Assault within the Fraternity Party Subculture: Sexual Assault and the Fraternity Subculture," *Sociology Compass* 9, no. 5 (May 2015): 386–99, https://doi.org/10.1111/soc4.12261; Sanday, *Fraternity Gang Rape*.

4. Antonia Abbey et al., "Alcohol and Dating Risk Factors for Sexual Assault among College Women," *Psychology of Women Quarterly* 20, no. 1 (1996): 147–169; Fedina, Holmes, and Backes, "Campus Sexual Assault"; Koss, Gidycz, and Wisniewski, "The Scope of Rape"; Alan M. Gross et al., "An Examination of Sexual Violence against College Women," *Violence against Women* 12, no. 3 (2006): 288–300; Mellins et al., "Sexual Assault Incidents among College Undergraduates"; Charlene L. Muehlenhard and Melaney A. Linton, "Date Rape and Sexual Aggression in Dating Situations: Incidence and Risk Factors," *Journal of Counseling Psychology* 34, no. 2 (1987): 186; Paige Hall Smith, Jacquelyn W. White, and Lindsay J. Holland, "A Longitudinal Perspective on Dating Violence among Adolescent and College-Age Women," *American Journal of Public Health* 93, no. 7 (2003): 1104–9.

5. Martha McCaughey and Jill Cermele, "Changing the Hidden Curriculum of Campus Rape Prevention and Education: Women's Self-Defense as a Key Protective Factor for a Public Health Model of Prevention," *Trauma, Violence, and Abuse* 18, no. 3 (July 2017): 287–302, https://doi.org/10.1177/1524838015611674; Laura Kipnis, *Unwanted Advances: Sexual Paranoia Comes to Campus*, first edition (New York: Harper, 2017); Michael A. Messner, "Bad Men, Good Men, Bystanders: Who Is the Rapist?," *Gender and Society* 30, no. 1 (February 2016): 57–66, https://doi.org/10.1177/0891243215608781.

6. Victoria L. Banyard, Mary M. Moynihan, and Elizabethe G. Plante, "Sexual Violence Prevention through Bystander Education: An Experimental Evaluation," *Journal of Community Psychology* 35, no. 4 (2007): 463–81.

7. Alexander Wamboldt et al., "Friends, Strangers, and Bystanders: Informal Practices of Sexual Assault Intervention," *Global Public Health* 14, no. 1 (May 7, 2018): 1–12, https://doi.org/10.1080/17441692.2018.1472290.

8. Kathleen A. Bogle, *Hooking Up: Sex, Dating, and Relationships on Campus* (New

York: New York University Press, 2008); Lisa Wade, *American Hookup: The New Culture of Sex on Campus* (W. W. Norton & Company, 2018).

9. Elizabeth A. Armstrong et al., "Is Hooking Up Bad For Young Women?" *Contexts*, http://contexts.org/articles/is-hooking-up-bad-for-young-women/.

10. Louisa Gilbert et al., "Situational Contexts and Risk Factors Associated with Incapacitated and Nonincapacitated Sexual Assaults among College Women," *Journal of Women's Health*, November 27, 2018, https://doi.org/10.1089/jwh.2018.7191.

11. Paula England, "Has the Surplus of Women over Men Driven the Increase in Premarital and Casual Sex among American Young Adults?," *Society* 49, no. 6 (October 18, 2012): 512–14, https://doi.org/10.1007/s12115-012-9594-0.

12. Christine A. Gidycz and Christina M. Dardis, "Feminist Self-Defense and Resistance Training for College Students: A Critical Review and Recommendations for the Future," *Trauma, Violence, and Abuse* 15, no. 4 (October 2014): 322–33, https://doi.org/10.1177/1524838014521026.

13. Kate Walsh et al., "Dual Measures of Sexual Consent: A Confirmatory Factor Analysis of the Internal Consent Scale and External Consent Scale," *Journal of Sex Research*, March 18, 2019, 1–9, https://doi.org/10.1080/00224499.2019.1581882.

14. Rachel Allison and Barbara J. Risman, "A Double Standard for 'Hooking Up': How Far Have We Come toward Gender Equality?," *Social Science Research* 42, no. 5 (September 2013): 1191–1206, https://doi.org/10.1016/j.ssresearch.2013.04.006; Laura Hamilton and Elizabeth A. Armstrong, "Gendered Sexuality in Young Adulthood Double Binds and Flawed Options," *Gender and Society* 23, no. 5 (October 1, 2009): 589–616, https://doi.org/10.1177/0891243209345829.

15. J. Ford and J. G. Soto-Marquez, "Sexual Assault Victimization among Straight, Gay/Lesbian, and Bisexual College Students," *Violence and Gender* 3, no. 2 (2016): 107–15; Alexander Wamboldt et al., "'It Was a War of Attrition': Queer and Trans Undergraduates' Practices of Consent and Experiences of Sexual Assault," in process.

16. Melanie Beres, "Sexual Miscommunication? Untangling Assumptions about Sexual Communication between Casual Sex Partners," *Culture, Health and Sexuality* 12, no. 1 (January 2010): 1–14, https://doi.org/10.1080/13691050903075226.

17. M. Burkett and K. Hamilton, "Postfeminist Sexual Agency: Young Women's Negotiations of Sexual Consent," *Sexualities* 15, no. 7 (2012): 815–33; Heather R. Hlavka, "Normalizing Sexual Violence: Young Women Account for Harassment and Abuse," *Gender and Society* 28, no. 3 (June 2014): 337–58, https://doi.org/10.1177/0891243214526468.

18. Rachael O'Byrne, Susan Hansen, and Mark Rapley, "'If a Girl Doesn't Say "No"...': Young Men, Rape and Claims of 'Insufficient Knowledge,'" *Journal of Community and Applied Social Psychology* 18, no. 3 (May 2008): 168–93, https://doi.org/10.1002/casp.922.

19. Mellins et al., "Sexual Assault Incidents among College Undergraduates."

20. Cindy Struckman-Johnson, "Forced Sex on Dates: It Happens to Men, Too," *Journal of Sex Research* 24, no. 1 (January 1988): 234–41, https://doi.org/10.1080/00224498809551418; Victoria L. Banyard et al., "Unwanted Sexual Contact on Campus: A Comparison of Women's and Men's Experiences," *Violence and Victims* 22, no. 1 (2007): 52–70; JA Turchik, "Sexual Victimization among Male College Students: Assault Severity, Sexual Functioning, and Health Risk Behaviors," *Psychology of Men and Masculinity* 13, no. 3 (2012): 243–55.

21. S. J. T. Hust, K. B. Rodgers, and B. Bayly, "Scripting Sexual Consent: Internalized Traditional Sexual Scripts and Sexual Consent Expectancies among College Students," *Family Relations* 66 (2017): 197–210.

22. Fields, *Risky Lessons*; Richardson, "Constructing Sexual Citizenship."

23. Burkett and Hamilton, "Postfeminist Sexual Agency."

24. Elizabeth A. Armstrong, Paula England, and Alison C. K. Fogarty, "Accounting for Women's Orgasm and Sexual Enjoyment in College Hookups and Relationships," *American Sociological Review* 77, no. 3 (June 1, 2012): 435–62, https://doi.org/10.1177/0003122412445802; Jane Gerhard, "Revisiting 'The Myth of the Vaginal Orgasm': The Female Orgasm in American Sexual Thought and Second Wave Feminism," *Feminist Studies* 26, no. 2 (2000): 449, https://doi.org/10.2307/3178545.

CHAPTER 2: UNDER ONE ROOF

1. Kelly B. Filipkowski, Kristin E. Heron, and Joshua M. Smyth, "Early Adverse Experiences and Health: The Transition to College," *American Journal of Health Behavior* 40, no. 6 (November 1, 2016): 717–28, https://doi.org/10.5993/AJHB.40.6.4.

2. Lesley Scanlon, Louise Rowling, and Zita Weber, "'You Don't Have like an Identity . . . You Are Just Lost in a Crowd': Forming a Student Identity in the First-Year Transition to University," *Journal of Youth Studies* 10, no. 2 (May 2007): 223–41, https://doi.org/10.1080/13676260600983684.

3. Candy Chan, "Can Columbia's Fraternities Survive the National Threat to Greek Life?," *Columbia Daily Spectator*, November 13, 2018, https://www.columbiaspectator.com/eye-lead/2018/11/14/can-columbias-fraternities-survive-the-national-threat-to-greek-life/.

4. American College Health Association, "American College Health Association-National College Health Assessment II: Reference Group Undergraduates Executive Summary Fall 2015" (Hanover, MD: American College Health Association, 2016).

5. David R. Reetz, Victor Barr, and Brian Krylowicz, "The Association for University and College Counseling Center Directors Annual Survey" (Indianapolis, IN: Association for University and College Counseling Center Directors, 2013).

6. American College Health Association, "American College Health Association-National College Health Assessment II: Reference Group Data Report Fall 2008." (Baltimore: American College Health Association, 2009); American College Health Association, "American College Health Association-National College Health Assessment Spring 2018 Reference Group Data Report" (Baltimore: American College Health Association, 2018).

7. Jaison R. Abel, Richard Deitz, and Yaqin Su, "Are Recent College Graduates Finding Good Jobs?," *The Federal Reserve Bank of New York: Current Issues in Economics and Finance* 20, no. 1 (2014): 1–8.

8. Jesus Cisneros, "College as the Great Liberator: Undocuqueer Immigrants' Meaning Making in and out of Higher Education," *Journal of Diversity in Higher Education* 12, no. 1 (March 2019): 74–84, https://doi.org/10.1037/dhe0000075.

9. Anthony A. Jack, *The Privileged Poor: Rich College, Poor Students, and the Gap Between Access and Inclusion* (Harvard University Press, 2019).

10. Marta Tienda, "Diversity ≠ Inclusion: Promoting Integration in Higher Education," *Educational Researcher* 42, no. 9 (2013): 467–75.

11. Columbia University, "Under1Roof," 2019, https://www.cc-seas.columbia.edu/OMA/diversityed/u1r.php.

12. Barnard College, "Fact Sheet"; These numbers don't add to 100% because students can pick more than one racial/ethnic category. Columbia University, "Class of 2022 Profile."

13. Mellins et al., "Sexual Assault Incidents among College Undergraduates.

14. Columbia University, "Class of 2022 Profile."

15. Darren Fishell, "Census Survey: Maine's Still the Oldest, Whitest State," *Bangor Daily News*, June 25, 2015, https://bangordailynews.com/2015/06/25/business/census-survey-maines-still-the-oldest-whitest-state/.

16. Office of Planning U.S. Department of Education Evaluation and Policy Development and Office of the Under Secretary, "Advancing Diversity and Inclusion in Higher Education: Key Data Highlights Focusing on Race and Ethnicity and Promising Practices" (Washington, DC: US Dept. of Education, 2016), https://www2.ed.gov/rschstat/research/pubs/advancing-diversity-inclusion.pdf.

17. Erwin Chemerinsky and Howard Gillman, *Free Speech on Campus*, Paperback edition (New Haven ; London: Yale University Press, 2018); Alan Charles Kors and Harvey A Silverglate, *The Shadow University: The Betrayal of Liberty on America's Campuses* (Portland, OR: Powells, 2000), http://www.myilibrary.com?id=899115.

18. Columbia University Office of the Planning and Research, "Columbia College and School of Engineering Undergraduate Fall Admissions Statistics, 2009–2018" (New York: Columbia University Office of the Provost, November 26, 2018), https://provost.columbia.edu/sites/default/files/content/Institutional%20Research/Statistical%20Abstract/opir_admissions_history.pdf.

19. William Deresiewicz, *Excellent Sheep: The Miseducation of the American Elite and the Way to a Meaningful Life*, First Free Press hardcover edition (New York: Free Press, 2014).

20. Ella Christophe, "Acceptance Rate Falls by One Third, Reaching Record Low of 18 Percent," *The Chicago Maroon*, April 2, 2010, https://www.chicagomaroon .com/2010/4/2/acceptance-rate-falls-by-one-third-reaching-record-low-of-18 -percent/; Dennis Rodkin, "College Comeback: The University of Chicago Finds Its Groove," *Chicago*, March 16, 2011, https://www.chicagomag.com/Chicago -Magazine/March-2011/College-Comeback-The-University-of-Chicago-Finds-Its -Groove/.

21. Shira Boss, "Class of 1987 Heralds New Era at Columbia," *Columbia College Today*, Spring 2012, https://www.college.columbia.edu/cct/archive/spring12/cover_story_0; Amy Callahan, "Columbia College Breaks Admissions Records Again," *Columbia University Record*, April 18, 1997, http://www.columbia.edu/cu/record/archives/ vol22/vol22_iss21/record2221.13.html; Michael Matier and Cathy Alvord, "Undergraduate Enrollment Trends Fall 1998" (Cornell University Institutional Research and Planning, 1998), https://dpb.cornell.edu/documents/1000023.pdf.

22. Matier and Alvord, "Undergraduate Enrollment Trends Fall 1998."

23. Collins English Dictionary, "Snowflake Generation," in *Collins English Dictionary* (Harper Collins, 2019), https://www.collinsdictionary.com/dictionary/english/ snowflake-generation; Claire Fox, *I Find That Offensive!*, Provocations (London: Biteback Publishing, 2016); Joel Stein, "Millennials: The Me Me Me Generation," *Time Magazine*, May 20, 2013, http://time.com/247/millennials-the-me-me-me -generation/.

24. Sarah E. Erb et al., "The Importance of College Roommate Relationships: A Review and Systemic Conceptualization," *Journal of Student Affairs Research and Practice* 51, no. 1 (January 1, 2014): 43–55, https://doi.org/10.1515/jsarp-2014-0004.

25. Dina Okamoto and G. Cristina Mora, "Panethnicity," *Annual Review of Sociology* 40 (2014): 219–39.

26. David Paulk, "Columbia's Chinese Students Targeted by Racist Vandalism," *Sixth Tone*, February 14, 2017, https://www.sixthtone.com/news/1932/columbia-chinese -students-targeted-by-racist-vandalism.

27. Aaron Holmes, "Grad Student Banned from Pupin for Homophobic, Transphobic Vandalism," *Columbia Daily Spectator*, accessed May 31, 2019, https://www .columbiaspectator.com/news/2017/04/10/physics-grad-student-banned-from -pupin-for-homophobic-transphobic-vandalism/.

28. Scott Jaschik, "Entering Campus Building While Black," *Inside Higher Education*, accessed May 22, 2019, https://www.insidehighered.com/news/2019/04/15/barnard -suspends-police-officers-after-incident-black-student.

29. Thomas J. Espenshade, Alexandria Walton Radford, and Chang Young Chung, *No*

Longer Separate, Not yet Equal: Race and Class in Elite College Admission and Campus Life (Princeton: Princeton University Press, 2009).

30. Alexander Wamboldt et al., "Wine Nights, 'Bro-Dinners,' and Jungle Juice: Disaggregating Practices of Undergraduate Binge Drinking," *Journal of Drug Issues*, forthcoming.

31. Jones, "What Teenagers Are Learning from Online Porn."

32. Mellins et al., "Sexual Assault Incidents among College Undergraduates."

CHAPTER 3: THE TOXIC CAMPUS BREW

1. Henry Wechsler, "Alcohol and the American College Campus: *A Report from the Harvard School of Public Health*," *Change: The Magazine of Higher Learning* 28, no. 4 (August 1996): 20–60, https://doi.org/10.1080/00091383.1996.9937758.

2. Thomas Vander Ven, *Getting Wasted: Why College Students Drink Too Much and Party so Hard* (New York and London: New York University Press, 2011).

3. Vander Ven.

4. In the methodological appendix we outline our ethical protocols for observing illegal or potentially harmful behaviors. As we explain, we did intervene if someone was clearly in imminent danger of harming themselves or others.

5. Wendy S. Slutske, "Alcohol Use Disorders among US College Students and Their Non–College-Attending Peers," *Archives of General Psychiatry* 62, no. 3 (March 1, 2005): 321, https://doi.org/10.1001/archpsyc.62.3.321; Wendy S. Slutske et al., "Do College Students Drink More Than Their Non-College-Attending Peers? Evidence From a Population-Based Longitudinal Female Twin Study," *Journal of Abnormal Psychology* 113, no. 4 (2004): 530–40, https://doi.org/10.1037/0021 -843X.113.4.530.

6. Paul K. Piff et al., "Higher Social Class Predicts Increased Unethical Behavior," *Proceedings of the National Academy of Sciences* 109, no. 11 (March 13, 2012): 4086, https://doi.org/10.1073/pnas.1118373109.

7. Columbia University Emergency Medical Service, "FAQ," 2019, https://cuems .columbia.edu/faq; Rahil Kamath and Peter Maroulis, "Confusion Surrounding Cost of CUEMS Discourages Students from Calling Free Service," *Columbia Daily Spectator*, December 7, 2017, https://www.columbiaspectator.com/news/2017/12/07/ confusion-surrounding-cost-of-cuems-discourages-students-from-calling/.

8. Barbara Alvarez Martin et al., "The Role of Monthly Spending Money in College Student Drinking Behaviors and Their Consequences," *Journal of American College Health* 57, no. 6 (n.d.): 587–96.

9. Henry Wechsler and Toben F. Nelson, "Binge Drinking and the American College Students: What's Five Drinks?," *Psychology of Addictive Behaviors* 15, no. 4 (2001): 287–91, https://doi.org/10.1037//0893-164X.15.4.287.

10. Henry Wechsler et al., "Trends in College Binge Drinking During a Period of Increased Prevention Efforts: Findings from 4 Harvard School of Public Health College Alcohol Study Surveys: 1993–2001," *Journal of American College Health*, no. 50 (2015): 5.

11. Mellins et al., "Sexual Assault Incidents among College Undergraduates.

12. Dafna Kanny et al., "Annual Total Binge Drinks Consumed by U.S. Adults, 2015," *American Journal of Preventive Medicine* 54, no. 4 (2018): 486–96, https://doi.org/10.1016/j.amepre.2017.12.021.

13. Justin Jager et al., "Historical Variation in Drug Use Trajectories across the Transition to Adulthood: The Trend toward Lower Intercepts and Steeper, Ascending Slopes," *Development and Psychopathology* 25, no. 2 (May 2013): 527–43, https://doi.org/10.1017/S0954579412001228.

14. Byron H. Atkinson and A. T. Brugger, "Do College Students Drink Too Much?," *The Journal of Higher Education* 30, no. 6 (June 1959): 305–12, https://doi.org/10.1080/00221546.1959.11777453.

15. Eugene J. Kanin, "Male Aggression in Dating-Courtship Relations," *American Journal of Sociology* 63, no. 2 (September 1957): 197–204, https://doi.org/10.1086/222177.

16. National Institute on Alcohol Abuse and Alcoholism (NIAAA), "Reducing Alcohol Problems on Campus: A Guide to Planning and Evaluation," 2002, https://www.collegedrinkingprevention.gov/media/finalhandbook.pdf.

17. Jennifer S. Hirsch, et al., *The Secret: Love, Marriage, and HIV* (Nashville: Vanderbilt University Press, 2009); Shamus R. Khan et al., " 'I Didn't Want to Be "That Girl" ': The Social Risks of Labeling, Telling, and Reporting Sexual Assault," *Sociological Science* 5 (July 12, 2018): 432–60, https://doi.org/10.15195/v5.a19.

18. Jennifer S. Hirsch et al., "The Social Constructions of Sexuality: Marital Infidelity and Sexually Transmitted Disease—HIV Risk in a Mexican Migrant Community," *American Journal of Public Health* 92, no. 8 (2002): 1227–37.

19. W. F. Flack, " 'The Red Zone': Temporal Risk for Unwanted Sex among College Students," *Journal of Interpersonal Violence* 23, no. 9 (2008): 1177–96; Matthew Kimble et al., "Risk of Unwanted Sex for College Women: Evidence for a Red Zone," *Journal of American College Health* 57, no. 3 (November 2008): 331–38, https://doi.org/10.3200/JACH.57.3.331-338.

20. William DeJong and Jason Blanchette, "Case Closed: Research Evidence on the Positive Public Health Impact of the Age 21 Minimum Legal Drinking Age in the United States," *Journal of Studies on Alcohol and Drugs, Supplement*, no. s17 (March 2014): 108–15, https://doi.org/10.15288/jsads.2014.s17.108; John Kindelberger and National Highway Traffic Safety Administration, "Calculating Lives Saved Due to Minimum Drinking Age Laws" (Washington, DC: NHTSA's National Center for tatistics and Analysis, March 2005).

21. Wechsler et al., "Trends in College Binge Drinking During a Period of Increased

Prevention Efforts: Findings from 4 Harvard School of Public Health College Alcohol Study Surveys: 1993–2001."

22. Columbia University, "Class of 2022 Profile"; Columbia University Office of the Planning and Research, "Columbia College and School of Engineering Undergraduate Fall Admissions Statistics, 2009–2018."

23. President's Commission on Slavery and the University, "Universities Studying Slavery," 2018, http://slavery.virginia.edu/universities-studying-slavery/.

24. Tienda, "Diversity ≠ Inclusion"; Natasha Kumar Warikoo, *The Diversity Bargain: And Other Dilemmas of Race, Admissions, and Meritocracy at Elite Universities* (Chicago ; London: The University of Chicago Press, 2016).

25. Adam E. Barry et al., "Alcohol Use and Mental Health Conditions among Black College Males: Do Those Attending Postsecondary Minority Institutions Fare Better Than Those at Primarily White Institutions?," *American Journal of Men's Health* 11, no. 4 (July 2017): 962–68, https://doi.org/10.1177/1557988316674840; Reginald Fennell, "Health Behaviors of Students Attending Historically Black Colleges and Universities: Results From the National College Health Risk Behavior Survey," *Journal of American College Health* 46, no. 3 (November 1997): 109–17, https://doi.org/10.1080/07448489709595596; Daniel Ari Kapner, "Alcohol and Other Drug Use at Historically Black Colleges and Universities" (Newton, MA: The Higher Education Center for Alcohol and Other Drug Abuse and Violence Prevention, 2008), https://files.eric.ed.gov/fulltext/ED537617.pdf.

26. Dong-Chul Seo and Kaigang Li, "Effects of College Climate on Students' Binge Drinking: Hierarchical Generalized Linear Model," *Annals of Behavioral Medicine* 38, no. 3 (December 1, 2009): 262–68, https://doi.org/10.1007/s12160-009-9150-3.

27. Diana M. Doumas and Aida Midgett, "Ethnic Differences in Drinking Motives and Alcohol Use among College Athletes," *Journal of College Counseling* 18, no. 2 (July 1, 2015): 116–29, https://doi.org/10.1002/jocc.12009.

28. Stephanie M. McClure, "Voluntary Association Membership: Black Greek Men on a Predominantly White Campus," *The Journal of Higher Education* 77, no. 6 (2006): 1036–57, https://doi.org/10.1353/jhe.2006.0053; Jenny M. Stuber, Joshua Klugman, and Caitlin Daniel, "Gender, Social Class, and Exclusion: Collegiate Peer Cultures and Social Reproduction," *Sociological Perspectives* 54, no. 3 (September 2011): 431–51, https://doi.org/10.1525/sop.2011.54.3.431.

29. Sanday, *Fraternity Gang Rape*.

30. Alexandra Robbins, *Fraternity: An inside Look at a Year of College Boys Becoming Men* (New York: Dutton, 2019); M. P. Koss and H. H. Cleveland, "Athletic Participation, Fraternity Membership, and Date Rape: The Question Remains—Self-Selection or Different Causal Processes?," *Violence against Women* 2, no. 2 (June 1, 1996): 180–90, https://doi.org/10.1177/1077801296002002005; Sanday, *Fraternity Gang Rape*.

31. Alyce Holland and Thomas Andre, "Athletic Participation and the Social Status of

Adolescent Males and Females," *Youth and Society* 25, no. 3 (March 1994): 388–407, https://doi.org/10.1177/0044118X94025003005.

32. Wamboldt et al., "Wine Night, 'Bro-Dinners,' and Jungle Juice."

33. Tristan Bridges, "A Very 'Gay' Straight?: Hybrid Masculinities, Sexual Aesthetics, and the Changing Relationship between Masculinity and Homophobia," *Gender and Society* 28, no. 1 (February 2014): 58–82, https://doi.org/10.1177/0891243213503901; Demetrakis Z. Demetriou, "Connell's Concept of Hegemonic Masculinity: A Critique," *Theory and Society* 30, no. 3 (2001): 337–61.

34. Demetriou, "Connell's Concept of Hegemonic Masculinity"; Tristan Bridges and C. J. Pascoe, "Hybrid Masculinities: New Directions in the Sociology of Men and Masculinities: Hybrid Masculinities," *Sociology Compass* 8, no. 3 (March 2014): 246–58, https://doi.org/10.1111/soc4.12134.

35. Wamboldt et al., "Wine Night, 'Bro-Dinners,' and Jungle Juice."

36. Abbey et al., "Alcohol and Dating Risk Factors for Sexual Assault among College Women"; Lance S Weinhardt and Michael P Carey, "Does Alcohol Lead to Sexual Risk Behavior? Findings from Event-Level Research," *Annual Review of Sex Research* 11 (2000): 125–57.

37. Centers for Disease Control and Prevention, U.S. Department of Health and Human Services, and National Center for Health Statistics, "Early Release of Selected Estimates Based on Data From the National Health Interview Survey, January–March 2016: Alcohol Consumption" (Atlanta: Centers for Disease Control, September 2017); National Institute on Alcohol Abuse and Alcoholism (NIAAA), "College Drinking—Fact Sheet—National Institute on Alcohol Abuse and Alcoholism," April 2015, http://pubs.niaaa.nih.gov/publications/CollegeFactSheet/CollegeFactSheet.pdf; Lisa Wade et al., "Ruling Out Rape," *Contexts*, May 21, 2014, https://contexts.org/articles/ruling-out-rape/; Wechsler, "Alcohol and the American College Campus."

38. Centers for Disease Control and Prevention, "All Injuries," May 3, 2017, https://www.cdc.gov/nchs/fastats/injury.htm; The Global Burden of Disease 2016 Injury Collaborators et al., "Global Mortality from Firearms, 1990–2016," *JAMA* 320, no. 8 (August 28, 2018): 792, https://doi.org/10.1001/jama.2018.10060.

39. Wamboldt et al., "Wine Nights, 'Bro-Dinners,' and Jungle Juice."

40. Antonia Abbey et al., "The Relationship between the Quantity of Alcohol Consumed and the Severity of Sexual Assaults Committed by College Men," *Journal of Interpersonal Violence* 18, no. 7 (2003): 813–33; Antonia Abbey et al., "Sexual Assault and Alcohol Consumption: What Do We Know about Their Relationship and What Types of Research Are Still Needed?," *Aggression and Violent Behavior* 9, no. 3 (2004): 271–303.

41. Molly K. Crossman, Alan E. Kazdin, and Krista Knudson, "Brief Unstructured Interaction with a Dog Reduces Distress," *Anthrozoös* 28, no. 4 (December 2015):

649–59, https://doi.org/10.1080/08927936.2015.1070008; Dasha Grajfoner et al., "The Effect of Dog-Assisted Intervention on Student Well-Being, Mood, and Anxiety," *International Journal of Environmental Research and Public Health* 14, no. 5 (May 5, 2017): 483, https://doi.org/10.3390/ijerph14050483.

42. Schalet, *Not under My Roof*; Kate Dawson, Saoirse Nic Gabhainn, and Pádraig MacNeela, "Toward a Model of Porn Literacy: Core Concepts, Rationales, and Approaches," *Journal of Sex Research*, January 9, 2019, 1–15, https://doi.org/10.1080/00224499.2018.1556238; Emily F. Rothman et al., "A Pornography Literacy Class for Youth: Results of a Feasibility and Efficacy Pilot Study," *American Journal of Sexuality Education* 13, no. 1 (January 2, 2018): 1–17, https://doi.org/10.1080/15546128.2018.1437100.

CHAPTER 4: WHAT IS SEX FOR?

1. Richard A. Cloward, *Delinquency and Opportunity : A Theory of Delinquent Gangs /*, ed. Lloyd E. Ohlin (Glencoe, IL: Free Press, 1960); Hirsch et al., *The Secret*.

2. Mellins et al., "Sexual Assault Incidents among College Undergraduates."

3. Elizabeth L. Paul and Kristen A. Hayes, "The Casualties of 'Casual' Sex: A Qualitative Exploration of the Phenomenology of College Students' Hookups," *Journal of Social and Personal Relationships* 19, no. 5 (2002): 639–61.

4. Laura M. Carpenter, *Virginity Lost: An Intimate Portrait of First Sexual Experiences* (New York: New York University, 2005); Janet Holland et al., "Deconstructing Virginity—Young People's Accounts of First Sex," *Sexual and Relationship Therapy* 15, no. 3 (August 2000): 221–32, https://doi.org/10.1080/14681990050109827.

5. Ted M. Brimeyer and William L. Smith, "Religion, Race, Social Class, and Gender Differences in Dating and Hooking Up among College Students," *Sociological Spectrum* 32, no. 5 (September 2012): 462–73, https://doi.org/10.1080/02732173.2012.694799; Amy M. Burdette et al., " 'Hooking Up' at College: Does Religion Make a Difference?," *Journal for the Scientific Study of Religion* 48, no. 3 (September 2009): 535–51, https://doi.org/10.1111/j.1468-5906.2009.01464.x; Ellen H. Zaleski and Kathleen M. Schiaffino, "Religiosity and Sexual Risk-Taking Behavior during the Transition to College," *Journal of Adolescence* 23, no. 2 (2000): 223–27.

6. Wade, *American Hookup*.

7. Elizabeth A. Armstrong, Paula England, and Alison C. K. Fogarty, "Accounting for Women's Orgasm and Sexual Enjoyment in College Hookups and Relationships," *American Sociological Review* 77, no. 3 (June 1, 2012): 435–62, https://doi.org/10.1177/0003122412445802; Burkett and Hamilton, "Postfeminist Sexual Agency"; April Burns, Valerie A. Futch, and Deborah L. Tolman, " 'It's Like Doing Homework': Academic Achievement Discourse in Adolescent Girls' Fellatio Narratives,"

Sexuality Research and Social Policy 8, no. 3 (September 2011): 239–51, https://doi
.org/10.1007/s13178-011-0062-1; Jane Gerhard, "Revisiting 'The Myth of the Vaginal Orgasm': The Female Orgasm in American Sexual Thought and Second Wave
Feminism," *Feminist Studies* 26, no. 2 (2000): 449, https://doi.org/10.2307/3178545;
Juliet Richters et al., "Sexual Practices at Last Heterosexual Encounter and Occurrence of Orgasm in a National Survey," *Journal of Sex Research* 43, no. 3 (August 1,
2006): 217–26, https://doi.org/10.1080/00224490609552320.

8. Marcel Mauss, *The Gift: The Form and Reason for Exchange in Archaic Societies.* New
York and London: W. W. Norton, 1990.

9. NYC LGBT Historic Sites Project, "Student Homophile League at Earl Hall,
Columbia University," 2017, http://www.nyclgbtsites.org/site/columbia-university/.

10. A. M. Burdette and T. D. Hill, "Religious Involvement and Transitions into Adolescent Sexual Activities," *Sociology of Religion* 70, no. 1 (March 1, 2009): 28–48,
https://doi.org/10.1093/socrel/srp011; Donna Freitas, *Sex and the Soul: Juggling Sexuality, Spirituality, Romance, and Religion on America's College Campuses,* updated
edition (Oxford and New York: Oxford University Press, 2015); S. Hardy, "Adolescent Religiosity and Sexuality: An Investigation of Reciprocal Influences," *Journal of Adolescence* 26, no. 6 (December 2003): 731–39, https://doi.org/10.1016/j
.adolescence.2003.09.003; Lisa Miller and Merav Gur, "Religiousness and Sexual
Responsibility in Adolescent Girls," *Journal of Adolescent Health* 31, no. 5 (November 2002): 401–6, https://doi.org/10.1016/S1054-139X(02)00403-2; Arland Thornton and Donald Camburn, "Religious Participation and Adolescent Sexual Behavior
and Attitudes," *Journal of Marriage and Family* 51, no. 3 (1989): 641–53, https://doi
.org/10.2307/352164.

11. Megan C. Lytle et al., "Association of Religiosity with Sexual Minority Suicide Ideation and Attempt," *American Journal of Preventive Medicine* 54, no. 5 (May 2018):
644–51, https://doi.org/10.1016/j.amepre.2018.01.019.

12. Holland et al., "Deconstructing Virginity"; Carpenter, *Virginity Lost,* 2005.

13. Sonia Livingstone, "Taking Risky Opportunities in Youthful Content Creation: Teenagers' Use of Social Networking Sites for Intimacy, Privacy and Self-
Expression," *New Media and Society* 10, no. 3 (June 2008): 393–411, https://doi.org/10
.1177/1461444808089415.

14. Finer and Philbin, "Trends in Ages at Key Reproductive Transitions in the United
States, 1951–2010."

15. Lisa M. Cookingham and Ginny L. Ryan, "The Impact of Social Media on the
Sexual and Social Wellness of Adolescents," *Journal of Pediatric and Adolescent Gyne-
cology* 28, no. 1 (February 2015): 2–5, https://doi.org/10.1016/j.jpag.2014.03.001;
Nicole B. Ellison, Charles Steinfield, and Cliff Lampe, "The Benefits of Facebook
'Friends': Social Capital and College Students' Use of Online Social Network Sites,"

Journal of Computer-Mediated Communication 12, no. 4 (July 2007): 1143–68, https://doi.org/10.1111/j.1083-6101.2007.00367.x.

16. Piotr S. Bobkowski, Jane D. Brown, and Deborah R. Neffa, "'Hit Me Up and We Can Get Down': US Youths' Risk Behaviors and Sexual Self-Disclosure in MySpace Profiles," *Journal of Children and Media* 6, no. 1 (February 2012): 119–34, https://doi.org/10.1080/17482798.2011.633412; Suzan M. Doornwaard et al., "Young Adolescents' Sexual and Romantic Reference Displays on Facebook," *Journal of Adolescent Health* 55, no. 4 (October 2014): 535–41, https://doi.org/10.1016/j.jadohealth.2014.04.002; Mansi Kanuga and Walter D. Rosenfeld, "Adolescent Sexuality and the Internet: The Good, the Bad, and the URL," *Journal of Pediatric and Adolescent Gynecology* 17, no. 2 (April 2004): 117–24, https://doi.org/10.1016/j.jpag.2004.01.015; Megan A Moreno, Malcolm Parks, and Laura P. Richardson, "What Are Adolescents Showing the World about Their Health Risk Behaviors on MySpace?," *Medscape General Medicine* 9, no. 4 (October 11, 2007): 9; Kaveri Subrahmanyam, David Smahel, and Patricia Greenfield, "Connecting Developmental Constructions to the Internet: Identity Presentation and Sexual Exploration in Online Teen Chat Rooms," *Developmental Psychology* 42, no. 3 (2006): 395–406, https://doi.org/10.1037/0012-1649.42.3.395; Johanna M. F. van Oosten, Jochen Peter, and Inge Boot, "Exploring Associations between Exposure to Sexy Online Self-Presentations and Adolescents' Sexual Attitudes and Behavior," *Journal of Youth and Adolescence* 44, no. 5 (May 2015): 1078–91, https://doi.org/10.1007/s10964-014-0194-8.

17. Terri L. Messman-Moore et al., "Sexuality, Substance Use, and Susceptibility to Victimization: Risk for Rape and Sexual Coercion in a Prospective Study of College Women," *Journal of Interpersonal Violence* 23, no. 12 (December 1, 2008): 1730–46, https://doi.org/10.1177/0886260508314336.

18. Herbert A. Simon, "Rational Choice and the Structure of the Environment," *Psychological Review* 63, no. 2 (1956): 129–38, https://doi.org/10.1037/h0042769.

19. C. Heldman and L. Wade, "Hook-Up Culture: Setting a New Research Agenda," *Sexuality Research and Social Policy*, no. 4 (2010): 323–33; Wade, *American Hookup*.

20. Matthew Chin et al., "Time for Sex: Examining Dimensions of Temporality in Sexual Consent among College Students," *Human Organization* 78, no. 4 (in press); Kanuga and Rosenfeld, "Adolescent Sexuality and the Internet."

CHAPTER 5: CONSENT

1. Some of the materials and analysis in this chapter are drawn from Jennifer S. Hirsch et al., "Social Dimensions of Sexual Consent among Cisgender Heterosexual College Students: Insights From Ethnographic Research," *Journal of Adolescent Health* 64, no. 1 (2018): 26–35, https://doi.org/10.1016/j.jadohealth.2018.06.011.

2. M. A. Beres, "'Spontaneous' Sexual Consent: An Analysis of Sexual Consent

Literature," *Feminism and Psychology* 17, no. 1 (2007): 93–108; K. N. Jozkowski and Z. D. Peterson, "College Students and Sexual Consent: Unique Insights," *Journal of Sex Research* 50, no. 6 (2013): 517–23.

3. Charlene L. Muehlenhard and Zoë D. Peterson, "Wanting and Not Wanting Sex: The Missing Discourse of Ambivalence," *Feminism and Psychology* 15, no. 1 (February 2005): 15–20, https://doi.org/10.1177/0959353505049698.

4. Heidi C. Fantasia et al., "Knowledge, Attitudes and Beliefs About Contraceptive and Sexual Consent Negotiation among College Women," *Journal of Forensic Nursing* 10, no. 4 (2014): 199–207; Hust, Rodgers, and Bayly, "Scripting Sexual Consent."

5. Burkett and Hamilton, "Postfeminist Sexual Agency"; H. C. Fantasia, "Really Not Even a Decision Any More: Late Adolescent Narratives of Implied Sexual Consent," *Journal of Forensic Nursing* 7, no. 3 (2011): 120–29; K. N. Jozkowski et al., "Gender Differences in Heterosexual College Students' Conceptualizations and Indicators of Sexual Consent: Implications for Contemporary Sexual Assault Prevention Education," *Journal of Sex Research* 51, no. 8 (2014): 904–16.

6. Antonia Abbey, "Alcohol-Related Sexual Assault: A Common Problem among College Students," *Journal of Studies on Alcohol and Drugs* 14 (2002): 118–28; American College Health Association, "American College Health Association-National College Health Assessment II: Undergraduate Student Reference Group Executive Summary Spring 2015" (Hanover, MD: American College Health Association, 2016).

7. M. A. Lewis et al., "Predictors of Hooking Up Sexual Behaviors and Emotional Reactions among U.S. College Students," *Archives of Sexual Behavior* 41, no. 5 (2011): 1219–29.

8. Hust, Rodgers, and Bayly, "Scripting Sexual Consent"; Jozkowski and Peterson, "College Students and Sexual Consent: Unique Insights."

9. "Affirmative Consent Laws (Yes Means Yes) State by State."

10. K. N Jozkowski, ""Yes Means Yes?" Sexual Consent Policy and College Students," *Change: The Magazine of Higher Learning* 47, no. 2 (2015): 16–23.

11. Charlene L. Muehlenhard et al., "The Complexities of Sexual Consent among College Students: A Conceptual and Empirical Review," *The Journal of Sex Research* 53, no. 4–5 (May 3, 2016): 457–87, https://doi.org/10.1080/00224499.2016.1146651.

12. Abbey, "Alcohol-Related Sexual Assault"; C. A. Franklin, "Physically Forced, Alcohol-Induced, and Verbally Coerced Sexual Victimization: Assessing Risk Factors among University Women," *Journal of Criminal Justice* 38, no. 2 (2010): 149–59.

13. Beres, "Sexual Miscommunication?"

14. Mellins et al., "Sexual Assault Incidents among College Undergraduates.

15. John H. Gagnon and William Simon, *Sexual Conduct: The Social Sources of Human Sexuality*, 2nd ed (New Brunswick, NJ: AldineTransaction, 2005); Hust, Rodgers, and Bayly, "Scripting Sexual Consent."

16. Fantasia, "Really Not Even a Decision Any More: Late Adolescent Narratives of

Implied Sexual Consent"; Jozkowski et al., "Gender Differences in Heterosexual College Students' Conceptualizations and Indicators of Sexual Consent."

17. Michelle Fine, "Sexuality, Schooling, and Adolescent Females: The Missing Discourse of Desire," *Harvard Educational Review* 58, no. 1 (April 1988): 29–54, https://doi.org/10.17763/haer.58.1.u0468k1v2n2n8242.

18. Jozkowski et al., "Gender Differences in Heterosexual College Students' Conceptualizations and Indicators of Sexual Consent."

19. Chin et al., "Time for Sex."

20. Charlene L. Muehlenhard and Stephen W. Cook, "Men's Self-Reports of Unwanted Sexual Activity," *Journal of Sex Research* 24, no. 1 (1988): 58–72.

21. Armstrong, England, and Fogarty, "Accounting for Women's Orgasm and Sexual Enjoyment in College Hookups and Relationships."

22. Some of the materials and analysis in this chapter are drawn from Alexander Wamboldt et al., "'It Was a War of Attrition:' Queer and Trans Undergraduates' Practices of Consent and Experiences of Sexual Assault," in process.

23. Pierre Bourdieu, *Outline of a Theory of Practice*, 25th printing, Cambridge Studies in Social and Cultural Anthropology 16 (Cambridge: Cambridge Univ. Press, 2010).

24. Espenshade, Radford, and Chung, *No Longer Separate, Not yet Equal*; Tienda, "Diversity ≠ Inclusion: Promoting Integration in Higher Education"; Warikoo, *The Diversity Bargain*.

25. Mike Godfrey and James W. Satterfield, "The Effects Athletic Culture Formation and Perceived Faculty Stereotypes in Higher Education," *Journal of Contemporary Athletics* 5, no. 2 (2011): 89–104; McClure, "Voluntary Association Membership"; Herbert D. Simons et al., "The Athlete Stigma in Higher Education," *College Student Journal* 41, no. 2 (June 2007): 251–73.

26. Rachel Allison and Barbara J. Risman, "'It Goes Hand in Hand with the Parties': Race, Class, and Residence in College Student Negotiations of Hooking Up," *Sociological Perspectives* 57, no. 1 (March 2014): 102–23, https://doi.org/10.1177/0731121413516608; Brimeyer and Smith, "Religion, Race, Social Class, and Gender Differences in Dating and Hooking Up among College Students"; B. K. Diamond-Welch, M. D. Hetzel-Riggin, and J. A. Hemingway, "The Willingness of College Students to Intervene in Sexual Assault Situations: Attitude and Behavior Differences by Gender, Race, Age, and Community of Origin," *Violence and Gender* 3, no. 1 (2016): 49–54; Carolyn J. Field, Sitawa R. Kimuna, and Marissa N. Lang, "The Relation of Interracial Relationships to Intimate Partner Violence by College Students," *Journal of Black Studies* 46, no. 4 (May 2015): 384–403, https://doi.org/10.1177/0021934715574804; Rashawn Ray and Jason A. Rosow, "Getting Off and Getting Intimate: How Normative Institutional Arrangements Structure Black and White Fraternity Men's Approaches toward Women," *Men and Masculinities* 12, no. 5 (August 1, 2010): 523–46, https://doi.org/10.1177/1097184X09331750; Amy

C. Wilkins, "Stigma and Status: Interracial Intimacy and Intersectional Identities among Black College Men," *Gender and Society* 26, no. 2 (April 2012): 165–89, https://doi.org/10.1177/0891243211434613.

27. Doumas and Midgett, "Ethnic Differences in Drinking Motives and Alcohol Use among College Athletes."

28. W. E. B. Du Bois, *The Souls of Black Folk* (New York: Vintage Books/Library of America, 1990).

29. Bruce Gross, "False Rape Allegations: An Assault on Justice," *Forensic Examiner* 18 (2009): 66–70; Eugene J. Kanin, "False Rape Allegations," *Archives of Sexual Behavior* 23, no. 1 (1994): 81–92; David Lisak, "False Allegations of Rape: A Critique of Kanin," October 2007, http://www.davidlisak.com/wp-content/uploads/pdf/SARFalseAllegationsofRape.pdf; Kimberly A. Lonsway, Joanne Archambault, and David Lisak, "False Reports: Moving beyond the Issue to Successfully Investigate and Prosecute Non-Stranger Sexual Assault" (Harrisburg, PA: National Sexual Violence Resource Center, 2009), https://www.nsvrc.org/publications/articles/false-reports-moving-beyond-issue-successfully-investigate-and-prosecute-non-s; Philip N. S. Rumney, "False Allegations of Rape," *The Cambridge Law Journal* 65, no. 01 (March 2006): 128–58, https://doi.org/10.1017/S0008197306007069; "Department of Justice: Sexual Assault False Reporting Overview," 2012, http://www.nsvrc.org/sites/default/files/Publications_NSVRC_Overview_False-Reporting.pdf.

CHAPTER 6: ACTS OF ENTITLEMENT, SELF-ABSORPTION, AND VIOLENCE

1. Andra Teten Tharp et al., "A Systematic Qualitative Review of Risk and Protective Factors for Sexual Violence Perpetration," *Trauma, Violence, and Abuse* 14, no. 2 (April 2013): 133–67, https://doi.org/10.1177/1524838012470031.

2. Gagnon and Simon, *Sexual Conduct*; Hust, Rodgers, and Bayly, "Scripting Sexual Consent."

3. Beres, "Sexual Miscommunication?"; Cindy Struckman-Johnson, David Struckman-Johnson, and Peter B. Anderson, "Tactics of Sexual Coercion: When Men and Women Won't Take No for an Answer," *Journal of Sex Research* 40, no. 1 (February 2003): 76–86, https://doi.org/10.1080/00224490309552168.

4. K. C. Basile, "Rape by Acquiescence: The Ways in Which Women 'Give In' to Unwanted Sex with Their Husbands," *Violence against Women* 5, no. 9 (1999): 1036–58; Brenda L. Russell and Debra L. Oswald, "Strategies and Dispositional Correlates of Sexual Coercion Perpetrated by Women: An Exploratory Investigation," *Sex Roles* 45, no. 1 (2001): 103–15.

5. Russell and Oswald, "Strategies and Dispositional Correlates of Sexual Coercion Perpetrated by Women."

6. Basile, "Rape by Acquiescence"; Heidi M. Zinzow and Martie Thompson, "Fac-

tors Associated with Use of Verbally Coercive, Incapacitated, and Forcible Sexual Assault Tactics in a Longitudinal Study of College Men," *Aggressive Behavior* 41, no. 1 (January 2015): 34–43, https://doi.org/10.1002/ab.21567.

7. Alletta Brenner, "Resisting Simple Dichotomies: Critiquing Narratives of Victims, Perpetrators, and Harm in Feminist Theories of Rape," *Harvard Journal of Law and Gender* 36 (2013): 503; K. F. McCartan, H. Kemshall, and J. Tabachnick, "The Construction of Community Understandings of Sexual Violence: Rethinking Public, Practitioner and Policy Discourses," *Journal of Sexual Aggression* 21, no. 1 (January 2, 2015): 100–116, https://doi.org/10.1080/13552600.2014.945976.

8. Antonia Abbey et al., "Attitudinal, Experiential, and Situational Predictors of Sexual Assault Perpetration," *Journal of Interpersonal Violence* 16, no. 8 (2001): 784–807; Antonia Abbey, Pam McAuslan, and Lisa Thomson Ross, "Sexual Assault Perpetration by College Men: The Role of Alcohol, Misperception of Sexual Intent, and Sexual Beliefs and Experiences," *Journal of Social and Clinical Psychology* 17, no. 2 (1998): 167–95; Antonia Abbey and Angela J. Jacques-Tiura, "Sexual Assault Perpetrators' Tactics: Associations with Their Personal Characteristics and Aspects of the Incident," *Journal of Interpersonal Violence* 26, no. 14 (September 2011): 2866–89, https://doi.org/10.1177/0886260510390955; Carolyn L. Brennan et al., "Evidence for Multiple Classes of Sexually Violent College Men," *Psychology of Violence* 9, no. 1 (January 2019): 48–55, https://doi.org/10.1037/vio0000179; Jacquelyn Campbell, "Campus Sexual Assault Perpetration: What Else We Need to Know," *JAMA Pediatrics*, July 13, 2015; Poco D. Kernsmith and Roger M. Kernsmith, "Female Pornography Use and Sexual Coercion Perpetration," *Deviant Behavior* 30, no. 7 (August 19, 2009): 589–610, https://doi.org/10.1080/01639620802589798; Sarah K. Murnen, Carrie Wright, and Gretchen Kaluzny, "If 'Boys Will Be Boys,' Then Girls Will Be Victims? A Meta-Analytic Review of the Research That Relates Masculine Ideology to Sexual Aggression," *Sex Roles* 46, no. 11/12 (2002): 359–75, https://doi .org/10.1023/A:1020488928736; Kevin M. Swartout et al., "Trajectory Analysis of the Campus Serial Rapist Assumption," *JAMA Pediatrics* 169, no. 12 (December 1, 2015): 1148, https://doi.org/10.1001/jamapediatrics.2015.0707; Tharp et al., "A Systematic Qualitative Review of Risk and Protective Factors for Sexual Violence Perpetration"; Emily K. Voller and Patricia J. Long, "Sexual Assault and Rape Perpetration by College Men: The Role of the Big Five Personality Traits," *Journal of Interpersonal Violence*, 2009, http://jiv.sagepub.com/content/early/2009/05/14/0886 260509334390.short.

9. Kate Walsh et al., "Prevalence and Correlates of Sexual Assault Perpetration and Ambiguous Consent in a Representative Sample of College Students," in press.

10. Kirkpatrick and Kanin, "Male Sex Aggression on a University Campus"; Koss, Gidycz, and Wisniewski, "The Scope of Rape"; Warshaw and Koss, *I Never Called It Rape.*

11. Laura M. Carpenter, *Virginity Lost: An Intimate Portrait of First Sexual Experiences* (New York: New York University, 2005); Holland et al., "Deconstructing Virginity."

12. Randy P. Auerbach et al., "WHO World Mental Health Surveys International College Student Project: Prevalence and Distribution of Mental Disorders," *Journal of Abnormal Psychology* 127, no. 7 (October 2018): 623–38, https://doi.org/10.1037/abn0000362; J. Hunt and D. Eisenberg, "Mental Health Problems and Help-Seeking Behavior among College Students," *Journal of Adolescent Health* 46 (2010): 3–10.

13. Michelle Cleary, Garry Walter, and Debra Jackson, " 'Not Always Smooth Sailing': Mental Health Issues Associated with the Transition from High School to College," *Issues in Mental Health Nursing* 32, no. 4 (March 2, 2011): 250–54, https://doi.org/10.3109/01612840.2010.548906; Terence Hicks and Samuel Heastie, "High School to College Transition: A Profile of the Stressors, Physical and Psychological Health Issues That Affect the First-Year On-Campus College Student," *Journal of Cultural Diversity* 15, no. 3 (2008): 143–47; Richard Kadison and Theresa Foy DiGeronimo, *College of the Overwhelmed: The Campus Mental Health Crisis and What to Do About It* (Wiley, 2004).

14. Armstrong et al., "Is Hooking Up Bad for Young Women?"; Heather Littleton et al., "Risky Situation or Harmless Fun? A Qualitative Examination of College Women's Bad Hook-up and Rape Scripts," *Sex Roles* 60, no. 11–12 (2009): 793–804; Elizabeth L. Paul, Brian McManus, and Allison Hayes, " 'Hookups': Characteristics and Correlates of College Students' Spontaneous and Anonymous Sexual Experiences," *Journal of Sex Research* 37, no. 1 (2000): 76–88; Wade, *American Hookup*.

15. Chin et al., "Time for Sex."

16. Rachel Shteir, "50 Shades of Ivy: Kink on Campus," *Observer*, March 6, 2015, https://observer.com/2015/03/50-shades-of-ivy-kink-on-campus/.

17. Hirsch et al., "Social Dimensions of Sexual Consent among Cisgender Heterosexual College Students."

18. Jones, "What Teenagers Are Learning from Online Porn"; Ethan A. Marshall, Holly A. Miller, and Jeff A. Bouffard, "Crossing the Threshold from Porn Use to Porn Problem: Frequency and Modality of Porn Use as Predictors of Sexually Coercive Behaviors," *Journal of Interpersonal Violence*, November 22, 2017, 088626051774354, https://doi.org/10.1177/0886260517743549; Paul J. Wright, Robert S. Tokunaga, and Ashley Kraus, "A Meta-Analysis of Pornography Consumption and Actual Acts of Sexual Aggression in General Population Studies: Pornography and Sexual Aggression," *Journal of Communication* 66, no. 1 (February 2016): 183–205, https://doi.org/10.1111/jcom.12201.

19. "Affirmative Consent Laws (Yes Means Yes) State by State."

20. Antonia Abbey, "Moving beyond Simple Answers to Complex Questions: How Does Context Affect Alcohol's Role in Sexual Assault Perpetration? A Commentary on Testa and Cleveland (2017)," *Journal of Studies on Alcohol and Drugs* 78 (2016):

14–15; Abbey, McAuslan, and Ross, "Sexual Assault Perpetration by College Men"; Maria Testa and Michael J. Cleveland, "Does Alcohol Contribute to College Men's Sexual Assault Perpetration? Between-and Within-Person Effects Over Five Semesters," *Journal of Studies on Alcohol and Drugs* 78, no. 1 (December 12, 2016): 5–13, https://doi.org/10.15288/jsad.2017.78.5.

21. Mellins et al., "Sexual Assault Incidents among College Undergraduates."

22. Struckman-Johnson, C., Struckman-Johnson, D., and Anderson, P. B., "Tactics of Sexual Coercion: When Men and Women Won't Take No for an Answer," *The Journal of Sex Research* 40, no. 1 (n.d.): 76–86.

23. Gagnon and Simon, *Sexual Conduct*.

24. R. W. Coulter et al., "Prevalence of Past-Year Sexual Assault Victimization among Undergraduate Students: Exploring Differences by and Intersections of Gender Identity, Sexual Identity, and Race/Ethnicity," *Prev Sci* Epub ahead of print (2017), https://doi.org/doi: 10.1007/s11121-017-0762-8; Jennifer S. Hirsch et al., "There Was Nowhere to Cry: Power, Precarity, and the Ecology of Student Well-Being," in development; Jack, *The Privileged Poor*; Mellins et al., "Sexual Assault Incidents among College Undergraduates"; Warikoo, *The Diversity Bargain*.

25. Deborah K. Lewis and Timothy C. Marchell, "Safety First: A Medical Amnesty Approach to Alcohol Poisoning at a U.S. University," *International Journal of Drug Policy* 17, no. 4 (July 2006): 329–38, https://doi.org/10.1016/j.drugpo.2006.02.007.

26. Alexandre Fachini et al., "Efficacy of Brief Alcohol Screening Intervention for College Students (BASICS): A Meta-Analysis of Randomized Controlled Trials," *Substance Abuse Treatment, Prevention, and Policy* 7, no. 1 (December 2012): 40, https://doi.org/10.1186/1747-597X-7-40.

27. Promoting Restorative Initiatives on Sexual Misconduct at Colleges and Universities Campus PRISM Project, "Next Steps for a Restorative Justice Approach to Campus-Based Sexual and Gender-Based Harassment, Including Sexual Violence" (Saratoga Springs, NY: Project on Restorative Justice at Skidmore College, December 2017), https://www.skidmore.edu/campusrj/documents/Next-Steps-for -RJ-Campus-PRISM.pdf; Jacqueline R. Piccigallo, Terry G. Lilley, and Susan L. Miller, "'It's Cool to Care about Sexual Violence': Men's Experiences with Sexual Assault Prevention," *Men and Masculinities* 15, no. 5 (December 2012): 507–25, https://doi.org/10.1177/1097184X12458590; Joan Tabachnick and Cordelia Anderson, "Accountability and Responsibility in the Era of #MeToo," *ATSA (Association for the Treatment of Sexual Abusers)* XXXI, no. 2 (Spring 2019), http://newsmanager .commpartners.com/atsa/issues/2019-03-13/2.html.

28. Cantor et al., "Report on the AAU Campus Climate Survey on Sexual Assault and Sexual Misconduct: Columbia University"; Mellins et al., "Sexual Assault Incidents among College Undergraduates.

29. Schneider and Hirsch, "Comprehensive Sexuality Education as a Primary Preven-

tion Strategy for Sexual Violence Perpetration"; Ronny A. Shtarkshall, John S. Santelli, and Jennifer S. Hirsch, "Sex Education and Sexual Socialization: Roles for Educators and Parents," *Perspectives on Sexual and Reproductive Health* 39, no. 2 (June 2007): 116–19, https://doi.org/10.1363/3911607.

CHAPTER 7: THE POWER OF THE GROUP

1. Barnard College, "Fact Sheet"; Columbia University, "Class of 2022 Profile."
2. Raewyn Connell, *Gender and Power: Society, the Person and Sexual Politics* (Cambridge [Cambridgeshire] : Polity Press, 1987); Gagnon and Simon, *Sexual Conduct*; Cicely Marston and Eleanor King, "Factors That Shape Young People's Sexual Behaviour: A Systematic Review," *The Lancet* 368, no. 9547 (November 4, 2006): 1581–86, https://doi.org/10.1016/S0140-6736(06)69662-1.
3. John T. P. Hustad et al., "Tailgating and Pregaming by College Students with Alcohol Offenses: Patterns of Alcohol Use and Beliefs," *Substance Use and Misuse* 49, no. 14 (December 6, 2014): 1928–33, https://doi.org/10.3109/10826084.2014 .949008; Jennifer E. Merrill et al., "Is the Pregame to Blame? Event-Level Associations Between Pregaming and Alcohol-Related Consequences," *Journal of Studies on Alcohol and Drugs* 74, no. 5 (September 2013): 757–64, https://doi.org/10.15288/ jsad.2013.74.757.
4. Mireille Cyr et al., "Intrafamilial Sexual Abuse: Brother–Sister Incest Does Not Differ from Father–Daughter and Stepfather–Stepdaughter Incest," *Child Abuse and Neglect* 26, no. 9 (September 2002): 957–73, https://doi.org/10.1016/S0145 -2134(02)00365-4; Kristi L. Hoffman, K. Jill Kiecolt, and John N. Edwards, "Physical Violence between Siblings: A Theoretical and Empirical Analysis," *Journal of Family Issues* 26, no. 8 (November 2005): 1103–30, https://doi.org/10 .1177/0192513X05277809.
5. N. C. Cantalupo, "Institution-Specific Victimization Surveys: Addressing Legal and Practical Disincentives to Gender-Based Violence Reporting on College Campuses," *Trauma, Violence, and Abuse* 15, no. 3 (2014): 227–41; Bonnie S. Fisher et al., "Reporting Sexual Victimization to the Police and Others: Results from a National-Level Study of College Women," *Criminal Justice and Behavior* 30, no. 1 (February 1, 2003): 6–38, https://doi.org/10.1177/0093854802239161; Lindsay M. Orchowski, Amy S. Untied, and Christine A. Gidycz, "Factors Associated with College Women's Labeling of Sexual Victimization," *Violence and Victims* 28, no. 6 (2013): 940–58; Marjorie R. Sable et al., "Barriers to Reporting Sexual Assault for Women and Men: Perspectives of College Students," *Journal of American College Health* 55 (2006): 157–62; Heidi M. Zinzow and Martie Thompson, "Barriers to Reporting Sexual Victimization: Prevalence and Correlates among Undergraduate Women," *ResearchGate* 20, no. 7 (October 1, 2011): 711–25, https://doi.org/10.1080/10926771.2011.613447.

6. Jason M. Fletcher and Marta Tienda, "High School Classmates and College Success," *Sociology of Education* 82, no. 4 (October 1, 2009): 287–314, https://doi.org/10.1177/003804070908200401; Lauren A. Rivera, *Pedigree: How Elite Students Get Elite Jobs*, first paperback printing with a new afterword by the author (Princeton and Oxford: Princeton University Press, 2016).

7. Matthijs Kalmijn, "Intermarriage and Homogamy: Causes, Patterns, Trends," *Annual Review of Sociology* 24, no. 1 (August 1998): 395–421, https://doi.org/10.1146/annurev.soc.24.1.395.

8. Margot Canaday, *The Straight State: Sexuality and Citizenship in Twentieth-Century America*, Politics and Society in Twentieth-Century America (Princeton, NJ: Princeton Univ. Press, 2009); Héctor Carrillo, "Imagining Modernity: Sexuality, Policy and Social Change in Mexico," *Sexuality Research and Social Policy* 4, no. 3 (September 2007): 74–91, https://doi.org/10.1525/srsp.2007.4.3.74.

9. Aaron C. Ahuvia and Mara B. Adelman, "Formal Intermediaries in the Marriage Market: A Typology and Review," *Journal of Marriage and the Family* 54, no. 2 (May 1992): 452, https://doi.org/10.2307/353076; Davor Jedlicka, "Formal Mate Selection Networks in the United States," *Family Relations* 29, no. 2 (April 1980): 199, https://doi.org/10.2307/584072.

10. Jennifer Hirsch and Holly Wardlow, *Modern Loves: The Anthropology of Romantic Courtship and Companionate Marriage* (Ann Arbor, MI: University of Michigan Press, 2006), https://doi.org/10.3998/mpub.170440.

11. Elizabeth E. Bruch and M. E. J. Newman, "Aspirational Pursuit of Mates in Online Dating Markets," *Science Advances* 4, no. 8 (August 1, 2018): eaap9815, https://doi.org/10.1126/sciadv.aap9815.

12. Bogle, *Hooking Up*.

13. Elizabeth A. Armstrong et al., "'Good Girls': Gender, Social Class, and Slut Discourse on Campus," *Social Psychology Quarterly* 77, no. 2 (June 1, 2014): 100–122, https://doi.org/10.1177/0190272514521220; Khan, *Privilege*.

14. Boeringer, "Influences of Fraternity Membership, Athletics, and Male Living Arrangements on Sexual Aggression"; C. A. Gidycz, J. B. Warkentin, and L. M. Orchowski, "Predictors of Perpetration of Verbal, Physical, and Sexual Violence: A Prospective Analysis of College Men," *Psychology of Men and Masculinity* 8, no. 2 (2007): 79–94; Koss and Cleveland, "Athletic Participation, Fraternity Membership, and Date Rape."

15. Eric Anderson, "Inclusive Masculinity in a Fraternal Setting," *Men and Masculinities* 10, no. 5 (August 2008): 604–20, https://doi.org/10.1177/1097184X06291907.

16. National Center for Education Statistics, "Table 303.70. Total Undergraduate Fall Enrollment in Degree-Granting Postsecondary Institutions, by Attendance Status, Sex of Student, and Control and Level of Institution: Selected Years, 1970 through 2026" (Washington, DC: Institute of Education Sciences, February 2017), https://

nces.ed.gov/programs/digest/d16/tables/dt16_303.70.asp; Jeremy E. Uecker and Mark D. Regnerus, "Bare Market: Campus Sex Ratios, Romantic Relationships, and Sexual Behavior," *The Sociological Quarterly* 51, no. 3 (August 2010): 408–35, https://doi.org/10.1111/j.1533-8525.2010.01177.x.

17. Mellins et al., "Sexual Assault Incidents among College Undergraduates.

18. Gidycz, Warkentin, and Orchowski, "Predictors of Perpetration of Verbal, Physical, and Sexual Violence"; Arrick Jackson, Katherine Gilliland, and Louis Veneziano, "Routine Activity Theory and Sexual Deviance among Male College Students," *Journal of Family Violence* 21, no. 7 (December 1, 2006): 449–60, https://doi.org/10 .1007/s10896-006-9040-4; Koss and Cleveland, "Athletic Participation, Fraternity Membership, and Date Rape"; Sarah K. Murnen and Marla H. Kohlman, "Athletic Participation, Fraternity Membership, and Sexual Aggression among College Men: A Meta-Analytic Review," *Sex Roles* 57, no. 1–2 (August 2, 2007): 145–57, https:// doi.org/10.1007/s11199-007-9225-1; Walsh et al., "Prevalence and Correlates of Sexual Assault Perpetration and Ambiguous Consent in a Representative Sample of College Students."

19. Flack, "'The Red Zone.'"

20. David H. Jernigan et al., "Assessing Campus Alcohol Policies: Measuring Accessibility, Clarity, and Effectiveness," *Alcoholism: Clinical and Experimental Research* 43, no. 5 (May 2019): 1007–15, https://doi.org/10.1111/acer.14017.

21. C. J. Pascoe and Jocelyn A. Hollander, "Good Guys Don't Rape: Gender, Domination, and Mobilizing Rape," *Gender and Society* 30, no. 1 (February 2016): 67–79, https://doi.org/10.1177/0891243215612707.

22. Alexander Wamboldt et al., "Feminists and Creeps: Collegiate Greek Life and Athletics, Hybrid Moral Masculinity, and the Politics of Sexuality and Gender," n.d.

23. Bridges, "A Very 'Gay' Straight?"; Demetriou, "Connell's Concept of Hegemonic Masculinity"; Bridges and Pascoe, "Hybrid Masculinities"; Robbins, *Fraternity*.

24. Hirsch et al., "There Was Nowhere to Cry."

25. Maya Perry, "The Constitution of a Community: Why Student Clubs Are Starting to Take Sexual Violence Response into Their Own Hands," *Columbia Daily Spectator*, February 24, 2019, https://www.columbiaspectator.com/eye-lead/2019/02/24/ the-constitution-of-a-community-why-student-clubs-are-starting-to-take-sexual -violence-response-into-their-own-hands/.

26. Fletcher and Tienda, "High School Classmates and College Success."

27. Messner, "Bad Men, Good Men, Bystanders."

28. Banyard, Moynihan, and Crossman, "Reducing Sexual Violence on Campus"; Mabry and Turner, "Do Sexual Assault Bystander Interventions Change Men's Intentions?"

29. Alexander Wamboldt et al., "Friends, Strangers, and Bystanders."

30. Mark Kleiman, *When Brute Force Fails: How to Have Less Crime and Less Punishment*

(Princeton, NJ: Princeton Univ. Press, 2010); Daniel S. Nagin, "Deterrence in the Twenty-First Century," *Crime and Justice* 42, no. 1 (August 2013): 199–263, https://doi.org/10.1086/670398.

31. Brenner, "Resisting Simple Dichotomies"; Piccigallo, Lilley, and Miller, "'It's Cool to Care about Sexual Violence'"; Brian Sweeney, "Party Animals or Responsible Men: Social Class, Race, and Masculinity on Campus," *International Journal of Qualitative Studies in Education* 27, no. 6 (July 3, 2014): 804–21, https://doi.org/10.1080/09518398.2014.901578.

32. Kipnis, *Unwanted Advances*; McCaughey and Cermele, "Changing the Hidden Curriculum of Campus Rape Prevention and Education"; Messner, "Bad Men, Good Men, Bystanders."

33. Sarah McMahon and Victoria L. Banyard, "When Can I Help? A Conceptual Framework for the Prevention of Sexual Violence Through Bystander Intervention," *Trauma, Violence, and Abuse* 13, no. 1 (January 2012): 3–14, https://doi.org/10.1177/1524838011426015.

34. Pascoe and Hollander, "Good Guys Don't Rape."

CHAPTER 8: THE AFTERMATH

1. Cecilia Mengo and Beverly M. Black, "Violence Victimization on a College Campus: Impact on GPA and School Dropout," *Journal of College Student Retention: Research, Theory and Practice* 18, no. 2 (August 2016): 234–48, https://doi.org/10.1177/1521025115584750; Sarah E Ullman, "Sexual Assault Victimization and Suicidal Behavior in Women: A Review of the Literature," *Aggression and Violent Behavior* 9, no. 4 (July 2004): 331–51, https://doi.org/10.1016/S1359-1789(03)00019-3; Zinzow and Thompson, "Barriers to Reporting Sexual Victimization."

2. Khan et al., "'I Didn't Want to Be "That Girl."'"

3. Hirsch et al., *The Secret*; Caroline M. Parker et al., "Social Risk, Stigma and Space: Key Concepts for Understanding HIV Vulnerability among Black Men Who Have Sex with Men in New York City," *Culture, Health and Sexuality* 19, no. 3 (March 4, 2017): 323–37, https://doi.org/10.1080/13691058.2016.1216604.

4. Shamus Khan et al., "Ecologically Constituted Classes of Sexual Assault: Constructing a Behavioral, Relational, and Contextual Model," n.p.; Mary P. Koss et al., "Stranger and Acquaintance Rape: Are There Differences in the Victim's Experience?," *Psychology of Women Quarterly* 12, no. 1 (1988): 1–24.

5. Sable et al., "Barriers to Reporting Sexual Assault for Women and Men."

6. Kaitlin M. Boyle, "Sexual Assault and Identity Disruption: A Sociological Approach to Posttraumatic Stress," *Society and Mental Health* 7, no. 2 (July 2017): 69–84, https://doi.org/10.1177/2156869317699249; Melanie S. Harned, "Understanding Women's Labeling of Unwanted Sexual Experiences with Dating Partners: A Qual-

itative Analysis," *Violence against Women* 11, no. 3 (2005): 374–413; Orchowski, Untied, and Gidycz, "Factors Associated with College Women's Labeling of Sexual Victimization."

7. "McCaskill: Campus Sexual Assault Survey Results a 'Wakeup Call' for Schools | U.S. Senator Claire McCaskill of Missouri," accessed May 4, 2015, http://www .mccaskill.senate.gov/media-center/news-releases/campus-sexual-assault-survey; Sharyn Potter et al., "Long-Term Impacts of College Sexual Assaults on Women Survivors' Educational and Career Attainments," *Journal of American College Health*, February 15, 2018, 1–37, https://doi.org/10.1080/07448481.2018.1440574; "It's On Us, a Growing Movement to End Campus Sexual Assault," The White House, accessed May 4, 2015, http://www.whitehouse.gov/blog/2014/09/24/its-us-growing -movement-end-campus-sexual-assault.

8. Rosemary Iconis, "Rape Myth Acceptance in College Students: A Literature Review," *Contemporary Issues in Education Research (CIER)* 1, no. 2 (2011): 47–52.

9. Sapana D. Donde, "College Women's Attributions of Blame for Experiences of Sexual Assault," *Journal of Interpersonal Violence* 32, no. 22 (November 2017): 3520–38, https://doi.org/10.1177/0886260515599659; Nicole K. Jeffrey and Paula C. Barata, "'He Didn't Necessarily Force Himself Upon Me, But . . . ': Women's Lived Experiences of Sexual Coercion in Intimate Relationships with Men," *Violence against Women* 23, no. 8 (July 2017): 911–33, https://doi.org/10.1177/1077801216652507; Lonsway, Archambault, and Lisak, "False Reports."

10. Armstrong, Hamilton, and Sweeney, "Sexual Assault on Campus"; Stephen Cranney, "The Relationship between Sexual Victimization and Year in School in U.S. Colleges: Investigating the Parameters of the 'Red Zone,'" *Journal of Interpersonal Violence* 30, no. 17 (October 2015): 3133–45, https://doi.org/10.1177/0886260514554425; Flack, "'The Red Zone' Temporal Risk for Unwanted Sex among College Students"; Kimble et al., "Risk of Unwanted Sex for College Women."

11. L. Kamin, "On the Length of Black Penises and the Depth of White Racism," in *Psychology and Oppression: Critiques and Proposals* (Johannesburg: Skotaville, 1993), 35–54.

12. Mellins et al., "Sexual Assault Incidents among College Undergraduates."

13. Mellins et al., "Sexual Assault Incidents among College Undergraduates."

14. Gilbert et al., "Situational Contexts and Risk Factors Associated with Incapacitated and Nonincapacitated Sexual Assaults among College Women."

15. Heather Littleton and Craig E. Henderson, "If She Is Not a Victim, Does That Mean She Was Not Traumatized? Evaluation of Predictors of PTSD Symptomatology among College Rape Victims," *Violence against Women* 15, no. 2 (2009): 148–67; Laura C. Wilson and Angela Scarpa, "The Unique Associations between Rape Acknowledgment and the DSM-5 PTSD Symptom Clusters," *Psychiatry Research* 257 (November 2017): 290–95, https://doi.org/10.1016/j.psychres.2017.07.055.

16. Sarah McMahon et al., "Campus Sexual Assault: Future Directions for Research," *Sexual Abuse* 31, no. 3 (April 2019): 270–95, https://doi.org/10.1177/1079063217750864; Potter, "Reducing Sexual Assault on Campus"; Malachi Willis and Kristen N. Jozkowski, "Barriers to the Success of Affirmative Consent Initiatives: An Application of the Social Ecological Model," *American Journal of Sexuality Education* 13, no. 3 (July 3, 2018): 324–36, https://doi.org/10.1080/15546128.2018.1443300.

17. Catherine Kaukinen, "The Help-Seeking Decisions of Violent Crime Victims: An Examination of the Direct and Conditional Effects of Gender and the Victim-Offender Relationship," *Journal of Interpersonal Violence* 17, no. 4 (April 2002): 432–56, https://doi.org/10.1177/0886260502017004006; Sable et al., "Barriers to Reporting Sexual Assault for Women and Men."

18. Briana M. Moore and Thomas Baker, "An Exploratory Examination of College Students' Likelihood of Reporting Sexual Assault to Police and University Officials: Results of a Self-Report Survey," *Journal of Interpersonal Violence* 33, no. 22 (November 2018): 3419–38, https://doi.org/10.1177/0886260516632357; Sable et al., "Barriers to Reporting Sexual Assault for Women and Men"; Zinzow and Thompson, "Barriers to Reporting Sexual Victimization."

19. Campbell, Dworkin, and Cabral, "An Ecological Model of the Impact of Sexual Assault on Women's Mental Health"; Kate Walsh et al., "Lifetime Prevalence of Gender-Based Violence in US Women: Associations with Mood/Anxiety and Substance Use Disorders," *Journal of Psychiatric Research* 62 (March 2015): 7–13, https://doi.org/10.1016/j.jpsychires.2015.01.002.

20. Lynn A. Addington and Callie Marie Rennison, "US National Crime Victimization Survey," in *Encyclopedia of Criminology and Criminal Justice*, ed. Gerben Bruinsma and David Weisburd (New York: Springer New York, 2014), 5392–5401, https://doi.org/10.1007/978-1-4614-5690-2_448; Ruth D. Peterson and William C. Bailey, "Rape and Dimensions of Socioeconomic Inequality in U.S. Metropolitan Areas," *Journal of Research in Crime and Delinquency* 29, no. 2 (1992): 162–77.

21. Fisher et al., "Reporting Sexual Victimization To The Police And Others Results From a National-Level Study of College Women"; Patricia A. Frazier and Beth Haney, "Sexual Assault Cases in the Legal System: Police, Prosecutor, and Victim Perspectives," *Law and Human Behavior* 20, no. 6 (1996): 607–28, https://doi.org/10.1007/BF01499234; Martie Thompson et al., "Reasons for Not Reporting Victimizations to the Police: Do They Vary for Physical and Sexual Incidents?," *Journal of American College Health: J of ACH* 55, no. 5 (April 2007): 277–82, https://doi.org/10.3200/JACH.55.5.277-282; Cassia Spohn and Katharine Tellis, "The Criminal Justice System's Response to Sexual Violence," *Violence against Women* 18, no. 2 (February 2012): 169–92, https://doi.org/10.1177/1077801212440020.

22. David Lisak et al., "False Allegations of Sexual Assault: An Analysis of Ten Years

of Reported Cases," *Violence against Women* 16, no. 12 (December 1, 2010): 1318–34, https://doi.org/10.1177/1077801210387747; Lonsway, Archambault, and Lisak, "False Reports"; Cassia Spohn, Clair White, and Katharine Tellis, "Unfounding Sexual Assault: Examining the Decision to Unfound and Identifying False Reports: Unfounding Sexual Assault," *Law and Society Review* 48, no. 1 (March 2014): 161–92, https://doi.org/10.1111/lasr.12060; Dana A. Weiser, "Confronting Myths about Sexual Assault: A Feminist Analysis of the False Report Literature: False Reports," *Family Relations* 66, no. 1 (February 2017): 46–60, https://doi.org/10.1111/fare.12235; Kate B. Wolitzky-Taylor et al., "Reporting Rape in a National Sample of College Women," *Journal of American College Health* 59, no. 7 (2011): 582–87; "Department of Justice: Sexual Assault False Reporting Overview."

23. Rebecca Campbell and Sheela Raja, "Secondary Victimization of Rape Victims: Insights From Mental Health Professionals Who Treat Survivors of Violence," *Violence and Victims* 14, no. 3 (1999): 261–75; Sable et al., "Barriers to Reporting Sexual Assault for Women and Men"; Zinzow and Thompson, "Barriers to Reporting Sexual Victimization."

24. Kristine A. Peace, Stephen Porter, and Leanne ten Brinke, "Are Memories for Sexually Traumatic Events 'Special'? A Within-Subjects Investigation of Trauma and Memory in a Clinical Sample," *Memory* 16, no. 1 (January 2008): 10–21, https://doi.org/10.1080/09658210701363583; Bessel A. Van Der Kolk, "Trauma and Memory: Trauma and Memory," *Psychiatry and Clinical Neurosciences* 52, no. S1 (September 1998): S57–69, https://doi.org/10.1046/j.1440-1819.1998.0520s5S97.x.

25. Tom J. Barry et al., "Meta-Analysis of the Association between Autobiographical Memory Specificity and Exposure to Trauma: Memory Specificity and Trauma," *Journal of Traumatic Stress* 31, no. 1 (February 2018): 35–46, https://doi.org/10.1002/jts.22263; Anke Ehlers and David M. Clark, "A Cognitive Model of Posttraumatic Stress Disorder," *Behaviour Research and Therapy* 38, no. 4 (April 2000): 319–45, https://doi.org/10.1016/S0005-7967(99)00123-0; Sarah L. Halligan et al., "Posttraumatic Stress Disorder Following Assault: The Role of Cognitive Processing, Trauma Memory, and Appraisals," *Journal of Consulting and Clinical Psychology* 71, no. 3 (2003): 419–31, https://doi.org/10.1037/0022-006X.71.3.419.

26. Judith Lewis Herman, "The Mental Health of Crime Victims: Impact of Legal Intervention," *Journal of Traumatic Stress* 16, no. 2 (April 2003): 159–66, https://doi.org/10.1023/A:1022847223135.

27. Campbell and Raja, "Secondary Victimization of Rape Victims."

28. Fisher et al., "Reporting Sexual Victimization To The Police And Others Results From a National-Level Study of College Women"; Spohn and Tellis, "The Criminal Justice System's Response to Sexual Violence"; Wolitzky-Taylor et al., "Reporting Rape in a National Sample of College Women."

29. Patricia C. Dunn, Karen Vail-Smith, and Sharon M. Knight, "What Date/Acquain-

tance Rape Victims Tell Others: A Study of College Student Recipients of Disclosure," *Journal of American College Health* 47, no. 5 (1999): 213–19.

30. Victoria L. Banyard et al., "Friends of Survivors: The Community Impact of Unwanted Sexual Experiences," *Journal of Interpersonal Violence* 25, no. 2 (February 2010): 242–56, https://doi.org/10.1177/0886260509334407; Kathryn A. Branch and Tara N. Richards, "The Effects of Receiving a Rape Disclosure: College Friends' Stories," *Violence against Women* 19, no. 5 (May 2013): 658–70, https://doi.org/10.1177/1077801213490509; Mellins et al., "Sexual Assault Incidents among College Undergraduates."

31. Mellins et al., "Sexual Assault Incidents among College Undergraduates."

32. Vicki Connop and Jenny Petrak, "The Impact of Sexual Assault on Heterosexual Couples," *Sexual and Relationship Therapy* 19, no. 1 (February 2004): 29–38, https://doi.org/10.1080/14681990410001640817; Evalina van wijk and Tracie C. Harrison, "Relationship Difficulties Postrape: Being a Male Intimate Partner of a Female Rape Victim in Cape Town, South Africa," *Health Care for Women International* 35, no. 7–9 (September 2014): 1081–1105, https://doi.org/10.1080/07399332.2014.916708.

33. Khan et al., "Ecologically Constituted Classes of Sexual Assault: Constructing a Behavioral, Relational, and Contextual Model."

34. Brenner, "Resisting Simple Dichotomies."

35. Tom Boellstorff, "But Do Not Identify as Gay: A Proleptic Genealogy of the MSM Category," *Cultural Anthropology* 26, no. 2 (May 2011): 287–312, https://doi.org/10.1111/j.1548-1360.2011.01100.x; Brenner, "Resisting Simple Dichotomies"; Jonathan Garcia et al., "The Limitations of 'Black MSM' as a Category: Why Gender, Sexuality, and Desire Still Matter for Social and Biomedical HIV Prevention Methods," *Global Public Health* 11, no. 7–8 (September 13, 2016): 1026–48, https://doi.org/10.1080/17441692.2015.1134616.

36. Elissa R. Weitzman, "Poor Mental Health, Depression, and Associations with Alcohol Consumption, Harm, and Abuse in a National Sample of Young Adults in College," *The Journal of Nervous and Mental Disease* 192, no. 4 (April 2004): 269–77, https://doi.org/10.1097/01.nmd.0000120885.17362.94; Heidi M. Zinzow et al., "Self-Rated Health in Relation to Rape and Mental Health Disorders in a National Sample of College Women," *Journal of American College Health* 59, no. 7 (2011): 588–94.

CHAPTER 9: GENDER AND BEYOND

1. Connell, *Gender and Power: Society, the Person and Sexual Politics*; Christina Linder, *Sexual Violence on Campus: Power-Conscious Approaches to Awareness, Prevention, and*

Response, Great Debates in Higher Education Ser. (Bingley, UK: Emerald Publishing Limited, 2018).

2. V. Banyard, "Who Will Help Prevent Sexual Violence: Creating an Ecological Model of Bystander Intervention," *Psychology of Violence* 1, no. 3 (2011): 216–29; Casey and Lindhorst, "Toward a Multi-Level, Ecological Approach to the Primary Prevention of Sexual Assault"; Potter, "Reducing Sexual Assault on Campus."

3. Elizabeth Armstrong and Jamie Budnick, "Sexual Assault on Campus: Part of Council of Contemporary Families' Online Symposium on Intimate Partner Violence," May 7, 2015, http://thesocietypages.org/ccf/2015/05/07/sexual-assault-on-campus/; Todd Crosset, "Male Athletes' Violence against Women: A Critical Assessment of the Athletic Affiliation, Violence against Women Debate," *Quest* 51, no. 3 (August 1999): 244–57, https://doi.org/10.1080/00336297.1999.10491684; Koss and Cleveland, "Athletic Participation, Fraternity Membership, and Date Rape"; Patricia Yancey Martin, "The Rape Prone Culture of Academic Contexts: Fraternities and Athletics," *Gender and Society* 30, no. 1 (February 2016): 30–43, https://doi.org/10.1177/0891243215612708; Merrill Melnick, "Male Athletes and Sexual Assault," *Journal of Physical Education, Recreation and Dance* 63, no. 5 (1992): 32–36.

4. Elizabeth A. Armstrong, Miriam Gleckman-Krut, and Lanora Johnson, "Silence, Power, and Inequality: An Intersectional Approach to Sexual Violence," *Annual Review of Sociology* 44, no. 1 (July 30, 2018): 99–122, https://doi.org/10.1146/annurev-soc-073117-041410; Crenshaw, "Demarginalizing the Intersection of Race and Sex; Linder, *Sexual Violence on Campus: Power-Conscious Approaches to Awareness, Prevention, and Response.*

5. Clayton M. Bullock and Mace Beckson, "Male Victims of Sexual Assault: Phenomenology, Psychology, Physiology," *Journal of the American Academy of Psychiatry and the Law* 39, no. 2 (2011): 197–205; Ford and Soto-Marquez, "Sexual Assault Victimization among Straight, Gay/Lesbian, and Bisexual College Students."

6. Crenshaw, "Demarginalizing the Intersection of Race and Sex: A Black Feminist Critique of Antidiscrimination Doctrine, Feminist Theory and Antiracist Politics."

7. Armstrong et al., "'Good Girls.'"

8. Basile, "Rape by Acquiescence"; Ann L Coker et al., "Physical and Mental Health Effects of Intimate Partner Violence for Men and Women," *American Journal of Preventive Medicine* 23, no. 4 (November 2002): 260–68, https://doi.org/10.1016/S0749-3797(02)00514-7; Patricia A. Resick, "The Psychological Impact of Rape," *Journal of Interpersonal Violence* 8, no. 2 (June 1993): 223–55, https://doi.org/10.1177/088626093008002005.

9. Franklin, "Physically Forced, Alcohol-Induced, and Verbally Coerced Sexual Victimization"; Genell Sandberg, Thomas L. Jackson, and Patricia Petretic-Jackson, "College Students' Attitudes Regarding Sexual Coercion and Aggression: Devel-

oping Educational and Preventive Strategies," *Journal of College Student Personnel*, 1987, http://psycnet.apa.org/psycinfo/1988-27979-001.

10. Andria G. M. Langenberg et al., "A Prospective Study of New Infections with Herpes Simplex Virus Type 1 and Type 2," *New England Journal of Medicine* 341, no. 19 (November 4, 1999): 1432–38, https://doi.org/10.1056/NEJM199911043411904.

11. Simons et al., "The Athlete Stigma in Higher Education."

12. Robb Willer et al., "Overdoing Gender: A Test of the Masculine Overcompensation Thesis," *American Journal of Sociology* 118, no. 4 (January 1, 2013): 980–1022, https://doi.org/10.1086/668417.

13. Pascoe and Hollander, "Good Guys Don't Rape."

14. Cranney, "The Relationship between Sexual Victimization and Year in School in U.S. Colleges"; Flack, "'The Red Zone'"; Kimble et al., "Risk of Unwanted Sex for College Women."

15. Ellison, Steinfield, and Lampe, "The Benefits of Facebook 'Friends.'"

16. Erb et al., "The Importance of College Roommate Relationships"; Hicks and Heastie, "High School to College Transition."

17. For more on these dynamics, see our paper, Wamboldt et al., "'It Was a War of Attrition': Queer and Trans Undergraduates' Practices of Consent and Experiences of Sexual Assault."

18. L. M. Johnson, T. L. Matthews, and S. L. Napper, "Sexual Orientation and Sexual Assault Victimization among US College Students," *Social Science Journal* 53, no. 2016 (2016): 174–83; E. F. Rothman, D. Exner, and A. Baughman, "The Prevalence of Sexual Assault against People Who Identify as Gay, Lesbian or Bisexual in the United States: A Systematic Review," *Trauma Violence and Abuse* 12, no. 2 (2011): 55–66.

19. C. Struckman-Johnson, D. Struckman-Johnson, and P. B. Anderson, "Tactics of Sexual Coercion: When Men and Women Won't Take No for an Answer."

20. Z. Nicolazzo, "'Just Go In Looking Good': The Resilience, Resistance, and Kinship-Building of Trans* College Students," *Journal of College Student Development* 57, no. 5 (2016): 538–56, https://doi.org/10.1353/csd.2016.0057.

21. Brimeyer and Smith, "Religion, Race, Social Class, and Gender Differences in Dating and Hooking Up among College Students"; Elizabeth Aura McClintock, "When Does Race Matter? Race, Sex, and Dating at an Elite University," *Journal of Marriage and Family* 72, no. 1 (February 2010): 45–72, https://doi.org/10.1111/j.1741-3737.2009.00683.x.

22. Diamond-Welch, Hetzel-Riggin, and Hemingway, "The Willingness of College Students to Intervene in Sexual Assault Situations."

23. Gilbert et al., "Situational Contexts and Risk Factors Associated with Incapacitated and Nonincapacitated Sexual Assaults among College Women."

24. Khan et al., "Ecologically Constituted Classes of Sexual Assault: Constructing a Behavioral, Relational, and Contextual Model."

25. Erin E. Ayala, Brandy Kotary, and Maria Hetz, "Blame Attributions of Victims and Perpetrators: Effects of Victim Gender, Perpetrator Gender, and Relationship," *Journal of Interpersonal Violence* 33, no. 1 (January 2018): 94–116, https://doi.org/10.1177/0886260515599160; Russell and Oswald, "Strategies and Dispositional Correlates of Sexual Coercion Perpetrated by Women."

26. Bullock and Beckson, "Male Victims of Sexual Assault"; David Lisak, "Men as Victims: Challenging Cultural Myths," *Journal of Traumatic Stress* 6, no. 4 (October 1, 1993): 577–80, https://doi.org/10.1002/jts.2490060414; Sable et al., "Barriers to Reporting Sexual Assault for Women and Men."

27. Andrea Dworkin, *Intercourse: The Twentieth Anniversary Edition* (New York: Basic-Books, 2007).

28. M. L. Hatzenbuehler, "The Social Environment and Suicide Attempts in Lesbian, Gay, and Bisexual Youth," *Pediatrics* 127, no. 5 (May 1, 2011): 896–903, https://doi.org/10.1542/peds.2010-3020.

CONCLUSIONS: FORMING SEXUAL CITIZENS

1. Jeffrey Drope et al., eds., *The Tobacco Atlas*, sixth ed. (Atlanta, GA: The American Cancer Society, Inc., 2018).

2. Joseph R. Gusfield, *The Culture of Public Problems: Drinking-Driving and the Symbolic Order* (Chicago: Univ. of Chicago Press, 1994).

3. Richard Klein, "An Analysis of Thirty-Five Years of Rape Reform: A Frustrating Search for Fundamental Fairness," *Akron Law Review* 41, no. 981 (2008), https://papers.ssrn.com/sol3/papers.cfm?abstract_id=2341690.

4. Elaine K. Martin, Casey T. Taft, and Patricia A. Resick, "A Review of Marital Rape," *Aggression and Violent Behavior* 12, no. 3 (May 2007): 329–47, https://doi.org/10.1016/j.avb.2006.10.003.

5. Briana Bierschbach, "This Woman Fought To End Minnesota's 'Marital Rape' Exception, And Won," National Public Radio, May 4, 2019, https://www.npr.org/2019/05/04/719635969/this-woman-fought-to-end-minnesotas-marital-rape-exception-and-won; Mattie Quinn, "Marital Rape Isn't Necessarily a Crime in 12 States," *Governing*, April 10, 2019, https://www.governing.com/topics/public-justice-safety/gov-marital-rape-states-ohio-minnesota.html; Sexual Trauma Services, "South Carolina Laws Regarding Sexual Assault and Consent" (Columbia, SC: Sexual Trauma Services, 2019), https://www.stsm.org/south-carolina-laws-regarding-sexual-assault-and-consent.

6. McGuire, *At the Dark End of the Street*.

7. Abbey, "Alcohol-Related Sexual Assault"; Antonia Abbey and Pam McAuslan, "A Longitudinal Examination of Male College Students' Perpetration of Sexual Assault," *Journal of Consulting and Clinical Psychology* 72, no. 5 (2004): 747; Banyard, "Who Will Help Prevent Sexual Violence"; Katie M. Edwards et al., "Rape Myths: History, Individual and Institutional-Level Presence, and Implications for Change," *Sex Roles* 65, no. 11–12 (December 2011): 761–73, https://doi.org/10.1007/s11199-011-9943-2; Kimberly A. Lonsway and Louise F. Fitzgerald, "Rape Myths: In Review," *Psychology of Women Quarterly* 18, no. 2 (June 1994): 133–64, https://doi.org/10.1111/j.1471-6402.1994.tb00448.x; Patricia Yancey Martin and Robert A. Hummer, "Fraternities and Rape on Campus," *Gender & Society* 3, no. 4 (1989): 457–473; Sandra L. Martin et al., "Women's Sexual Orientations and Their Experiences of Sexual Assault before and during University," *Women's Health Issues* 21, no. 3 (May 2011): 199–205, https://doi.org/10.1016/j.whi.2010.12.002; Muehlenhard et al., "The Complexities of Sexual Consent among College Students"; Murnen, Wright, and Kaluzny, "If 'Boys Will Be Boys,' Then Girls Will Be Victims?"; Tharp et al., "A Systematic Qualitative Review of Risk and Protective Factors for Sexual Violence Perpetration"; Catherine J. Vladutiu, Sandra L. Martin, and Rebecca J. Macy, "College- or University-Based Sexual Assault Prevention Programs: A Review of Program Outcomes, Characteristics, and Recommendations," *Trauma, Violence, and Abuse* 12, no. 2 (April 2011): 67–86, https://doi.org/10.1177/1524838010390708; Henry Wechsler et al., "Health and Behavioral Consequences of Binge Drinking in College. A National Survey of Students at 140 Campuses," *JAMA* 272, no. 21 (December 7, 1994): 1672–77.

8. Jennifer S. Hirsch and Claude Ann Mellins, "Sexual Health Initiative to Foster Transformation (SHIFT) Final Report" (New York: Columbia University, March 2019), https://www.mailman.columbia.edu/sites/default/files/shift_final_report_4-11-19.pdf.

9. Jessup-Anger, Lopez, and Koss, "History of Sexual Violence in Higher Education."

10. Randall Waechter and Van Ma, "Sexual Violence in America: Public Funding and Social Priority," *American Journal of Public Health* 105, no. 12 (October 15, 2015): 2430–37, https://doi.org/10.2105/AJPH.2015.302860.

11. Khan et al., "'I Didn't Want to Be "That Girl.'"

12. John Braithwaite, *Restorative Justice and Responsive Regulation*, Studies in Crime and Public Policy (Oxford: Oxford University Press, 2002); Mary P. Koss, Jay K. Wilgus, and Kaaren M. Williamsen, "Campus Sexual Misconduct: Restorative Justice Approaches to Enhance Compliance with Title IX Guidance," *Trauma, Violence and Abuse* 15, no. 3 (April 27, 2014): 242–57, https://doi.org/10.1177/1524838014521500; Mary Koss, "Restorative Justice Responses to Sexual Assault," February 20, 2008, http://dev.vawnet.org/materials/restorative-justice-responses-sexual-assault.

13. E. Bernstein, "The Sexual Politics of the 'New Abolitionism,'" *Differences* 18, no. 3 (January 1, 2007): 128–51, https://doi.org/10.1215/10407391-2007-013.

14. Patrick Sharkey, *Uneasy Peace: The Great Crime Decline, the Renewal of City Life, and the next War on Violence* (New York: W. W. Norton & Company, 2018); Sara Wakefield and Christopher Uggen, "Incarceration and Stratification," *Annual Review of Sociology* 36, no. 1 (June 2010): 387–406, https://doi.org/10.1146/annurev.soc.012809.102551.

15. Robert J. Sampson, "Neighborhoods and Violent Crime: A Multilevel Study of Collective Efficacy," *Science* 277, no. 5328 (August 15, 1997): 918–24, https://doi.org/10.1126/science.277.5328.918.

16. National Institute on Alcohol Abuse and Alcoholism (NIAAA), "Reducing Alcohol Problems on Campus."

17. Fachini et al., "Efficacy of Brief Alcohol Screening Intervention for College Students (BASICS)."

18. Campbell, Dworkin, and Cabral, "An Ecological Model of the Impact of Sexual Assault on Women's Mental Health"; Mary P. Koss and Mary R. Harvey, *The Rape Victim: Clinical and Community Interventions (2nd ed.)*, vol. 14, Sage Library of Social Research, vol. 185 (Thousand Oaks, CA: Sage Publications, Inc, 1991); Sarah E. Ullman et al., "Trauma Histories, Substance Use Coping, PTSD, and Problem Substance Use among Sexual Assault Victims," *Addictive Behaviors* 38 (2013): 2219–23.

19. Hirsch et al., "There Was Nowhere to Cry."

20. Auerbach et al., "WHO World Mental Health Surveys International College Student Project"; Claudia Vadeboncoeur, Nicholas Townsend, and Charlie Foster, "A Meta-Analysis of Weight Gain in First Year University Students: Is Freshman 15 a Myth?," *BMC Obesity* 2, no. 1 (December 2015): 22, https://doi.org/10.1186/s40608-015-0051-7.

21. Information Insurance Institute, "Facts + Statistics: Mortality Risk" (New York: Information Insurance Institute, 2017), https://www.iii.org/fact-statistic/facts-statistics-mortality-risk#Odds%20Of%20Death%20In%20The%20United%20States%20By%20Selected%20Cause%20Of%20Injury,%202017%20(1); Justin Pope, "The College Graduation Swim Test Has Gone Belly-Up," *Los Angeles Times*, June 18, 2006, https://www.latimes.com/archives/la-xpm-2006-jun-18-adna-swim18-story.html.

22. Mellins et al., "Sexual Assault Incidents among College Undergraduates."

23. John S. Santelli et al., "Does Sex Education before College Protect Students from Sexual Assault in College?," *PLOS ONE* 13, no. 11 (November 14, 2018): e0205951, https://doi.org/10.1371/journal.pone.0205951.

24. Schneider and Hirsch, "Comprehensive Sexuality Education as a Primary Prevention Strategy for Sexual Violence Perpetration."

25. Leslie Kantor and Nicole Levitz, "Parents' Views on Sex Education in Schools: How Much Do Democrats and Republicans Agree?," ed. Ehsan U Syed, *PLOS ONE* 12, no. 7 (July 3, 2017): e0180250, https://doi.org/10.1371/journal.pone.0180250;

Lindberg, Maddow-Zimet, and Boonstra, "Changes in Adolescents' Receipt of Sex Education, 2006–2013."

26. Laura Dwyer-Lindgren et al., "Inequalities in Life Expectancy among US Counties, 1980 to 2014: Temporal Trends and Key Drivers," *JAMA Internal Medicine* 177, no. 7 (July 1, 2017): 1003, https://doi.org/10.1001/jamainternmed.2017.0918.

27. "Sexual and Reproductive Health Care: A Position Paper of the Society for Adolescent Health and Medicine," *Journal of Adolescent Health* 54, no. 4 (April 1, 2014): 491–96, https://doi.org/10.1016/j.jadohealth.2014.01.010.

28. Kantor and Levitz, "Parents' Views on Sex Education in Schools"; Lindberg, Maddow-Zimet, and Boonstra, "Changes in Adolescents' Receipt of Sex Education, 2006–2013."

29. Rothman et al., "A Pornography Literacy Class for Youth."

30. Jones, "What Teenagers Are Learning from Online Porn."

31. Shtarkshall, Santelli, and Hirsch, "Sex Education and Sexual Socialization."

32. Ester di Giacomo et al., "Estimating the Risk of Attempted Suicide among Sexual Minority Youths: A Systematic Review and Meta-Analysis," *JAMA Pediatrics* 172, no. 12 (December 1, 2018): 1145–52, https://doi.org/10.1001/jamapediatrics.2018.2731.

33. Mark L. Hatzenbuehler and Bruce G. Link, "Introduction to the Special Issue on Structural Stigma and Health," *Social Science and Medicine* 103 (February 2014): 1–6, https://doi.org/10.1016/j.socscimed.2013.12.017.

34. Potter, "Reducing Sexual Assault on Campus."

METHODOLOGICAL APPENDIX

1. Hirsch and Mellins, "Sexual Health Initiative to Foster Transformation (SHIFT) Final Report."

2. Hirsch et al., "Transforming the Campus Climate."

3. Nicholas Wolferman et al., "The Advisory Board Perspective from a Campus Community-Based Participatory Research Project on Sexual Violence," *Progress in Community Health Partnerships: Research, Education, and Action* 13, no. 1 (2019): 115–19, https://doi.org/10.1353/cpr.2019.0014.

BIBLIOGRAPHY

Abbey, Antonia. "Alcohol-Related Sexual Assault: A Common Problem among College Students." *Journal of Studies on Alcohol and Drugs* 14 (2002): 118–28.

———. "Moving beyond Simple Answers to Complex Questions: How Does Context Affect Alcohol's Role in Sexual Assault Perpetration? A Commentary on Testa and Cleveland (2017)." *Journal of Studies on Alcohol and Drugs* 78 (2016): 14–15.

Abbey, Antonia, A. Monique Clinton-Sherrod, Pam McAuslan, Tina Zawacki, and Philip O. Buck. "The Relationship between the Quantity of Alcohol Consumed and the Severity of Sexual Assaults Committed by College Men." *Journal of Interpersonal Violence* 18, no. 7 (2003): 813–33.

Abbey, Antonia, and Angela J. Jacques-Tiura. "Sexual Assault Perpetrators' Tactics: Associations with Their Personal Characteristics and Aspects of the Incident." *Journal of Interpersonal Violence* 26, no. 14 (September 2011): 2866–89. https://doi.org/10.1177/0886260510390955.

Abbey, Antonia, and Pam McAuslan. "A Longitudinal Examination of Male College Students' Perpetration of Sexual Assault." *Journal of Consulting and Clinical Psychology* 72, no. 5 (2004): 747.

Abbey, Antonia, Pam McAuslan, and Lisa Thomson Ross. "Sexual Assault Perpetration by College Men: The Role of Alcohol, Misperception of Sexual Intent, and Sexual Beliefs and Experiences." *Journal of Social and Clinical Psychology* 17, no. 2 (1998): 167–95.

Abbey, Antonia, Pam McAuslan, Tina Zawacki, A. Monique Clinton, and Philip O. Buck. "Attitudinal, Experiential, and Situational Predictors of Sexual Assault Perpetration." *Journal of Interpersonal Violence* 16, no. 8 (2001): 784–807.

Abbey, Antonia, Lisa Thomson Ross, Donna McDuffie, and Pam McAuslan. "Alcohol and Dating Risk Factors for Sexual Assault among College Women." *Psychology of Women Quarterly* 20, no. 1 (1996): 147–69.

Abbey, Antonia, Tina Zawacki, Philip O. Buck, A. Monique Clinton, and Pam McAuslan. "Sexual Assault and Alcohol Consumption: What Do We Know about Their Relationship and What Types of Research Are Still Needed?" *Aggression and Violent Behavior* 9, no. 3 (2004): 271–303.

Abel, Jaison R., Richard Deitz, and Yaqin Su. "Are Recent College Graduates Finding Good Jobs?" *The Federal Reserve Bank of New York: Current Issues in Economics and Finance* 20, no. 1 (2014): 1–8.

Abu-Odeh, Desiree, Constance Nathanson, and Shamus Khan. "Bureaucratization of Sex at Columbia and Barnard, 1955 to 1990." *Social Science History*, forthcoming.

Addington, Lynn A., and Callie Marie Rennison. "US National Crime Victimization Survey." In *Encyclopedia of Criminology and Criminal Justice*, edited by Gerben Bruinsma and David Weisburd, 5392–5401. New York: Springer New York, 2014. https://doi.org/10.1007/978-1-4614-5690-2_448.

"Affirmative Consent Laws (Yes Means Yes) State by State." AffirmativeConsent.com. Accessed July 17, 2017. http://affirmativeconsent.com/affirmative-consent-laws -state-by-state/.

Ahuvia, Aaron C., and Mara B. Adelman. "Formal Intermediaries in the Marriage Market: A Typology and Review." *Journal of Marriage and the Family* 54, no. 2 (May 1992): 452. https://doi.org/10.2307/353076.

Allison, Rachel, and Barbara J. Risman. "A Double Standard for 'Hooking Up': How Far Have We Come toward Gender Equality?" *Social Science Research* 42, no. 5 (September 2013): 1191–1206. https://doi.org/10.1016/j.ssresearch.2013.04.006.

———. "'It Goes Hand in Hand with the Parties': Race, Class, and Residence in College Student Negotiations of Hooking Up." *Sociological Perspectives* 57, no. 1 (March 2014): 102–23. https://doi.org/10.1177/0731121413516608.

Alvarez Martin, Barbara, Thomas P. McCoy, Heather Champion, Maria T. Parries, Robert H. Durant, Ananda Mitra, and Scott Rhodes. "The Role of Monthly Spending Money in College Student Drinking Behaviors and Their Consequences." *Journal of American College Health* 57, no. 6 (n.d.): 587–96.

American College Health Association. "American College Health Association-National College Health Assessment II: Reference Group Data Report Fall 2008." Baltimore: American College Health Association, 2009.

———. "American College Health Association-National College Health Assessment II: Reference Group Undergraduates Executive Summary Fall 2015." Hanover, MD: American College Health Association, 2016.

———. "American College Health Association-National College Health Assessment II: Undergraduate Student Reference Group Executive Summary Spring 2015." Hanover, MD: American College Health Association, 2016.

———. "American College Health Association-National College Health Assessment Spring 2018 Reference Group Data Report." Baltimore: American College Health Association, 2018.

Anderson, Eric. "Inclusive Masculinity in a Fraternal Setting." *Men and Masculinities* 10, no. 5 (August 2008): 604–20. https://doi.org/10.1177/1097184X06291907.

Anderson, Nick. "At First, 55 Schools Faced Sexual Violence Investigations. Now the List Has Quadrupled." *Washington Post*, January 18, 2017.

Armstrong, Elizabeth A., Paula England, and Alison C. K. Fogarty. "Accounting for Women's Orgasm and Sexual Enjoyment in College Hookups and Relationships." *American Sociological Review* 77, no. 3 (June 1, 2012): 435–62. https://doi.org/10 .1177/0003122412445802.

Armstrong, Elizabeth A., Miriam Gleckman-Krut, and Lanora Johnson. "Silence, Power, and Inequality: An Intersectional Approach to Sexual Violence." *Annual Review of Sociology* 44, no. 1 (July 30, 2018): 99–122. https://doi.org/10.1146/annurev-soc-073117 -041410.

Armstrong, Elizabeth A., Laura Hamilton, Paula Engl, | August 5, and 2010 | Summer 2010. "Is Hooking Up Bad For Young Women?" *Contexts*, http://contexts.org/ articles/is-hooking-up-bad-for-young-women/.

Armstrong, Elizabeth A., Laura Hamilton, and Brian Sweeney. "Sexual Assault on Campus: A Multilevel, Integrative Approach to Party Rape." *Social Problems* 53, no. 4 (2006): 483–99. https://doi.org/10.1525/sp.2006.53.4.483.

Armstrong, Elizabeth A., and Laura T. Hamilton. *Paying for the Party: How College Maintains Inequality.* Cambridge, MA: Harvard University Press, 2013.

Armstrong, Elizabeth A., Laura T. Hamilton, Elizabeth M. Armstrong, and J. Lotus Seeley. "'Good Girls': Gender, Social Class, and Slut Discourse on Campus." *Social Psychology Quarterly* 77, no. 2 (June 1, 2014): 100–122. https://doi.org/10.1177/0190272514521220.

Atkinson, Byron H., and A. T. Brugger. "Do College Students Drink Too Much?" *The Journal of Higher Education* 30, no. 6 (June 1959): 305–12. https://doi.org/10.1080/00221546 .1959.11777453.

Auerbach, Randy P., Philippe Mortier, Ronny Bruffaerts, Jordi Alonso, Corina Benjet, Pim Cuijpers, Koen Demyttenaere, et al. "WHO World Mental Health Surveys International College Student Project: Prevalence and Distribution of Mental Disorders." *Journal of Abnormal Psychology* 127, no. 7 (October 2018): 623–38. https:// doi.org/10.1037/abn0000362.

Axinn, William George, Maura Elaine Bardos, and Brady Thomas West. "General Population Estimates of the Association between College Experience and the Odds of Forced Intercourse." *Social Science Research* 70 (February 2018): 131–43. https://doi .org/10.1016/j.ssresearch.2017.10.006.

Ayala, Erin E., Brandy Kotary, and Maria Hetz. "Blame Attributions of Victims and Perpetrators: Effects of Victim Gender, Perpetrator Gender, and Relationship."

Journal of Interpersonal Violence 33, no. 1 (January 2018): 94–116. https://doi.org/10.1177/0886260515599160.

Banyard, V. "Who Will Help Prevent Sexual Violence: Creating an Ecological Model of Bystander Intervention." *Psychology of Violence* 1, no. 3 (2011): 216–29.

Banyard, Victoria L., Mary M. Moynihan, and Maria T. Crossman. "Reducing Sexual Violence on Campus: The Role of Student Leaders as Empowered Bystanders." *Journal of College Student Development* 50, no. 4 (2009): 446–57.

Banyard, Victoria L., Mary M. Moynihan, and Elizabethe G. Plante. "Sexual Violence Prevention through Bystander Education: An Experimental Evaluation." *Journal of Community Psychology* 35, no. 4 (2007): 463–81.

Banyard, Victoria L., Mary M. Moynihan, Wendy A. Walsh, Ellen S. Cohn, and Sally Ward. "Friends of Survivors: The Community Impact of Unwanted Sexual Experiences." *Journal of Interpersonal Violence* 25, no. 2 (February 2010): 242–56. https://doi.org/10.1177/0886260509334407.

Banyard, Victoria L., Sally Ward, Ellen S. Cohn, Elizabethe G. Plante, Cari Moorhead, and Wendy Walsh. "Unwanted Sexual Contact on Campus: A Comparison of Women's and Men's Experiences." *Violence and Victims* 22, no. 1 (2007): 52–70.

Barnard College. "Fact Sheet," 2019. https://barnard.edu/pressroom/fact-sheet.

Barry, Adam E., Zachary Jackson, Daphne C. Watkins, Janelle R. Goodwill, and Haslyn E. R. Hunte. "Alcohol Use and Mental Health Conditions among Black College Males: Do Those Attending Postsecondary Minority Institutions Fare Better Than Those at Primarily White Institutions?" *American Journal of Men's Health* 11, no. 4 (July 2017): 962–68. https://doi.org/10.1177/1557988316674840.

Barry, Tom J., Bert Lenaert, Dirk Hermans, Filip Raes, and James W. Griffith. "Meta-Analysis of the Association Between Autobiographical Memory Specificity and Exposure to Trauma: Memory Specificity and Trauma." *Journal of Traumatic Stress* 31, no. 1 (February 2018): 35–46. https://doi.org/10.1002/jts.22263.

Basile, K. C. "Rape by Acquiescence: The Ways in Which Women 'Give in' to Unwanted Sex with Their Husbands." *Violence against Women* 5, no. 9 (1999): 1036–58.

Beres, M. A. "'Spontaneous' Sexual Consent: An Analysis of Sexual Consent Literature." *Feminism and Psychology* 17, no. 1 (2007): 93–108.

Beres, Melanie. "Sexual Miscommunication? Untangling Assumptions about Sexual Communication between Casual Sex Partners." *Culture, Health and Sexuality* 12, no. 1 (January 2010): 1–14. https://doi.org/10.1080/13691050903075226.

Bernstein, E. "The Sexual Politics of the 'New Abolitionism.'" *Differences* 18, no. 3 (January 1, 2007): 128–51. https://doi.org/10.1215/10407391-2007-013.

Bierschbach, Briana. "This Woman Fought To End Minnesota's 'Marital Rape' Exception, And Won." National Public Radio, May 4, 2019. https://www.npr.org/2019/05/04/719635969/this-woman-fought-to-end-minnesotas-marital-rape-exception-and-won.

Bobkowski, Piotr S., Jane D. Brown, and Deborah R. Neffa. "'Hit Me Up and We Can Get Down': US Youths' Risk Behaviors and Sexual Self-Disclosure in MySpace Profiles." *Journal of Children and Media* 6, no. 1 (February 2012): 119–34. https://doi.org/10.1080/17482798.2011.633412.

Boellstorff, Tom. "But Do Not Identify as Gay: A Proleptic Genealogy of the MSM Category." *Cultural Anthropology* 26, no. 2 (May 2011): 287–312. https://doi.org/10.1111/j.1548-1360.2011.01100.x.

Boeringer, Scott B. "Influences of Fraternity Membership, Athletics, and Male Living Arrangements on Sexual Aggression." *Violence against Women* 2, no. 2 (June 1, 1996): 134–47. https://doi.org/10.1177/1077801296002002002.

Bogle, Kathleen A. *Hooking Up: Sex, Dating, and Relationships on Campus.* New York: New York University Press, 2008.

Boss, Shira. "Class of 1987 Heralds New Era at Columbia." *Columbia College Today.* Spring 2012. https://www.college.columbia.edu/cct/archive/spring12/cover_story_0.

Bourdieu, Pierre. *Outline of a Theory of Practice.* 25th printing. Cambridge Studies in Social and Cultural Anthropology 16. Cambridge: Cambridge Univ. Press, 2010.

Boyle, Kaitlin M. "Sexual Assault and Identity Disruption: A Sociological Approach to Posttraumatic Stress." *Society and Mental Health* 7, no. 2 (July 2017): 69–84. https://doi.org/10.1177/2156869317699249.

———. "Social Psychological Processes That Facilitate Sexual Assault within the Fraternity Party Subculture: Sexual Assault and the Fraternity Subculture." *Sociology Compass* 9, no. 5 (May 2015): 386–99. https://doi.org/10.1111/soc4.12261.

Braithwaite, John. *Restorative Justice and Responsive Regulation.* Studies in Crime and Public Policy. Oxford: Oxford University Press, 2002.

Branch, Kathryn A., and Tara N. Richards. "The Effects of Receiving a Rape Disclosure: College Friends' Stories." *Violence against Women* 19, no. 5 (May 2013): 658–70. https://doi.org/10.1177/1077801213490509.

Brennan, Carolyn L., Kevin M. Swartout, Bradley L. Goodnight, Sarah L. Cook, Dominic J. Parrott, Martie P. Thompson, Amie R. Newins, Sarah R. B. Barron, Joana Carvalho, and Ruschelle M. Leone. "Evidence for Multiple Classes of Sexually Violent College Men." *Psychology of Violence* 9, no. 1 (January 2019): 48–55. https://doi.org/10.1037/vio0000179.

Brenner, Alletta. "Resisting Simple Dichotomies: Critiquing Narratives of Victims, Perpetrators, and Harm in Feminist Theories of Rape." *Harvard Journal of Law and Gender* 36 (2013): 503.

Bridges, Tristan. "A Very 'Gay' Straight?: Hybrid Masculinities, Sexual Aesthetics, and the Changing Relationship between Masculinity and Homophobia." *Gender and Society* 28, no. 1 (February 2014): 58–82. https://doi.org/10.1177/0891243213503901.

Bridges, Tristan, and C. J. Pascoe. "Hybrid Masculinities: New Directions in the Sociology of Men and Masculinities: Hybrid Masculinities." *Sociology Compass* 8, no. 3 (March 2014): 246–58. https://doi.org/10.1111/soc4.12134.

Brimeyer, Ted M., and William L. Smith. "Religion, Race, Social Class, and Gender Differences in Dating and Hooking Up among College Students." *Sociological Spectrum* 32, no. 5 (September 2012): 462–73. https://doi.org/10.1080/02732173.2012 .694799.

Bronfenbrenner, U. "Toward an Experimental Ecology of Human Development." *American Psychologist* 32, no. 7 (1977): 513–31.

Brownmiller, Susan. *Against Our Will: Men, Women, and Rape.* Reprinted edition. New York: Ballantine Books, 1993.

Bruch, Elizabeth E., and M. E. J. Newman. "Aspirational Pursuit of Mates in Online Dating Markets." *Science Advances* 4, no. 8 (August 1, 2018): eaap9815. https://doi .org/10.1126/sciadv.aap9815.

Bullock, Clayton M., and Mace Beckson. "Male Victims of Sexual Assault: Phenomenology, Psychology, Physiology." *Journal of the American Academy of Psychiatry and the Law* 39, no. 2 (2011): 197–205.

Burdette, A. M., and T. D. Hill. "Religious Involvement and Transitions into Adolescent Sexual Activities." *Sociology of Religion* 70, no. 1 (March 1, 2009): 28–48. https:// doi.org/10.1093/socrel/srp011.

Burdette, Amy M., Christopher G. Ellison, Terrence D. Hill, and Norval D. Glenn. " 'Hooking Up' at College: Does Religion Make a Difference?" *Journal for the Scientific Study of Religion* 48, no. 3 (September 2009): 535–51. https://doi.org/10.1111/j .1468-5906.2009.01464.x.

Burkett, M., and K. Hamilton. "Postfeminist Sexual Agency: Young Women's Negotiations of Sexual Consent." *Sexualities* 15, no. 7 (2012): 815–33.

Burns, April, Valerie A. Futch, and Deborah L. Tolman. " 'It's Like Doing Homework': Academic Achievement Discourse in Adolescent Girls' Fellatio Narratives." *Sexuality Research and Social Policy* 8, no. 3 (September 2011): 239–51. https://doi.org/10 .1007/s13178-011-0062-1.

Callahan, Amy. "Columbia College Breaks Admissions Records Again." *Columbia University Record*, April 18, 1997. http://www.columbia.edu/cu/record/archives/vol22/ vol22_iss21/record2221.13.html.

Campbell, Jacquelyn. "Campus Sexual Assault Perpetration: What Else We Need to Know." *JAMA Pediatrics*, July 13, 2015.

Campbell, Rebecca, Emily Dworkin, and Giannina Cabral. "An Ecological Model of the Impact of Sexual Assault on Women's Mental Health." *Trauma, Violence, and Abuse*, 2009. http://tva.sagepub.com/content/early/2009/05/10/1524838009334456.short.

Campbell, Rebecca, and Sheela Raja. "Secondary Victimization of Rape Victims: Insights From Mental Health Professionals Who Treat Survivors of Violence." *Violence and Victims* 14, no. 3 (1999): 261–75.

Campus PRISM Project, Promoting Restorative Initiatives on Sexual Misconduct
    at Colleges and Universities. "Next Steps for a Restorative Justice Approach to
    Campus-Based Sexual and Gender-Based Harassment, Including Sexual Vio-
    lence." Saratoga Springs, NY: Project on Restorative Justice at Skidmore College,
    December 2017. https://www.skidmore.edu/campusrj/documents/Next-Steps-for
    -RJ-Campus-PRISM.pdf.

Canaday, Margot. *The Straight State: Sexuality and Citizenship in Twentieth-Century Amer-
    ica*. Politics and Society in Twentieth-Century America. Princeton, NJ: Princeton
    Univ. Press, 2009.

Cantalupo, N. C. "Institution-Specific Victimization Surveys: Addressing Legal and
    Practical Disincentives to Gender-Based Violence Reporting on College Cam-
    puses." *Trauma, Violence, and Abuse* 15, no. 3 (2014): 227–41.

Cantor, David, Bonnie Fisher, Susan Chibnall, Reanne Townsend, Lee, Hyunshik, Carol
    Bruce, and Gail Thomas. "Report on the AAU Campus Climate Survey on Sexual
    Assault and Sexual Misconduct: Columbia University." Rockville, MD: The Amer-
    ican Association of Universities, September 21, 2015.

Carpenter, Laura M. *Virginity Lost: An Intimate Portrait of First Sexual Experiences*. New
    York: New York University, 2005.

———. *Virginity Lost: An Intimate Portrait of First Sexual Experiences*. New York: New
    York University, 2005.

Carrillo, Héctor. "Imagining Modernity: Sexuality, Policy and Social Change in Mexico."
    Sexuality Research and Social Policy 4, no. 3 (September 2007): 74–91. https://doi
    .org/10.1525/srsp.2007.4.3.74.

Casey, Erin A., and Taryn P. Lindhorst. "Toward a Multi-Level, Ecological Approach
    to the Primary Prevention of Sexual Assault: Prevention in Peer and Community
    Contexts." *Trauma, Violence and Abuse* 10, no. 2 (April 2009): 91–114. https://doi
    .org/10.1177/1524838009334129.

Centers for Disease Control and Prevention. "All Injuries," May 3, 2017. https://www.cdc
    .gov/nchs/fastats/injury.htm.

Centers for Disease Control and Prevention, U.S. Department of Health and Human
    Services, and National Center for Health Statistics. "Early Release of Selected Esti-
    mates Based on Data From the National Health Interview Survey, January–March
    2016: Alcohol Consumption." Atlanta: Centers for Disease Control, September
    2017.

Chan, Candy. "Can Columbia's Fraternities Survive the National Threat to Greek Life?"
    Columbia Daily Spectator, November 13, 2018. https://www.columbiaspectator
    .com/eye-lead/2018/11/14/can-columbias-fraternities-survive-the-national-threat
    -to-greek-life/.

Chemerinsky, Erwin, and Howard Gillman. *Free Speech on Campus*. Paperback edition.
    New Haven ; London: Yale University Press, 2018.

Chin, Matthew, Alexander Wamboldt, Shamus R. Khan, Claude Ann Mellins, and Jennifer S. Hirsch. "Time for Sex: Examining Dimensions of Temporality in Sexual Consent among College Students." *Human Organization* 78, no. 4 (In press).

Christophe, Ella. "Acceptance Rate Falls by One Third, Reaching Record Low of 18 Percent." *The Chicago Maroon*. April 2, 2010. https://www.chicagomaroon.com/2010/4/2/acceptance-rate-falls-by-one-third-reaching-record-low-of-18-percent/.

Cisneros, Jesus. "College as the Great Liberator: Undocuqueer Immigrants' Meaning Making in and out of Higher Education." *Journal of Diversity in Higher Education* 12, no. 1 (March 2019): 74–84. https://doi.org/10.1037/dhe0000075.

Cleary, Michelle, Garry Walter, and Debra Jackson. "'Not Always Smooth Sailing': Mental Health Issues Associated with the Transition from High School to College." *Issues in Mental Health Nursing* 32, no. 4 (March 2, 2011): 250–54. https://doi.org/10.3109/01612840.2010.548906.

Cloward, Richard A. *Delinquency and Opportunity : A Theory of Delinquent Gangs /.* Edited by Lloyd E. Ohlin. Glencoe, Ill. : Free Press, 1960.

Coker, Ann L., Keith E. Davis, Ileana Arias, Sujata Desai, Maureen Sanderson, Heather M. Brandt, and Paige H. Smith. "Physical and Mental Health Effects of Intimate Partner Violence for Men and Women." *American Journal of Preventive Medicine* 23, no. 4 (November 2002): 260–68. https://doi.org/10.1016/S0749-3797(02)00514-7.

Coker, Ann L., Diane R. Follingstad, Heather M. Bush, and Bonnie S. Fisher. "Are Interpersonal Violence Rates Higher among Young Women in College Compared with Those Never Attending College?" *Journal of Interpersonal Violence* 31, no. 8 (May 2016): 1413–29. https://doi.org/10.1177/0886260514567958.

Collins English Dictionary. "Snowflake Generation." In *Collins English Dictionary.* Harper Collins, 2019. https://www.collinsdictionary.com/dictionary/english/snowflake-generation.

Columbia University. "Class of 2022 Profile," May 1, 2018. https://undergrad.admissions.columbia.edu/classprofile/2022.

———. "Under1Roof," 2019. https://www.cc-seas.columbia.edu/OMA/diversityed/u1r.php.

Columbia University Emergency Medical Service. "FAQ," 2019. https://cuems.columbia.edu/faq.

Columbia University Office of the Planning and Research. "Columbia College and School of Engineering Undergraduate Fall Admissions Statistics, 2009–2018." New York: Columbia University Office of the Provost, November 26, 2018. https://provost.columbia.edu/sites/default/files/content/Institutional%20Research/Statistical%20Abstract/opir_admissions_history.pdf.

Combahee River Collective. "Combahee River Collective Statement." In *Home Girls: A Black Feminist Anthology*, edited by Barbara Smith, 264–74. New York: Kitchen Table—Women of Color Press, 1983.

Connell, Raewyn. *Gender and Power: Society, the Person and Sexual Politics.* Cambridge [Cambridgeshire] : Polity Press, 1987.

Connop, Vicki, and Jenny Petrak. "The Impact of Sexual Assault on Heterosexual Couples." *Sexual and Relationship Therapy* 19, no. 1 (February 2004): 29–38. https://doi.org/10.1080/14681990410001640817.

Cookingham, Lisa M., and Ginny L. Ryan. "The Impact of Social Media on the Sexual and Social Wellness of Adolescents." *Journal of Pediatric and Adolescent Gynecology* 28, no. 1 (February 2015): 2–5. https://doi.org/10.1016/j.jpag.2014.03.001.

Coulter, R. W., C. Mair, E. Miller, J. R. Blosnich, D. D. Matthews, and H. L. McCauley. "Prevalence of Past-Year Sexual Assault Victimization among Undergraduate Students: Exploring Differences by and Intersections of Gender Identity, Sexual Identity, and Race/Ethnicity." *Prev Sci* Epub ahead of print (2017). https://doi.org/doi: 10.1007/s11121-017-0762-8.

Cranney, Stephen. "The Relationship Between Sexual Victimization and Year in School in U.S. Colleges: Investigating the Parameters of the 'Red Zone.'" *Journal of Interpersonal Violence* 30, no. 17 (October 2015): 3133–45. https://doi.org/10.1177/0886260514554425.

Crenshaw, Kimberle. "Demarginalizing the Intersection of Race and Sex: A Black Feminist Critique of Antidiscrimination Doctrine, Feminist Theory and Antiracist Politics." *University of Chicago Legal Forum* 1989, no. 1 (1989): 139–67.

Crosset, Todd. "Male Athletes' Violence against Women: A Critical Assessment of the Athletic Affiliation, Violence against Women Debate." *Quest* 51, no. 3 (August 1999): 244–57. https://doi.org/10.1080/00336297.1999.10491684.

Crossman, Molly K., Alan E. Kazdin, and Krista Knudson. "Brief Unstructured Interaction with a Dog Reduces Distress." *Anthrozoös* 28, no. 4 (December 2015): 649–59. https://doi.org/10.1080/08927936.2015.1070008.

Cyr, Mireille, John Wright, Pierre McDuff, and Alain Perron. "Intrafamilial Sexual Abuse: Brother–Sister Incest Does Not Differ from Father–Daughter and Stepfather–Stepdaughter Incest." *Child Abuse and Neglect* 26, no. 9 (September 2002): 957–73. https://doi.org/10.1016/S0145-2134(02)00365-4.

Dasha Grajfoner, Emma Harte, Lauren Potter, and Nicola McGuigan. "The Effect of Dog-Assisted Intervention on Student Well-Being, Mood, and Anxiety." *International Journal of Environmental Research and Public Health* 14, no. 5 (May 5, 2017): 483. https://doi.org/10.3390/ijerph14050483.

Dawson, Kate, Saoirse Nic Gabhainn, and Pádraig MacNeela. "Toward a Model of Porn Literacy: Core Concepts, Rationales, and Approaches." *The Journal of Sex Research*, January 9, 2019, 1–15. https://doi.org/10.1080/00224499.2018.1556238.

DeGue, Sarah, Linda Anne Valle, Melissa K. Holt, Greta M. Massetti, Jennifer L. Matjasko, and Andra Teten Tharp. "A Systematic Review of Primary Prevention Strategies for Sexual Violence Perpetration." *Aggression and Violent Behavior* 19 (2014): 346–62.

DeJong, William, and Jason Blanchette. "Case Closed: Research Evidence on the Positive Public Health Impact of the Age 21 Minimum Legal Drinking Age in the United States." *Journal of Studies on Alcohol and Drugs, Supplement,* no. s17 (March 2014): 108–15. https://doi.org/10.15288/jsads.2014.s17.108.

Demetriou, Demetrakis Z. "Connell's Concept of Hegemonic Masculinity: A Critique." *Theory and Society* 30, no. 3 (2001): 337–61.

"Department of Justice: Sexual Assault False Reporting Overview," 2012. http://www .nsvrc.org/sites/default/files/Publications_NSVRC_Overview_False-Reporting.pdf.

Deresiewicz, William. *Excellent Sheep: The Miseducation of the American Elite and the Way to a Meaningful Life.* First Free Press hardcover edition. New York: Free Press, 2014.

Diamond-Welch, B. K., M. D. Hetzel-Riggin, and J. A. Hemingway. "The Willingness of College Students to Intervene in Sexual Assault Situations: Attitude and Behavior Differences by Gender, Race, Age, and Community of Origin." *Violence and Gender* 3, no. 1 (2016): 49–54.

Dilulio, John J. Fill Churches, Not Jails: Youth Crime and "Superpredators" (1996).

Doherty, Shannen, and Cypress Hill. "Is It Date Rape?" *Saturday Night Live,* season 19. NBC, October 2, 1993.

Donde, Sapana D. "College Women's Attributions of Blame for Experiences of Sexual Assault." *Journal of Interpersonal Violence* 32, no. 22 (November 2017): 3520–38. https://doi.org/10.1177/0886260515599659.

Doornwaard, Suzan M., Megan A. Moreno, Regina J.J.M. van den Eijnden, Ine Vanwesenbeeck, and Tom F. M. ter Bogt. "Young Adolescents' Sexual and Romantic Reference Displays on Facebook." *Journal of Adolescent Health* 55, no. 4 (October 2014): 535–41. https://doi.org/10.1016/j.jadohealth.2014.04.002.

Doumas, Diana M., and Aida Midgett. "Ethnic Differences in Drinking Motives and Alcohol Use among College Athletes." *Journal of College Counseling* 18, no. 2 (July 1, 2015): 116–29. https://doi.org/10.1002/jocc.12009.

Drope, Jeffrey, Neil W. Schluger, Zachary Cahn, Jacqui Drope, Stephen Hamill, Farhad Islami, Alex Liber, Nigar Nargis, and Michael Stoklosa, eds. *The Tobacco Atlas.* Sixth ed. Atlanta, GA: The American Cancer Society, Inc., 2018.

Du Bois, W. E. B. *The Souls of Black Folk.* New York: Vintage Books/Library of America, 1990.

Dunn, Patricia C., Karen Vail-Smith, and Sharon M. Knight. "What Date/Acquaintance Rape Victims Tell Others: A Study of College Student Recipients of Disclosure." *Journal of American College Health* 47, no. 5 (1999): 213–19.

Dworkin, Andrea. *Intercourse: The Twentieth Anniversary Edition.* New York: BasicBooks, 2007.

Dwyer-Lindgren, Laura, Amelia Bertozzi-Villa, Rebecca W. Stubbs, Chloe Morozoff, Johan P. Mackenbach, Frank J. van Lenthe, Ali H. Mokdad, and Christopher J. L. Murray. "Inequalities in Life Expectancy among US Counties, 1980 to 2014: Temporal Trends and Key Drivers." *JAMA Internal Medicine* 177, no. 7 (July 1, 2017): 1003. https://doi.org/10.1001/jamainternmed.2017.0918.

Edwards, Katie M., Jessica A. Turchik, Christina M. Dardis, Nicole Reynolds, and Christine A. Gidycz. "Rape Myths: History, Individual and Institutional-Level Presence, and Implications for Change." *Sex Roles* 65, no. 11–12 (December 2011): 761–73. https://doi.org/10.1007/s11199-011-9943-2.

Ehlers, Anke, and David M. Clark. "A Cognitive Model of Posttraumatic Stress Disorder." *Behaviour Research and Therapy* 38, no. 4 (April 2000): 319–45. https://doi.org/10.1016/S0005-7967(99)00123-0.

Eilperin, Juliet. "Seeking to End Rape on Campus, White House Launches 'It's On Us.'" *Washington Post*, September 19, 2014. http://www.washingtonpost.com/blogs/post-politics/wp/2014/09/19/seeking-to-end-rape-on-campus-wh-launches-its-on-us/.

Elizabeth Armstrong and Jamie Budnick. "Sexual Assault on Campus: Part of Council of Contemporary Families' Online Symposium on Intimate Partner Violence," May 7, 2015. http://thesocietypages.org/ccf/2015/05/07/sexual-assault-on-campus/.

Ellison, Nicole B., Charles Steinfield, and Cliff Lampe. "The Benefits of Facebook 'Friends': Social Capital and College Students' Use of Online Social Network Sites." *Journal of Computer-Mediated Communication* 12, no. 4 (July 2007): 1143–68. https://doi.org/10.1111/j.1083-6101.2007.00367.x.

England, Paula. "Has the Surplus of Women over Men Driven the Increase in Premarital and Casual Sex among American Young Adults?" *Society* 49, no. 6 (October 18, 2012): 512–14. https://doi.org/10.1007/s12115-012-9594-0.

Epstein, Steven, and Héctor Carrillo. "Immigrant Sexual Citizenship: Intersectional Templates among Mexican Gay Immigrants to the USA." *Citizenship Studies* 18, no. 3–4 (April 3, 2014): 259–76. https://doi.org/10.1080/13621025.2014.905266.

Erb, Sarah E., Keith D. Renshaw, Jerome L. Short, and Jeffrey W. Pollard. "The Importance of College Roommate Relationships: A Review and Systemic Conceptualization." *Journal of Student Affairs Research and Practice* 51, no. 1 (January 1, 2014): 43–55. https://doi.org/10.1515/jsarp-2014-0004.

Espenshade, Thomas J., Alexandria Walton Radford, and Chang Young Chung. *No Longer Separate, Not yet Equal: Race and Class in Elite College Admission and Campus Life.* Princeton: Princeton University Press, 2009.

Fachini, Alexandre, Poliana P Aliane, Edson Z Martinez, and Erikson F Furtado. "Efficacy of Brief Alcohol Screening Intervention for College Students (BASICS): A Meta-Analysis of Randomized Controlled Trials." *Substance Abuse Treatment, Prevention, and Policy* 7, no. 1 (December 2012): 40. https://doi.org/10.1186/1747-597X-7-40.

Fantasia, H. C. "Really Not Even a Decision Any More: Late Adolescent Narratives of Implied Sexual Consent." *Journal of Forensic Nursing* 7, no. 3 (2011): 120–29.

Fantasia, Heidi C., Melissa A Sutherland, Holly Fontenot, and Janet A. Ierardi. "Knowledge, Attitudes and Beliefs About Contraceptive and Sexual Consent Negotiation among College Women." *Journal of Forensic Nursing* 10, no. 4 (2014): 199–207.

Fedina, Lisa, Jennifer Lynne Holmes, and Bethany L. Backes. "Campus Sexual Assault: A Systematic Review of Prevalence Research From 2000 to 2015." *Trauma, Violence, and Abuse* 19, no. 1 (January 1, 2018): 76–93. https://doi.org/10.1177/1524838016631129.

Fennell, Reginald. "Health Behaviors of Students Attending Historically Black Colleges and Universities: Results From the National College Health Risk Behavior Survey." *Journal of American College Health* 46, no. 3 (November 1997): 109–17. https://doi.org/10.1080/07448489709595596.

Fenton, Reuven, and Danika Fears. "Columbia Profs Creep out Students by Watching Them Drink for Sex Study." *New York Post*, October 21, 2015. https://nypost.com/2015/10/21/columbia-profs-creeping-out-students-by-watching-them-drink/.

Field, Carolyn J., Sitawa R. Kimuna, and Marissa N. Lang. "The Relation of Interracial Relationships to Intimate Partner Violence by College Students." *Journal of Black Studies* 46, no. 4 (May 2015): 384–403. https://doi.org/10.1177/0021934715574804.

Fields, Jessica. *Risky Lessons: Sex Education and Social Inequality*. New Brunswick, NJ : Rutgers University Press, 2008.

Filipkowski, Kelly B., Kristin E. Heron, and Joshua M. Smyth. "Early Adverse Experiences and Health: The Transition to College." *American Journal of Health Behavior* 40, no. 6 (November 1, 2016): 717–28. https://doi.org/10.5993/AJHB.40.6.4.

Fine, Michelle. "Sexuality, Schooling, and Adolescent Females: The Missing Discourse of Desire." *Harvard Educational Review* 58, no. 1 (April 1988): 29–54. https://doi.org/10.17763/haer.58.1.u0468k1v2n2n8242.

Finer, Lawrence B. "Trends in Premarital Sex in the United States, 1954–2003." *Public Health Reports* 122, no. 1 (January 2007): 73–78. https://doi.org/10.1177/003335490712200110.

Finer, Lawrence B., and Jesse M. Philbin. "Trends in Ages at Key Reproductive Transitions in the United States, 1951–2010." *Women's Health Issues* 24, no. 3 (May 2014): e271–79. https://doi.org/10.1016/j.whi.2014.02.002.

Fishell, Darren. "Census Survey: Maine's Still the Oldest, Whitest State." *Bangor Daily News*, June 25, 2015. https://bangordailynews.com/2015/06/25/business/census-survey-maines-still-the-oldest-whitest-state/.

Fisher, Bonnie S., Francis T. Cullen, and Michael G. Turner. "The Sexual Victimization of College Women: Research Report." Washington, DC: Department of Justice, National Inst. of Justice, Bureau of Justice Statistics, 2000. http://eric.ed.gov/?id=ED449712.

Fisher, Bonnie S., Leah E. Daigle, Francis T. Cullen, and Michael G. Turner. "Reporting Sexual Victimization to the Police and Others: Results From a National-Level Study of College Women." *Criminal Justice and Behavior* 30, no. 1 (February 1, 2003): 6–38. https://doi.org/10.1177/0093854802239161.

Flack, W. F. "'The Red Zone': Temporal Risk for Unwanted Sex among College Students." *Journal of Interpersonal Violence* 23, no. 9 (2008): 1177–96.

Fletcher, Jason M., and Marta Tienda. "High School Classmates and College Success." *Sociology of Education* 82, no. 4 (October 1, 2009): 287–314. https://doi.org/10.1177/003804070908200401.

Ford, J., and J. G. Soto-Marquez. "Sexual Assault Victimization among Straight, Gay/Lesbian, and Bisexual College Students." *Violence and Gender* 3, no. 2 (2016): 107–15.

Foubert, John D., Angela Clark-Taylor, and Andrew F. Wall. "Is Campus Rape Primarily a Serial or One-Time Problem? Evidence From a Multicampus Study." *Violence against Women*, March 18, 2019, 107780121983382. https://doi.org/10.1177/1077801219833820.

Fox, Claire. *I Find That Offensive!* Provocations. London: Biteback Publishing, 2016.

Franklin, C. A. "Physically Forced, Alcohol-Induced, and Verbally Coerced Sexual Victimization: Assessing Risk Factors among University Women." *Journal of Criminal Justice* 38, no. 2 (2010): 149–59.

Frazier, Patricia A., and Beth Haney. "Sexual Assault Cases in the Legal System: Police, Prosecutor, and Victim Perspectives." *Law and Human Behavior* 20, no. 6 (1996): 607–28. https://doi.org/10.1007/BF01499234.

Freitas, Donna. *Sex and the Soul: Juggling Sexuality, Spirituality, Romance, and Religion on America's College Campuses.* Updated edition. Oxford and New York: Oxford University Press, 2015.

Gagnon, John H., and William Simon. *Sexual Conduct: The Social Sources of Human Sexuality.* 2nd ed. New Brunswick [N.J.]: AldineTransaction, 2005.

Garcia, Jonathan, Richard G. Parker, Caroline Parker, Patrick A. Wilson, Morgan Philbin, and Jennifer S. Hirsch. "The Limitations of 'Black MSM' as a Category: Why Gender, Sexuality, and Desire Still Matter for Social and Biomedical HIV Prevention Methods." *Global Public Health* 11, no. 7–8 (September 13, 2016): 1026–48. https://doi.org/10.1080/17441692.2015.1134616.

Gerhard, Jane. "Revisiting 'The Myth of the Vaginal Orgasm': The Female Orgasm in American Sexual Thought and Second Wave Feminism." *Feminist Studies* 26, no. 2 (2000): 449. https://doi.org/10.2307/3178545.

Giacomo, Ester di, Micheal Krausz, Fabrizia Colmegna, Flora Aspesi, and Massimo Clerici. "Estimating the Risk of Attempted Suicide among Sexual Minority Youths: A Systematic Review and Meta-Analysis." *JAMA Pediatrics* 172, no. 12 (December 1, 2018): 1145–52. https://doi.org/10.1001/jamapediatrics.2018.2731.

Gibson, Megan. "I Am Woman, Hear Me Roar: Take Back the Night." *Time*, August 12, 2011.

Gidycz, Christine A., J. B. Warkentin, and L. M. Orchowski. "Predictors of Perpetration of Verbal, Physical, and Sexual Violence: A Prospective Analysis of College Men." *Psychology of Men and Masculinity* 8, no. 2 (2007): 79–94.

Gidycz, Christine A., and Christina M. Dardis. "Feminist Self-Defense and Resistance

Training for College Students: A Critical Review and Recommendations for the
Future." *Trauma, Violence, and Abuse* 15, no. 4 (October 2014): 322–33. https://doi
.org/10.1177/1524838014521026.

Giele, Janet Zollinger, and Glen H. Elder, eds. *Methods of Life Course Research: Qualitative and Quantitative Approaches.* Thousand Oaks, CA: Sage Publications, 1998.

Gilbert, Louisa, Aaron L. Sarvet, Melanie Wall, Kate Walsh, Leigh Reardon, Patrick
Wilson, John Santelli, et al. "Situational Contexts and Risk Factors Associated with
Incapacitated and Nonincapacitated Sexual Assaults among College Women." *Jour-
nal of Women's Health*, November 27, 2018. https://doi.org/10.1089/jwh.2018.7191.

Godfrey, Mike, and James W. Satterfield. "The Effects Athletic Culture Formation and
Perceived Faculty Stereotypes in Higher Education." *Journal of Contemporary Athletics* 5, no. 2 (2011): 89–104.

Gross, Alan M., Andrea Winslett, Miguel Roberts, and Carol L. Gohm. "An Examination of Sexual Violence against College Women." *Violence against Women* 12, no. 3
(2006): 288–300.

Gross, Bruce. "False Rape Allegations: An Assault on Justice." *Forensic Examiner* 18
(2009): 66–70.

Gusfield, Joseph R. *The Culture of Public Problems: Drinking-Driving and the Symbolic
Order.* Chicago: Univ. of Chicago Press, 1994.

Guttmacher Institute. "Adolescent Sexual and Reproductive Health in the United
States." New York: Guttmacher Institute, September 2017. https://www.guttmacher
.org/fact-sheet/american-teens-sexual-and-reproductive-health.

———. "American Adolescents' Sources of Sexual Health Information." New York:
Guttmacher Institute, December 2017. https://www.guttmacher.org/fact-sheet/
facts-american-teens-sources-information-about-sex.

Guzzo, Karen Benjamin. "Trends in Cohabitation Outcomes: Compositional Changes
and Engagement among Never-Married Young Adults: Trends in Cohabitation Outcomes." *Journal of Marriage and Family* 76, no. 4 (August 2014): 826–42. https://doi
.org/10.1111/jomf.12123.

Halligan, Sarah L., Tanja Michael, David M. Clark, and Anke Ehlers. "Posttraumatic
Stress Disorder Following Assault: The Role of Cognitive Processing, Trauma Memory, and Appraisals." *Journal of Consulting and Clinical Psychology* 71, no. 3 (2003):
419–31. https://doi.org/10.1037/0022-006X.71.3.419.

Hamilton, Laura, and Elizabeth A. Armstrong. "Gendered Sexuality in Young Adulthood Double Binds and Flawed Options." *Gender and Society* 23, no. 5 (October 1,
2009): 589–616. https://doi.org/10.1177/0891243209345829.

Hardy, S. "Adolescent Religiosity and Sexuality: An Investigation of Reciprocal Influences." *Journal of Adolescence* 26, no. 6 (December 2003): 731–39. https://doi.org/10
.1016/j.adolescence.2003.09.003.

Harned, Melanie S. "Understanding Women's Labeling of Unwanted Sexual Experiences with Dating Partners: A Qualitative Analysis." *Violence against Women* 11, no. 3 (2005): 374–413.

Hatzenbuehler, M. L. "The Social Environment and Suicide Attempts in Lesbian, Gay, and Bisexual Youth." *Pediatrics* 127, no. 5 (May 1, 2011): 896–903. https://doi.org/10.1542/peds.2010-3020.

Hatzenbuehler, Mark L., and Bruce G. Link. "Introduction to the Special Issue on Structural Stigma and Health." *Social Science and Medicine* 103 (February 2014): 1–6. https://doi.org/10.1016/j.socscimed.2013.12.017.

Heise, Lori L. "Violence against Women: An Integrated, Ecological Framework." *Violence against Women* 4, no. 3 (June 1, 1998): 262–90. https://doi.org/10.1177/1077801298004003002.

Heldman, C., and L. Wade. "Hook-Up Culture: Setting a New Research Agenda." *Sexuality Research and Social Policy*, no. 4 (2010): 323–33.

Herman, Judith Lewis. "The Mental Health of Crime Victims: Impact of Legal Intervention." *Journal of Traumatic Stress* 16, no. 2 (April 2003): 159–66. https://doi.org/10.1023/A:1022847223135.

Hicks, Terence, and Samuel Heastie. "High School to College Transition: A Profile of the Stressors, Physical and Psychological Health Issues That Affect the First-Year On-Campus College Student." *Journal of Cultural Diversity* 15, no. 3 (2008): 143–47.

Hirsch, Jennifer S. *A Courtship after Marriage: Sexuality and Love in Mexican Transnational Families*. Berkeley: University of California Press, 2003.

Hirsch, Jennifer S. "Desire across Borders: Markets, Migration, and Marital HIV Risk in Rural Mexico." *Culture, Health and Sexuality* 17, no. S1 (2015): 20–33. https://doi.org/10.1080/13691058.2014.963681.

Hirsch, Jennifer S., Jennifer Higgins, Margaret E. Bentley, and Constance A. Nathanson. "The Social Constructions of Sexuality: Marital Infidelity and Sexually Transmitted Disease—HIV Risk in a Mexican Migrant Community." *American Journal of Public Health* 92, no. 8 (2002): 1227–37.

Hirsch, Jennifer S., Shamus R. Khan, Alexander Wamboldt, and Claude A. Mellins. "Social Dimensions of Sexual Consent among Cisgender Heterosexual College Students: Insights From Ethnographic Research." *Journal of Adolescent Health* 64, no. 1 (2018): 26–35. https://doi.org/10.1016/j.jadohealth.2018.06.011.

Hirsch, Jennifer S., and Claude Ann Mellins. "Sexual Health Initiative to Foster Transformation (SHIFT) Final Report." New York: Columbia University, March 2019. https://www.mailman.columbia.edu/sites/default/files/shift_final_report_4-11-19.pdf.

Hirsch, Jennifer S., Leigh Reardon, Shamus Khan, John S. Santelli, Patrick A. Wilson, Louisa Gilbert, Melanie Wall, and Claude A Mellins. "Transforming the Campus Climate: Advancing Mixed-Methods Research on the Social and Cultural Roots of Sexual Assault on a College Campus." *Voices:* 13, no. 1 (2018): 23–54. https://doi.org/10.1111/voic.12003.

Hirsch, Jennifer S., Alexander Wamboldt, Shamus R. Khan, Melanie M. Wall, Chen Chen, Leigh Reardon, and Claude Ann Mellins. "There Was Nowhere to Cry: Power, Precarity, and the Ecology of Student Well-Being." In development.

Hirsch, Jennifer S., Holly Wardlow, Daniel Smith, Harriet Phinney, Shanti Parikh, and Constance Nathanson, eds. *The Secret: Love, Marriage, and HIV.* Nashville: Vanderbilt University Press, 2010.

Hirsch, Jennifer, and Holly Wardlow. *Modern Loves: The Anthropology of Romantic Courtship and Companionate Marriage.* Ann Arbor, MI: University of Michigan Press, 2006. https://doi.org/10.3998/mpub.170440.

Hlavka, Heather R. "Normalizing Sexual Violence: Young Women Account for Harassment and Abuse." *Gender and Society* 28, no. 3 (June 2014): 337–58. https://doi.org/10.1177/0891243214526468.

Hoffman, Kristi L., K. Jill Kiecolt, and John N. Edwards. "Physical Violence between Siblings: A Theoretical and Empirical Analysis." *Journal of Family Issues* 26, no. 8 (November 2005): 1103–30. https://doi.org/10.1177/0192513X05277809.

Holland, Alyce, and Thomas Andre. "Athletic Participation and the Social Status of Adolescent Males and Females." *Youth and Society* 25, no. 3 (March 1994): 388–407. https://doi.org/10.1177/0044118X94025003005.

Holland, Janet, Caroline Ramazanoglu, Sue Sharpe, and Rachel Thomson. "Deconstructing Virginity—Young People's Accounts of First Sex." *Sexual and Relationship Therapy* 15, no. 3 (August 2000): 221–32. https://doi.org/10.1080/14681990050109827.

Holmes, Aaron. "Grad Student Banned from Pupin for Homophobic, Transphobic Vandalism." *Columbia Daily Spectator.* Accessed May 31, 2019. https://www.columbiaspectator.com/news/2017/04/10/physics-grad-student-banned-from-pupin-for-homophobic-transphobic-vandalism/.

Hunt, J., and D. Eisenberg. "Mental Health Problems and Help-Seeking Behavior among College Students." *Journal of Adolescent Health* 46 (2010): 3–10.

Hust, S. J. T., K. B. Rodgers, and B. Bayly. "Scripting Sexual Consent: Internalized Traditional Sexual Scripts and Sexual Consent Expectancies among College Students." *Family Relations* 66 (2017): 197–210.

Hustad, John T. P., Nadine R. Mastroleo, Rachel Urwin, Suzanne Zeman, Linda LaSalle, and Brian Borsari. "Tailgating and Pregaming by College Students with Alcohol Offenses: Patterns of Alcohol Use and Beliefs." *Substance Use and Misuse* 49, no. 14 (December 6, 2014): 1928–33. https://doi.org/10.3109/10826084.2014.949008.

Iconis, Rosemary. "Rape Myth Acceptance in College Students: A Literature Review." *Contemporary Issues in Education Research (CIER)* 1, no. 2 (2011): 47–52.

Information Insurance Institute. "Facts + Statistics: Mortality Risk." New York: Information Insurance Institute, 2017. https://www.iii.org/fact-statistic/facts-statistics-mortality-risk#Odds%20Of%20Death%20In%20The%20United%20States%20By%20Selected%20Cause%20Of%20Injury,%202017%20(1).

"It's On Us, a Growing Movement to End Campus Sexual Assault." The White House. Accessed May 4, 2015. http://www.whitehouse.gov/blog/2014/09/24/its-us-growing -movement-end-campus-sexual-assault.

Jack, Anthony A. *The Privileged Poor: Rich College, Poor Students, and the Gap between Access and Inclusion.* Harvard University Press, 2019.

Jackson, Arrick, Katherine Gilliland, and Louis Veneziano. "Routine Activity Theory and Sexual Deviance among Male College Students." *Journal of Family Violence* 21, no. 7 (December 1, 2006): 449–60. https://doi.org/10.1007/s10896-006-9040-4.

Jager, Justin, John E. Schulenberg, Patrick M. O'Malley, and Jerald G. Bachman. "Historical Variation in Drug Use Trajectories across the Transition to Adulthood: The Trend toward Lower Intercepts and Steeper, Ascending Slopes." *Development and Psychopathology* 25, no. 2 (May 2013): 527–43. https://doi.org/10.1017/S0954579412001228.

Jaschik, Scott. "Entering Campus Building While Black." *Inside Higher Education.* Accessed May 22, 2019. https://www.insidehighered.com/news/2019/04/15/barnard -suspends-police-officers-after-incident-black-student.

Jeanne Clery Disclosure of Campus Security Policy and Campus Crime Statistics Act of 1990, 20 U.S.C. § §1092(f) (2018).

Jedlicka, Davor. "Formal Mate Selection Networks in the United States." *Family Relations* 29, no. 2 (April 1980): 199. https://doi.org/10.2307/584072.

Jeffrey, Nicole K., and Paula C. Barata. "'He Didn't Necessarily Force Himself Upon Me, But . . . ': Women's Lived Experiences of Sexual Coercion in Intimate Relationships with Men." *Violence against Women* 23, no. 8 (July 2017): 911–33. https://doi .org/10.1177/1077801216652507.

Jernigan, David H., Kelsey Shields, Molly Mitchell, and Amelia M. Arria. "Assessing Campus Alcohol Policies: Measuring Accessibility, Clarity, and Effectiveness." *Alcoholism: Clinical and Experimental Research* 43, no. 5 (May 2019): 1007–15. https://doi.org/10.1111/acer.14017.

Jerolmack, Colin, and Shamus Khan. "Talk Is Cheap: Ethnography and the Attitudinal Fallacy." *Sociological Methods and Research* 43, no. 2 (May 1, 2014): 178–209. https:// doi.org/10.1177/0049124114523396.

Jessup-Anger, Jody, Elise Lopez, and Mary P. Koss. "History of Sexual Violence in Higher Education: History of Sexual Violence in Higher Education." *New Directions for Student Services* 2018, no. 161 (March 2018): 9–19. https://doi.org/10.1002/ss.20249.

Johnson, L. M., T. L. Matthews, and S. L. Napper. "Sexual Orientation and Sexual Assault Victimization among US College Students." *The Social Science Journal* 53, no. 2016 (2016): 174–83.

Johnston, Lynda, and Robyn Longhurst. *Space, Place, and Sex: Geographies of Sexualities.* Lanham: Rowman & Littlefield, 2010.

Jones, Maggie. "What Teenagers Are Learning from Online Porn." *New York Times*, February 7, 2018. https://www.nytimes.com/2018/02/07/magazine/teenagers-learning -online-porn-literacy-sex-education.html.

Jozkowski, K. N. ""Yes Means Yes?" Sexual Consent Policy and College Students." *Change: The Magazine of Higher Learning* 47, no. 2 (2015): 16–23.

Jozkowski, K. N., and Z. D. Peterson. "College Students and Sexual Consent: Unique Insights." *Journal of Sex Research* 50, no. 6 (2013): 517–23.

Jozkowski, K. N., Z. D. Peterson, S. A. Sanders, B Dennis, and M. Reece, M. "Gender Differences in Heterosexual College Students' Conceptualizations and Indicators of Sexual Consent: Implications for Contemporary Sexual Assault Prevention Education." *Journal of Sex Research* 51, no. 8 (2014): 904–16.

Kadison, Richard, and Theresa Foy DiGeronimo. *College of the Overwhelmed: The Campus Mental Health Crisis and What to Do About It*. Wiley, 2004.

Kalmijn, Matthijs. "Intermarriage and Homogamy: Causes, Patterns, Trends." *Annual Review of Sociology* 24, no. 1 (August 1998): 395–421. https://doi.org/10.1146/ annurev.soc.24.1.395.

Kamath, Rahil, and Peter Maroulis. "Confusion Surrounding Cost of CUEMS Discourages Students from Calling Free Service." *Columbia Daily Spectator*, December 7, 2017. https://www.columbiaspectator.com/news/2017/12/07/confusion-surrounding -cost-of-cuems-discourages-students-from-calling/.

Kamin, L. "On the Length of Black Penises and the Depth of White Racism." In *Psychology and Oppression: Critiques and Proposals*, 35–54. Johannesburg: Skotaville, 1993.

Kanin, Eugene J. "False Rape Allegations." *Archives of Sexual Behavior* 23, no. 1 (1994): 81–92.

———. "Male Aggression in Dating-Courtship Relations." *American Journal of Sociology* 63, no. 2 (September 1957): 197–204. https://doi.org/10.1086/222177.

Kanny, Dafna, Timothy S. Naimi, Yong Liu, Hua Lu, and Robert D. Brewer. "Annual Total Binge Drinks Consumed by U.S. Adults, 2015." *American Journal of Preventive Medicine* 54, no. 4 (2018): 486–96. https://doi.org/10.1016/j.amepre.2017.12.021.

Kantor, Leslie, and Nicole Levitz. "Parents' Views on Sex Education in Schools: How Much Do Democrats and Republicans Agree?" Edited by Ehsan U Syed. *PLOS ONE* 12, no. 7 (July 3, 2017): e0180250. https://doi.org/10.1371/journal.pone .0180250.

Kanuga, Mansi, and Walter D. Rosenfeld. "Adolescent Sexuality and the Internet: The Good, the Bad, and the URL." *Journal of Pediatric and Adolescent Gynecology* 17, no. 2 (April 2004): 117–24. https://doi.org/10.1016/j.jpag.2004.01.015.

Kapner, Daniel Ari. "Alcohol and Other Drug Use at Historically Black Colleges and Universities." Newton, MA: The Higher Education Center for Alcohol and Other Drug Abuse and Violence Prevention, 2008. https://files.eric.ed.gov/fulltext/ED537617.pdf.

Karjane, Heather M., Bonnie Fisher, and Francis T. Cullen. *Sexual Assault on Campus:*

What Colleges and Universities Are Doing about It. US Department of Justice, Office of Justice Programs, National Institute of Justice, 2005. https://www.ncjrs.gov/App/abstractdb/AbstractDBDetails.aspx?id=205521.

Kaukinen, Catherine. "The Help-Seeking Decisions of Violent Crime Victims: An Examination of the Direct and Conditional Effects of Gender and the Victim-Offender Relationship." *Journal of Interpersonal Violence* 17, no. 4 (April 2002): 432–56. https://doi.org/10.1177/0886260502017004006.

Kernsmith, Poco D., and Roger M. Kernsmith. "Female Pornography Use and Sexual Coercion Perpetration." *Deviant Behavior* 30, no. 7 (August 19, 2009): 589–610. https://doi.org/10.1080/01639620802589798.

Khan, Shamus. *Privilege: The Making of an Adolescent Elite at St. Paul's School.* First paperback printing. Princeton Studies in Cultural Sociology. Princeton, NJ: Princeton Univ. Press, 2011.

Khan, Shamus R., Jennifer S. Hirsch, Alexander Wamboldt, and Claude A. Mellins. "'I Didn't Want to Be "That Girl"': The Social Risks of Labeling, Telling, and Reporting Sexual Assault." *Sociological Science* 5 (July 12, 2018): 432–60. https://doi.org/10.15195/v5.a19.

Khan, Shamus, Aaron L. Sarvet, Tse-Hwei Choo, Melanie Wall, Kate Walsh, John Santelli, Patrick Wilson, et al. "Ecologically Constituted Classes of Sexual Assault: Constructing a Behavioral, Relational, and Contextual Model," n.p.

Kimble, Matthew, Andrada D. Neacsiu, William F. Flack, and Jessica Horner. "Risk of Unwanted Sex for College Women: Evidence for a Red Zone." *Journal of American College Health* 57, no. 3 (November 2008): 331–38. https://doi.org/10.3200/JACH.57.3.331-338.

Kindelberger, John, and National Highway Traffic Safety Administration. "Calculating Lives Saved Due to Minimum Drinking Age Laws." Washington, DC: NHTSA's National Center for tatistics and Analysis, March 2005.

Kipnis, Laura. *Unwanted Advances: Sexual Paranoia Comes to Campus.* First edition. New York: Harper, 2017.

Kirkpatrick, Clifford, and Eugene Kanin. "Male Sex Aggression on a University Campus." *American Sociological Review* 22, no. 1 (February 1957): 52. https://doi.org/10.2307/2088765.

Kleiman, Mark. *When Brute Force Fails: How to Have Less Crime and Less Punishment.* Princeton, NJ: Princeton Univ. Press, 2010.

Klein, Richard. "An Analysis of Thirty-Five Years of Rape Reform: A Frustrating Search for Fundamental Fairness." *Akron Law Review* 41, no. 981 (2008). https://papers.ssrn.com/sol3/papers.cfm?abstract_id=2341690#.

Kors, Alan Charles, and Harvey A Silverglate. *The Shadow University: The Betrayal of Liberty on America's Campuses.* Portland, OR: Powells, 2000. http://www.myilibrary.com?id=899115.

Koss, M. P., and H. H. Cleveland. "Athletic Participation, Fraternity Membership, and Date Rape: The Question Remains—Self-Selection or Different Causal Processes?" *Violence against Women* 2, no. 2 (June 1, 1996): 180–90. https://doi.org/10.1177/1077801296002002005.

Koss, Mary. "Restorative Justice Responses to Sexual Assault," February 20, 2008. http://dev.vawnet.org/materials/restorative-justice-responses-sexual-assault.

Koss, Mary P., Thomas E. Dinero, Cynthia A. Seibel, and Susan L. Cox. "Stranger and Acquaintance Rape: Are There Differences in the Victim's Experience?" *Psychology of Women Quarterly* 12, no. 1 (1988): 1–24.

Koss, Mary P., Christine A. Gidycz, and Nadine Wisniewski. "The Scope of Rape: Incidence and Prevalence of Sexual Aggression and Victimization in a National Sample of Higher Education Students." *Journal of Consulting and Clinical Psychology* 55, no. 2 (1987): 162–70.

Koss, Mary P., and Mary R. Harvey. *The Rape Victim: Clinical and Community Interventions (2nd ed.)*, vol. xiv. Sage Library of Social Research, vol. 185. Thousand Oaks, CA: Sage Publications, Inc, 1991.

Koss, Mary P., Jay K. Wilgus, and Kaaren M. Williamsen. "Campus Sexual Misconduct: Restorative Justice Approaches to Enhance Compliance with Title IX Guidance." *Trauma, Violence and Abuse* 15, no. 3 (April 27, 2014): 242–57. https://doi.org/10.1177/1524838014521500.

Krebs, Christopher P., Christine H. Lindquist, Tara D. Warner, Bonnie S. Fisher, and Sandra L Martin. "The Campus Sexual Assault Study (CSA) Final Report: Performance Period: January 2005 through December 2007." Rockville, MD: National Institute of Justice, 2007.

Langenberg, Andria G. M., Lawrence Corey, Rhoda L. Ashley, Wai Ping Leong, and Stephen E. Straus. "A Prospective Study of New Infections with Herpes Simplex Virus Type 1 and Type 2." *New England Journal of Medicine* 341, no. 19 (November 4, 1999): 1432–38. https://doi.org/10.1056/NEJM199911043411904.

Lerner, Gerda, ed. *Black Women in White America: A Documentary History*. New York: Vintage Books, 1992.

Lewis, Deborah K., and Timothy C. Marchell. "Safety First: A Medical Amnesty Approach to Alcohol Poisoning at a U.S. University." *International Journal of Drug Policy* 17, no. 4 (July 2006): 329–38. https://doi.org/10.1016/j.drugpo.2006.02.007.

Lewis, M. A., H. Granato, J. A. Blayney, T. W. Lostutter, and J. R. Kilmer. "Predictors of Hooking Up Sexual Behaviors and Emotional Reactions among U.S. College Students." *Archives of Sexual Behavior* 41, no. 5 (2011): 1219–29.

Lindberg, Laura Duberstein, Isaac Maddow-Zimet, and Heather Boonstra. "Changes in Adolescents' Receipt of Sex Education, 2006–2013." *Journal of Adolescent Health* 58, no. 6 (June 2016): 621–27. https://doi.org/10.1016/j.jadohealth.2016.02.004.

Linder, Christina. *Sexual Violence on Campus: Power-Conscious Approaches to Awareness,*

Prevention, and Response. Great Debates in Higher Education Ser. Bingley, UK: Emerald Publishing Limited, 2018.

Lisak, David. "False Allegations of Rape: A Critique of Kanin," October 2007. http://www.davidlisak.com/wp-content/uploads/pdf/SARFalseAllegationsofRape.pdf.

———. "Men as Victims: Challenging Cultural Myths." *Journal of Traumatic Stress* 6, no. 4 (October 1, 1993): 577–80. https://doi.org/10.1002/jts.2490060414.

Lisak, David, Lori Gardinier, Sarah C. Nicksa, and Ashley M. Cote. "False Allegations of Sexual Assault: An Analysis of Ten Years of Reported Cases." *Violence against Women* 16, no. 12 (December 1, 2010): 1318–34. https://doi.org/10.1177/1077801210387747.

Littleton, Heather, and Craig E. Henderson. "If She Is Not a Victim, Does That Mean She Was Not Traumatized? Evaluation of Predictors of PTSD Symptomatology among College Rape Victims." *Violence against Women* 15, no. 2 (2009): 148–67.

Littleton, Heather, Holly Tabernik, Erika J. Canales, and Tamika Backstrom. "Risky Situation or Harmless Fun? A Qualitative Examination of College Women's Bad Hook-up and Rape Scripts." *Sex Roles* 60, no. 11–12 (2009): 793–804.

Livingstone, Sonia. "Taking Risky Opportunities in Youthful Content Creation: Teenagers' Use of Social Networking Sites for Intimacy, Privacy and Self-Expression." *New Media and Society* 10, no. 3 (June 2008): 393–411. https://doi.org/10.1177/1461444808089415.

Lonsway, Kimberly A., Joanne Archambault, and David Lisak. "False Reports: Moving beyond the Issue to Successfully Investigate and Prosecute Non-Stranger Sexual Assault." Harrisburg, PA: National Sexual Violence Resource Center, 2009. https://www.nsvrc.org/publications/articles/false-reports-moving-beyond-issue-successfully-investigate-and-prosecute-non-s.

Lonsway, Kimberly A., and Louise F. Fitzgerald. "Rape Myths: In Review." *Psychology of Women Quarterly* 18, no. 2 (June 1994): 133–64. https://doi.org/10.1111/j.1471-6402.1994.tb00448.x.

Lytle, Megan C., John R. Blosnich, Susan M. De Luca, and Chris Brownson. "Association of Religiosity with Sexual Minority Suicide Ideation and Attempt." *American Journal of Preventive Medicine* 54, no. 5 (May 2018): 644–51. https://doi.org/10.1016/j.amepre.2018.01.019.

Mabry, A., and M. M. Turner. "Do Sexual Assault Bystander Interventions Change Men's Intentions? Applying the Theory of Normative Social Behavior to Predicting Bystander Outcomes." *Journal of Health Communication* 21, no. 3 (2015): 276–92.

MacKinnon, Catharine A. "Feminism, Marxism, Method, and the State: Toward Feminist Jurisprudence." *Signs: Journal of Women in Culture and Society* 8, no. 4 (July 1983): 635–58. https://doi.org/10.1086/494000.

Marshall, Ethan A., Holly A. Miller, and Jeff A. Bouffard. "Crossing the Threshold from Porn Use to Porn Problem: Frequency and Modality of Porn Use as Predictors of Sexually Coercive Behaviors." *Journal of Interpersonal Violence*, November 22, 2017, 088626051774354. https://doi.org/10.1177/0886260517743549.

Marston, Cicely, and Eleanor King. "Factors That Shape Young People's Sexual Behaviour: A Systematic Review." *The Lancet* 368, no. 9547 (November 4, 2006): 1581–86. https://doi.org/10.1016/S0140-6736(06)69662-1.

Martin, Elaine K., Casey T. Taft, and Patricia A. Resick. "A Review of Marital Rape." *Aggression and Violent Behavior* 12, no. 3 (May 2007): 329–47. https://doi.org/10.1016/j.avb.2006.10.003.

Martin, Patricia Yancey. "The Rape Prone Culture of Academic Contexts: Fraternities and Athletics." *Gender and Society* 30, no. 1 (February 2016): 30–43. https://doi.org/10.1177/0891243215612708.

Martin, Patricia Yancey, and Robert A. Hummer. "Fraternities and Rape on Campus." *Gender and Society* 3, no. 4 (1989): 457–73.

Martin, Sandra L., Bonnie S. Fisher, Tara D. Warner, Christopher P. Krebs, and Christine H. Lindquist. "Women's Sexual Orientations and Their Experiences of Sexual Assault before and during University." *Women's Health Issues* 21, no. 3 (May 2011): 199–205. https://doi.org/10.1016/j.whi.2010.12.002.

Matier, Michael, and Cathy Alvord. "Undergraduate Enrollment Trends Fall 1998." Cornell University Institutional Research and Planning, 1998. https://dpb.cornell.edu/documents/1000023.pdf.

Mauss, Marcel. *The Gift: The Form and Reason for Exchange in Archaic Societies.* New York and London: W. W. Norton, 1990.

McCartan, K. F., H. Kemshall, and J. Tabachnick. "The Construction of Community Understandings of Sexual Violence: Rethinking Public, Practitioner and Policy Discourses." *Journal of Sexual Aggression* 21, no. 1 (January 2, 2015): 100–116. https://doi.org/10.1080/13552600.2014.945976.

"McCaskill: Campus Sexual Assault Survey Results a 'Wakeup Call' for Schools | U.S. Senator Claire McCaskill of Missouri." Accessed May 4, 2015. http://www.mccaskill.senate.gov/media-center/news-releases/campus-sexual-assault-survey.

McCaughey, Martha, and Jill Cermele. "Changing the Hidden Curriculum of Campus Rape Prevention and Education: Women's Self-Defense as a Key Protective Factor for a Public Health Model of Prevention." *Trauma, Violence, and Abuse* 18, no. 3 (July 2017): 287–302. https://doi.org/10.1177/1524838015611674.

McClintock, Elizabeth Aura. "When Does Race Matter? Race, Sex, and Dating at an Elite University." *Journal of Marriage and Family* 72, no. 1 (February 2010): 45–72. https://doi.org/10.1111/j.1741-3737.2009.00683.x.

McClure, Stephanie M. "Voluntary Association Membership: Black Greek Men on a Predominantly White Campus." *The Journal of Higher Education* 77, no. 6 (2006): 1036–57. https://doi.org/10.1353/jhe.2006.0053.

McGuire, Danielle L. *At the Dark End of the Street: Black Women, Rape, and Resistance- a New History of the Civil Rights Movement from Rosa Parks to the Rise of Black Power.* New York: Alfred A. Knopf, 2010.

McMahon, Sarah, and Victoria L. Banyard. "When Can I Help? A Conceptual Framework for the Prevention of Sexual Violence Through Bystander Intervention." *Trauma, Violence, and Abuse* 13, no. 1 (January 2012): 3–14. https://doi.org/10.1177/1524838011426015.

McMahon, Sarah, Leila Wood, Julia Cusano, and Lisa M. Macri. "Campus Sexual Assault: Future Directions for Research." *Sexual Abuse* 31, no. 3 (April 2019): 270–95. https://doi.org/10.1177/1079063217750864.

Mellins, Claude A., Kate Walsh, Aaron L. Sarvet, Melanie Wall, Louisa Gilbert, John S. Santelli, Martie Thompson, et al. "Sexual Assault Incidents among College Undergraduates: Prevalence and Factors Associated with Risk." *PLOS ONE* 12, no. 11 (2017): e0186471. https://doi.org/10.1371/journal.pone.0186471.

Melnick, Merrill. "Male Athletes and Sexual Assault." *Journal of Physical Education, Recreation and Dance* 63, no. 5 (1992): 32–36.

Mengo, Cecilia, and Beverly M. Black. "Violence Victimization on a College Campus: Impact on GPA and School Dropout." *Journal of College Student Retention: Research, Theory and Practice* 18, no. 2 (August 2016): 234–48. https://doi.org/10.1177/1521025115584750.

Merrill, Jennifer E., Leah N. Vermont, Rachel L. Bachrach, and Jennifer P. Read. "Is the Pregame to Blame? Event-Level Associations Between Pregaming and Alcohol-Related Consequences." *Journal of Studies on Alcohol and Drugs* 74, no. 5 (September 2013): 757–64. https://doi.org/10.15288/jsad.2013.74.757.

Messman-Moore, Terri L., Aubrey A. Coates, Kathryn J. Gaffey, and Carrie F. Johnson. "Sexuality, Substance Use, and Susceptibility to Victimization: Risk for Rape and Sexual Coercion in a Prospective Study of College Women." *Journal of Interpersonal Violence* 23, no. 12 (December 1, 2008): 1730–46. https://doi.org/10.1177/0886260508314336.

Messner, Michael A. "Bad Men, Good Men, Bystanders: Who Is the Rapist?" *Gender and Society* 30, no. 1 (February 2016): 57–66. https://doi.org/10.1177/0891243215608781.

Miller, Lisa, and Merav Gur. "Religiousness and Sexual Responsibility in Adolescent Girls." *Journal of Adolescent Health* 31, no. 5 (November 2002): 401–6. https://doi.org/10.1016/S1054-139X(02)00403-2.

Moore, Briana M., and Thomas Baker. "An Exploratory Examination of College Students' Likelihood of Reporting Sexual Assault to Police and University Officials: Results of a Self-Report Survey." *Journal of Interpersonal Violence* 33, no. 22 (November 2018): 3419–38. https://doi.org/10.1177/0886260516632357.

Moreno, Megan A., Malcolm Parks, and Laura P. Richardson. "What Are Adolescents Showing the World about Their Health Risk Behaviors on MySpace?" *Medscape General Medicine* 9, no. 4 (October 11, 2007): 9.

Muehlenhard, Charlene L., and Stephen W. Cook. "Men's Self-Reports of Unwanted Sexual Activity." *Journal of Sex Research* 24, no. 1 (1988): 58–72.

Muehlenhard, Charlene L., Terry P. Humphreys, Kristen N. Jozkowski, and Zoë D.

Peterson. "The Complexities of Sexual Consent among College Students: A Conceptual and Empirical Review." *The Journal of Sex Research* 53, no. 4–5 (May 3, 2016): 457–87. https://doi.org/10.1080/00224499.2016.1146651.

Muehlenhard, Charlene L., and Melaney A. Linton. "Date Rape and Sexual Aggression in Dating Situations: Incidence and Risk Factors." *Journal of Counseling Psychology* 34, no. 2 (1987): 186.

Muehlenhard, Charlene L., and Zoë D. Peterson. "Wanting and Not Wanting Sex: The Missing Discourse of Ambivalence." *Feminism and Psychology* 15, no. 1 (February 2005): 15–20. https://doi.org/10.1177/0959353505049698.

Murnen, Sarah K., and Marla H. Kohlman. "Athletic Participation, Fraternity Membership, and Sexual Aggression among College Men: A Meta-Analytic Review." *Sex Roles* 57, no. 1–2 (August 2, 2007): 145–57. https://doi.org/10.1007/s11199-007-9225-1.

Murnen, Sarah K., Carrie Wright, and Gretchen Kaluzny. "If 'Boys Will Be Boys,' Then Girls Will Be Victims? A Meta-Analytic Review of the Research That Relates Masculine Ideology to Sexual Aggression." *Sex Roles* 46, no. 11/12 (2002): 359–75. https://doi.org/10.1023/A:1020488928736.

Nagin, Daniel S. "Deterrence in the Twenty-First Century." *Crime and Justice* 42, no. 1 (August 2013): 199–263. https://doi.org/10.1086/670398.

National Center for Education Statistics. "Fast Facts." Washington, DC: Institute of Education Sciences, 2018. https://nces.ed.gov/fastfacts/display.asp?id=372.

———. "Table 303.70. Total Undergraduate Fall Enrollment in Degree-Granting Postsecondary Institutions, by Attendance Status, Sex of Student, and Control and Level of Institution: Selected Years, 1970 through 2026." Washington, DC: Institute of Education Sciences, February 2017. https://nces.ed.gov/programs/digest/d16/tables/dt16_303.70.asp.

National Institute on Alcohol Abuse and Alcoholism (NIAAA). "College Drinking—Fact Sheet—National Institute on Alcohol Abuse and Alcoholism," April 2015. http://pubs.niaaa.nih.gov/publications/CollegeFactSheet/CollegeFactSheet.pdf.

———. "Reducing Alcohol Problems on Campus: A Guide to Planning and Evaluation," 2002. https://www.collegedrinkingprevention.gov/media/finalhandbook.pdf.

Nicolazzo, Z. "'Just Go In Looking Good': The Resilience, Resistance, and Kinship-Building of Trans* College Students." *Journal of College Student Development* 57, no. 5 (2016): 538–56. https://doi.org/10.1353/csd.2016.0057.

NYC LGBT Historic Sites Project. "Student Homophile League at Earl Hall, Columbia University," 2017. http://www.nyclgbtsites.org/site/columbia-university/.

O'Byrne, Rachael, Susan Hansen, and Mark Rapley. "'If a Girl Doesn't Say "No" . . .': Young Men, Rape and Claims of 'Insufficient Knowledge.'" *Journal of Community and Applied Social Psychology* 18, no. 3 (May 2008): 168–93. https://doi.org/10.1002/casp.922.

Okamoto, Dina, and G. Cristina Mora. "Panethnicity." *Annual Review of Sociology* 40 (2014): 219–39.

Oosten, Johanna M. F. van, Jochen Peter, and Inge Boot. "Exploring Associations between Exposure to Sexy Online Self-Presentations and Adolescents' Sexual Attitudes and Behavior." *Journal of Youth and Adolescence* 44, no. 5 (May 2015): 1078–91. https://doi.org/10.1007/s10964-014-0194-8.

Orchowski, Lindsay M., Amy S. Untied, and Christine A. Gidycz. "Factors Associated with College Women's Labeling of Sexual Victimization." *Violence and Victims* 28, no. 6 (2013): 940–58.

Parker, Caroline M., Jonathan Garcia, Morgan M. Philbin, Patrick A. Wilson, Richard G. Parker, and Jennifer S. Hirsch. "Social Risk, Stigma and Space: Key Concepts for Understanding HIV Vulnerability among Black Men Who Have Sex with Men in New York City." *Culture, Health and Sexuality* 19, no. 3 (March 4, 2017): 323–37. https://doi.org/10.1080/13691058.2016.1216604.

Pascoe, C. J., and Jocelyn A. Hollander. "Good Guys Don't Rape: Gender, Domination, and Mobilizing Rape." *Gender and Society* 30, no. 1 (February 2016): 67–79. https://doi.org/10.1177/0891243215612707.

Paul, Elizabeth L., and Kristen A. Hayes. "The Casualties of 'Casual' Sex: A Qualitative Exploration of the Phenomenology of College Students' Hookups." *Journal of Social and Personal Relationships* 19, no. 5 (2002): 639–61.

Paul, Elizabeth L., Brian McManus, and Allison Hayes. "'Hookups': Characteristics and Correlates of College Students' Spontaneous and Anonymous Sexual Experiences." *Journal of Sex Research* 37, no. 1 (2000): 76–88.

Paulk, David. "Columbia's Chinese Students Targeted by Racist Vandalism." *Sixth Tone*, February 14, 2017. https://www.sixthtone.com/news/1932/columbia-chinese-students-targeted-by-racist-vandalism.

Peace, Kristine A., Stephen Porter, and Leanne ten Brinke. "Are Memories for Sexually Traumatic Events 'Special'? A Within-Subjects Investigation of Trauma and Memory in a Clinical Sample." *Memory* 16, no. 1 (January 2008): 10–21. https://doi.org/10.1080/09658210701363583.

Perry, Maya. "The Constitution of a Community: Why Student Clubs Are Starting to Take Sexual Violence Response into Their Own Hands." *Columbia Daily Spectator*, February 24, 2019. https://www.columbiaspectator.com/eye-lead/2019/02/24/the-constitution-of-a-community-why-student-clubs-are-starting-to-take-sexual-violence-response-into-their-own-hands/.

Peterson, Cora, Sarah DeGue, Curtis Florence, and Colby N. Lokey. "Lifetime Economic Burden of Rape among U.S. Adults." *American Journal of Preventive Medicine* 52, no. 6 (2017): 691–701. https://doi.org/10.1016/j.amepre.2016.11.014.

Peterson, Ruth D., and William C. Bailey. "Rape and Dimensions of Socioeconomic

Inequality in U.S. Metropolitan Areas." *Journal of Research in Crime and Delinquency* 29, no. 2 (1992): 162–77.

Piccigallo, Jacqueline R., Terry G. Lilley, and Susan L. Miller. "'It's Cool to Care about Sexual Violence': Men's Experiences with Sexual Assault Prevention." *Men and Masculinities* 15, no. 5 (December 2012): 507–25. https://doi.org/10.1177/1097184X12458590.

Piff, Paul K., Daniel M. Stancato, Stéphane Côté, Rodolfo Mendoza-Denton, and Dacher Keltner. "Higher Social Class Predicts Increased Unethical Behavior." *Proceedings of the National Academy of Sciences* 109, no. 11 (March 13, 2012): 4086. https://doi.org/10.1073/pnas.1118373109.

Pope, Justin. "The College Graduation Swim Test Has Gone Belly-Up." *Los Angeles Times*, June 18, 2006. https://www.latimes.com/archives/la-xpm-2006-jun-18-adna-swim18-story.html.

Potter, Sharyn, Rebecca Howard, Sharon Murphy, and Mary M. Moynihan. "Long-Term Impacts of College Sexual Assaults on Women Survivors' Educational and Career Attainments." *Journal of American College Health*, February 15, 2018, 1–37. https://doi.org/10.1080/07448481.2018.1440574.

Potter, Sharyn J. "Reducing Sexual Assault on Campus: Lessons From the Movement to Prevent Drunk Driving." *American Journal of Public Health* 106, no. 5 (2016): 822–29.

President's Commission on Slavery and the University. "Universities Studying Slavery," 2018. http://slavery.virginia.edu/universities-studying-slavery/.

Quinn, Mattie. "Marital Rape Isn't Necessarily a Crime in 12 States." *Governing*, April 10, 2019. https://www.governing.com/topics/public-justice-safety/gov-marital-rape-states-ohio-minnesota.html.

Ray, Rashawn, and Jason A. Rosow. "Getting Off and Getting Intimate: How Normative Institutional Arrangements Structure Black and White Fraternity Men's Approaches Toward Women." *Men and Masculinities* 12, no. 5 (August 1, 2010): 523–46. https://doi.org/10.1177/1097184X09331750.

Reetz, David R., Victor Barr, and Brian Krylowicz. "The Association for University and College Counseling Center Directors Annual Survey." Indianapolis, IN: Association for University and College Counseling Center Directors, 2013.

Resick, Patricia A. "The Psychological Impact of Rape." *Journal of Interpersonal Violence* 8, no. 2 (June 1993): 223–55. https://doi.org/10.1177/088626093008002005.

Reynolds, Celene. "The Mobilization of Title IX across U.S. Colleges and Universities, 1994–2014." *Social Problems* 66, no. 2 (May 1, 2019): 245–73. https://doi.org/10.1093/socpro/spy005.

Richardson, Diane. "Constructing Sexual Citizenship: Theorizing Sexual Rights." *Critical Social Policy* 20, no. 1 (February 1, 2000): 105–35. https://doi.org/10.1177/026101830002000105.

Richters, Juliet, Richard de Visser, Chris Rissel, and Anthony Smith. "Sexual Practices at Last Heterosexual Encounter and Occurrence of Orgasm in a National Survey." *The Journal of Sex Research* 43, no. 3 (August 1, 2006): 217–26. https://doi.org/10.1080/00224490609552320.

Rivera, Lauren A. *Pedigree: How Elite Students Get Elite Jobs.* First paperback printing with a new afterword by the author. Princeton and Oxford: Princeton University Press, 2016.

Robbins, Alexandra. *Fraternity: An inside Look at a Year of College Boys Becoming Men.* New York, New York: Dutton, 2019.

Rodkin, Dennis. "College Comeback: The University of Chicago Finds Its Groove." *Chicago*, March 16, 2011. https://www.chicagomag.com/Chicago-Magazine/March-2011/College-Comeback-The-University-of-Chicago-Finds-Its-Groove/.

Rothman, Emily F., D. Exner, and A. Baughman. "The Prevalence of Sexual Assault against People Who Identify as Gay, Lesbian or Bisexual in the United States: A Systematic Review." *Trauma Violence and Abuse* 12, no. 2 (2011): 55–66.

Rothman, Emily F., Avanti Adhia, Tiffany T. Christensen, Jennifer Paruk, Jessica Alder, and Nicole Daley. "A Pornography Literacy Class for Youth: Results of a Feasibility and Efficacy Pilot Study." *American Journal of Sexuality Education* 13, no. 1 (January 2, 2018): 1–17. https://doi.org/10.1080/15546128.2018.1437100.

Rumney, Philip N. S. "False Allegations of Rape." *The Cambridge Law Journal* 65, no. 01 (March 2006): 128–58. https://doi.org/10.1017/S0008197306007069.

Russell, Brenda L., and Debra L. Oswald. "Strategies and Dispositional Correlates of Sexual Coercion Perpetrated by Women: An Exploratory Investigation." *Sex Roles* 45, no. 1 (2001): 103–15.

Russlynn, A. "Dear Colleague Letter." U.S. Department of Education, Office for Civil Rights, April 4, 2011.

Sable, Marjorie R., Fran Danis, Denise L. Mauzy, and Sarah K. Gallagher. "Barriers to Reporting Sexual Assault for Women and Men: Perspectives of College Students." *Journal of American College Health* 55 (2006): 157–62.

Sampson, Robert J. *Great American City: Chicago and the Enduring Neighborhood Effect.* Chicago: University of Chicago Press, 2011.

———. "Neighborhoods and Violent Crime: A Multilevel Study of Collective Efficacy." *Science* 277, no. 5328 (August 15, 1997): 918–24. https://doi.org/10.1126/science.277.5328.918.

Sanday, Peggy. *Fraternity Gang Rape: Sex, Brotherhood, and Privilege on Campus.* NYU Press, 2007.

Sandberg, Genell, Thomas L. Jackson, and Patricia Petretic-Jackson. "College Students' Attitudes Regarding Sexual Coercion and Aggression: Developing Educational and Preventive Strategies." *Journal of College Student Personnel*, 1987. http://psycnet.apa.org/psycinfo/1988-27979-001.

Sanders, Stephanie, Brandon J. Hill, William L. Yarber, Cynthia A. Graham, Richard A.

Crosby, and Robin R. Milhausen. "Misclassification Bias: Diversity in Conceptualisations about Having 'Had Sex.'" *Sexual Health* 7, no. 1 (2010): 31–34.

Santelli, John S., Stephanie A. Grilo, Tse-Hwei Choo, Gloria Diaz, Kate Walsh, Melanie Wall, Jennifer S. Hirsch, et al. "Does Sex Education before College Protect Students from Sexual Assault in College?" *PLOS ONE* 13, no. 11 (November 14, 2018): e0205951. https://doi.org/10.1371/journal.pone.0205951.

Santelli, John S., Leslie M. Kantor, Stephanie A. Grilo, Ilene S. Speizer, Laura D. Lindberg, Jennifer Heitel, Amy T. Schalet, et al. "Abstinence-Only-Until-Marriage: An Updated Review of U.S. Policies and Programs and Their Impact." *Journal of Adolescent Health* 61, no. 3 (September 2017): 273–80. https://doi.org/10.1016/j.jadohealth.2017.05.031.

Scanlon, Lesley, Louise Rowling, and Zita Weber. "'You Don't Have like an Identity . . . You Are Just Lost in a Crowd': Forming a Student Identity in the First-Year Transition to University." *Journal of Youth Studies* 10, no. 2 (May 2007): 223–41. https://doi.org/10.1080/13676260600983684.

Schalet, Amy T. *Not under My Roof: Parents, Teens, and the Culture of Sex*. Chicago: University of Chicago Press, 2011.

Schneider, Madeline, and Jennifer S. Hirsch. "Comprehensive Sexuality Education as a Primary Prevention Strategy for Sexual Violence Perpetration." *Trauma, Violence, and Abuse*, May 2, 2018, 1–17. https://doi.org/10.1177/1524838018772855.

Scully, Regina Kulik, Paul Blavin, Kirby Dick, Amy Ziering, Thaddeus Wadleigh, Aaron Kopp, and Miriam Cutler. *The Hunting Ground*. Anchor Bay Entertainment, Inc., 2015.

Seo, Dong-Chul, and Kaigang Li. "Effects of College Climate on Students' Binge Drinking: Hierarchical Generalized Linear Model." *Annals of Behavioral Medicine* 38, no. 3 (December 1, 2009): 262–68. https://doi.org/10.1007/s12160-009-9150-3.

"Sexual and Reproductive Health Care: A Position Paper of the Society for Adolescent Health and Medicine." *Journal of Adolescent Health* 54, no. 4 (April 1, 2014): 491–96. https://doi.org/10.1016/j.jadohealth.2014.01.010.

Sexual Trauma Services. "South Carolina Laws Regarding Sexual Assault and Consent." Columbia, SC: Sexual Trauma Services, 2019. https://www.stsm.org/south-carolina-laws-regarding-sexual-assault-and-consent.

Sharkey, Patrick. *Uneasy Peace: The Great Crime Decline, the Renewal of City Life, and the next War on Violence*. New York: W. W. Norton & Company, 2018.

Shtarkshall, Ronny A., John S. Santelli, and Jennifer S. Hirsch. "Sex Education and Sexual Socialization: Roles for Educators and Parents." *Perspectives on Sexual and Reproductive Health* 39, no. 2 (June 2007): 116–19. https://doi.org/10.1363/3911607.

Shteir, Rachel. "50 Shades of Ivy: Kink on Campus." *Observer*, March 6, 2015. https://observer.com/2015/03/50-shades-of-ivy-kink-on-campus/.

Simon, Herbert A. "Rational Choice and the Structure of the Environment." *Psychological Review* 63, no. 2 (1956): 129–38. https://doi.org/10.1037/h0042769.

Simons, Herbert D., Corey Bosworth, Scott Fujita, and Mark Jensen. "The Athlete Stigma in Higher Education." *College Student Journal* 41, no. 2 (June 2007): 251–73.

Sinozich, Sofi, and Lynn Langton. "Rape and Sexual Assault among College-Age Females, 1995–2013." Washington, DC: Bureau of Justice Statistics, U.S. Department of Justice, December 11, 2014. https://www.bjs.gov/index.cfm?ty=pbdetail&iid=5176.

Sloane, Wick. "Veterans at Elite Colleges, 2016." *Chronicle of Higher Education*, November 11, 2016. https://www.insidehighered.com/views/2016/11/11/how-many-veterans-do-elite-colleges-enroll-not-enough-essay.

Slutske, Wendy S. "Alcohol Use Disorders among US College Students and Their Non–College-Attending Peers." *Archives of General Psychiatry* 62, no. 3 (March 1, 2005): 321. https://doi.org/10.1001/archpsyc.62.3.321.

Slutske, Wendy S., Erin E. Hunt-Carter, Rachel E. Nabors-Oberg, Kenneth J. Sher, Kathleen K. Bucholz, Pamela A. F. Madden, Andrey Anokhin, and Andrew C. Heath. "Do College Students Drink More Than Their Non-College-Attending Peers? Evidence From a Population-Based Longitudinal Female Twin Study." *Journal of Abnormal Psychology* 113, no. 4 (2004): 530–40. https://doi.org/10.1037/0021-843X.113.4.530.

Smith, Daniel Jordan, and Benjamin C. Mbakwem. "Antiretroviral Therapy and Reproductive Life Projects: Mitigating the Stigma of AIDS in Nigeria." *Social Science and Medicine* 71, no. 2 (July 2010): 345–52. https://doi.org/10.1016/j.socscimed.2010.04.006.

Smith, Paige Hall, Jacquelyn W. White, and Lindsay J. Holland. "A Longitudinal Perspective on Dating Violence among Adolescent and College-Age Women." *American Journal of Public Health* 93, no. 7 (2003): 1104–9.

Spohn, Cassia, and Katharine Tellis. "The Criminal Justice System's Response to Sexual Violence." *Violence against Women* 18, no. 2 (February 2012): 169–92. https://doi.org/10.1177/1077801212440020.

Spohn, Cassia, Clair White, and Katharine Tellis. "Unfounding Sexual Assault: Examining the Decision to Unfound and Identifying False Reports: Unfounding Sexual Assault." *Law and Society Review* 48, no. 1 (March 2014): 161–92. https://doi.org/10.1111/lasr.12060.

Stein, Joel. "Millennials: The Me Me Me Generation." *Time Magazine*, May 20, 2013. http://time.com/247/millennials-the-me-me-me-generation/.

Struckman-Johnson, C., D. Struckman-Johnson, and P. B. Anderson. "Tactics of Sexual Coercion: When Men and Women Won't Take No for an Answer." *The Journal of Sex Research* 40, no. 1 (n.d.): 76–86.

Struckman-Johnson, Cindy. "Forced Sex on Dates: It Happens to Men, Too." *Journal of Sex Research* 24, no. 1 (January 1988): 234–41. https://doi.org/10.1080/00224498809551418.

Struckman-Johnson, Cindy, David Struckman-Johnson, and Peter B. Anderson. "Tactics of Sexual Coercion: When Men and Women Won't Take No for an Answer."

Journal of Sex Research 40, no. 1 (February 2003): 76–86. https://doi.org/10.1080/00224490309552168.

Stuber, Jenny M., Joshua Klugman, and Caitlin Daniel. "Gender, Social Class, and Exclusion: Collegiate Peer Cultures and Social Reproduction." *Sociological Perspectives* 54, no. 3 (September 2011): 431–51. https://doi.org/10.1525/sop.2011.54.3.431.

Subrahmanyam, Kaveri, David Smahel, and Patricia Greenfield. "Connecting Developmental Constructions to the Internet: Identity Presentation and Sexual Exploration in Online Teen Chat Rooms." *Developmental Psychology* 42, no. 3 (2006): 395–406. https://doi.org/10.1037/0012-1649.42.3.395.

Swartout, Kevin M., Mary P. Koss, Jacquelyn W. White, Martie P. Thompson, Antonia Abbey, and Alexandra L. Bellis. "Trajectory Analysis of the Campus Serial Rapist Assumption." *JAMA Pediatrics* 169, no. 12 (December 1, 2015): 1148. https://doi.org/10.1001/jamapediatrics.2015.0707.

Sweeney, Brian. "Party Animals or Responsible Men: Social Class, Race, and Masculinity on Campus." *International Journal of Qualitative Studies in Education* 27, no. 6 (July 3, 2014): 804–21. https://doi.org/10.1080/09518398.2014.901578.

Tabachnick, Joan, and Cordelia Anderson. "Accountability and Responsibility in the Era of #MeToo." *ATSA (Association for the Treatment of Sexual Abusers)* XXXI, no. 2 (Spring 2019). http://newsmanager.commpartners.com/atsa/issues/2019-03-13/2.html.

Testa, Maria, and Michael J. Cleveland. "Does Alcohol Contribute to College Men's Sexual Assault Perpetration? Between-and Within-Person Effects Over Five Semesters." *Journal of Studies on Alcohol and Drugs* 78, no. 1 (December 12, 2016): 5–13. https://doi.org/10.15288/jsad.2017.78.5.

Thaler, Richard H., and Cass R. Sunstein. *Nudge: Improving Decisions about Health, Wealth, and Happiness.* Rev. and expanded ed. New York: Penguin Books, 2009.

Tharp, Andra Teten, Sarah DeGue, Linda Anne Valle, Kathryn A. Brookmeyer, Greta M. Massetti, and Jennifer L. Matjasko. "A Systematic Qualitative Review of Risk and Protective Factors for Sexual Violence Perpetration." *Trauma, Violence, and Abuse* 14, no. 2 (April 2013): 133–67. https://doi.org/10.1177/1524838012470031.

The Global Burden of Disease 2016 Injury Collaborators, Mohsen Naghavi, Laurie B. Marczak, Michael Kutz, Katya Anne Shackelford, Megha Arora, Molly Miller-Petrie, et al. "Global Mortality from Firearms, 1990–2016." *JAMA* 320, no. 8 (August 28, 2018): 792. https://doi.org/10.1001/jama.2018.10060.

The National Museum of African-American History and Culture. "The Scottsboro Boys," 2019. https://nmaahc.si.edu/blog/scottsboro-boys.

Thompson, Martie, Dylan Sitterle, George Clay, and Jeffrey Kingree. "Reasons for Not Reporting Victimizations to the Police: Do They Vary for Physical and Sexual Incidents?" *Journal of American College Health: J of ACH* 55, no. 5 (April 2007): 277–82. https://doi.org/10.3200/JACH.55.5.277-282.

Thornton, Arland, and Donald Camburn. "Religious Participation and Adolescent Sexual

Behavior and Attitudes." *Journal of Marriage and Family* 51, no. 3 (1989): 641–53. https://doi.org/10.2307/352164.

Tienda, Marta. "Diversity ≠ Inclusion: Promoting Integration in Higher Education." *Educational Researcher* 42, no. 9 (2013): 467–75.

Title IX, 20 U.S.C. Education Amendments Act of 1972. §§1681–1688.

Turchik, JA. "Sexual Victimization among Male College Students: Assault Severity, Sexual Functioning, and Health Risk Behaviors." *Psychology of Men and Masculinity* 13, no. 3 (2012): 243–55.

Uecker, Jeremy E., and Mark D. Regnerus. "Bare Market: Campus Sex Ratios, Romantic Relationships, and Sexual Behavior." *The Sociological Quarterly* 51, no. 3 (August 2010): 408–35. https://doi.org/10.1111/j.1533-8525.2010.01177.x.

Ullman, Sarah E. "Sexual Assault Victimization and Suicidal Behavior in Women: A Review of the Literature." *Aggression and Violent Behavior* 9, no. 4 (July 2004): 331–51. https://doi.org/10.1016/S1359-1789(03)00019-3.

Ullman, Sarah E., Mark Relyea, Liana Peter-Hagene, and Amanda L. Vasquez. "Trauma Histories, Substance Use Coping, PTSD, and Problem Substance Use among Sexual Assault Victims." *Addictive Behaviors* 38 (2013): 2219–23.

U.S. Department of Education, Office of Planning, Evaluation and Policy Development and Office of the Under Secretary. "Advancing Diversity and Inclusion in Higher Education: Key Data Highlights Focusing on Race and Ethnicity and Promising Practices." Washington, DC: US Dept. of Education, 2016. https://www2.ed.gov/rschstat/research/pubs/advancing-diversity-inclusion.pdf.

Vadeboncoeur, Claudia, Nicholas Townsend, and Charlie Foster. "A Meta-Analysis of Weight Gain in First Year University Students: Is Freshman 15 a Myth?" *BMC Obesity* 2, no. 1 (December 2015): 22. https://doi.org/10.1186/s40608-015-0051-7.

Van Der Kolk, Bessel A. "Trauma and Memory: Trauma and Memory." *Psychiatry and Clinical Neurosciences* 52, no. S1 (September 1998): S57–69. https://doi.org/10.1046/j.1440-1819.1998.0520s5S97.x.

Vander Ven, Thomas. *Getting Wasted: Why College Students Drink Too Much and Party so Hard.* New York ; London: New York University Press, 2011.

Violence Against Women Act of 1993:, 42 U.S.C § §13701-14040 (1994).

Vladutiu, Catherine J., Sandra L. Martin, and Rebecca J. Macy. "College- or University-Based Sexual Assault Prevention Programs: A Review of Program Outcomes, Characteristics, and Recommendations." *Trauma, Violence, and Abuse* 12, no. 2 (April 2011): 67–86. https://doi.org/10.1177/1524838010390708.

Voller, Emily K., and Patricia J. Long. "Sexual Assault and Rape Perpetration by College Men: The Role of the Big Five Personality Traits." *Journal of Interpersonal Violence,* 2009. http://jiv.sagepub.com/content/early/2009/05/14/0886260509334390.short.

Wade, Lisa. *American Hookup: The New Culture of Sex on Campus.* W. W. Norton & Company, 2018.

Wade, Lisa, Brian Sweeney, Amelia Seraphia Derr, Michael A. Messner, and Carol Burke. "Ruling Out Rape." *Contexts*, May 21, 2014. https://contexts.org/articles/ruling-out-rape/.

Waechter, Randall, and Van Ma. "Sexual Violence in America: Public Funding and Social Priority." *American Journal of Public Health* 105, no. 12 (October 15, 2015): 2430–37. https://doi.org/10.2105/AJPH.2015.302860.

Wakefield, Sara, and Christopher Uggen. "Incarceration and Stratification." *Annual Review of Sociology* 36, no. 1 (June 2010): 387–406. https://doi.org/10.1146/annurev.soc.012809.102551.

Walsh, Kate, Sara Honickman, Zerbrina Valdespino-Hayden, and Sarah R. Lowe. "Dual Measures of Sexual Consent: A Confirmatory Factor Analysis of the Internal Consent Scale and External Consent Scale." *Journal of Sex Research*, March 18, 2019, 1–9. https://doi.org/10.1080/00224499.2019.1581882.

Walsh, Kate, Katherine M. Keyes, Karestan C. Koenen, and Deborah Hasin. "Lifetime Prevalence of Gender-Based Violence in US Women: Associations with Mood/Anxiety and Substance Use Disorders." *Journal of Psychiatric Research* 62 (March 2015): 7–13. https://doi.org/10.1016/j.jpsychires.2015.01.002.

Walsh, Kate, Aaron Sarvet, Melanie Wall, Louisa Gilbert, John S Santelli, Shamus R. Khan, Martie Thompson, Leigh Reardon, Jennifer S. Hirsch, and Claude Ann Mellins. "Prevalence and Correlates of Sexual Assault Perpetration and Ambiguous Consent in a Representative Sample of College Students." In press.

Wamboldt, Alexander, Jessie V. Ford, Shamus R. Khan, Jennifer S. Hirsch, and Claude Ann Mellins. "'It Was a War of Attrition': Queer and Trans Undergraduates' Practices of Consent and Experiences of Sexual Assault." In process.

Wamboldt, Alexander, Shamus Khan, Claude Ann Mellins, Melanie M. Wall, Leigh Reardon, and Jennifer S. Hirsch. "Wine Night, 'Bro-Dinners,' and Jungle Juice: Disaggregating Practices of Undergraduate Binge Drinking." *Journal of Drug Issues*, June 27, 2019, 002204261985754. https://doi.org/10.1177/0022042619857549.

Wamboldt, Alexander, Shamus R. Khan, Claude A. Mellins, and Jennifer S. Hirsch. "Feminists and Creeps: Collegiate Greek Life and Athletics, Hybrid Moral Masculinity, and the Politics of Sexuality and Gender," n.d.

Wamboldt, Alexander, Shamus R. Khan, Claude Ann Mellins, and Jennifer S. Hirsch. "Friends, Strangers, and Bystanders: Informal Practices of Sexual Assault Intervention." *Global Public Health* 14, no. 1 (May 7, 2018): 1–12. https://doi.org/10.1080/17441692.2018.1472290.

———. "Wine Nights, 'Bro-Dinners,' and Jungle Juice: Disaggregating Practices of Undergraduate Binge Drinking." *Journal of Drug Issues*. Forthcoming.

Warikoo, Natasha Kumar. *The Diversity Bargain: And Other Dilemmas of Race, Admissions, and Meritocracy at Elite Universities*. Chicago ; London: The University of Chicago Press, 2016.

Warshaw, Robin, and Mary P Koss. *I Never Called It Rape: The Ms. Report on Recognizing, Fighting, and Surviving Date and Acquaintance Rape*. New York: Harper/Perennial, 1994.

Wechsler, Henry. "Alcohol and the American College Campus: *A Report from the Harvard School of Public Health*." *Change: The Magazine of Higher Learning* 28, no. 4 (August 1996): 20–60. https://doi.org/10.1080/00091383.1996.9937758.

Wechsler, Henry, A. Davenport, G. Dowdall, B. Moeykens, and S. Castillo. "Health and Behavioral Consequences of Binge Drinking in College. A National Survey of Students at 140 Campuses." *JAMA* 272, no. 21 (December 7, 1994): 1672–77.

Wechsler, Henry, JE Lee, M Kuo, M Seibring, TF Nelson, and H Lee. "Trends in College Binge Drinking During a Period of Increased Prevention Efforts: Findings from 4 Harvard School of Public Health College Alcohol Study Surveys: 1993–2001." *Journal of American College Health*, no. 50 (2015): 5.

Wechsler, Henry, and Toben F. Nelson. "Binge Drinking and the American College Students: What's Five Drinks?" *Psychology of Addictive Behaviors* 15, no. 4 (2001): 287–91. https://doi.org/10.1037//0893-164X.15.4.287.

Weinhardt, Lance S., and Michael P Carey. "Does Alcohol Lead to Sexual Risk Behavior? Findings from Event-Level Research." *Annual Review of Sex Research* 11 (2000): 125–57.

Weiser, Dana A. "Confronting Myths About Sexual Assault: A Feminist Analysis of the False Report Literature: False Reports." *Family Relations* 66, no. 1 (February 2017): 46–60. https://doi.org/10.1111/fare.12235.

wijk, Evalina van, and Tracie C. Harrison. "Relationship Difficulties Postrape: Being a Male Intimate Partner of a Female Rape Victim in Cape Town, South Africa." *Health Care for Women International* 35, no. 7–9 (September 2014): 1081–1105. https://doi.org/10.1080/07399332.2014.916708.

Wilkins, Amy C. "Stigma and Status: Interracial Intimacy and Intersectional Identities among Black College Men." *Gender and Society* 26, no. 2 (April 2012): 165–89. https://doi.org/10.1177/0891243211434613.

Willer, Robb, Christabel L. Rogalin, Conlon Bridget, and Michael T. Wojnowicz. "Overdoing Gender: A Test of the Masculine Overcompensation Thesis." *American Journal of Sociology* 118, no. 4 (January 1, 2013): 980–1022. https://doi.org/10.1086/668417.

Willis, Malachi, and Kristen N. Jozkowski. "Barriers to the Success of Affirmative Consent Initiatives: An Application of the Social Ecological Model." *American Journal of Sexuality Education* 13, no. 3 (July 3, 2018): 324–36. https://doi.org/10.1080/15546128.2018.1443300.

Wilson, Laura C., and Angela Scarpa. "The Unique Associations between Rape Acknowledgment and the DSM-5 PTSD Symptom Clusters." *Psychiatry Research* 257 (November 2017): 290–95. https://doi.org/10.1016/j.psychres.2017.07.055.

Wilson, Patrick A., Shamus R. Khan, Jennifer S. Hirsch, and Claude A. Mellins. "Using a Daily Diary Approach to Examine Quality of Sex and the Temporal Ordering of Stressful Events, Substance Use, and Sleep Patterns among College Students.," In process.

Wolferman, Nicholas, Trendha Hunter, Jennifer S. Hirsch, Shamus R. Khan, Leigh Reardon, and Claude A. Mellins. "The Advisory Board Perspective from a Campus Community-Based Participatory Research Project on Sexual Violence." *Progress in Community Health Partnerships: Research, Education, and Action* 13, no. 1 (2019): 115–19. https://doi.org/10.1353/cpr.2019.0014.

Wolitzky-Taylor, Kate B., Heidi S. Resnick, Ananda B. Amstadter, Jenna L. McCauley, Kenneth J. Ruggiero, and Dean G. Kilpatrick. "Reporting Rape in a National Sample of College Women." *Journal of American College Health* 59, no. 7 (2011): 582–87.

Wright, Paul J., Robert S. Tokunaga, and Ashley Kraus. "A Meta-Analysis of Pornography Consumption and Actual Acts of Sexual Aggression in General Population Studies: Pornography and Sexual Aggression." *Journal of Communication* 66, no. 1 (February 2016): 183–205. https://doi.org/10.1111/jcom.12201.

Zaleski, Ellen H., and Kathleen M. Schiaffino. "Religiosity and Sexual Risk-Taking Behavior during the Transition to College." *Journal of Adolescence* 23, no. 2 (2000): 223–27.

Zinzow, Heidi M., Ananda B. Amstadter, Jenna L. McCauley, Kenneth J. Ruggiero, Heidi S. Resnick, and Dean G. Kilpatrick. "Self-Rated Health in Relation to Rape and Mental Health Disorders in a National Sample of College Women." *Journal of American College Health* 59, no. 7 (2011): 588–94.

Zinzow, Heidi M., and Martie Thompson. "Barriers to Reporting Sexual Victimization: Prevalence and Correlates among Undergraduate Women." *ResearchGate* 20, no. 7 (October 1, 2011): 711–25. https://doi.org/10.1080/10926771.2011.613447.

———. "Factors Associated with Use of Verbally Coercive, Incapacitated, and Forcible Sexual Assault Tactics in a Longitudinal Study of College Men." *Aggressive Behavior* 41, no. 1 (January 2015): 34–43. https://doi.org/10.1002/ab.21567.

Zweig, Janine M., Bonnie L. Barber, and Jacquelynne S. Eccles. "Sexual Coercion and Well-Being in Young Adulthood: Comparisons by Gender and College Status." *Journal of Interpersonal Violence* 12, no. 2 (April 1997): 291–308. https://doi.org/10.1177/088626097012002009.

INDEX